KANT'S EARLY C

This book offers first-time translations of the initial (1781–89) critical reactions to Kant's philosophy. Also included is a selection of writings by Kant's contemporaries who took on the task of defending the critical philosophy against early attacks.

Kant's first critics took an empiricist stance toward his philosophy and articulated concerns that are still with us in current interpretations of Kant. The first aim of this collection is to show in detail how Kant was understood and misunderstood by his contemporaries. The second aim is to reveal the sorts of arguments that Kant and his first disciples mounted in their defense of the theoretical philosophy. A third overriding aim of the book is to contribute to an understanding of the development of Kant's critical philosophy after its initial formulation in the *Critique of Pure Reason*, and in particular why Kant made the changes he did in the second edition of the work in 1787.

This collection, which includes a glossary of key terms and biographical sketches of the critics on both sides of the debate, is a major addition to Kant scholarship and should be seen as a companion volume to the *Cambridge Edition of the Works of Immanuel Kant.*

Brigitte Sassen is Assistant Professor of Philosophy at McMaster University.

KANT'S EARLY CRITICS

The Empiricist Critique
of the
Theoretical Philosophy

TRANSLATED AND EDITED BY
BRIGITTE SASSEN
McMaster University

CAMBRIDGE UNIVERSITY PRESS
Cambridge, New York, Melbourne, Madrid, Cape Town, Singapore, São Paulo

Cambridge University Press
The Edinburgh Building, Cambridge CB2 8RU, UK

Published in the United States of America by Cambridge University Press, New York

www.cambridge.org
Information on this title: www.cambridge.org/9780521781671

First published 2000
This digitally printed version 2007

A catalogue record for this publication is available from the British Library

Library of Congress Cataloguing in Publication data
Sassen, Brigitte, 1960–
Kant's early critics : the empiricist critique of the theoretical philosophy /
Brigitte Sassen.
p. cm.
Companion volume to: Cambridge edition of the works of Immanuel Kant.
Includes bibliographical references and index.
ISBN 0-521-78167-1
1. Kant, Immanuel, 1724–1804. Kritik der reinen Vernunft.
2. Empiricism. 3. Knowled,
Theory of.
4. Reason. 5. Causation. I. Title.

B2779.S26 2000
193–dc21

99-059882

ISBN 978-0-521-78167-1 hardback
ISBN 978-0-521-03764-8 paperback

Contents

Acknowledgments *page vii*
Frequently Cited Texts and Abbreviations *ix*

Introduction: Major Trends in the Early Empiricist Reception of Kant's Critical Philosophy 1

I. Feder/Garve and Garve

The Göttingen Review
[Anonymous], *Zugabe zu den Göttingischen Anzeigen von gelehrten Sachen* (January 19, 1782): 40–8 53

The Garve Review
Christian Garve, "*Critique of Pure Reason* by Immanuel Kant" *AdB* supplements to vols. 37–52 (1783): 838–62. 59

II. The Transcendental Aesthetic

Dietrich Tiedemann, "On the Nature of Metaphysics: An Examination of Professor Kant's Principles – Against the Aesthetic" *Hessische Beyträge zur Gelehrsamkeit und Kunst* 1 (1785), 113–30. 81

[Hermann Andreas Pistorius], "*Elucidations of Professor Kant's 'Critique of Pure Reason,'* by Johann Schultze" *AdB* 66/1 (1786): 92–123. 93

Johann Georg Heinrich Feder, *On Space and Causality: An Examination of the Kantian Philosophy*, 1–64, 84*–91* 106

[Anonymous], "*On Space and Causality: An Examination of the Kantian Philosophy* by Johann Georg Heinrich Feder" *ALZ* (28 January 1788): 249–54. 127

Friedrich Gottlob Born, *Investigation into the First Grounds of the Doctrine of the Senses*, 87–92 133

III. Idealism

Johann Georg Heinrich Feder, *On Space and Causality: An Examination of the Kantian Philosophy*, 61–83*, 114–18 139

J. C. G. Schaumann, *On the Transcendental Aesthetic: A Critical Attempt*, 131–75 155

Friedrich Heinrich Jacobi, "On Transcendental Idealism" *David Hume über den Glauben oder Idealismus und Realismus*, 209–30 169

[Hermann Andreas Pistorius], "*Critique of Pure Reason* by Immanuel Kant"
AdB 81/2 (1788): 343–54. 176
Friedrich Gottlob Born, *Investigation into the First Grounds of the Doctrine of the Senses*, 117–20, 141–53 183

IV. The Categories
C. G. Selle, "Attempt at a Proof That There Are No Pure Concepts of Reason That Are Independent of Experience"
Berlinische Monatsschrift (1784): 565–75. 193
Dietrich Tiedemann, "Continuation of the Examination of Professor Kant's Thoughts About the Nature of Metaphysics – Against the Analytic"
Hessische Beyträge zur Gelehrsamkeit und Kunst 1 (1785) 233–48. 199
[Johann Schultz], "*Institutiones Logicae et Metaphysica* by Jo. Aug. Henr. Ulrich"
ALZ (13 December 1785): 297–9. 210
Gottlob August Tittel, *On Kantian Forms of Thought or Categories*, 3–41, 103–11 215

V. Empiricism vs. Purism
Carl Christian Erhard Schmid, "Some Remarks About Empiricism and Purism in Philosophy Occasioned by Selle's *Principles of Pure Philosophy*"
Appendix to the *Dictionary for Easier Use of Kant's Writing*, 619–68 233
[Hermann Andreas Pistorius], "On Carl Christian Erhard Schmid's Essay About Kant's Purism and Selle's Empiricism"
AdB 88/1 (1789): 104–22. 255

Appendices
A: About the Authors 270
B: Biographical Sketches of Figures in Early Kant Reception 275

Notes 279
Glossary 304
Bibliography 319
Index 326

Acknowledgments

I began work on this project some years ago, while holding a Social Sciences and Humanities Research Council of Canada postdoctoral fellowship at the University of Western Ontario, and am grateful to the Council for its support. I would also like to thank my colleagues at McMaster University for granting me a teaching reduction during the final stages of this project that made possible a speedy completion and revision of the manuscript.

This collection would not have been possible without the assistance of the staff at archives and research libraries. Staff at the Thomas Fischer Rare Book Room at the University of Toronto gave me first access to much of the material translated here, and the staff at the Archives and Research Collections at McMaster University was immensely helpful during the final stages of the project.

Although translation, more than other academic work, is a solitary pursuit, I benefited greatly from the support and advice of colleagues. I thank Andrew Brook and Alison Wylie for early encouragement. Three anonymous readers for Cambridge University Press made several helpful comments and suggestions, and Sara Black did an outstanding job of editing. Finally, my thanks go, in particular, to Lorne Falkenstein, who supported the project from the start, and took on the onerous task of reading all the translations in draft form. His knowledge of Kant and his sensitivity to the language prevented serious errors, and his suggestions for alternate formulations helped to make the translations more English than they would otherwise have been. It goes without saying that any errors and instances of overly Germanic style are due to my own obstinacy rather than advice I received.

Frequently Cited Texts and Abbreviations

AdB	*Allgemeine deutsche Bibliothek*
Ak	Immanuel Kant, *Gesammelte Schriften*, 27+ vols. Berlin: de Gruyter and predecessors, 1900–.
ALZ	*Allgemeine Literatur-Zeitung*
Briefwechsel	Immanuel Kant, *Briefwechsel*, Otto Schöndorffer and Rudolf Malter, eds., 3rd ed. Hamburg: Felix Meiner Verlag, 1986.
FGr	Feder/Garve review
KdrV A	Immanuel Kant, *Kritik der reinen Vernunft*. Riga: Hartknoch, 1781. Unless otherwise noted, the references to the *Kritik* Kant's critics provide are to this edition of the *Critique*.
KdrV B	Immanuel Kant, *Kritik der reinen Vernunft*, 2nd ed. Riga: Hartknoch, 1787.
KEC	*Kant's Early Critics*
NAdB	*Neue Allgemeine deutsche Bibliothek*
Prolegomena	Immanuel Kant, *Prolegomena zu einer jeden künftigen Metaphysik, die als Wissenschaft wird auftreten können*. Benno Erdmann, ed. Ak. IV, 253–83. Unlike the pagination of the *Critique*, that of the *Prolegomena* was not standard at the time. References that Kant's contemporaries provide have been supplemented by references to this standard edition.

Introduction

Major Trends in the Early Empiricist Reception of Kant's Critical Philosophy

There can be no doubt that the initial reception of the *Critique of Pure Reason* was quite different from what Kant had expected and hoped for. His correspondence from 1781 and 1782 clearly demonstrates that he had hoped, perhaps expected, that certain of his contemporaries, particularly Mendelssohn and Tetens, would subject the work to serious study and that they would ultimately endorse it.[1] Nothing, however, was to be heard from Johann Tetens, and Moses Mendelssohn soon "put the book aside," citing age and ill health.[2] Even worse, not only was there no word from Mendelssohn and Tetens, in 1781 there was no word from anyone, aside, that is, from the obligatory announcements and short summaries gleaned mostly from the Table of Contents, certainly not from serious study.[3] And although 1782 did bring the first review, this was, as is well known, the Göttingen or Feder/Garve review,[4] hardly the sort of assessment that Kant had hoped for. His bitter disappointment is evident in his efforts to involve others, notably Johann Schultz[5] and even Mendelssohn,[6] in the review and evaluation of the work, as it is evident also in his very public reaction to the Göttingen review in the *Prolegomena* Appendix.

But Kant's disappointment was premature. For after the initial, perhaps stunned, silence, reviews of and even commentaries on the critical philosophy began to appear in ever increasing numbers, so much so that by the mid 1780s Kant criticism had become a striving concern. Even the major review journals had become involved. Friedrich Nicolai's *Allgemeine deutsche Bibliothek* was soon known as the forum for Kant criticism, and the newly published *Allgemeine Literatur-Zeitung* was committed to the defense of the critical philosophy.[7] Still, initially at least, the reaction was negative. Kant's contemporaries could for the most part simply not understand a philosophy according to which the understanding, as Kant's first reviewer, Johann Feder, states in amazement, "makes objects."[8] This is still evident in the reviews of the *Prolegomena* in 1783 and 1784,[9] but public assessment began to shift in 1785, with the publication of the pro-Kantian *Allgemeine Literatur-*

Zeitung, and by 1786, when Karl Leonhard Reinhold's *Briefe über die Kantische Philosophie* began to appear (in installments) in the *Teutsche Merkur*, it came to be firmly on Kant's side, at least for a time.[10]

Notice, however, that the eventual endorsement of the critical philosophy did not amount to an acceptance of the theoretical philosophy. Reinhold's *Briefe* had a broad impact on early Kant reception because they spoke to the pantheism controversy. By demonstrating that it is practical, not theoretical, reason that functions as the arbitrator in religious matters, Reinhold showed the relevance of Kant's critique of reason to a then vehemently argued debate (the question of the proof of the existence of God) and in this way managed to popularize Kant's philosophy. But this also came somewhat at the expense of the theoretical philosophy, which Kant's contemporaries had yet to come to terms with. To the extent that they did so at all, this occurred in its transformation into nineteenth century idealism, to which public attention turned in the 1790s. This shift involved first a focus on Reinhold and his *Elementarphilosophie*,[11] and, in short order, a turn to Johann Gottlieb Fichte, Friedrich Wilhelm Schelling, and Georg Wilhelm Friedrich Hegel and, with that, to the development of nineteenth century idealism.[12]

A survey of the material that Kant's contemporaries produced between 1782 and 1793 reveals that the early reception of the theoretical philosophy can be divided into three trends. These accord with broader trends in the turbulent period that characterized the late Enlightenment in Germany. The first two trends are backward looking and amount to attempts to valorize different parts of the tradition against what their adherents took to be Kant's attack. First on the scene were those popular philosophers who were influenced by British empiricism, notably John Locke and David Hume, and by Scottish common sense philosophy. They, including Feder, Christian Garve, Hermann Andreas Pistorius, Christian Gottlieb Selle, Dietrich Tiedemann, Gottlob August Tittel, and Adam Weishaupt, constitute the early empiricist reception of the critical philosophy that dominated the scene from 1782 to about 1788. The second wave of early Kant criticism lasted from late 1788, when the first issues of Eberhard's *Philosophisches Magazin* were published, to roughly 1793. It was dominated by the defenders of the Leibnizian/Wolffian philosophy, notably Johann August Eberhard, Johann Gebhard Ehrenreich Maaß, and Johann Christoph Schwab. The "rationalist" reception of the critical philosophy gained prominence, of course, with Kant's response to the first issue of Eberhard's *Philosophisches Magazin* in the *Entdeckung*[13] just as the "empiricist" reception had been popularized by Kant's *Prolegomena* response to Feder.

At roughly the same time that the rationalists were taking on the critical philosophy, a third trend of early Kant reception emerged. Strictly speaking this amounted to a complex of trends that are here taken together because they are best described as forward looking. Not concerned with valorizing some aspect of the philosophical tradition, these "critics" sought to develop the critical philosophy further. Interestingly, they initially appeared as disciples who sought to defend Kant against earlier attacks. Kant certainly saw them as supporters and was bitterly disappointed when they began to develop the critical philosophy in ways that he thought unacceptable. This is evident in his reaction to Reinhold whose "completion" of the critical philosophy in the *Elementarphilosophie* might have been undertaken in the spirit of defense, indeed, seems to have been taken as such by other contemporaries,[14] but Reinhold's efforts appeared as a betrayal to Kant. It is evident in his reaction to Fichte, who, in the process of defending Kant against Gottlob Ernst Schulze's skeptical attack in the *Aenesidemus*, articulated the principles that would become the cornerstone of the development of nineteenth century idealism.[15] It is evident also in his reaction to Beck and Maimon, who similarly proceeded to suggest improvements and further developments of the critical philosophy.[16] It is instructive that Kant, when asked in 1797 who his best defender was, named Schultz, his first and overall most faithful expositor, and not either Reinhold, Jakob Sigismund Beck, or even Fichte.[17]

This is not to say, of course, that all Kant's early critics could be clearly assigned to one or the other of these trends or that they exhausted all the philosophical movements that governed German philosophy at the end of the eighteenth century. In these divisions, Johann Georg Hamann, Friedrich Heinrich Jacobi, and Johann Gottfried Herder, are noticeable by their absence, as is the pantheism controversy. It is true that Hamann's "*Metakritik*,"[18] a critique of Kant's philosophy that is based on a philosophy of language, though not published until 1800, was circulated widely in manuscript form and as such was likely known to Kant,[19] and that Kant was at least peripherally involved both in the debate with Herder[20] and in the pantheism controversy.[21] Moreover, the controversy or, as already noted and more to the point, Reinhold's Kantian answer to that controversy in his *Briefe über die Kantische Philosophie* contributed to the widespread acceptance of the critical philosophy.[22] However, these developments had a role to play in the constitution of the context within which the critical philosophy was read, but they had little influence on the development of the theoretical philosophy after its initial formulation in the first edition of the *Critique of Pure Reason* and were only to a small extent relevant to its reception. In a volume that presents the very early reception of Kant's theoretical philosophy, as this one does, this material is of relatively less importance than the material that speaks directly to the reception of that philosophy is.

The texts translated in this volume were published by Kant's contemporaries between 1782 and 1789. They stem largely from the first (empiricist) wave of early Kant criticisms that began in 1782, with the publication of the Feder/Garve review. Even though the endpoint of this approach to the criticism of Kant's philosophy is not as clearly marked, I selected 1789 in large part because the first complete volume of Eberhard's *Philosophisches Magazin*,[23] the voice piece of the second ("rationalist") wave of early Kant reception, was published in that year. To be sure, the early empiricist criticisms did not magically end in 1789,[24] but Kant's and public attention in general did shift for a time to the second-wave, rationalist reception and in short order to the emergence of idealism that began in the early 1790s.

My focus on texts from the early empiricist reception of the critical philosophy was prompted by two considerations. The first had to do with space and representativeness. Quite simply, there is too much material to represent more than one of the three identified approaches to Kant criticism in a single volume. The second point is of greater interest. Although both the rationalist criticisms of Kant's theoretical philosophy and the transition to idealism have been documented to some extent in the English literature – the rationalist critique in Allison's translation of Kant's *Entdeckung* and the transition to idealism in di Giovanni and Harris's *Between Kant and Hegel* – comparatively little information is available on the early empiricist reception. Yet from the point of view of the relevance that the work of Kant's contemporaries had for the development of Kant's philosophy, it is arguably the most significant work in early Kant criticism. It set the tone of early Kant reception, identified the issues that quickly came to dominate it and that are still discussed in contemporary Kant interpretation, and, perhaps most importantly, was instrumental in the additions and revisions that distinguish the second edition of the *Critique* from the first.

Even with the limited focus of this volume, the amount of material produced is much too vast to include more than a representative sample. I made every effort to include texts and portions of texts that are both historically and philosophically interesting. Among these are texts that are "firsts" either in terms of time of publication or in terms of criticism. The former includes the first review of the *Critique* (the Göttingen or Feder/Garve review) and Garve's original version of that review; among the latter I count the materials that were the first to raise telling and sometimes persistent objections, such as the neglected alternative argument that views space as both an a priori form of intuition and a property of things in themselves first advanced by Pistorius. I hope in this way to convey a sense of how Kant's theoretical philosophy was read by his empiricist critics, as well as a sense of what they found particularly troubling in his philosophy.[25] In addition, I included some representative responses to specific criticisms that Kant's early defenders formulated on his behalf. These are not always the best responses that could be given – Schaumann's response to Feder's idealism charge, for instance, serves to endorse, not dispel, the problem of affection – but they do tell us how Kant was read by his very early disciples and defenders. As it turns out, they tend to endorse the early interpretations of the critical philosophy but reject the objections that early critics associated with these interpretations.

The texts that are included in this collection were assigned to sections that reflect the order of their appearance and their sometimes overlapping major concerns – the Transcendental Aesthetic, the idealist implications of Kant's thought, and the Transcendental Analytic. The very first section contains the Feder/Garve and Garve reviews – the two clear "firsts" in terms of appearance – and the final section is devoted to a text by a defender (Schmid) and one by a critic (Pistorius). Both seek to come to terms with the difference between the empiricist approach to metaphysical and epistemological matters, on the one hand, and what has by this time been identified as Kant's purism on the other, thus neatly summing up the nature of the empiricist critique of Kant's philosophy.

Because it is the aim of this volume to let early critics and defenders speak for themselves, the following introductory remarks are largely limited to background and contexts, and to the major concerns and trends in interpretation that each text presents. Special attention is, however, devoted to the few texts to which Kant responded directly. The introduction ends with a brief account of periodical publication in late eighteenth century Germany, paying particular attention to the two major review journals in which much of the early debate was published.

FEDER/GARVE AND GARVE

The first two reviews that appeared after the publication of the *Critique of Pure Reason* and that dealt with its content were, as noted, the Göttingen or Feder/Garve review and Garve's much longer and more comprehensive original version of that review.[26] Both reviews are interesting for what they say about the *Critique of Pure Reason*, and for what they say is wrong with the *Critique of Pure Reason*. The FGr is interesting, as well, for what Kant says, both about the reviewer's interpretation of his work and about why its objections are misguided. It is an important piece, moreover, because, as the first and long-awaited (by Kant, at any rate) assessment of the *Critique of Pure Reason*, it, along with Kant's public and vitriolic reaction in the *Prolegomena* Appendix,[27] set the tone for early Kant reception for some time to come.

Here we might note that it was, in some measure, unfortunate that the Göttingen review was published at all. It set early Kant reception on a combative and contentious course (for which Kant was also to blame). Matters might have been different had Garve's version been the first review of the content of the *Critique* to be published, because it was written much more soberly, very much in the mode of a student who, admiring the teacher, tries to comprehend some new and difficult material. And given that one of Kant's chief objections to the FGr was not that it got his views wrong but that it presented his conclusions in so brief and stark a fashion as to make them appear ridiculous,[28] he might well have been much more positively impressed by Garve's thorough exposition of the main points of the *Critique* and the reasons leading Kant to make these points. But we must at least consider the possibility that he might not have been. Although Kant's response to Garve's letter that explains his role in the FGr[29] is very generous – he praises Garve's fairness, identifies him as one of the people who, along with Mendelssohn and Tetens, could bring metaphysics to its completion, and takes the questions he raises in his letter[30] seriously – he had not at this time read the review.[31] His reaction might have been different had the original review been available to him and had its publication not been preceded by the Feder fiasco. For Garve is obviously uncomfortable with many of the same things that Feder also claims to be uncomfortable with, for instance, Kant's apparent inability to differentiate dreams from experience,[32] and the failure, in their eyes, of the argument of the Fourth Paralogism.[33] Unlike the FGr, his version does not directly accuse the critical philosophy of idealism, but he is clearly suspicious that it not only fails to refute idealism but actually translates into it. It is hard to believe that, in the face of his grave disappointment at the silence that greeted the *Critique*, Kant would not have reacted negatively to this review as well. Hamann's report that Kant "was not satisfied with it [Garve's review] and thought that he had been treated like an imbecile"[34] is instructive, though, in the absence of any other evidence, it is hard to confirm whether this was indeed Kant's ultimate sentiment.

Feder

By way of content, the FGr is notorious for its charge that the *Critique* is a system of "higher idealism" and for its comparison of Kant's position with that of Berkeley. But aside from Kant's reaction to those charges in the *Prolegomena* Appendix, there is little reason for this specific notoriety. The review only mentions George Berkeley once, in passing, and the comparison is far from thoroughgoing. It amounts to no more than the remark that "[o]ne basic pillar of the Kantian system rests on these concepts of sensations as mere modifications of ourselves (on which *Berkeley*, too, principally builds his idealism), and of space and time."[35] Thus, both space and time and the operations of understanding (presumably, the "other pillar") are implicitly acknowledged as *non-Berkeleyan* elements of Kant's account, and the comparison is restricted to the observation that Kant happened to agree with Berkeley in taking the remaining element, sensation, to be a mere modification of the subject. As for the charge of "higher idealism," that is no more than an insult, one that Kant might have done well to ignore.

Given his focus on the idealism objection, Kant's response pays no attention to the account that the review provides of the *Critique* or, for that matter, to the single substantive objection that remains when it is divested of all insults and rhetorical flourishes. According to the review, the *Critique of Pure Reason* presents all knowledge as arising when understanding constructs a representation of objects by combining sensations, which are "mere modifications of ourselves," in accord with its own laws. The process is a multistage one. First, understanding combines "a multiplicity of small successive alterations of our soul"[36] to constitute sensations; then it arranges sensations in time, as cause and effect, and in space, as a world of interacting objects. Both material things and minds are objects that come to be constituted through this process. Because the laws understanding follows in this process of constitution are used to bring experience into being, they cannot be learned from experience but must be a priori.

The objection raised here, anticipating what would become a standard empiricist objection in the years to come, is that it is hard to see how we can come to distinguish reality from illusion through the *mere* employment of the understanding, without there being anything in the sensations that might guide this employment and dictate that the combination be carried out in one way in preference to others.[37] If the synthetic operations of understanding are not guided by what is given in sensation, then it makes no difference to understanding what particular sensory content is given when it goes on to synthesize that content. It is unclear, then, just what determines understanding to combine sensations in one way rather than another.

Because this became a standard objection, it is unfortunate that Kant did not address it, preferring instead to enumerate the insults he perceived in the review (among them, that the reviewer did not even call him *Mr.* Kant) and to engage in ad hominem attacks on the anonymous reviewer. It is instructive (and perhaps disturbing) that he appeared to let most of the basic picture of his account go unchallenged. He complained not that the review got him wrong but that it presented the main theses of the *Critique* in a long, sketchy list of bald unsupported assertions (which cannot even be understood when so taken out of their context), occasionally interspersing criticisms, but nowhere relating or engaging the arguments for the claims. His comments on the content of the review are limited to the brief critical comments contained in the opening and closing paragraphs (in translation). So he objected to the idealism charge and to the comparison with Berkeley (which he identified as the sole peculiar or noteworthy aspects) but ignored the worry about the role of sensations in the constitution of experience and the assertion that he took sensations to be assigned to locations in space and time by understanding.

Kant responded to the idealism charge by differentiating his idealism from the idealism he took to be Berkeley's. Truth, he claimed, rests on universal and necessary laws, laws that Berkeley, given that experience is only a posteriori for him, could find only in pure understanding and reason. So the kind of idealism advocated by Berkeley is, for Kant, a "mystic and visionary" idealism of the sort originally propounded by the Eleatics. It is really a sort of intellectualism or Platonism, which consists in the assertion that truth can only be known through pure understanding and reason and not through the senses. The *Critique*, by contrast, takes experience to contain a priori elements (space, time, and the pure concepts of understanding), which "prescribe their law to all possible experience a priori"[38] and so serve as a foundation for truth. As a consequence, it explodes the sort of "idealism" held by Berkeley.

Of course, the less that is said about the adequacy of this characterization of Berkeley's predicament, the better.[39] Berkeley would not accept that truth must rest on universal and necessary laws any more than he would accept Kant's characterization of his position. Nor does the FGr, which recognizes "our strongest and most enduring *sensations*"[40] as an acceptable, even if not always completely satisfactory, criterion of truth. This is an empiricist commitment that Kant, in light of his challenge to the author of the review to produce "synthetic a priori principles," seems to have missed. Indeed, the review seems quite willing to recognize Kant's characterization of the critical enterprise (namely, the identification of certain a priori elements that "prescribe their law to all possible experience"), though the authors, like later critics, may have been reluctant to accept that it is correct.

In any case, however indignantly Kant's answer might have repudiated the rhetoric and insults of the FGr, it is hard to see how it actually served to dispel the reading of the *Critique* the review proposed and, by implication, offer a satisfactory answer to the one substantive charge that the review made. For if truth is determined by the a priori elements in experience and *is not* in any way guided by sensations (which, being a posteriori, would undermine the "truth" of any principle they determined, according to the underlying premise that truth requires universal and necessary principles), then the FGr is right – Kant took experience to be the product of the imposition of spatiotemporal and categorial form on a kind of indifferent, sensory prime matter. And what determines that this imposition should be carried out in one way rather than another – that this sensation be placed to the left rather than the right of that one? Ironically this raises the problem of the distinction between truth and illusion – between right and wrong ways of constituting experience – in an even more virulent form. Given their interpretation of the critical enterprise and the support that interpretation appears to receive from Kant's *Prolegomena* response, it is not hard to see why Kant's empiricist critics would return to this issue time and again.[41]

Garve

Since the *Göttingen* review was fashioned from Garve's original version, it is not surprising that many of the charges the former intimates are in Garve's review as well, albeit more respectfully formulated. Now admittedly, Garve's idealism charge was not by far as explicitly (or insultingly) articulated,[42] but he still insinuated that the refutation of idealism in the Fourth Paralogism is a failure. Moreover, Garve expressed even more explicitly the view that Kant's position is that sensations are mere alterations in us, that understanding "makes" objects by a multistage process of synthesis of sensations in accord with its own laws, and that the difference between objective and subjective experience has to do with the fact that in the former case sensations are assigned to locations in space and time.

In addition, in his own evaluation at the close of the review, Garve attacked Kant's a priorism. He charged that rather than seek to obtain general concepts and laws by abstraction from experience, Kant tried to derive them all from space and time, previously established to be subjective laws of our sensory capacity and criteria for the objectivity of representations. Garve considers it incredible that space and time should be so "fruitful" – in part because our sensations of sound, taste, and touch lead us to know objects even though they are not spatial; in part because dreams and fantasies exhibit spatial structure.[43] Though the charges are strained, the general point, that Kant tried to take too much of experience to be constituted a priori, was one that has been repeated in many variants down through the years.[44]

Garve's review also contained early statements of a number of other objections that became classic. He objected to Kant's introduction of a new terminology, which he saw as a kind of sophistical ploy, used to obfuscate claims that, if stated in plain language, would sound too paradoxical.[45] He was particularly concerned, in this regard, with Kant's description of space and time as subjective "conditions" of sensible intuition – a term that he assumed that Kant used to obfuscate the status he truly gave to them: that of innate dispositions to imprint a certain form on all our impressions.[46] That Garve expressed particular dissatisfaction with this issue is instructive. It indicates that he, like many of his contemporaries, understood Kant's project to be a psychological, not an epistemic one. That is, he understood the critical project as one that sought to delineate the manner in which the mind actually processes sensations when working them up into representations of objects in space. If he had interpreted the project epistemically, by contrast, he would have seen it as identifying conditions that must be satisfied for knowledge of a certain type to arise, regardless of what particular mechanisms may be involved.[47]

Garve also raised a number of other points concerning objections that later critics treated in more detail. He questioned the basis for the Table of Categories, arguing that rather than being drawn from the nature of understanding they are obtained merely by analogy and association and the kind of hindsight that looks for what it thinks it has a need for,[48] and complained about what is now called Kant's architectonic – his tendency to impose the structure of the Table of Categories on his investigations. In addition, Garve presented a stinging indictment of Kant's resolution of the Third and Fourth Antinomies and his approach to the problems of freedom and the existence of God: "the author takes certain principles to be higher and more sacred than his systems, and, in certain decisions, has more regard for the consequences he wants at all costs to maintain than for the principles he has set down."[49] Behind this observation was the charge that a faith in these matters, grounded in a merely moral necessity, was impossible after the speculative proofs of them have been determined.

On the whole, Garve's review is quite an impressive piece of work. In spite of the fact that he did not fully understand or appreciate all aspects of the *Critique*, he did his best to give a fair and thorough account of it. And, as I have pointed out, the objections he raised, for the most part, became standard objections raised by the early empiricist critics of Kant. The review is certainly interesting for this reason, as it is interesting also in view of the role it played in the Göttingen review.

THE TRANSCENDENTAL AESTHETIC

Not surprisingly, the three early empiricist critics included in Section II – Tiedemann, Feder, and Pistorius – voiced the widespread suspicion of what they took to be Kant's central claim regarding space (and time) – its a priori origin. Each attacked Kant's position and backed up his attack by a plea for an alternative conception and origin. For Feder and Tiedemann, the alternative was a standard empiricist conception, for Pistorius it was a more complex one involving subjective and objective elements. Moreover, Tiedemann was content to argue that the empiricist account of space is preferable to the a priori one and to show that the individual arguments of the Metaphysical Exposition (in A) fail to establish their point, whereas both Feder and Pistorius had a broader aim of showing that the alternative each favored is not just preferable to but is, in fact, consistent with the arguments of the Metaphysical Exposition. By implication, they tried to show that Kant was not only misguided in holding the nativist conception of space but, more devastatingly, that even if he were correct, his arguments failed to show that this is so.

In the course of the examination of the Transcendental Aesthetic, these early critics raised objections that became classic. Two points are noteworthy here. First, both Tiedemann and Feder thought that the first argument came dangerously close to being trivially true.[50] Interestingly, this point seems to be endorsed by the author of the *ALZ* review of Feder's text included here. In his zealous effort to defend the argument, the reviewer pushed it in a direction that even Feder hesitated to assume Kant had intended: that of taking the point to be the unassailable, but also trivial, thesis that *space* is required if we are to represent the objects of our experience as being *spatial* in nature. Second, as noted, both Tiedemann and Feder attempted to defend an empirical origin of space – Tiedemann appealed to the senses of sight and touch and Feder provided a tantalizing, though unfortunately not a clearly worked out allusion to the possibility that the concept of space may be developed by appeal to feelings of motion in combination with retinal images.

These texts do more, however, than raise particular objections to the Transcendental Aesthetic. Each also serves to bring to light salient issues to which early empiricist critics appealed in their attack on the Kantian system. Tiedemann's examination is noteworthy as an early instance of an attack on Kant's claim that mathematical judgments are synthetic; Feder and Pistorius stand out for bringing the research on the Molyneux question to bear on the question of the origin of the concept of space. Pistorius gave powerful expression to the three most serious objections to Kant's theoretical philosophy in the first part of the *Critique*: the problem of affection generally associated with Jacobi,[51] the problem of the neglected alternative usually attributed to Adolf Trendelenburg,[52] and the problem of subjectivity, which has antecedents in comments on Kant's Inaugural Dissertation made by Mendelssohn, Johann Heinrich Lambert, and Schultz.[53] Additionally, the debate between Feder and some of Kant's defenders revealed the prevalence of the temporal-psychological interpretation of Kant's claim that space is a priori, indicating thereby how at least this aspect of the Transcendental Aesthetic was read by Kant's contemporaries in general.

Tiedemann

Taking its cue from the *Prolegomena*, Tiedemann's essay is, as noted, particularly noteworthy for an early instance of an attack on Kant's claim that mathematical (arithmetical and geometrical) judgments are synthetic.[54] With regard to arithmetical judgments, Tiedemann claimed that $7 + 5 = 12$ is analytic because the concept of twelve units may be analyzed into a group of seven units and a group of five. Here the "analysis" to which the concept of twelve is subjected is actually a division of a whole into its mereological parts, rather than an identification of the specific differentiae defining a concept, but Tiedemann was explicit that the one deserves to be called an analysis as much as the other. In making this assertion, he might be thought to be begging the question against Kant, who could have insisted that the operations are *not* the same. But by spurring his Kantian opponents to be more explicit about why this should be so, Tiedemann at least advanced the discussion.

Tiedemann then explained that some geometrical propositions result from the composition and division of larger figures, and so are analytic for the reasons already given. Others, such as the proposition that the shortest distance between two points is a straight line, have a different status. His examination of this type of proposition involved an implicit appeal to Hume, who had earlier observed that some relations can be discovered simply by inspecting and comparing the terms that are to be related, without having to consult experience any further.[55] Thus, I can discover that crimson is more like scarlet than like green, that one note is higher or lower than another, or that salt is not sweet, simply by having and inspecting the concepts concerned. In a sense, these propositions are analytic because they follow merely from an inspection of the concepts to be compared. Of course, the *concepts* must originally have been given through experience, but the *judgment* that the concepts exhibit a certain relation to one another is not itself based on experience. As Tiedemann pointed out, "[w]hen the relation and connection of concepts is understood on the basis of those concepts alone, when all experience is excluded from it, and when in all this we clearly recognize that no other combination is possible, then . . . we do not ask further about the origin of concepts."[56]

In contrast, that one thing should be the cause of another, should be identified as a later state of another, or should be placed before rather than after it cannot be determined simply by inspecting our concepts. Some further reference to the manner in which the objects answering to these concepts are presented in experience is required. Thus, propositions involving relations like cause, effect, identity, and contiguity are synthetic in a sense in which propositions involving relations of similarity and difference are not. In the latter case, one needs experience only to learn of the terms to be compared and the relation is then evident from comparison – or, as one might put it, by "analysis" of the already given concepts – whereas in the former experience is required not merely to exhibit the terms but also to exhibit the relation.

Tiedemann tried to exploit this difference to account for the principle that a straight line is the shortest distance between two points.[57] When we are asked to identify the line that is the shortest distance between two points, we compare the straight one with all the possible crooked ones, and it is simply evident by comparison – or "analysis" – that the straight line is the shortest of them all.

Of course, Kant would object that the comparison Tiedemann envisioned is not possible without intuition. We do not compare our *concepts* of straight and crooked lines with one another; rather, we apply ink to paper or build images in our imaginations to picture straight and crooked lines as they appear in space in accord with their concepts, and we then compare these *images* with one another. Here, the results of the comparison are tacitly influenced by the structure of the space in which the lines are pictured; therefore, we are not simply analyzing or comparing our concepts but comparing objects as they appear in space in accord with these concepts.[58]

In spite of the problems and misinterpretations that we might find in the essay today, it generated a great deal of attention, largely, I suspect, because it was the first sustained attack on the Transcendental Aesthetic. By the time the first part of Tiedemann's three-part examination appeared in 1785, Kant's contemporaries had become quite interested in the critical philosophy and were struggling to come to terms with it. Given, however, that little had as yet been published, and given also that Tiedemann presented the essay as answering Kant's *Prolegomena* invitation that one examine his system and identify any problems,[59] the essay proved to be a welcome opportunity to engage, in this case, the Transcendental Aesthetic. Reaction to the essay was predictably mixed, ranging from approval,[60] to prompt critique in the pro-Kantian *Allgemeine Literatur-Zeitung*,[61] to a devastating assessment on the part of Kant. As he put it in a letter to Johann Bering, "[i]n his ostensive refutations Mr. Tiedemann has shown so little comprehension of the question to be addressed, so little insight into the principles that are decisive in its resolution, and should I say this, so little ability for pure philosophical investigations, . . . that I believe he will avoid further attempts of this kind."[62]

Pistorius

Pistorius's piece is a review of Schultz's *Erläuterungen* – largely a paraphrase of the *Critique* with a few hints, as Schultz put it, for a closer examination of the Kantian system.[63] As a review of an early "commentary" on the *Critique* rather than an examination of some portion of it, it differs to some extent from the other essays/reviews considered so far. Pistorius's comments sprang, he claimed, from Schultz's failure to address the most serious objection to Kant's philosophy – the problem of subjectivity – and was, therefore, not solely focused on the Transcendental Aesthetic. However, because he took Kant's emphasis on the subjective status of space and time as being chiefly responsible for generating the problem of subjectivity (and the problem of affection), much of what he said in the review ended up being addressed to the Transcendental Aesthetic. He discussed other problems, which have for reasons of brevity been excluded here, including, in particular, the solution (or, in his view, the failure of the ostensive solution) of the Third Antinomy.[64]

In the course of setting out his criticism of the Transcendental Aesthetic, Pistorius offered an interpretation that is in some measure more sophisticated than that of other critics. He began by demonstrating why the subjectivity of space (and time) generates the problem it does, proceeded to demonstrate an alternate conception that, he claimed, was consistent with Kant's arguments, and ended by setting out the advantages it had over Kant's merely subjective conception. His alternate conception is interesting for two reasons. First, rather than simply endorse the empiricist conception of space (and time), his alternative appealed to an empirical *and* a priori origin, thus attributing to it a dual objective *and* subjective nature against what he described as Kant's merely subjective one (and the empiricist merely objective one). Second, it is a conception that tries to come to terms with the question of just what it means to call space a priori in the first place.

The concern that drove Pistorius in virtually all his work on Kant, his defenders, and his critics, has to do with the relation or connection of what he called the intelligible (objective) world (the world of things in themselves) and the sensible world (the world of appearances). Thinking that on the Kantian system the connection cannot be maintained (and, by implication, that the existence of "the objective intelligible world is as good as destroyed for us"[65]), he asked why may we not grant that Kant's argument for the subjectivity of space and time have some force, but allow that space and time might be *both* subjective and objective – both forms of sensibility and features of things in themselves. The charge that Kant neglected to consider this alternative was just the "neglected alternative argument" that was later to be popularized by Trendelenburg.[66] Now, Pistorius did not so much accuse Kant of neglecting an alternative, as he simply devoted his efforts to trying to make a case that there really was an alternative to be made out and that, even though it was not the only possible account that could be given, it is preferable to the account Kant provided.

Pistorius's main suggestion was that certain general features of space and time may be grounded in the way we are constituted (or our limitation as he called it, thereby offering a tantalizing hint for a possible interpretation of Kant's claim that space is a priori – albeit one he did not further develop), whereas the specific way in which these features are determined may be grounded in the objects that affect us.[67] Now admittedly, this was not an easy position to work out. If the general features of space and time are due to us, then we may still wonder whether these are features that we prescribe to things in themselves, thus constraining the manner of their existence. If we say that things in themselves just happen to accord with the general spatial and temporal features we "impose" or "legislate," one wonders about the fortuitous harmony between the sensible and the objective world Pistorius's account would seem to presuppose. And if this were Pistorius's position, the objection he raised to Kant in a subsequent essay, namely, that the Copernican Revolution arbitrarily supposed that nature conformed to our cognition,[68] would apply to his account as well.

There is a great deal more in Pistorius's essay, but even these few remarks should be sufficient to indicate the persistent concern animating this and other discussions he undertook. It is perhaps unfortunate that Pistorius, although known through reviews in the *Allgemeine deutsche Bibliothek* initialed Rk, Sg, Wo, and Zk,[69] only played a critical role in the early reception of the Kantian philosophy.[70] Without a university position and being located in an even greater *isolation* from the heart of German academic life than Kant (he was a pastor on the island of Rügen in the Baltic Sea), Pistorius did not have the influence he should perhaps have had. It is difficult to know, accordingly, whether his reviews were widely read or eagerly awaited. Kant himself referred to Pistorius with approval, but only in connection with his moral philosophy.[71]

Feder

Like Tiedemann's essay, Feder's book, especially the portion commenting on the Transcendental Aesthetic, garnered a great deal of attention, not surprisingly given his role in the Göttingen review, which Feder did not try to hide. But that was not the only reason the book was noticed. Feder was quite well respected in his own right at the time,[72] although he lost a great deal of that respect over his role in early Kant criticism. So it made sense that his contemporaries would await the promised examination, that they would review it,[73] and that those who had by this time become Kantians would try to convert Feder as well by responding to his arguments.[74] And although Kant vowed after the *Prolegomena* that he would not engage his critics again, a vow he perhaps unfortunately only broke once, in the *Entdeckung*, he at least considered writing a response to his empiricist critics, notably Feder and Tittel.[75]

The portion of Feder's book devoted to the examination of the Transcendental Aesthetic is noteworthy for its thorough examination of the arguments of the Metaphysical Exposition (in A) and as an example of an early paraphrase of Kant's arguments. The language is simple and direct and is probably the best expression of how these arguments would have been most naturally read and understood by Kant's contemporaries. This is true also for the overall reading of the Transcendental Aesthetic. Feder's text reveals that the standard empiricist interpretation of Kant's conception of space (and time) as a priori was a temporal-psychological rather than a logical-epistemic one. So he thought that the representation is not merely a condition of the possibility of sensory experience, as it would be on the epistemic reading, but a representation that we must have "before" any particular intuitions or sensations of outer sense and that we cannot have abstracted from those representations.[76] Interpreted in this light, Kant is understood as a nativist about the origin of our idea of space, and it is this nativism that Feder and the empiricist critics in general chiefly object to.[77]

The view that Kant had intended to take a position on the psychological origin of our representation of space, while not perhaps as widely endorsed today as it was by Kant's contemporaries,[78] has a long and important history. The history of the development of the theory of visual perception in the ninteenth century, for instance, cannot be disengaged from this reading of Kant, as many of the principal players such as Jakob Friedrich Fries, Rudolf Hermann Lotze, and Hermann von Helmholtz were explicitly concerned to engage it.[79] Feder stood at the forefront of this tradition. In recent years, the early psychological reading has been reintroduced (in more sophisticated form) and defended.[80]

Significantly, it is a reading that was accepted, indeed endorsed, by Kant's contemporary defenders. The *Allgemeine Literatur-Zeitung* review of this portion of *On Space and Causality* that is included in this volume[81] is in this respect as interesting for what it does not say as for what it does. The author set out to defend Kant against Feder's attack but did not take Feder to task over his temporal and psychological interpretation of what Kant meant by calling space a priori. On the contrary, the reviewer engaged Feder at that same level and attempted to defend Kant by appealing to the same sorts of empirical arguments that Feder used to attack him.

The general endorsement of the temporal-psychological reading of Kant rather than the logical-epistemic one is also evident in their respective treatment of the Molyneux question.[82] Feder appealed to the research surrounding this issue in order to further cement the empirical nature/origin of the representation of space. He argued that the a priori origin of the concept of space cannot be squared with the empirical evidence of the difficulty newly sighted adults have in identifying the space they see with the space they feel. Contrary to Kant's claims about the essential unity of space in the later expositions, he argued that there might in fact be two distinct kinds of space: one given empirically through sensations of touch and the other given empirically through sensations of vision, though common elements might subsequently be abstracted from the two. He faults Kant for not having considered this research, thinking, no doubt, that had Kant done so he could not have taken space to have an a priori origin.

In his response to Feder's appeal to research on the Molyneux question and his critique of Kant's failure to consider it, Born charged that Feder failed to distinguish the empirical representation of space, which is determined through visual and tangible experience, from pure intuition. However, rather than represent pure intuition as an epistemic or sensible condition of the possibility of experience, Born represented it as an indeterminate representation that lies in the mind antecedent to all empirical experiences. To the extent that he did so, he held the same temporal-psychological understanding of Kant's position as did Feder and the author of the *ALZ* review.[83] One cannot help but wonder how Kant himself understood his claim that space is a priori.

In the context of his discussion of idealism, Feder returned briefly to his criticism of Kant's concept of space. §22 has therefore been included in this section rather than the next one. Here Feder sought to make two points: (1) that Kant was wrong to assume that simply because space is infinitely divisible, the objects in space must also be infinitely divisible,[84] and (2) though Feder hesitated to say so, that Kant was inconsistent in holding that empty space cannot be a possible object of perception while simultaneously affirming, in the second argument of the Metaphysical Expositions, that space can somehow be thought or given independently of objects.[85] Feder's treatment of both points was excellent, indeed, it would make *On Space and Causality* an important book, even if no other portion of it did.

IDEALISM

The selections contained in Section III can be divided into those that speak to the A-edition of the *Critique* and the *Prolegomena* and those that take issue with the second edition, specifically its Refutation of Idealism. The first focus is represented by Feder and Jacobi, the second by Pistorius. Defenders are Schaumann, who addresses his remarks to Feder, and Born, whose defense takes issue with both Feder and Pistorius.

The selections included in this section demonstrate that, with respect to the issue of idealism, Kant and his empiricist critics did not so much fail to understand each other, as they talked past each other. As a consequence, each side in the debate was unwilling (perhaps unable) to appreciate the other's concerns. This was evident in the respective terms in which the debate was framed. Even though Kant presented transcendental idealism in epistemological terms – we can have certain knowledge but only of appearances – his critics took issue with what they understood to be the ontological implications of restricting knowledge to appearances – the very existence of transcendentally real things becomes dubious. In response to his *Prolegomena* response to the FGr, they might have been willing to concede that his position was not Berkeley's,[86] but they still insisted that it translated into the empirical or skeptical idealism Kant associated with Descartes.[87] No matter how certain we might be of appearances, the means by which this certainty is attained – the a priori forms of intuition and categories – makes it in principle impossible to have access to things in themselves. Unlike Kant, they thought that such access was necessary if our position was not to be idealist, and, more importantly, if we were to have viable knowledge of the world. To give voice to their suspicions, they asked repeatedly what appearances were; how, if at all, they were distinct from mere representations in us; and how we could possibly live in a world about which we cannot know anything.

Kant's published responses did not help matters.[88] Unwilling to concede the ontological idealism his critics charged, indeed, unwilling (or unable) to deal with this dimension of their criticism, Kant emphasized the very epistemological benefits of his position that were at the heart of their suspicions. And when, in the B-Refutation, he finally provided the sort of proof of the existence of actual things that could have laid matters to rest, if successful, the questions about the nature of appearances, of actual things in space, reappeared with renewed vigor, along with the charges of ambiguity already familiar from the first section. For, they wondered, what could actual things in space be in the Kantian system, if not appearances, that is, on their interpretation, if not representations.[89] It should not come as a surprise that, faced with the implications of Kant's philosophical approach and his apparent inability to address their concerns, his empiricist contemporaries tended to make a plea for a kind of common-sense realism.

Feder

Feder's reflections on idealism in *On Space and Causality* constituted his response to the attack against the Göttingen review Kant launched in the *Prolegomena*. Stooping neither to the tone of apparent amazement that anyone could say the sorts of things Kant said that we find in his initial review nor to the polemical invective Kant employed against him, Feder delivered a set of reflections that are representative of a measured and mature assessment of the passages from the A-edition Fourth Paralogism and their echoes in the *Prolegomena*. Feder agreed with much of what Kant said, and, not surprisingly, the respects in which he agreed with Kant are the respects in which Kant's position resembled the empiricist position to which Feder adhered (for instance, that we do not *directly* know things in themselves, and that our knowledge is at least in part determined by the sensible apparatus),[90] but he drew the line at what he thought was the extreme (and in his eyes unwarranted) idealist inference he took Kant to draw from these points: that we cannot have any knowledge of actual (mind-independent) things existing outside of us. Against this position he defended a common-sense realist one.

In his defense of a realist position against Kant, Feder took an interesting intermediary position between Locke's representative realism and Berkeley's direct realism. As Locke would have done, he conceded to Kant that we do not *directly* know things in themselves, but only the representations they bring about in us.[91] But he disagreed with Kant over whether the representations that merely appear to us refer to objects that exist independently of us, or whether we are warranted in actually asserting the existence of such objects by inference from our sensations. On Feder's interpretation, transcendental idealism, asserting that "bodies are mere representations in us,"[92] forbids *any* reference to transcendentally real things, and he did his best to show that this is contrary to common sense. Now, Feder recognized that Kant occasionally claimed that the notion of appearances carries with it the idea of something that appears.[93] However, he regarded this as inconsistent with the consequences of Kant's doctrine of the subjectivity of space and time and everything in it, which precludes any knowledge of the existence of things in themselves as causes of our representations in contrast to, say, God or the invention of our minds or a kind of "manicheanism" – by which he presumably meant some combination of the former two possibilities.[94]

Feder's defense of his realist position also involved an appeal to the dual distinctions between primary and secondary qualities[95] and between acts of perception and objects of perception.[96] The position he articulated with respect to these distinctions hints at that taken by Reid.[97] Our terminology for both primary and secondary qualities is ambiguous, Feder claimed, sometimes referring to the sensible quality that appears to us, sometimes to the power or ability in the object to affect us in this way (in the case of secondary qualities) or to the actual – as opposed to the perspectively relative – qualities of the object (in the case of primary qualities). And when we talk about our perception of the qualities as they are in objects, we need to distinguish between the act of perception, which is in the mind, and the object thought of or represented through this act. Like Reid, Feder suggested that the belief in an external object resulting from the process of perception may not consist in the existence of a mental object – a copy or image of this object that comes to inhere in the mind as a representation resulting from the process of perception – but may instead be a judgment that consists in the act of asserting the existence of an object as it is outside of the mind, an object possessing something like the primary qualities exhibited by our sensations, and some merely relatively denominated "power" to bring about our sensations of the secondary qualities. This judgment has the status of a basic or axiomatic principle that arises in us as a result of the process of perception and that cannot be further justified.

Although Feder appreciated the problems with which Kant (and others) dealt, there can be no question where he stood with respect to Kant. He thought that Kant has gone too far from common sense and from actual objects. One comment in particular vividly illustrates what he took to be the absurdity of Kant's position. He wondered how anyone could seriously think that "Göttingen is something in me, a mere representation or modification of myself, that the wall on which I am taking a walk is in me, that the view over meadows and fields to the mountains, and the sun and moon [are in me]."[98] To the extent that Kant was driven to this position by his overall philosophical approach, which Feder thought was the case, this approach must be rejected.

Schaumann

Although the next piece in this selection was not the next to be published (Jacobi's classic piece precedes it by some two years), Schaumann's lengthy "letter" to Feder appended to his *On the Transcendental Aesthetic* is a response to the latter's charge that the transcendental philosophy is "simply idealistic" and must be read in connections with both Feder's original review and the subsequent reaffirmation of that charge. Schaumann provided the kind of defense of Kant that had become standard by this time, particularly since it echoed the defense Kant himself gave in the *Prolegomena*. Unfortunately, he placed the sort of interpretation on Kant's work that opened it up to Jacobi's classic statement of the problem of affection – according to Vaihinger the most serious objection that has yet been raised against Kant.[99] And this means, in turn, that in spite of the fact that it preceded Schaumann's defense, Jacobi's piece must be read as the culmination of this first part of the idealism debate rather than simply a cog in it.

Schaumann's role in early Kant reception is a minor one. *On the Transcendental Aesthetic*, to which the "letter" to Feder was appended, was his first publication, written when he was a teacher at a school in Halle (he was latter called to a professorship in Gießen), and given that it appeared toward the end of the first, namely empiricist, wave of early Kant reception, the book was largely ignored.[100] Schaumann acknowledged equal respect and admiration for Kant and Feder,[101] and he was clearly one of Kant's early defenders who sought to convert Feder to the Kantian philosophy.

In spite of the "minor" role Schaumann played in early Kant reception, his piece is a fascinating study of the difficulties and interpretive challenges that Kant's position posed for the average reader at the time, and it is still a rewarding piece for anyone concerned to study the idealism problem in Kant and the complexities surrounding it. Echoing a point Kant had already made, Schaumann insisted that the *Critique* did not deny the existence of material objects, as idealism did. It merely affirmed that the immediate objects of our knowledge are representations that are subjective states of our own minds and that exist only in us.[102] Schaumann thus took Kant to be, if not an idealist, at least a representationalist – a philosopher who supposes that there are intermediate representative entities standing between the objects in the external world and the subject, and that knowledge is directly of these representations.

Now, insofar as he did this, Schaumann seemed to be granting the main point to Feder. Even if Kant's position was not characterized by the view that material objects do not exist, on Schaumann's interpretation it is the view that the only "objects" that can be known to exist are our own representations, which are subjective states in us that cannot be supposed to exist unperceived or independently of all perceivers. The only difference between the Kantianism that emerges here and simple idealism is that Kant's position is epistemological whereas simple idealism is ontological. Kant, that is, confined himself to making a claim about what we can know, whereas simple idealism makes a claim about what can exist. Both claims, however, are perfectly compatible with one another.

Aware that this picture could not stand, Schaumann mounted two interconnected lines of argument to give it a more realistic cast. With regard to the distinction between "real" and "imaginary" representations, Schaumann dealt with a point made by Kant in the *Prolegomena*, although he cashed it out in a significantly different way. Rather than appeal to the a priori status of space as establishing the, for him, important difference between Kant's position and that of Berkeley,[103] Schaumann appealed to sensation. "Real" appearances, he claimed, are those that are discovered through sensation, the rest are imaginary.[104] The answer is not a happy one. Quite apart from the problem posed by the dreaming argument, which Schaumann did not consider, his position was open to the objection that inner sense, which might well include the awareness of the products of imagination, was as much a "sense" for Kant as outer sense. At the very least, then, the attempt to found a reality/illusion distinction on sense requires more explanation and support than Schaumann thought it necessary to provide. It is an interesting question why Schaumann did not pursue the line Kant himself suggests in the *Prolegomena*. It might be that he simply did not understand it.

Schaumann's second line of argument was a version of Kant's argument of affection.[105] Even though the core thesis of the *Critique* is that we only know our own perceptions, which are mere representations in us, Schaumann argued that the *Critique* allowed that the existence of some transcendental object distinct from us may be immediately affirmed on the basis of some causal inference. Something else must exist as the cause of the sensations that constitute the matter of our intuitions, and the *Critique* took this to be a real, a posteriori element of our experience that we ourselves are not responsible for. At the very least, we can conceive or form the idea of such a thing, though we cannot describe it in any way, or take it to bear any resemblance to our representations.[106] Of course, if we are to do more than merely think that there might be objects distinct from our representations, Kant was still stuck with having to affirm that we can only know our own representations, and not having a position that differs significantly from simple idealism. But if, on the contrary, we are to have any assurance that there actually are transcendental objects distinct from ourselves, then the causal inference cannot be merely problematic, but must assure us of the actual existence of these objects. Schaumann, who set himself the difficult task of addressing a criticism Kant himself was unable to address in a satisfactory way (at least in the eyes of his contemporaries)[107] waffled between these two alternatives and never came up with a clear position.

Schaumann's appeal to causality invited the charge that Jacobi had already made earlier, that an appeal to the category of cause to make claims about the noumenal world was a violation of the *Critique*'s claims, so that Kant could not in fact consistently draw the distinction between what arises in us as sensation and what is an a priori form contributed by the subject.

Jacobi

Jacobi, who was not among Kant's empiricist critics, attacked the critical philosophy in light of his attack on the Enlightenment faith in reason.[108] Nevertheless, the vehement critique of the A-edition Fourth Paralogism he mounted in the text at hand brought the empiricist idealism critique out with greater clarity than other critics were able to provide. It may be that he was able to do so because he was unencumbered by a desire to defend reason or common sense. At any rate, he set out to examine the charge that Kant's philosophy is manifestly idealistic and even solipsistic. And he concluded that, whatever Kant or his defenders may say, it must be. Insofar as Kant tried in any way to even hint that there are things in themselves distinct from us, he contradicted himself.

Kant's distinction between sensation, as matter of intuition, and space and time, as its forms, already constituted such a hint, Jacobi observed, and insofar as it did so that distinction itself must be jettisoned. All our representations must be considered to simply be in us, even if the cost is an admission of solipsism.

Jacobi observed that Kant attributed space and time to the constitution of the subject's receptive capacities and sensation to the activity of the affecting objects. But how, he went on to ask, could Kant say that sensations are the effects of some object on the senses of the subject if he denied that we can have any knowledge of things in themselves? To be consistent, Kant would have had to admit that we have no idea what corresponds to or causes our sensations. It might be a whole collection of things (different ones for different sensations) that are distinct from the subject and act on its organs. It might be one thing that divinely inspires the subject with different appearances. It might be the subject itself. It might be nothing at all. Kant could not consistently prefer one of these explanations to any of the others and still abide by his core claims about the bounds of our knowledge.

Nor could he try to salvage the distinction between matter and form of intuition by grounding it in the distinction between receptivity and spontaneity. Just as one cannot think of a downslope without thinking of an upslope, so one cannot think of receptivity or passivity without thinking both of something that is affected and of its being affected by something else. Thus, the notion that we are receptive always carries with it the thought of something distinct from us that acts on us, and knowledge of that sort is expressly denied by Kant.

Today, Jacobi's challenge to Kant is known largely through his epigrammatic pronouncement that it is impossible to find a way into the Kantian philosophy without the thing in itself, and impossible to stay there with it.[109] But this piece as a whole mounted a powerful and profound challenge to Kant's A-edition and *Prolegomena* arguments refuting idealism and demonstrated just how difficult it must have been for Kants' disciples to mount a successful defense to Kant's early critics. It deserves a wide reading.

Pistorius

Pistorius's review of the second edition of the *Critique* was limited to two points: the Copernican turn in metaphysics Kant claimed to have initiated[110] and his new refutation of idealism.[111] His remarks on the Copernican turn highlight what the empiricists took to be the root cause of everything that was wrong with Kant's philosophical approach, and his condemnation of the Refutation demonstrates why any effort Kant made to escape the idealist implications of the turn must end in failure.

Pistorius's remarks about the Copernican turn recalled earlier concerns about empirical guidedness.[112] It was a turn, he thought, that Kant simply could not make as thoroughly as he would have liked. The only way objects could truly conform to our knowledge is if they are considered to be a kind of Aristotelian prime matter that can be molded in any way we like by the processing operations of the mind. But considered as such, objects do not contain anything to guide the process of apprehension. There is nothing in the objects that will determine that they will be seen as red rather than blue, as square rather than circular, as on the left rather than on the right, as causally sequential in accord with a rule rather than reciprocally simultaneous, and so on. Under such conditions it is entirely up to us whether to constitute the world in one way rather than another. And that, Pistorius thought, left Kant with two choices: either to accept that his approach entailed a philosophy that was simply idealist in nature, or, if he wanted to maintain the realist thesis that objects play some role in guiding and determining the content of our knowledge and the manner in which our a priori forms and categories are applied, to abandon the Copernican turn. The realist thesis entails that our knowledge conforms to objects rather than the other way around and so is inconsistent with the Copernican Revolution.

The Refutation of Idealism is the only real addition to the second edition of the *Critique*, Pistorius went on to say, and it did not seem to cohere with the Copernican turn at all because that, as he thought he had already established, necessarily implied simple idealism, not its refutation. That Kant purported to refute idealism is, moreover, inconsistent with his claim that the things that cause our representations of external objects can never be known, and that to identify these things with objects that correspond to our representation rather than ideas in the mind of God or the products of the subject's own inspiration can never be anything more than problematic. To say that things in themselves *must* exist as the causes of the representations that immediate self-consciousness reveals to us is, first, to subsume things in themselves under the category of necessity, and second, to treat them as being spatially and temporally determined. Both are contrary to Kant's prescriptions.

Of course, one might respond that the "external" objects that the Refutation proves to exist are not things in themselves, but merely appearances in space.[113] To this reply Pistorius had two answers: the first was that Kant himself did not clearly distinguish between the two, but simply spoke of "the existence of outer objects,"[114] an expression that equivocated between things in themselves actually existing outside of me, and appearances merely imagined by me to exist outside of me as a result of some inference. Pistorius's second answer drew on the first. Were we to in fact disambiguate Kant's pronouncements and take the Refutation to merely establish the existence of apparent things, the whole exercise would be a farce, and an affirmation rather than a refutation of idealism, since these very objects were ones that Kant insisted only have being in us.[115] To claim with any seriousness that an experience of outer objects is a prior condition of any consciousness of the representations in our mind when the experience of outer objects being referred to is not a direct perception of things in themselves, but is itself among the representations in our minds that we are conscious of is to get caught in a vicious circle.

Like Feder's and Jacobi's critiques of the A-edition and the *Prolegomena*, Pistorius's objections to the Refutation left Kant and his defenders with a significant challenge. Kant did not take up this challenge in his work produced for publication, but he returned to the issue of idealism several times in his unpublished notes.[116] One set of notes in particular, R5653 and 5654, dated to the period immediately following the *Critique* and Pistorius's review of it,[117] began with the argument of the refutation, but took it an essential step farther. Mounting a complex transcendental argument, Kant now tied the existence of objects that are truly distinct from us to the awareness we indubitably have of persisting objects outside of us in space (as per the B-Refutation).[118] It is not clear, of course, whether Kant drafted this argument specifically in response to Pistorius's criticism, or, for that matter, whether this argument successfully addressed Pistorius's concerns, but it is instructive that he returned to this issue again, even after having provided the official Refutation of Idealism.

Born

The final selection in this section is by Born, a Professor of Philosophy at Leizig and one of Kant's early defenders.[119] The text was primarily directed at Adam Weishaupt, one of Kant's empiricist critics whose three texts appeared in 1788,[120] in other words, when the empiricist trend of early Kant criticism was drawing to a close. §36, however, entitled "On Idealism" was aimed at Feder, who was here named the chief anti-Kantian, and §41 took Pistorius's review of the B-edition, which, Born noted, came his way shortly before the book went to press.[121]

Born's reply to Feder opened by charging that no one can rightly accept Kant's premises concerning the limits of sensible knowledge without accepting his conclusions that the objects of our knowledge are all appearances.[122] But this was hardly to the point. Kant's opponents did not accept the premises as generously as Born supposed, and the point they wished to emphasize was that *if* one accepted the premises then one ought to own up to being an idealist, and not pretend to affirm the existence of the mind-independent external world.

When it came to differentiating Kant's position from the idealism with which he was charged, Born provided the two-pronged response that had become standard by this time. So he argued, first, that whereas the idealist denied that anything existed but minds and their representations, the Kantian held that actual objects existed outside of us, but that we only knew their effects.[123] This ignored the force of the critics' (Feder, Jacobi, and Pistorius) point that if we only know "their" effects, then we are hardly in a position to say that "they" are objects outside of rather than products of our minds or ideas seen in the mind of God.

Born's second response was to claim that for Kant the world of the senses was certainly something actual and that there was a real distinction to be drawn within the Kantian system between this world and a merely illusory or fantastic world created by our imaginations.[124] But this was again hardly to the point. The issue the critics raise is the issue of realism and idealism, not the issue of reality and illusion. One can be an idealist and still provide, within an idealist system, for a distinction between ideas of sense and ideas of imagination, or reality and illusion. The point that Kant's critics made against him was that it did him no good to protest that he was capable of drawing a distinction between those of our representations that we refer to as the real world and those that we take to be illusory if the representations in the former class are not direct perceptions of things in themselves, but are still appearances supposed to exit only in us. They granted Kant his distinction between reality and illusion but still observe that the way he drew it committed him to an idealist construal of "reality." At least in his published work, Kant never seemed to have seen through things this far. Neither did his defenders.

Ultimately, the failure of Kant's defenders (and Kant himself) to come to terms with the idealism objection made nothing so clear as that Kant lacked a viable, or at least a clearly worked out, notion of intentionality. Lacking that notion Kant could not, as Reid could, say that we have representations that are *of* an object, that the representation is in the mind where it exists only when it is thought, but that the object is somewhere else and has a different sort of existence – that the representation consists in the act of referring to or thinking of an object distinct from itself, and is not itself an object that the mind knows.[125] Kant's talk of "appearance" was his own confused substitute for the notion of an intentional object. Appearances are representations in us that are themselves the objects of the mind's awareness. The critics pushed Kant on this matter and asked him how, if appearances exist only in us, he could claim to be a realist, rather than an idealist with a viable reality/illusion distinction. If we had direct perception of external objects, there would be no question of Kant's entitlement to deny idealism. But because he held that all our knowledge is only of objects that are themselves representations had by the mind, it is not clear with what right he could deny idealism. Reid's middle way of holding that the representations that are in us are not themselves the objects that appear to us and maintaining instead that the objects that appear to us are intentional objects that are thought *of* through the act of representing would have provided Kant with a sense of "appearance" that could have answered the idealism critique. It would have allowed him to claim that the object is not literally in us, but only the representation, whereas the object is rather what the representation is intentionally directed to refer to and so has a different sort of existence than that of a purely mental state – even if not the existence of a thing in itself.

Admittedly, this is a controversial point, especially considering that others have found a notion of intentionality in Kant's writings.[126] However, even if we grant an interpretation that ascribes a concept of intentionality to Kant, it would still be true that he did not articulate the notion with sufficient clarity to allow his critics and defenders to see that it might address the idealism objection. Indeed, we may wonder whether he was altogether clear on this position himself. In light of this observation, we can hardly fault his contemporaries for reading him as they did.

To return for a moment to Born's text, his reply to Pistorius's review was ultimately no more successful than his earlier response to Feder. He completely neglected the first of Pistorius's chief concerns: that any sense of empirical guidedness is incompatible with the assertion that objects must conform to our cognitive capacities. The claim that actual things can be supposed to exist outside us because we can sense their effects was made as if it were entirely problematic,[127] and the answer to the charge of idealism was made to consist in the assertion that Kant was able to draw the distinction between those representations in us we denominate "real" and those that are imaginary. As Born understood this distinction, it was one that was drawn between representations that are not products of our will and those that are.[128] That Pistorius asked how it was even possible to draw this distinction in this way if *all* objects are supposed to conform to us, as the Copernican turn claimed, went unnoticed.

Born also failed to appreciate Pistorius's worry about the Refutation. He faulted Pistorius for reading the Refutation as an attempt to demonstrate the existence of transcendental objects in space. But this was false. Pistorius in fact argued, on Kantian grounds, that the outer objects whose existence had presumably been demonstrated could not be the distinct transcendental objects that would refute idealism and went on to charge that the nature of these objects remained ambiguous. Born attempted to disambiguate the argument by providing a strained grammatical analysis that he nonetheless denominated "very clear" in its meaning.[129] Kant's claim, he insisted, was always that the objects that appear to us in space must have something "outside" of us, in the sense of being distinct from our representation, as their ground, never that objects that are said through one side of the mouth to be things in themselves, and through the other to be outside of us in the spatial sense, must exist. The main problem with this reading was that it bore no obvious relation to what the Refutation appeared to be directed to prove. That is that the consciousness of my own inner states presupposes an awareness of appearances that are literally in space, not that awareness of appearances that are quite literally in space presupposes the existence of objects that are distinct from ourselves in some spatial or nonspatial sense. That Born should read the Refutation as he did lent some credence to Pistorius's ambiguity charge.

However flawed the respective arguments and interpretations in the idealism debates might have been, they demonstrated that the empiricist approach to epistemological (and metaphysical) matters on the one hand, and what came to be identified as Kant's purist approach[130] on the other, are fundamentally at odds with each other. This is also evident in the next two sections, which are devoted to the widespread criticism of the Transcendental Analytic, in particular, of its Table of Categories, and to comparisons between empiricism and purism.

THE CATEGORIES

In the discussions of the Transcendental Analytic included in this section, specifically of its Table of Categories, the major concerns of Kant's contemporaries centered around the origin, nature, and applicability of the categories and principles. Overall, their attack was two pronged: (1) They disputed the necessity of a priori concepts and principles, much as they had already disputed that space and time must be a priori forms of intuition. (2) Perhaps more interestingly, they argued that even if we were to grant the necessity of something like a priori concepts, at least two problems remained. First, Kant had yet to demonstrate satisfactorily the accuracy and completeness of the Table of Categories. As it stood, or so the argument went, the selection of the categories was arbitrary. Second, the applicability of the categories remained in question. It was not clear what the link was between categories and intuitions and how empty forms of understanding could be applied to sensations. Kant was aware of this problem and tried to address it through the doctrine of the schematism,[131] but his contemporaries were not able to follow him here. Indeed, the doctrine of the schematism was left largely out of consideration by Kant's empiricist critics.

Selle

On first sight, Selle's short essay may not appear to bear a relation to Kant. Indeed, the essay appears as just what its title promises, an "attempt at a proof that there are no pure concepts of reason that are independent of experience" and seems to serve more as a statement of an extreme Lockean position on knowledge than a contribution to the debate with Kant. However, it would be premature to dismiss it for that reason. For Selle may not have engaged Kant directly, but he nevertheless had Kant in mind when he complained that "[p]eople did not want to be content with probabilities, and found them unworthy of genuine philosophy."[132] His short essay, accordingly, and his later *Principles of Pure Philosophy*,[133] which similarly does not engage Kant directly, were presented as empiricist (Lockean) alternatives to the Kantian approach. Certainly they were taken as such by Kant's contemporaries, both his critics and his defenders, who saw Selle as one of the chief representatives of the empiricist position and who also viewed his work as relevant to understanding the reception of the critical philosophy.[134] Hausius included the essay in his 1793 collection of materials pertaining to the reception of Kant's philosophy, the first and admittedly somewhat haphazard collection of its kind.[135] Perhaps more tellingly, Selle's *Principles of Pure Philosophy* was taken by Kant's defenders as the centrally important text against which Kant's purist approach must defend itself. Carl Christian Erhard Schmid, the author of the first dictionary of Kantian terminology,[136] addressed his comparison of the empiricist and the purist philosophical approach to Selle's *Principles of Pure Philosophy*. Although apparently peripheral, accordingly, Selle's texts must be taken into consideration in any account of the early reception of the critical philosophy. And given that the *Principles* are too long to be included here, the short "proof" that takes its place must serve as a substitute.

Selle was emphatic that experience is the only source and guarantee of cognition. His proof, accordingly, amounted to a demonstration that a priori concepts are simply not required. Now, since reason, Selle's term for both understanding and reason, arrives at knowledge either analytically or synthetically, this involves showing that a priori concepts are not necessary for either analytic or synthetic judgments, ultimately because both are grounded in experience. More specifically, a priori concepts are not required for analytic judgments because those are based on the principle of noncontradiction, which is grounded, in turn, in nothing more than generalized empirical observation of the rules that those of sound mind follow in their reasoning.[137] Selle did not consider how we differentiate a sound mind from an unsound one, but some appeal to an empirically demonstrated ability to thrive might charitably be ascribed to him.

Selle's demonstration that synthetic knowledge, too, is based only on experience (and therefore does not require a priori concepts) was more complex. He began with the claim that particular judgments/propositions (i.e., those that concern objects) cannot be universal and necessary. He then went on to argue that the sorts of judgments that have been deemed synthetic and yet universal and necessary and that have therefore been taken to be in need of a priori concepts do not require such concepts because they are, in fact, analytic. He demonstrated this claim with reference to the principle of sufficient reason, arguing that it is an analytic principle that is based, in turn, on the principle of noncontradiction.[138] And, as we already know, that principle is grounded in experience.

To be sure, Selle can only maintain the analytic nature of the principle of sufficient reason, and with that, of universal judgments generally deemed synthetic, by claiming that the principle really states no more than that what exists, exists either through itself or through something else.[139] Arguably, Kant proposed to prove the synthetic a priori status of something more specific: that whatever comes to be must be preceded by something else upon which it follows in accord with a rule[140] (i.e., that this particular happening must be a specific instance of a succession that always happens between these two types of events), which is a truth, Selle *claimed*, that can only ever be taught by experience.[141] One could fault him for failing to engage Kant's claim to the contrary, as one could also fault him for failing to engage Kant's claim that we can demonstrate synthetic *a priori* truths by analyzing the conditions of the possibility of experience. But doing so would amount to our failure to appreciate just what Selle was doing in this short essay: to present a counterpart to Kant, an alternative empiricist account of knowledge. Selle's failure to engage Kant must be seen in the light of his conviction that any "philosophy of pure reason" other than the "analysis of identical propositions" is "a fruitless and useless enterprise" and ultimately "nothing but [a] collection . . . of identical words."[142]

Tiedemann

Tiedemann's essay on the Transcendental Analytic is the second part of his three part examination of the theoretical philosophy. Like the first part, its arguments might be deemed somewhat lacking in rigor, clarity, and persuasiveness. But just as in the first portion of the essay, Tiedemann managed to identify some of the central themes that are representative of the empiricist interpretation of the Analytic.

Much of what is in Selle's essay can also be found in Tiedemann's, albeit in more elaborate form, not surprisingly, since Tiedemann did engage Kant's texts. Like Selle, he appealed to the principle of sufficient reason to dispute Kant's claim that a priori principles of understanding are required for our knowledge of the world. And also like Selle, he made this point by claiming that the principle of sufficient reason is analytic, and not a function of an a priori law of understanding that we bring to experience. Just as his earlier proofs for the analytic nature of geometrical propositions involved a claim that such propositions are based only on an analysis of concepts, so the principle of sufficient reason is said to be analytic because it, as well, requires only an analysis of concepts, in this case the concept of a contingent thing and its determinations. A rather painstaking analysis demonstrated that the attribution of properties to such a thing without sufficient reason is a patent absurdity and, by implication, that "there must be a sufficient reason for what is contingent."[143]

Tiedemann was quite proud to have doubted and, at least in his mind, successfully refuted what he took to be Kant's main proposition (that a priori principles are required), no doubt thinking that this endorsed his empiricist stance, namely that laws deemed universal are either analytically true or spring from experience, but his examination actually became more interesting when he turned to the ostensive consequence of this main proposition: that "there are no a priori principles whatsoever that apply to objects of experience."[144] Tiedemann realized that as it stood this was not actually Kant's claim, that Kant denied only that a priori principles are applicable to things in themselves, but the distinction between things in themselves and appearances is not one he could accept. For once that distinction was granted, the objective reference to transcendentally real things that he thought was required for any knowledge to be genuine disappeared. The distinction entailed that the order and regularity the Kantian laws of understanding afforded, an order and regularity that Tiedemann agreed was necessary for knowledge, amounted in the end to no more than an order and regularity of representations. It did not, indeed, could not translate into an order and regularity of sensations.[145] So even if the distinction allowed Kant to address some central problems, any advantage it brought to the critical philosophy was more than offset by the prize the approach as a whole had to pay. In substantially less lucid form, this was a version of a charge that Pistorius would later raise with regard to the Copernican turn,[146] and that Kant's contemporaries in general associated with his *a priorism*. In essence, Tiedemann and other contemporaries simply could not understand how the application of merely *subjective* laws of thought could translate into an *objective* order of experience.

One could charge here that Tiedemann had, at the very least, failed to appreciate the power of the critical approach, and although it is true that he did not have the most sophisticated comprehension of various aspects of the critical philosophy, his concern spoke to the fundamental incompatibility between the principles of empiricism and the principles of purism that had already emerged in various other selections. Adhering to the former, Tiedemann, like other early empiricist critics, was simply unable to accept the alternative the critical philosophy afforded.

Schultz

Both Schultz's review and its inclusion in this volume might be thought surprising. The piece itself is surprising because Schultz, Kant's best friend (and frequent dinner companion), was also one of his most committed defenders, and as noted earlier, the author of the first paraphrase of the *Critique*, the *Erläuterungen*.[147] In view of his commitment to Kant's defense, it is surprising that he wrote a review, even an anonymous one, that was as critical of Kant as this one was. Its inclusion in this volume might be thought surprising because it is a review of Johann August Ulrich's *Institutiones logicae et metaphysicae*, and Ulrich was not an adherent of the empiricist tradition, but rather of the Leibnizian-Wolffian tradition. Still, Ulrich's role in early Kant reception was quite complex. As one of the first people to lecture on Kant (at Jena), he seemed initially to be one of Kant's defenders. But it is questionable just how far his early endorsement of Kant went. Whatever his initial commitment might have been, by the late 1780s, he had become a decided critic of the Kantian philosophy, so much so that every one of his lectures (an astounding six lectures per day) involved a critique of Kant. Moreover, the criticisms in the *Institutiones*, which appeared in 1785, suggested that there might have been other reasons for his initial apparent adherence than the conversion to Kant's philosophy.[148] In spite of these concerns, however, Schultz's review is interesting in the context of this collection because it demonstrated fundamentally the same worries regarding the categories as the empiricist critics did, and because one of the subsequent critics, Tittel, took up the response Kant gave to Schultz in the B-Deduction (though Tittel seems not to have been aware that the remarks he referred to were a response specifically to Schultz).

It must have seemed a betrayal to Kant that Schultz went as far as he did in his endorsement of Ulrich's criticism,[149] particularly in the pro-Kantian *Allgemeine Literatur-Zeitung*.[150] Schultz began by noting with approval the extent to which Ulrich agreed with Kant up to the categories, and continued to note, again with approval, the respects in which he disagreed with Kant beyond that, stating that he "found his own doubts reflected in many of the author's doubts."[151] These doubts concerned particularly the necessary applicability of temporal form to things in themselves and the necessity of treating consciousness as a thing in itself. That Schultz should have been so openly critical – even in a respectful fashion – is surprising until we remember that both of the criticisms that have been mentioned echo the original criticisms Mendelssohn and Lambert made of the Inaugural Dissertation and that Schultz raised as well in his own review of that work,[152] and that Schultz had always been uncomfortable with the categories.[153] As well, we should at least consider that he was reluctant to be critical of Ulrich who seems, at this time, to be one of Kant's supporters.

Schultz was not entirely uncritical of Ulrich, however. He faulted Ulrich for not considering the Deduction of the Categories, but not without taking the opportunity to reiterate the charge of obscurity he had already made elsewhere, and that may have been instrumental in Kant's decision to rewrite it.[154]

Schultz went on to raise a further problem with the Transcendental Deduction and the proofs of the principles. Was Kant's claim, he asked, that the objective reality of the categories be required for any experience whatsoever to be possible, or was it just that it was required for any experience of objects to be possible? The former alternative seems unacceptable, on the one hand, because Kant himself denied it when he said that the categories are not required for judgments of perception,[155] and, on the other, because it seems intrinsically implausible that we should not be able to hear one note after another without first seeing this succession of sounds as an instance of a necessary regularity,[156] or perceive first sunlight and then warmth without first having to think the former to be the cause of the latter.[157] Taking the claim to be just that the objective validity of the categories is required for an experience of objects, however, threatens to reduce it to an identity and to beg the question against Hume, who asked what reason we have to suppose that we ever encounter what exist unperceived or are real causes. To "answer" these worries by asserting that *if* we are to perceive objects and causes, *then* we must presuppose the objective validity of the categories hardly seems adequate. Schultz supported this by suggesting that the order *could* be a function of the preestablished harmony of representations, so that whatever order the categories are thought to *impose* according to Kant is in fact only learned a posteriori from the apparent lawfulness we have access to, an objection that Kant would surely have to deal with.

Surprisingly, given his reluctance, after the Feder fiasco, to respond to his critics, Kant did in fact respond to Schultz on two occasions in his published work. In the Preface to the *Anfangsgründe*, he inserted a long footnote by way of a response.[158] Unfortunately, however, Kant chose to defend himself ad hominem by charging that Ulrich and the anonymous reviewer, who are described as "deeply examining" and "deeply probing," respectively, were in no position to make the complaints they did, given the other things they were willing to accept about his system, rather than by responding directly to the charges.[159] Nor is the passage that appears at the end of the B-Deduction any more satisfactory. For here, as at the close of the reply in the *Anfangsgründe*, he only emphasized the very point that Schultz found less than satisfactory: that on his assumption the categories would not have the requisite necessity.[160] But while the passage might not satisfy as a reply to Schultz's review, it struck a chord with other critics who took it up in their own engagement with the Transcendental Analytic. One such contemporary was Gottlob August Tittel.

Tittel

Tittel, a professor of philosophy at Karlsruhe and later of theology at Jena, belonged to Feder's empiricist school and was, like Selle, very much an adherent of Locke's version of empiricism. He published books on Kant's moral philosophy[161] and his theoretical philosophy.[162] Although Kant's defender Johann Biester dismissed Tittel as "a weak shadow of the weak Feder,"[163] and Ludwig Heinrich Jakob wrote that Tittel did not understand Kant's metaphysics,[164] Kant thought that the objections he raised in his work on the moral philosophy of sufficient importance to require a response. The response ended up as no more than a footnote in the Preface to the *Critique of Practical Reason*.[165] Still, it indicates that Kant himself did not think that Tittel could be as easily dismissed as his contemporaries might have liked.[166]

The objections Tittel raised in *Kantische Denkformen und Kategorien* spoke to the concerns that Kant's empiricist critics in general had, and were at least in part, concerns that are still with us today.[167] These objections concerned the selection of the categories, the unity and completeness of the Table of Categories, their nature, and their applicability.

With regard to the selection, Tittel claimed that the changes Kant made to the Aristotelian categories did not in any way constitute an improvement and charges that the architectonic unity Kant found in the Table of Categories is only there because Kant put it there.[168] And Tittel was simply unwilling to accept that the principle of identification is anything other than arbitrary. Indeed, he thought that it amounted to no more than an appeal to very elementary logic, which could not provide any guarantee of the completeness of the Table of Categories.[169] It is unbelievable, he added in his own polemical move, that "the great Aristotle"[170] should have missed something so basic, as he thought Kant believed.

This introductory point is effective in a polemical sense, but the point that Tittel deemed of relatively more importance had to do with what the categories are and how they can be applicable to sensations. Making a point that is analogous to one about the nature of space and time as a priori forms of intuition that was made with regard to the Transcendental Aesthetic, Tittel was quite dismayed that he could not find a satisfactory answer to his question of just what pure forms are.[171] The two interpretations that Tittel found acceptable – the view that emerges from Schultz's review of Ulrich, namely, that the categories are innate concepts or laws of thought that accord with outer objects as a function of preestablished harmony,[172] and the strict empiricist position, which Tittel favored, according to which the categories are general concepts that have been abstracted from experience,[173] are also not, as he realized, interpretations that Kant would allow to stand. The first alternative was rejected by way of a paraphrase of Kant's *Critique* response to Schultz,[174] the second by the obvious fact that the empiricist account is incompatible with the a priori status of the categories.[175]

Having rejected both of these positions on behalf of Kant, Tittel asked, in apparent desperation, "what then may these forms be?"[176] The answer he thought Kant would give to this question, that the categories are empty forms of thought, was unsatisfactory both because it really made no sense and because it led to inconsistencies in Kant's position. Although Tittel approved of Kant's claim that as empty forms the categories are meaningless independent of experience, he also thought that Kant could not consistently hold that the categories are only applicable to and meaningful through experience, yet also regulative of it.[177] And similarly, if the categories are empty forms, then their very generality would make any application to experience impossible. Tittel illustrated this with respect to the concept of causality. There is nothing in the category, he claimed, that would allow us to determine that it is properly applicable to one sequence of events, the motion of balls, but not another, the appearance of a comet and a war.[178] Here, however, Tittel misunderstood Kant. For the point of the Second Analogy is not to identify particular causes and effects, but to establish the general point that any event must have a cause, namely, that any event must be seen as an instance of rule-governed succession. What the particular cause is in each case can only be determined through experience just as only experience can tell us that we have inappropriately invoked the concept of cause in a particular instance.[179]

By conflating the particular and the general and suggesting, by implication, that there cannot be, for Kant, any significant role for experience in knowledge, Tittel managed to make Kant's position appear unsustainable. We could fault him for misunderstanding Kant's arguments, but he is in this regard hardly alone. In fact, the difficulties Tittel had with Kant's categories are representative of the difficulties Kant's early empiricist critics in general had when it came to identifying the nature and applicability of the categories. Ultimately, these difficulties, like the difficulties Kant's empiricist critics had with the idealist implications of Transcendental Idealism, speak to nothing so much as to the fundamental incommensurability, at the time, of the empiricist approach on the one hand and Kant's approach on the other. It is not surprising, accordingly, that Tittel completed the final section of the book, a brief comparison of Locke and Kant on the matter of laws of thought, with a resounding condemnation of the categories:

> . . . the decision must fall against **Kant** and his system, and the final result of everything cannot be otherwise than that the Kantian pure concepts of understanding or categories, . . . , and what is to be further developed from them, must be counted among the number of nonentities.[180]

EMPIRICISM VERSUS PURISM

The final two comparative selections in this collection bring the empiricist critique of the critical philosophy to a close. By 1788 and 1789, when these texts were published, it must have been evident to Kant's contemporaries that the empiricist critique juxtaposes two apparently incompatible approaches to epistemological and metaphysical matters, and they tended to take a strong stance on one or the other of these approaches. It is in light of this aim that we find overall comparisons of the empiricist approach with Kant's purist approach like the ones contained in the final section of this collection. Here it is in some measure unfortunate that the comparisons were undertaken by partisans of one or the other of these philosophical approaches. Schmid, the author of the first selection in this section, was a committed Kantian, and Tittel, who compared Kant and Locke with respect to the question of the laws of thought at the end of the final selection in the previous section, was a committed empiricist. Neither of these authors made a secret of his commitment, but given that these commitments were already in place, they were unable to consider whether these approaches were in fact as incompatible as Kant's early critics and defenders seemed to think. These comparisons do not afford the opportunity to consider whether there could be a position such as a mitigated empiricism, or a mitigated purism, even though the latter is arguably the position that Kant might have wanted to defend.[181] Kant's contemporaries could hardly be faulted for adopting a strong stance on the preferred approach, but the final word in this collection went to Kant's most reflective and moderate empiricist critic, who was likely to provide the most even-handed overall assessment and comparison of the two approaches: Hermann Pistorius.

Schmid

There is no question where Schmid stood with regard to the choice between empiricism and purism. As his *Critik der reinen Vernunft im Grundrisse* and his *Wörterbuch zum leichteren Gebrauch der Kantischen Schriften* demonstrate, he was a committed defender and expositor of Kant's philosophy. His essay itself involved a (partisan) comparison not merely of the two approaches, but of the two approaches as articulated by two representatives – Kant, of course, as the representative of the purist approach and Selle as the representative of the empiricist approach. It is interesting that Schmid chose Selle, rather than, say, Feder or Weishaupt,[182] as the representative of empiricism. For Selle, as we have already seen, took an extreme Lockean position rather than a more moderate empiricist one. It may be that the choice was motivated by nothing other than date of publication,[183] but it may also be that Schmid thought the comparison of Kant's position with an extreme empiricist one would make his task of defending Kant easier. Alternatively, perhaps Schmid was simply motivated by a desire to bring out the contrast and apparent incommensurability most clearly and chose the most extreme position to do so.

The essay itself involves the systematic presentation of the answers Schmid thought Kant and Selle, respectively, would give to a series of questions regarding the nature of sensibility, understanding, and reason; their relation to one another and to objects; and the knowledge/certainty each affords. Schmid does little by way of evaluation, apparently preferring to let the strength of the one position and the weakness of the other emerge on its own; however, he does at least indirectly emphasize the advantages that the Kantian (purist) philosophy has, in his eyes, over empiricism, thinking no doubt that those advantages made an endorsement of Kant's philosophy inevitable.

To the extent that Schmid offered a defense of purism, he praised its greater consistency[184] and emphasized that it is only in view of purism's a priori elements that we can have certainty.[185] Empiricism, by contrast, which rejected the a priori, necessarily led to "scepticism with regard to even the most general laws of nature."[186] Schmid made this point repeatedly throughout the essay, but he never considered whether scepticism, or even the comparative universality that Kant's empiricist critics endorsed, was the correct position, even though he may find it unpalatable. In addition and again on Kantian grounds, Schmid faulted empiricism for its claim that we can know the existence of God and the predicates of God and made it clear, again, that in his eyes Kant's appeals to practical reason and faith provided much better grounds than the empiricist inferential demonstrations.[187]

It is instructive, though in view of Schmid's aim not surprising, that he had very little to say about the role that sensations play in our cognition. Yes, we must be affected by things, and yes, our intuition must be ordered in space and time, but Schmid was much more concerned about clarifying the nature and role of the a priori elements of cognition (in this case, the intuition of space) than telling us just what the role of sensations is in relation to these elements. To the extent that he mentioned the fact that we must be affected by objects,[188] he simply restated or paraphrased what Kant said, and left matters at that, ignoring that what Kant said was precisely what had given rise to the empiricists' questions.

Pistorius

Here, as in his other work, Pistorius proceeded in a thoughtful and reflective manner. He followed the answers Schmid gave to his series of questions on Selle's and Kant's behalf, but was not content to do little more than repeat the comparison, albeit one that favored empiricism, not purism. He responded, in particular, to the scepticism charge, arguing that it was in fact Kant's philosophy, not empiricism, that endorsed scepticism. Here he appealed to empiricism's trust in the senses, to the constancy of outer things, and, in good Humean fashion, to our psychological makeup, which makes it impossible for us not to expect that identical cases are identical, and similar cases similar.[189] Highlighting what is at the heart of the empiricist discontent with Kant's philosophy, he claimed that the equally subjective *and* objective grounds of knowledge that empiricism appeals to is in fact much superior to the merely subjective grounds (the laws of our cognitive capacities) that constitute the basis of knowledge on his (their) understanding of purism. No matter how "universal" such grounds are, they do not "really" pertain to objects. Here Pistorius took the opportunity to reiterate a complaint he had already made in his review of the second edition of the *Critique*,[190] namely that on purely purist grounds, nature could be constituted in any way.

Although Pistorius, like Schmid, thought of Kant as a "purist" and, as was already evident from his earlier selections, faulted the critical philosophy on that ground, he made rather more of the empirical elements of Kant's philosophy than Schmid acknowledged and than Schmid might have liked. Significantly, Pistorius told us that the difference between purism and empiricism was a function of the degree to which the mind is active or passive,[191] and while he thought that the Kantian approach in general allowed for too little passivity, he also thought that Schmid's interpretation of Kant was less purist than the common one. For Schmid, according to Pistorius, "importantly concedes that the objects also do something, and consequently brings Kantian purism much closer to empiricism."[192] It is unlikely that this interpretation pleased Schmid.

In spite of these remarks, however, Pistorius, along with his other contemporaries, clearly thought that purism and empiricism constituted two conflicting and largely incompatible philosophical systems. Their difference was evident in what Pistorius thought their basic presuppositions were – the unchangeability of the nature of subjects according to purism and the unchangeability of the nature of objects for empiricism. As Pistorius noted in conclusion, the question of which set of presuppositions was correct was not one that could be settled, rather, "those acquainted with the issues will have to decide about their value."[193] It was clear where Pistorius and the empiricist critics in general stood on this point, as it was clear also just where Kant and his defenders stood.

THE ROLE OF THE *ADB* AND THE *ALZ* IN EARLY KANT RECEPTION

I will end this Introduction with a brief description of periodical publication in late eighteenth century Germany. My particular focus here will be on the two national review journals in which much of the debate of early Kant reception was published – the *Allgemeine deutsche Bibliothek* and the *Allgemeine Literatur-Zeitung*.

From the contemporary perspective, periodical publication in Philosophy in Kant's time was a curious practice. Perhaps most notably, there were few scholarly journals devoted solely to Philosophy, and those that did exist were generally short-lived and often served the editor's agenda.[194] The *Philosophische Bibliothek* edited by Johann Feder and Christoph Meiners, for instance, was limited to four volumes, which appeared yearly between 1788 and 1791 and functioned, as Feder specified in his autobiography, as a "standing army" against the Kantians.[195] Accordingly, a large portion of each volume was reserved for the editors' (generally Feder's) own essays, and the other material (book reviews, excerpts from foreign texts and notices) appears to have been selected with a view to cementing Feder's position in the dispute with Kant and the Kantians. Similarly, the *Philosophisches Magazin* (1788–92) and subsequent *Philosophisches Archiv* (1792–95) were edited by Eberhard and served as the voice piece of the rationalist critique of Kant. The major authors here were Eberhard, Maaß, and Schwab. Aside from their periodic appearance, these volumes have little similarity with contemporary journal publication. It would be better, accordingly, to see these apparently specialized Philosophy journals not as journals but as vehicles for the defense of a given editor's position (respectively, the empiricist and the rationalist critique of Kant's philosophy).

In spite of this agenda, however, these quasi periodicals were of far less significance in early Kant reception than the general periodicals in which philosophical material was also published. It is true that the first volume of the *Philosophisches Magazin* was widely noticed, but I suspect that this was due more to Kant's reply to it in the *Entdeckung* than to the journal itself.[196] In contrast, the general periodicals were attractive quite independently of any reply Kant or anyone else might have made to a given contribution. Like their philosophical counterparts, general periodicals were often short-lived, although some, such as the *Göttingische Anzeigen von gelehrten Sachen* (1739–1801),[197] the *Berlinische Monatsschrift* (1783–1811), and the *Teutsche Merkur* (1773–1810) had surprising staying power. Although not solely or even primarily Philosophy journals, the *Berlinische Monatsschrift* and the *Teutsche Merkur* likely come closest to publishing original philosophical material in journal format in late eighteenth century Germany.[198] In 1786 and 1787, the *Teutsche Merkur* published Reinhold's *Briefe über die Kantische Philosophy*, and thus contributed significantly to popularizing the critical philosophy.[199] The *Berlinische Monatsschrift* did so as well by publishing several of Kant's shorter essays ("Reply to the Question: What Is Enlightenment?" appeared in December of 1784; "Idea of a Universal History from a Cosmopolitan Point of View" appeared in November of the same year.) Unlike the general review journals that will be considered later, however, the *Berlinische Monatsschrift* was not a partisan publication.[200] Other voices could be heard as well, including those of Kant's critics. Selle's short "Attempt at a Proof That There Are No Pure Concepts of Reason Independently of Experience" which, as I have already argued, was directed against Kant, appeared in the same issue as Kant's Enlightenment essay (December 1784).[201] As well, the *Berlinische Monatsschrift*, which considered itself an Enlightenment publication,[202] made as much room for Mendelssohn (among others) as it made for Kant.

Although some general periodicals published original material, the life blood of general periodical publication in late eighteenth century Germany was the book review. At that time, a variety of local and national periodic publications sought to familiarize their readers with books published in the preceding year(s). Local publications, such as the *Königsbergische Gelehrte und Politische Zeitungen*, where Schultz published his review of Kant's Inaugural Dissertation,[203] might focus primarily or even exclusively on authors from the regions and use local reviewers, but this was not necessarily the case. As we know, one of these periodicals, the *Göttingische Anzeigen von gelehrten Sachen*, published the first review of the *Critique*, the Feder/Garve or Göttingen review.

Even though a given local periodical might have played a role in early Kant reception, the two already identified national publications, the *AdB* and the *ALZ*, were central, particularly in the early years. On the face of things, they were strikingly similar. Modeled on the British review journals, particularly the *Monthly Review* (1749–1845),[204] they had fundamentally the same aim: to publish generally accessible reviews of all books that had been published in German and/or Germany during the preceding year(s) and to do so in a roughly orderly rotation of subject fields.[205] Additionally, each professed a commitment to such values as comprehensiveness, timeliness, and impartiality, and each defended the practice of the anonymous review. Given these similarities, we must consider how they differed, why two at least apparently similar national review journals were deemed necessary in late eighteenth century Germany, and, in the context of this volume, what their respective roles were in early Kant reception.

There are some obvious differences between the two journals, though one wonders just how significant they might have been for the question at hand. Published from 1765 to 1806, the *AdB* was the older and more conservative of the two publications. For most of its existence, it was published and edited by its founder, Friedrich Nicolai, a publisher, bookseller, and adherent of the Enlightenment. In 1792 Nicolai passed the journal on to Karl Ernst Bohn, under the name *Neue Allgemeine deutsche Bibliothek*,[206] though it reverted to Nicolai in 1800. Founded by a group of literary and academic figures including poet Christoph Gottfried Wieland, Ferdinand Justin Bertuch, a bookseller and legation councillor in Weimar, and Christian Gottfried Schütz, professor of Poetry and Rhetoric at Jena, the *ALZ* began publication in 1785 under the primary editorship of Schütz.[207] The *AdB* was published in standard quarterly installments with numerous supplementary volumes, whereas the *ALZ* appeared six days a week in newspaper format, and in 1787 added an *Intelligenzblatt* [Announcer] for notices and general information about the publishing and academic world.[208] Perhaps more significantly, although both periodicals might have valued comprehensiveness and timeliness, the *AdB* soon had a five-year backlog – a problem with any publication that tries to keep its readership informed about recent publications – and found itself publishing a varying number of supplementary volumes that did not, however, properly come to terms with the backlog.[209] The *ALZ* managed better in both respects, perhaps because of its daily newspaper format,[210] perhaps because of the policy, articulated by Schütz in his preliminary report to the first issue of the second publication year, of grouping works deemed less significant and inferior together for purposes of review.[211]

In the preliminary material each of the editors published, Schütz placed comparatively greater emphasis on the value of impartiality than Nicolai did in his 1765 Preface. For Nicolai and the *AdB*, impartiality seems to have been largely a matter of the diversity and respectability of the reviewers.[212] Schütz, by contrast, went so far as to present "impartiality" as "the first law of our *Literatur-Zeitung*,"[213] and to consider how such impartiality can be guaranteed. Here he quickly acknowledged that one may not be able to guarantee the impartiality of any one reviewer but insisted that one can do so with respect to the journal as a whole, provided that it takes certain precautions. The need to specify some of these precautions might be thought surprising, but Schütz emphasized, first, that a given reviewer was not to review either his own work or that of a friend. In addition, a journal that wanted to guarantee impartiality had to employ established scholars because, in Schütz's view at least, such scholars not only lent respectability to a journal but, in view of their demonstrated knowledge and judgment, were likely to write impartial or objective reviews. Interestingly, nothing was said about the editor's own stance and the influence that might have on the overall objectivity of the journal.

In this context, both Nicolai and Schütz also defended the practice of the anonymous review in order to facilitate the reader's ability to make a judgment on the basis of a reasoned review rather than on the basis of the person and status of the reviewer. Although the anonymity of a reviewer was at the time one of the worst kept secrets especially in the case of negative or controversial reviews, the context of eighteenth-century German academic life made this practice perhaps more important than it might be today. The scholarly community was quite small and often given to gossip.[214] At the very least, a negatively reviewed author's reaction to the review (and the supposed reviewer) is an indication that the practice was a useful one. Consider here Kant's reaction to Feder and the Göttingen review, and Herder's reaction to Kant and the *ALZ* over the review of the *Ideen*.[215]

These differences, however, are only minor, and, more to the point, they do not tell us either why the *AdB* began to fail as early as 1783[216] (in other words, before the announcement and appearance of its main competition, the *ALZ*), or, for that matter, why a new review journal was thought necessary not only by its founders, but also by its readers.[217] One wonders about the factors that allowed one journal to flourish even as its counterpart failed. It might be tempting here to claim that the increase in the number of specialized scientific and technical journals in the late eighteenth century made the general review periodical superfluous,[218] but even if increasing specialization might explain a decrease in the interest in *general* review publications, this would not show why one of two apparently similar review journal succeeded while the other one failed. At the very least, the *ALZ* must have managed to reinvigorate the practice of the general review, and one wonders what it did that the *AdB* did not do.

A potentially more promising answer to this series of questions might point to the editors and their respective attitude toward the critical philosophy. However, even though this claim might be gratifying to a Kantian, it would also be overly simplistic. At the most, the attitude toward Kant and Kant criticism that Nicolai and Schütz, respectively, hold is a symptom of what is really at the ground of success and failure, not a cause.

The cause of the decrease in interest in the *AdB* was likely its overall conservatism, which is evident in the journal's format (book and page format rather than larger newspaper pages and column print)[219] and font (gothic rather than roman type),[220] as well as in the comparatively greater emphasis the journal places on some subject fields at the expense of others. From its beginning, the journal was little interested in reviewing works of literature, and the reviews that were produced tended to be negative.[221] In view of the drastic increase in the production of literary work during the *AdB*'s lifetime, an increase that was matched by the interest of the reading public, the *AdB*'s failure to similarly increase the rate by which such works were reviewed[222] showed a startling insensitivity toward the trends at the time.

More important in this context is that the *AdB*'s conservatism also showed itself in Nicolai's and his reviewers' attitudes toward the critical philosophy. Nicolai, very much an adherent of Enlightenment popular philosophy, its suspicion of technical terminology, and by implication its value of clarity,[223] was negatively inclined toward both Kant and the Kantians. So he complained about the incomprehensibility of Kant's texts, claiming that Kant "often writes obscurely and vaguely, and is cumbersome in his own mother tongue."[224]

To make matters worse, as the literary and philosophical scene changed, it became more and more difficult to find the desired established and dependable people willing to take on the task of writing reviews for what was then quickly becoming a rather conservative publication, and the torch came to be passed on to younger, less experienced, and, by implication, less respected colleagues. In other words, even if the *AdB*'s initial success had been a function of its reviewers, this could now no longer be the case. Coupled with problems in the production of the journal,[225] these factors made it an increasingly less desirable publication.

All of this is in stark contrast to the *ALZ*, whose founding members seem to have been rather more in tune with the trends of the time than

Nicolai was. This is evident in its new format and progressive stance, as it is also evident in view of the Schütz's commitment to the critical philosophy. He apparently used Kant's ideas in his lectures as early as 1782,[226] invited several of Kant's leading disciples (among them Reinhold, Schultz, and Schmid) to participate in the journal,[227] and corresponded with Kant, asking him for advice, seeking his approval for various of his projects, informing him of upcoming reviews and books to be reviewed, and repeatedly asking for his involvement.[228] Although Kant did contribute at the outset with a (critical) review of Herder's *Ideen*, he soon pleaded other involvement, and left the defense of his philosophy and the critique of his critics to his favorite defender, Johann Schultz.

The editors' attitude was reflected in the supposedly impartial journals via the choice of reviewers. The *AdB*'s reviewers were the representatives of the traditions and included the empiricist, the rationalist, and the popular philosophers. Among them are Eberhard, who later spearheaded the rationalist critique of Kant with his *Philosophisches Magazin*[229]; Garve, whose initial review echoes (or predates) Nicolai's complaint about the obscurity of Kant's technical terminology[230]; and Pistorius, who continued to bring Humean objections and Humean examples to bear on his reading of the critical philosophy[231] in his multiple and generally very reflective reviews of virtually all of Kant's works and the work of his various defenders. Aside from Pistorius, one of the most faithful reviewers of Philosophy was Dietrich Tiedemann, the author of the three-part examination of the *Critique* included here (in part),[232] who participated for a large portion of the *AdB*'s and *NAdB*'s existence.

As already noted, many of the philosophical reviewers for the *ALZ* were selected in view of the editor's commitment to defend the critical philosophy. The most notable reviewer was likely Reinhold, whose *Briefe über die Kantische Philosophie* contributed significantly to awakening the reader's interest in Kant and his critical thought. Also notable is Schultz, who similarly made a significant contribution to the acceptance of the critical philosophy with his 1784 *Erläuterungen* and later *Prüfung*. In view of the generally positive stance toward the critical philosophy, the fact that not every one of its reviews unquestioningly endorsed Kant's position goes some distance to lending credence to the claim to impartiality,[233] even if this is not a claim that can be accepted without acknowledging the fact that the editor and the journal are rather positively inclined toward Kant and the Kantians.

It is an interesting footnote to the history of the *AdB* and the *ALZ* that, in spite of its initially progressive stance, the latter too came to be accused of conservatism before long. This was at least in part a function of its continued adherence to the critical philosophy, which led to a critique of the then new literary and philosophical trends.[234] In 1803 Schütz moved to Halle, taking the *ALZ* with him,[235] and Goethe founded the *Jenaische Allgemeine Literatur-Zeitung* to take its place. It became the home for critics of the old *ALZ* (Schelling, August Wilhelm Schlegel, Friedrich Schleiermacher, and others).[236] Still, in spite of its eventual conservatism, its initially progressive stance, particularly the defense of the critical philosophy, contributed to the *ALZ*'s success. And that contributed, in turn, to the popularity of the Kantian philosophy.[237]

NOTE ON TRANSLATIONS

These translations follow the conventions of the Cambridge editions of the works of Immanuel Kant. As a consequence, I have indicated emphasis, to the extent that I have been able to identify it – some of the original texts are rather badly faded – through bold type and foreign words through italics. This is not to imply that the authors included here follow that same typographical convention. Not surprisingly, given that these conventions were not standard at the time, they did not. Some use emphasis rather more liberally than others, some indicate it through *Sperrdruck* (spaced type), others use *Fettdruck* (variably sized bold type), and yet others employ italics. Moreover, some of the authors emphasize personal names, others do not; indeed, in some texts the name(s) of the reviewed author(s) are, after an initial use, indicated only through the first letter of the last name. Even though I have imposed uniformity on the indication of emphasis, I have retained the variable practice of either highlighting or abbreviating a given philosopher's name.

Similarly, the attached glossary is in large part that of the Cambridge editions. There is no guarantee, of course, that Kant's contemporaries understood his technical terminology or that they used it either consistently or as he did. Still, I have for the most part treated the texts as if such an accord exists, noting significant deviations as they occur. Additionally, I have generally translated technical terms in the same way. This includes terms that are at times used variably. The term *Wirklichkeit* (actuality), for instance, is used on occasion, certainly by Kant and likely by his contemporaries as well, in the sense of *Realität* (reality). While both the Kemp Smith and the Guyer/Wood translations of the *Critique* try to capture this variability by translating *Wirklichkeit* as either "actuality" or "reality"; I have not done so, preferring to render *Wirklichkeit* consistently as "actuality" and to leave the decision about whether it is to be read as "actuality" or "reality" in a given context to the readers.

One of the biggest problems for the readers at the time was likely the lack of accuracy in the citations. The authors appeared, on occasion, to be sloppy and careless, providing citations that deviated to various degrees from the originals. I assume this is the case because they took the citations from notes they had taken, not from the original text. In the cases in which the errors are minor and do not impact on the meaning, I have translated the citations as they provided them without remarking on the deviations. In more serious cases, I have provided notes regarding errors made, and, when it seemed necessary, supplied the original text.

In general and whenever possible, the translations are based either on the original text or on a facsimile reprint edition of the original. Facsimile reprints of monographs and of the "periodical" publications pertaining to the critical philosophy (the *Philosophisches Magazin*, *Philosophisches Archiv*, *Philosophische Bibliothek*) are available in the Aetas Kantiana edition (for further detail see the Bibliography). Reprints of reviews published between 1781 and 1787 are available in Landau's collection (see Bibliography). Although I have initially based my translations of some of the reviews on the Landau reprints, I have also consulted the original texts in either text (*AdB*) or text and microfiche (*ALZ*) format. Unless otherwise noted, the pagination provided in the translations is that of the original, as indicated on the title page preceding each of the five sections that order this collection.

Section I

Feder/Garve and Garve

[Anonymous]. "*Critique of Pure Reason* by Immanuel Kant. 1781. 856 pages in Octavo." *Zugabe zu den Göttingischen Anzeigen von gelehrten Sachen* (January 19, 1782): 40–8 53

Reprinted in Immanuel Kant, *Prolegomena*, Karl Vorländer, ed. (Hamburg: Felix Meiner Verlag), 167–74; and Landau, *Rezensionen*, 10–17.

Christian Garve, "*Critique of Pure Reason* by Immanuel Kant. Riga, 1781. 856 pages in 8." *AdB*, supplement to vols. 37–52 (1783): 838–62 59

Reprinted in Landau, *Rezensionen*, 34–55.

The Göttingen Review

Critique of Pure Reason by Immanuel Kant. 1781. 856 Pages in Octavo.

This work, which always exercises the understanding of its readers – even if it does not always instruct it – which often strains their attention to the point of exhaustion, which aids them from time to time with well-chosen examples or rewards them with unexpected and generally useful inferences, is a system of higher or, as the author calls it, Transcendental Idealism. This idealism encompasses spirit and matter in the same manner, transforms the world and ourselves into representations, and lets all objects arise from appearances by having understanding connect them in **one** series of experience and having reason attempt, necessarily although unsuccessfully, to extend and unify them into **one** full and complete world system.

The author's system rests on roughly the following main propositions. All our cognition springs from certain modifications of ourselves, which we call sensations. We have no idea where they occur or what causes them. If there is an actual thing in which the representations inhere, or if they are created by actual things that exist independently of us, we still do not know the least predicate of either the one or the other. Nonetheless, we assume there are objects: we speak of ourselves, we speak of bodies as actual things, we believe that we know both, and we make judgments about them. What allows us to do so is that the various appearances have something in common. In view of this commonality, they unify themselves with one another and differentiate themselves from what we call **ourselves**. Thus we take intuitions of outer sense [41] as things and events outside of us because they occur beside each other in a certain space and follow each other in a certain time. That is actual for us which we represent to ourselves as in some place and at some time. Space and time themselves are not something actual outside of us. Nor are they relations or abstract concepts. Rather, they are subjective laws of our representative capacity, forms of sensation, and subjective conditions of sensible intuition. One basic pillar of the Kantian system rests on these concepts of sensations as mere modifications of ourselves (on which **Berkeley**, too, principally builds his idealism), and of space and time.

Understanding makes objects out of **sensible appearances**, which are distinguished from other representations only through the subjective condition that space and time are combined with them. It **makes** them. For it is what first unifies a multiplicity of small successive alterations of our soul into complete sensations; it is what then combines these complete sensations in time in such a manner that they follow each other as cause and effect. In this way, each attains its appointed place in infinite time, and together they attain the composure and solidity of actual things. It is understanding as well, finally, that, by means of an additional connection, differentiates simultaneous objects, which stand in reciprocal causal relations to one another, from successive objects, where one is dependent on the other in a one-sided fashion only. By thus bringing order, regularity of succession, and reciprocity into sensible intuitions, it creates nature in the proper sense and determines the laws of nature in accord with its own. These laws of understanding are older than the appearances to which they are applied. [42] Hence there are a priori concepts of understanding. We pass over the author's attempt to illuminate the work of understanding further through its reduction to four main functions and four main concepts that depend on them. These are quality, quantity, relation, and modality. Each of these, in turn, encompasses simpler concepts. In combination with the representations of time and space, these concepts are supposed to generate the principles of experiential knowledge. These are the widely known principles of logic and ontology expressed in accord with the author's idealist restrictions. It is shown, by and by, how Leibniz arrived at his monadology, but the criticisms that are advanced to oppose it, can, for the most part, be obtained independently of the author's transcendental idealism.

The main result of everything the author has noted about the work of understanding is supposed to be the following: that the right use of pure understanding is to apply its concepts to sensible appearances to form **experience** through their combination, and that it is a misuse of understanding, and an undertaking that will never succeed, to try to infer from concepts the existence and properties of those objects that we can never experience. (According to the author, experience, contrary to mere fancy and dreams, is [composed] of sensible intuitions combined with concepts of understanding. We admit, however, that we do not comprehend how the distinction of what is actual from what is imagined and merely possible, a distinction that is generally so easy for human understanding, could be sufficiently grounded in the **mere** application of concepts of understanding without assuming **one** mark of actuality in sensation itself. This is the case particularly in view of the fact that for those who are dreaming as well as for those who are awake, visions and fantasies can occur as [43] outer appearances in space and time, and, in general, as combined with one another in a most orderly fashion, sometimes even to all appearances in a more orderly fashion than actual events.)

In addition to understanding, there is, however, yet another power that now emerges for the processing of representations. That power is **reason**. It applies itself to the collected concepts of understanding just as understanding applies itself to appearances. Just as understanding contains the rules in accord with which particular phenomena are brought into the series of a cohesive experience, so reason seeks the highest principles by means of which these series can be unified in a complete world whole. And just as understanding creates a chain of objects out of sensations in such a way that they are connected like the parts of time and space, but where the last link always refers back to earlier or more distant ones, so reason seeks to extend this chain to its first or farthest link; it seeks the beginning and the limit of things. The first law of reason is that where there is something conditioned, the series of conditions must either be given in its totality or ascend to something unconditioned. According to this law, reason goes beyond experience in two ways. First, seeking the completion of the series, it wants to extend the series of things that we experience much farther than experience itself can go. Second, it also wants to lead us to things the like of which we have never experienced – to the unconditioned, the absolutely necessary, the unlimited. However, since they are [44] only supposed to serve understanding as a rule to **proceed continuously** in the exploration of nature, all principles of reason lead either to illusion or to contradictions when they are extended to show actual things and their properties.

The author now applies this general judgment to all the main topics of speculative psychology, cosmology, and theology. The particular way in which he does this and seeks to justify himself cannot be made completely evident by what follows, but we will give a rough outline. In psychology fallacious inferences arise when determinations that, properly speaking, belong only to thoughts as thoughts are taken to be properties of the thinking being. The proposition: **I think**, the sole source of all of rational psychology, does not contain a predicate of the **I**, of the being itself. It asserts merely a certain determination of thoughts, namely, their connection through consciousness. Thus, from it nothing can be inferred about the real properties of that being that is represented by the I. From the fact that the concept of **myself** is the subject of many propositions but can never become the predicate of any one of them, it is inferred that the **I**, the thinking being, is a substance; even though that word has been designated to indicate only the persisting in outer intuition. From the fact that there are not parts outside of parts found in my thoughts, it is inferred that the soul is simple. However, simplicity cannot occur in what is to be considered actual, that is, what is to be considered an object of outer intuition, because the condition of the latter is that it is in space, that it fills a space. The personality of the soul is inferred from the identity of consciousness. But could it not be the case that a series of substances transmit their consciousness and their thoughts to each other, just as they communicate their motions? (This is an objection that was also [45] made by Hume and long before him.) Finally, on the basis of the difference between the consciousness of ourselves and the intuition of outer things, a fallacious inference regarding the ideality of the latter is drawn. For inner sensations do not provide us with absolute predicates of ourselves any more than outer sensations do of bodies. In this way the common, or, as the author calls it, empirical idealism is ostensively refuted, not through a proof of the existence of bodies but through the abolition of the privilege that the conviction of our own existence was supposed to have over that of outer things.

The contradictions in cosmology are supposedly unavoidable as long as we regard the world as an objective reality and seek to grasp it as a complete whole. The infinity of its past duration, of its extension, and of its divisibility are taken to be incomprehensible to understanding, they offend it because it does not find the resting place that it seeks. And reason does not find an adequate ground to stop at any one point. The unification the author finds here, the true law of reason is, if we understand him correctly, that while reason advises understanding to continuously seek causes of causes, and parts of parts, with the intention of attaining the completion of the system of things, it nevertheless warns it not to assume that any one cause or any one part, each of which it finds through experience, is the last or first. This is the law of approximation, which encompasses both unattainability and constant approximation.

The result of the critique of natural theology is very similar to the previous result. Propositions that seem to affirm actualities are transformed into rules that merely prescribe a certain procedure to understanding. [46] The only new thing the author adds at this point is an appeal to practical interest. He permits moral ideas to turn the scale where speculation has left both sides of the balance equally heavy or, perhaps more appropriately, equally empty. Speculation reveals the following: all thought of a limited reality is similar to that of a limited space. Just as that could not be possible if there were no infinite general space, so a determinate finite reality would not be possible if there were no general infinite reality constituting the ground of all determinations, that is, of the limitations of particular things. Both, however, are true only of our concepts; both indicate only a law of our understanding, specifically, to what extent one representation presupposes another. In his examination, the author finds all other proofs, which are designed to demonstrate more, faulty and insufficient. Given that we understand it least, we leave aside the manner in which the author finally seeks to ground common modes of thought through moral concepts after he has deprived them of speculative grounds. There is certainly a way, which is grounded in our nature, to connect concepts of the true and the most universal laws of thought to the most universal concepts and principles of right action and by this means to prevent or correct the exuberance of speculation. But we do not recognize this way in the author's presentation.

The last part of the work, which contains the Doctrine of Method, shows first what pure reason should guard against, [47] and second, the rules it should take its cue from. The first is the **Discipline**, the second the **Canon** of Pure Reason. We cannot present the content in any detail, but it can for the most part be gleaned from what has already been said.

The book as a whole can certainly serve to expose the most considerable difficulties of speculative philosophy. It can also provide much material for salutary reflection to all those builders and defenders of metaphysical systems who all too proudly and boldly depend on their imagined pure reason. However, the author does not seem to us to have chosen the middle path between exuberant skepticism and dogmatism, the right middle path, which leads back to the most natural manner of thought with reassurance, even if not always with complete satisfaction. Both, it seems to us, are characterized by sure signs. First, the right use of understanding must accord with the most universal concept of right action, with the basic law of our moral nature, and hence with the furtherance of blessedness. As becomes quickly clear, understanding has to be applied in accord with its own basic laws. These find contradiction unacceptable and necessitate grounds for assent – indeed, prevailing and enduring grounds if there are contrary indications. It similarly follows from this that we have to adhere to our strongest and most enduring **sensations** or the strongest and most enduring semblance [*Schein*] as our reality. This is what common sense does. How does the reasoner lose this way? By bringing the **two kinds** of **sensations**, the inner and the outer, together, [48] melting them or transforming each into the other. Thus materialism, anthropomorphism, and so on arise when the cognition of inner sensation is transformed into and mixed up with the form of outer sensation. Thus also idealism when outer sensation loses its rightful place beside inner sensation, when it is denied its character. Skepticism does now one of these things, now the other in order to confuse and undermine everything. In a sense our author does the same; he denies the rights of inner sensation by demanding that the concepts of substance and actuality belong to outer sensation alone. But his idealism is even more in conflict with the laws of outer sensation and the language and mode of representation arising out of them in accord with our nature. When, as the author himself asserts, understanding merely processes sensations and does not deliver new knowledge, then it acts in accord with its first law when, in everything that concerns actuality, it is governed more by sensations than it governs them. And when, to assume the most extreme position with the idealist, everything of which we can know and say something is merely representation and law of thought, when representations in us, modified and ordered in accord with certain laws are just that which we call object and world, why then the fight against this commonly accepted language, **why** then and **from where** this idealist differentiation?

The Garve Review

Critique of Pure Reason by Immanuel Kant. Riga, 1781. 856 Pages in 8.

The philosophical writings Mr. Kant has so far presented to the public have shown him to be one of the deepest and most thorough of thinkers and a man whose fine and fruitful imagination often offers apt and well-chosen images for the most abstract concepts, thus making them [839] comprehensible and often even engaging also for the less perspicacious reader. But although the depth of his philosophical genius has not been revealed in any of his works to the degree to which it has been in this one, it is in most of its parts much less agreeably and popularly presented. This is the case, we think, not because his style has changed, but because most of the material he treats here is intrinsically too far removed from what is evident to sense and intuition to be made perspicacious even with the greatest effort on his part. The real purpose of this work is to determine the limits of reason, and its content consists in showing that reason goes beyond these limits whenever it asserts something about the actuality of any one thing. However, the abolition of all systems naturally produces a new one. There are certain principles that human beings cannot do without or that they cannot give up. Thus, when one believes one has found them to be invalid in all the senses in which they have hitherto been used, one is bound to seek a new meaning for them. After one has destroyed all those systems of ideas in which they have hitherto been preserved, one must explicitly erect a new system for them.

In order to make his system comprehensible, the author has also found it necessary to introduce a new terminology. It would be impossible to use that terminology here in a short account of his system. But it may be equally impossible to express the author's thoughts in all their uniqueness by means of words proper to a more popular philosophy. His terminology is the thread of Ariadne without which even the most perspicacious mind would not be able to lead his readers through the dark labyrinth of abstract speculation. Even if the reader does not always see clearly, he nevertheless feels comforted that he still holds the thread in his hand and hopes for an exit. However much one may attempt to bring the daylight of common sense into these dark solitary pathways, it is seldom able to illuminate them sufficiently to make visible the path that one has previously found through a kind of feeling. [840]

Still, it must be possible to connect this type of knowledge with our previous representations somehow since it doubtless did arise from them, even if only accidentally. It must be translatable, accordingly, into a more common language, though perhaps with some loss of precision. Here, then, is the system of the author as it has formed itself in the mind of this reviewer. He hopes that the changes that it has suffered thereby are at least not greater or more detrimental than those that it would have to suffer in the mind of every other reader if it is to be comprehensible or applicable.

All our cognition springs from certain modifications of ourselves, which we call sensations. We have no idea where they occur or what causes them. If there is an actual thing in which the representations inhere, or if they are created by actual things that exist independently of us, we still do not know the least predicate of either the one or the other. Nonetheless, we assume there are objects: we speak of ourselves, we speak of bodies as actual things, we believe that we know both, and we make judgments about them. By what wonderful artifice does nature arrange it that a series of alterations in us transforms itself into a series of things outside of us? How does it happen that in the face of the total dissimilarity of representations and objects (if the latter exist), the former still lead to the latter and seem to afford knowledge of them? That is the mystery Mr. Kant sets out to explain. The first question is: what belongs to sight, hearing, in a word, outer sensation? The second: what is required in order to form concepts of objects out of the appearances of the eye, the impressions of the ear, or, to put this differently, in order to form the kind of knowledge of objects that we have? Certain determinate modifications of our organs are required for mere appearances. But we abstract from them here. They are singular and particular in every sensation, but we seek the universal; they constitute the matter of appearances, [but] we seek its form. Still, they do have something in common, and this is precisely [841] what allows them to occur to us as outer appearances. This is that we place them all in a certain **space**, as things, and that we place them at a certain **time**, as events. **That** is actual for us which we represent to ourselves as **in some place** and **at some time**. Among all other representations space and time have an entirely individual and distinct nature. They are not something actual outside of us – for otherwise there would be infinite substances, which nonetheless have no properties. They are not concepts of relations – for relations are subsequent to the things that are related and cannot be thought without them. Space and time, however, precede all things because things can only be represented in them. They can be thought even when we remove all things. Nor are they abstract concepts – for there is no multiplicity of spaces, no multiplicity of times whose similarities would have been collected. There is one general space, one infinite time, and particular spaces and times are not kinds of this general space and infinite time, but only delimited portions.

What remains but that space and time are subjective laws of our representative capacity, forms of sensation, dispositions of our nature, which imprints the stamp of its two general forms on all impressions through which it is modified? – There is something too familiar connected with all of these words, and consequently, when so expressed, this opinion still appears strange. The author says: space and time are subjective conditions of sensible intuition, and as a matter of fact, the difficulty does disappear when strange ideas are expressed by less familiar words.

This is one of the basic pillars of the Kantian system. Data for objects are delivered through appearances. They are differentiated from other representations only through the subjective condition that space and time are combined with them. All our concepts of existent objects must be tested, accordingly, to determine whether they can cohere with the representations of space and time.

Understanding forms objects out of these appearances. It itself forms them, for it is what unifies a multiplicity of small successive alterations of our soul into complete sensations; it is what then combines these complete sensations in time in such a manner that they follow each other as cause and effect. [842] In this way, each attains its appointed place in infinite time, and together they attain the composure and solidity of actual things. It is understanding, finally, that, by means of an additional connection, differentiates simultaneous from successive objects. By thus bringing order, regularity of succession, and reciprocity into the sensible intuitions, it produces, indeed, creates nature in the proper sense and determines the laws of nature in accord with its own.

Sensible intuitions, by themselves, provide mere dreams. Concepts of understanding, by themselves, provide only a rule of order without the things that have to be ordered; sensible intuitions combined with concepts provide objects: apparent actualities. These laws of understanding are older than the appearances to which they are applied. Hence, there are a priori concepts of understanding. Mr. Kant specifies four general functions of understanding and derives from these four general concepts, which are applicable to appearances. These are the categories of quality, quantity, relation, and modality. The first contains reality, negation, and limitation; the second the universal, the particular, and the singular; the third, inherence, causality, and reciprocity; the fourth, possibility, existence, and necessity. (But on what basis does this division rest? What demonstrates its completeness? If these are a priori concepts of understanding and not just a posteriori logical classifications of predicates, then they must be derived from the nature of understanding. Does it not seem to be the case that, even in the most profound system, fundamental concepts often arise merely by association and that the mind is only employed to justify them through the unexpected applications that it knows to make of them?)

Understanding has a dual task in the transformation of sensible images into experiential knowledge. It forms concepts by ordering appearances in accord with the categories, and it produces principles, which are nothing other than expressions of its own laws and the rule of sensible intuition. To form concepts of objects three things are required: (1) successive impressions must be combined into one sensation of that sense; [843] (2) a multiplicity of complete sensations must be combined into one perception with the aid of imagination, which renews the past intuition while a new one presents itself; (3) a multiplicity of perceptions must be unified through the consciousness of ourselves, as belonging to one and **the same I**. In order for principles to be formed, the categories must be schematized, to use a new expression of the author. That is, they must be made more intuitable [or] immediately applicable to appearances and that happens through their combination with the representations of space and time as the conditions of intuition.

Analytic principles[1] are those that merely unfold the already given concept of the subject; synthetic ones are those that add a new predicate to the subject concept. The latter can only arise when the subject is intuited. (In order to discover something new in a thing, one must see it.) None of the categories have any employment, accordingly, unless they are schematized. The first analytic principle is that of contradiction. It says nothing more than that where I cancel one function of understanding through another, I do not employ any. The general synthetic principle affirms that all a priori cognitions, which are necessary in the formulation of an experience, and all concepts, without which appearances do not produce objects or without which objects cannot be brought into cohesive totalities, must be considered objectively valid.

When the category quantity is combined with space and time, the following axiom emerges: everything that exists (namely, in appearance) has extensive magnitude in space and time. Nothing can be represented as existing if it does not fill a certain space and a duration. – From the connection of the concept of quality with the determinations of time and place [*Ort*] the principle, that each sensed thing (each thing that is actual in appearance) must have an inner magnitude, a degree of reality, is developed. – By means of an application of this principle, one can show that the difference of specific gravity cannot be explained merely through more or less empty spaces in bodies, but that it could be a function of the different degrees of reality of their [844] basic parts. When the third category, that of relation, namely, substantiality, inherence, and reciprocity, is compared with the three main determinations of time, namely, persistence, succession, and simultaneity, then three principles emerge. The author calls them analogies of experience. (1) The substantial element in all appearances is nothing other than the persisting in relation to which other representations, which constitute accidents, change. The order of what is changeable, that is, time, is only perceptible through the persisting in which it is, just as quickly passing shadow images must have a ground against which their movement is seen. Accordingly, just as the concept of time is necessary for each existence, so is the persistence of substances. The concepts of creation and destruction would be, for us, a suspension of all thought and thus an absurdity. (2) Everything that happens must follow after something else out of which it flows in accord with a rule. For wherever there is **one** point of time, there is also a previous one. This previous point cannot be empty. The succession, however, between the previous and successive points must be regular because time is a continuous magnitude.[2] (3) Everything that is simultaneous must stand in reciprocal community. – Even simultaneous things make successive impressions. So how does understanding differentiate them from successive things? By means of a different type of connection. – And what difference can occur but that in the case of successive things the influence is one-sided, forward only from cause to effect, whereas for simultaneous things it becomes double and reciprocal?

Finally, if one applies the category of modality, namely, existence, **possibility**, and necessity, to the determinations that lie at the ground of intuition, one will find that these words, too, merely describe certain differences in our representations and cannot be applied to things in themselves with this signification in mind. That is **possible** for us which can be experienced, which accords with the formal conditions of experience. **Actual** is that which accords with the material conditions of experience, that is, that which is immediately intuited or that of which one understands clearly that were one placed at a different location or a different point in time one would experience it. Finally, **necessary** is that which is connected with the actual in accord with the [845] universal laws on which all experience rests. As a result, nothing is necessary but the effects that follow causes. Hence, we only ever comprehend the necessity of states of affairs, alterations, and events, not of substances. Those are never effects, they are what is persistent and everlasting in relation to which the alternation of causes and effects first becomes perceptible. All things, therefore, that we consider and name as objects, are only appearances, put together by understanding in accord with its own laws, by means of the function expressed in the category, and connected throughout according to space and time. The concepts of existence and substance, along with all those that attach to them, arise when the laws of pure understanding (which brings unity and system to appearances) operate, as it were, in unison with the laws of intuition, as required by the determinations of time and place [*Ort*]. Whether apart from these objects, which are nothing but impressions modified by the rules of understanding and intuition, there are other objects, which one could call **things in themselves** because their existence would be independent of the manner of our representation, is completely unknown to us. These things, if they exist, are without all predicates for us, hence nothing. At the same time, we are virtually forced, by another law of our understanding, to assume them problematically. This is precisely what has occasioned the differentiation between phenomena and noumena in the old, true meaning. These are words that indicate an inescapable and yet unanswerable question. –

We have drawn the principles thus far delineated from the categories by, as it were, substantializing them in appearances. The pure representations of understanding can, however, also be compared to each other without any reference to objects. As a matter of fact, that is what reflection means. The relations that we then find contained under them are nothing other than those of identity and difference, of the inner and the outer, of agreement and contradiction, and those, finally, of the determinable and the determined or of matter and form. Because, however, representations have a dual character, one when they are present only in pure understanding, as expressions of its functions, [846] another insofar as they are applied to appearances, insofar as they are, as it were, wrapped up in sensations, the previously mentioned relations also attain a dual sense. (1) Thought through the concepts of pure understanding, difference can only lie in the difference of characteristics because, apart from these, a concept contains nothing. In intuitions difference lies in the distinction of place [*Ort*] and time because they are the conditions of sensible intuition. – (2) When understanding seeks the inner nature of things independently of sensible appearances, it finds nothing but its **own conceit**, which it could call just that. The inner nature of things as they occur for us in intuition signifies the first and most universal of its relations, such as attractive and repulsive force. (3) Agreement in mere concepts is absence of contradiction. The latter lies in the affirmation and denial of the same predicate. Agreement in objects of appearance is the possible unification of forces without the reciprocal removal of their effects, and contradiction is the direct contraposition of forces. (4) For understanding as well as for intuition, matter is the data of sensations, the particular modifications of ourselves. For understanding, form consists in the universal a priori concepts or categories; for phenomena, form consists in space and time.

Leibniz's famous metaphysical principles can be derived from and refuted by the combination of these two manners of representation of the said relations. Because he could not count two concepts of things when he did not find a predicate in one that the other lacked, he inferred even of objects of sensibility that we could not think two where there were no differences of properties. He did not notice that in the latter case differences are added that concepts lack, those of space and time, the determinations that properly speaking constitute objects. Because he could not think an inner nature of things other than thought itself by means of understanding, he assigned the power of representation to each of his substances and formed monads, without becoming aware that objects of sensibility, which are nothing but representations and which, accordingly, are composed of nothing but relations, do not have a true **inner nature**. [847] Finding all concepts that do not contradict each other thinkable, he inferred that all realities must necessarily accord with each other, and from this proved the possibility of a perfect being. But he did not consider that real things that do not contradict each other can, like two opposed motions, still destroy each other in actuality. – All these and similar metaphysical delusions develop, accordingly, because one does not investigate in which faculty the representations are compared with one another. Relations that are true in the concepts of pure understanding may not be applied to what is actual, that is, to objects of intuition, without the addition of the special determinations that are dependent on spatial and temporal existence.

At this point we ascend the summit of metaphysical height in order to investigate: what is **Something**? What do we mean when we speak of an object, of a thing? Nothing but a representation given through sensible intuition, processed and brought under concepts by understanding. **Nothing**, accordingly, should indicate an absence of one of these two conditions of what is real. This absence can happen either when these conditions are missing altogether or when we merely omit them. When the concept of understanding is completely removed through contradiction, the outcome is a *nihil negativum*; when sensible intuition is missing because there is no impression, the outcome is a *nihil privativum*. By contrast, when we ourselves separate them from each other, then concepts without sensible intuition arise, *entia rationis*, or intuitions without concepts, *entia imaginaria*. An instance of the latter is empty space.

From all this, it is clear that the right use of pure understanding is to apply its concepts to sensible appearances to form **experience** through their combination and that it is a misuse of understanding, and an undertaking that will never succeed, to try to infer the existence and properties of those objects that we can never experience from concepts. Our author names this misuse Dialectic or the transcendental use of reason. The second part of this work is devoted to the investigation of the latter.

At this point, a further power and a further processing of our representations is introduced. Its source lies in reason. [848] It applies itself to the already collected concepts of understanding just as understanding applies itself to appearances. Just as understanding contains the rules in accord with which particular phenomena are brought into the series of cohesive experience, so reason seeks the highest principles by means of which these series can be unified in a complete world whole. And just as understanding creates a chain of objects out of sensations in such a way that they are connected like the parts of time and space, but where the last link always refers back to earlier and more distant ones, so reason seeks to extend this chain to its first or farthest link; it seeks the beginning and the limit of things.[3]

Here the term **conditions**, which the author has chosen, serves him very well. It is a term that he uses to sum up everything that must be assumed if a thing or representation is to be understood. Thus the previous time is a condition of future time, cause of effect, the part of the whole. Understanding applied to appearances leads us everywhere from conditioned to conditions, which are, in turn, conditioned, and stops there. The first law of reason is that where there is something conditioned, the series of conditions must either be given in its totality or ascend to something unconditioned. We sense the necessity of this law of nature, but is it a law of things considered in themselves as it is a subjective rule of our understanding? Reason goes beyond experience in two ways. First, seeking the completion of the series, it wants to extend the series of things that we experience much farther than experience itself can go. Second, it also wants to lead us to things the like of which we have never experienced – to the unconditioned, the absolutely necessary, the unlimited.

Reason seeks the totality of conditions with respect to (1) the thinking subject itself, (2) appearances or the objects of sensibility, (3) things in themselves or transcendental objects, which understanding presupposes but does not know. [849]

From this arise the deliberations of reason, about the **soul, the world, and God**.

The author manages to find some connection between the logical rules of reason's syllogisms and these metaphysical investigations that quite escapes us. The fact that the major premise must be universal is for him a ground for reason's search for universality, for the total completion of the world series. The categorical syllogism leads him to psychology, the hypothetical to cosmology, the disjunctive to theology. This reviewer has to admit that he does not know how to follow the author on this path.

The general result of these investigations is as follows: the principles of reason lead to illusion or contradictions when they are extended to show actual things and their properties. However, they are useful and indispensable when they serve understanding as a rule to proceed continuously in the exploration of nature. In psychology, fallacious inferences arise when determinations that, properly speaking, belong only to thoughts as thoughts are taken to be properties of the thinking being. **I think** is the sole source of all rational psychology. This proposition does not contain a predicate of the **I**, of the being itself. It asserts merely a certain determination of thoughts, namely, their connection through consciousness. Thus, from it nothing can be inferred about the real properties of that being that is represented by the **I**.

[1] From the fact that the concept of **myself** is the subject of many propositions but can never become the predicate of any one of them, it is inferred that the **I**, the thinking being, is a substance; even though that word has been designated to indicate only the persisting in outer intuition. (2) From the fact that there are not parts outside of parts found in my thoughts, it is inferred that the soul is simple. However, simplicity cannot occur in what is to be considered actual, that is, in what is to be considered an object of outer intuition, since the condition of the latter is that it is in space, that it fills a space. (3) The

personality of the soul is inferred from the identity of consciousness. But could it not be the case that a series of substances transmit their consciousness and their thoughts to each other, just as they communicate their motions? (This single metaphor does more to illuminate the author's ideas [850] than any general explanations.) (4) Finally, on the basis of the difference between the consciousness of ourselves and the intuition of outer things, a fallacious inference regarding the ideality of the latter is drawn. The author requires all his ingenuity to make only somewhat comprehensible how idealism with regard to the world of bodies, which he identifies as empirical idealism, can be refuted by transcendental idealism. Everything that this reviewer has been able to understand of this is summarized as follows. The idealist distinguishes the sensations of inner and outer sense by imagining that those of inner sense represent actual things, those of outer sense only effects of things, the causes of which are uncertain. The transcendental idealist does not recognize such a differentiation. He understands that our inner sense does not provide us with absolute predicates of ourselves any more than outer sense does of bodies, insofar as both are considered things in themselves. Consequently, for him our sensations resemble a series of alternating paintings that no more teach us the true properties of the painter than they teach us those of the painted objects. In one word, transcendental idealism does not demonstrate the existence of bodies, it merely abolishes the privilege that the conviction of our own existence is supposed to have over that of outer things.

In psychology the illusion of reason is merely one sided, in cosmology it occurs just as necessarily on two sides that are opposed to each other, thus creating contradictions that can never be resolved. For reason seeks the completion of the series of all objects connected in the world. (1) Seeking completion with respect to duration and extension, it asks about the beginning and limit of the world. (2) Seeking completion with respect to composition, it asks whether matter is infinitely divisible or consists of simple elements. (3) Seeking completion with respect to causality, it asks whether there are free causes or whether an alteration is always conditioned by another one into infinity. (4) Seeking completion with respect to the absolute existence of things, it seeks an absolutely necessary thing. In all these questions, contradictions are inevitable because reason and understanding have entirely opposed needs, make entirely different demands. [851]

If one closes these series at some arbitrary point and assumes a first member, then reason finds the standstill too sudden, the series too short and seeks higher members. If one wants to let the series continue to infinity, then they seem too long, incomprehensible, and hence absurd to understanding. A world without beginning and limit, a composite without elements, effects without free causes, [and] accidental things without a necessary one offend understanding because it does not find the resting place that it seeks. And yet it offends reason when one takes any one thing as the first, as the simple, as free, or as necessary because it cannot find a reason why one should stop with this rather than with any other one.[4]

These contradictions are resolved once one knows the true use of reason, once it is restricted to illuminating the path understanding has to take in the formation and use of its experiential knowledge. Then reason's principles will not assert how things are but merely prescribe to understanding how it is to treat them, and this treatment can often be reciprocal and necessary on each side.

It is not contradictory that reason advises understanding on the one hand to continuously seek causes of causes, and parts of parts, with the intention of attaining the completion of the system of things, and yet warns it on the other hand not to assume that any one cause or any one part, each of which it finds through experience, is the last or first. This is the law of approximation, which encompasses both unattainability and constant approximation. However, as soon as these regulative principles are taken as assertions about the things themselves, they must necessarily lead to contradictions. Through this discovery, these contradictions are resolved in the following manner. The first two antinomies, which concern merely the limits of magnitude, the beginning of the world and the divisibility of matter, are solved by showing that both opposing positions are false. There is no such world and no such division as is assumed by both antinomies. There are only appearances through which the regress can in fact be constantly extended and yet never completed. **World** is only another word for the [852] series of representations given to human beings through experience. That series can neither continue into infinity nor ever completely close itself for us. The two other antinomies, of freedom and the original being, concern the limit, the outermost of things, but as far as causality, not magnitude, is concerned. They can both be true at the same time. The series of changes can be a function of actions that have a dual character, a sensible one insofar as they belong as appearances to the events in the world and, as such, necessarily lead back to other, earlier ones, and an intellectual one insofar as they originate from an unknown **Something**, which we call the transcendental [thing], the thing in itself. By virtue of this second character they can be free. One finds a trace of this special kind of causality in the concept of **Ought**, in the **commanding** function of reason. It is a type of necessity distinguished from any other by being clearly recognized in an action even when its opposite has actually happened through the necessity of natural causes. Just as substances in the world can have an intellectual character by virtue of which their actions are free, though in another respect they were naturally necessary as phenomena, so there can be a complete intellectual substance apart from the series of accidents, which grounds them without limiting them. (It is impossible to clearly present the resolution that Mr. Kant wants to initiate in a few short words and impossible, I believe, to clearly comprehend it. But this is clear: that the author takes certain principles to be higher and more sacred than his systems, and, in certain decisions, has more regard for the consequences he wants at all costs to maintain than for the principles he has set down.) The final completion of the series, which reason demands, is one that leads it highest and farthest from the world of the senses. It is of things considered absolutely or in themselves and constitutes the ground of natural theology.

The result of the critique of natural theology is very similar to the previous result. Propositions that seem to affirm actualities are transformed into rules that merely prescribe a certain procedure to understanding. The only new thing the author adds at this point is an appeal to practical interest. [853] He finally permits moral ideas to turn the scale where speculation has left both sides of the balance equally heavy or, perhaps more appropriately, equally empty. Speculation reveals the following: all thought of a limited reality is similar to that of a limited space. Just as that could not be possible if there were no infinite general space in which the figure sets limits, so a determinate finite reality would not be possible if there were no general infinite reality constituting the ground of all determinations, that is, of the limitations of particular things. – Both, however, are true only of our concepts; both indicate only a law of our understanding, specifically, to what extent one representation presupposes another. – In his examination, the author finds all other proofs, which are designed to demonstrate more, insufficient. The first, the ontological proof, argues for the necessary existence of a God in an a priori fashion, on the basis of the concept of highest perfection, which encompasses all realities, including existence. This proof has two faults. First, we do not comprehend the inner possibility of this most perfect being, that is, whether and how all realities can be combined in one substance. Second, we do not comprehend the necessity of the existence of any being, no matter what predicates it has. We find a contradiction only when one of the predicates of a subject cancels another, but never when the subject is destroyed along with its predicates. Existence is not a new predicate, not an addition to the concept of a thing; hence, it cannot be viewed as either agreeing with it or contradicting it.

The cosmological proof, which argues for the existence of a God on the basis of the existence of an arbitrary series of accidental things, first expands the principle of causality beyond the appearances of the world, from which alone it is inferred and for which alone it is true. Second, it collapses into and presupposes the ontological proof because, in the end, a connection does always have to be demonstrated between necessity and highest perfection for the said substance; – a connection that cannot be demonstrated because we do not ever connect necessary existence to the concept of any thing and [854] because we cannot prove that highest perfection is inherently possible.

The physico-theological proof, which proceeds on the basis of the perfection of this our world, (1) does not make its cause God, rather, it makes this cause perfect or imperfect according to the good and evil that are in the world. (2) It again appeals to the cosmological and ontological proofs in order to complete what cannot be inferred on the basis of the properties of the world.

What remains of all this speculative theology? Nothing but a rule for understanding: seek incessantly the source of all realities, the unconditioned being, by ascending from condition to condition, but do not ever believe that you have found it in any actually experienced thing.

These speculations are now supplemented by moral concepts that are entirely necessary and true a priori. They show us that a certain manner of action is **right** – and present it at the same time as **entitling us to blessedness**. Through these two ideas they lead us to a connection of things where happiness must be distributed according to worthiness, and this system, which one could call the kingdom of grace, has God at its head.

How wise and happy is the nature of humanity; this reviewer cried when he arrived at this part of the book! After having stumbled over each small stone that he encountered on the path of speculation, he jumps over entire rocks and cliffs as soon as the stronger interest of virtue calls him back to the cleared road of common sense. It is certainly true that only moral feeling makes the thought of God important to us, that only the perfection of the former improves our theology. But that it should be possible to hold onto this feeling and the truth grounded in it after one has abandoned all other sensations that refer to the existence of things, along with the theory developed therefrom; that one should be able to live in the kingdom of grace after that of nature has disappeared before our eyes; [855] that, I believe, is something that only very few human beings will have the head or the heart to accept.

In this critique of all speculative theology, the author shows also, by means of some examples, how understanding makes laws of nature from its own laws; how even the greater adherence of understanding to one or another of its principles causes it also to consider nature from different sides. That we must not needlessly multiply the number of kinds; that we presuppose similarities in all species by means of which they can be brought under common genera, and in all properties possible modifications by means of which they provide further subspecies; all of this emerges from the dual law of our nature. One of these prescribes laws for the systematic order of our representations, the other demands that we presuppose the same systematic unity in the nature of things that our nature demands of the concepts of things.

Our world, then, is constituted by concepts drawn out of appearances, connected in experience by understanding, never entirely brought into a complete system, but for this purpose continually treated by reason; to make this our business is the result of our entire cosmology and theology.

The last part of the work, which contains the Doctrine of Method, shows first what pure reason should guard against, and second, the rules it should take its cue from. The first is the **Discipline**, the second the **Canon** of Pure Reason. The exploration of the dogmatic use of pure reason leads to a comparison of the mathematical and philosophical methods, which is instructive even for those who cannot comprehend the author's complete system. Mathematics is the only science that can make its universal concepts intuitable without in the least depriving them of their universality. Philosophy cannot do so except by examples taken from experience and these always involve the limitations of that particular circumstance. The drawn triangle presents the universal concept of triangle so completely, and includes so little apart from that universality, that it must be considered a pure intuition of the concept. The concept of force or cause [856] presented through an example adds so much that is extraneous and particular to the universal that it is difficult to keep the latter in view. In Mathematics the concept is **constituted** by the definition because it is a construction of our own understanding. It has necessity for that reason. In Philosophy the definition is only supposed to clarify a concept that already lies in our soul, and the definition is for that reason superfluous; further, a true definition cannot be found of either experiences or ideas of pure understanding. In Mathematics we have axioms because concepts can be intuited in their universality, that is, a priori, and in this way certain propositions are immediately evident. Philosophy, which cannot make its ideas intuitable except a posteriori through experience, does not have such axioms. – Finally, only Mathematics has demonstrations in which each step of reasoning is accompanied by intuition.

The second use of reason, to dispute and polemize, is useful when the discovery of necessary and irresolvable contradictions in its assertions leads it, finally, to the discovery of the limits within which it must remain. – Its third use, the formulation of hypotheses, extends only to the application of known affairs of nature to new phenomena, not to thinking up new causes. This third use is apt when the hypothesis explains the phenomenon completely, and when it does not need to appeal to further hypotheses to account for those aspects of the phenomenon which the original hypothesis did not sufficiently cover, or which it even contradicted. The hypothesis of the actuality of a highest being that serves as the explanation of the world fails on both counts. It is a being of a different nature than anything we have experienced. Nor does it explain everything; the imperfections of and disorders in the world require new supplementary hypotheses.

All this leads, finally, to the Canon of Pure Understanding [*Verstandes*], which consists of its highest purpose, namely, morality or worthiness for blessedness.

That we recognize a certain conduct as absolutely worthy of blessedness, and that this worthiness, more than blessedness itself, is the final purpose of nature, will both be less evident to many readers than some of the propositions that the author's critique has rejected. [857]

What we cannot know on speculative grounds reason enjoins us to believe because it provides us with a priori certain and necessary rules of conduct. These, however, could not be true, or could at least not be motivating powers of our will, if there were no God and no afterlife, that is, if there were no intelligible creator of the world and no state in which blessedness and desert are always together.

It is not necessary to anticipate the judgment that the reader who has followed the account up to this point will make of this system. Without a doubt, the system reveals problems that have never been completely resolved, indeed, cannot ever be completely resolved, and thus helps us to clearer insights into the limits of our understanding. From this point of view, the book is very important. It accomplishes in some of its articles what the reviewer has long wished for: to demonstrate, through a comparison of clashing systems, that it is impossible to completely satisfy reason in any one of them. – But the author wants to do more! He seeks to resolve these difficulties through an artificial new turn, by changing all things we call objects into types of representations and transforming the laws of things into subjective rules of our power of thought. And just as this method can never be brought to complete evidence and can thus not be useful in investigations or in life, so can it even less be freed of difficulties, equally great or perhaps greater than those which it was supposed to remedy.

The first basis of the whole system is the new perspective in which the author places the concepts of space and time. As subjective conditions of sensible appearances, which is what he considers them to be, they have two characteristics: first, they lie in us. They are forms, laws of our capacity of sensation. Second, they are what distinguishes those representations that present something to us as **actual**, as an object outside of us, from the rest. Once he believed he had found the specific thing that applies to our idea of existences, and through which it is, as it were, grounded, he proceeded from this principle in order to derive all universal ontological and cosmological principles, which [858] affirm something of actual things and which others consider to be abstractions from experience, from the peculiar determinations of space and time. When we assume something substantial in outer appearances, when we presuppose causes for all alterations, believe all simultaneous things to stand in reciprocity, in all these cases this happens, though we are not conscious of it, because time and space, without which nothing can appear as an object of sense, encompass all these concepts. Never before have space and time been rendered so fruitful for philosophical truths as they have by our author.

In fact there are hardly two such extraordinary, peculiar and incomprehensible ideas in the whole sphere of our knowledge. None of the theories about them, which one has thus far adopted, are satisfactory. To view them as things is impossible for understanding, to view them as relations is impossible for our imagination. They seem to be independent of and to precede outer sensations, but cannot be derived from inner sensations either. These are the difficulties that present themselves. But are they resolved when one turns space and time into a law or a condition of intuition? Is it more comprehensible how a subjective form of our thought presents itself as an object outside of us, for so space, even empty space, appears to imagination? Do the words, **law**, subjective form, **condition** of intuition, when used to designate a special kind of representation rather than a modification of our representations, show more than that this representation is found in us but that we do not know how to discover its cause in sensations as we have been able to do for others? Is this not basically an admission of our ignorance, the realization of the impossibility of resolving the difficulties, an admission that honors the philosopher? Such an admission is a true victory for him, but it cannot possibly become the basis for as many inferences.

And is the distance between the concepts of space and time and all other concepts of pure understanding really as large as the author supposes? It seems to this reviewer that he sees the route by which the author reached this separation. He saw the [859] apodeictic certainty of Mathematics, an apodeictic certainty that is singular to it among all human knowledge. He saw that it is the only science in which universal concepts can be made intuitable in all their purity. Going deeper into this difference he believed that he had discovered a special type of intuition that he called intuition a priori because, by means of it, without the aid of experience, universal concepts can be demonstrated in a manner that is otherwise possible only for objects of sensibility. This peculiarity of Mathematics and particularly of Geometry, he inferred, cannot come from anywhere but the special nature of its object, **space**, and because space and time are completely analogous concepts, this a priori intuition must be special to both of them and only them. Now it appeared to him that he understood the nature of the ideas of pure understanding and the appearances of the senses because he believed he had found the medium by which both are connected. The concepts of space and time belong to neither, but when they and all their implications are added to the ideas of pure understanding, the principles develop, and these can, in turn, be applied to the appearances of the senses so as to transform them into true cognitions. First, however, the author does not seem to have noticed that this whole theory is calculated only for the sense of sight, and that hearing, tasting, and touching, which do not involve space or an intuition a priori, should not allow us to think of something **actual**, of an object in this manner. Further, as similar as space and time supposedly are, and even though both, as the author puts it, are intuited a priori, how is it that the intuitable aspect of time has hardly led us to any particular proposition, whereas that of space has allowed us to develop a whole science, Geometry?

Is perhaps this a priori intuition, which is peculiar to and so fruitful for the author, nothing other than a sensible image of a concept of understanding, a sensible image that is so simple that what is particular and individual in the image strikes the mind so slightly that it does not diminish the attention to the universal? – And if that is the case, are the intuition of a drawn triangle in Geometry and that of a fact in Philosophy so radically different? [860] – I think not! Both are examples taken from experience. The former example, however, contains so little that is foreign, so few interesting supplementary conditions and determinations that, when intuiting it, it is extremely easy for us to abstract from everything that does not belong to the universal concept. In philosophical examples, by contrast, we find so many foreign additions, and the special conditions of a case strike us to such a degree that the attention is completely withdrawn from the universal characteristics of the concept and a confusion of both is avoided only with greatest effort.

Finally, even if we do concede all the distinctions the author advances, it nevertheless seems that he has not yet sufficiently explained (as he intended) how we arrive at the representation or conviction of something existing through the laws of our own nature. For neither the concepts of space and time, nor the categories combined with them, are particular to the conditions of alertness and sensation in which alone we assume existing objects; we can find them also in novels, fantasies, and dreams, even in the fantasies of the insane. Whenever we dream, we see what is represented just as well in time and space, in succession, in reciprocity, in short, in accord with the laws of our spirit, and yet we do not in the end recognize it as actual. – The difference between these two states, between sensation and the prevailing fantasy, which the author did not consider, seems to have always led understanding most clearly to the actuality of certain objects because it realized that subjective laws on their own cannot explain the manner and succession of those representations that are considered by all (and with the strongest reason) to be actual objects.

The proposition that has been elaborated in the author's system is in fact the long known proposition that our sensations do not teach us anything of the qualities of things but are merely alterations of ourselves, caused by certain qualities of things unknown to us. Nevertheless (particularly as far as the sense of sight is concerned), these modifications of ourselves appear as objects outside of us. Here, accordingly, is the first and greatest contradiction of sensibility and reason. The former says: there are [861] things and we know their properties, the latter shows clearly that we know nothing of these properties and consequently makes the existence of the things themselves doubtful. – Up to this point, the investigation of the actuality of things is at the same time an exploration of our nature, and we quickly reach that limit beyond which we cannot advance.

But it is hard to see what advantage can spring from following and developing this idea of reason further because the contradiction between it and sensibility, which always accompanies it, can never be resolved. We would have reached a true knowledge of ourselves and things if we could unify both. According to a claim the author himself makes, it is not the business of understanding to provide us with new cognition; instead it must process the sensations delivered to it, and so it appears that, with respect to actual things, understanding would do well to entrust itself to sensation. When, as the author himself affirms, understanding merely processes sensations and does not deliver new knowledge, then it acts in accord with its first laws when in everything that concerns reality it is governed more by sensations than it governs them. Moreover, when two things are completely identical *correlata*, like two expressions in Algebra, then it does not matter which of the two I use, which of them I take as definition to explain the other one. They would then be nothing but two words for one object and one, quite reasonably, tends to use the more familiar. Thus, when the representations in us, modified, ordered, and connected according to this or that law, are completely identical with what we call objects, of which we speak and with which all our intelligence and science concerns itself, then it is completely irrelevant whether we reduce things to ideas, or transform ideas into things. The latter is more in accord with our nature – and is so much a part of our language that we cannot express ourselves in any other way.

It would be impossible to accompany all parts of this work with the reflections they occasioned. The cosmological and theological [862] investigations are perhaps clearer. Here the author himself attempted to resolve the difficulties which he had created or set into greater light.

Section II

The Transcendental Aesthetic

Dietrich Tiedemann, "On the Nature of Metaphysics: An Examination of Professor Kant's Principles – Against the Aesthetic," *Hessische Beyträge zur Gelehrsamkeit und Kunst* 1 (1785), 113–30 81

Reprinted in Hausius, *Materialien*, vol. 2, 53 – 76. (The translation and pagination are based on this reprint edition.)

[Hermann Andreas Pistorius], "*Elucidations of Professor Kant's 'Critique of Pure Reason,'* by Johann Schultze, Prussian court chaplain. Königsberg: Dengel, 1784. 8, 254 pages." *AdB*, 66/1 (1786): 92–123 93

Reprinted in Landau, *Rezensionen*, 326–52.

Johann Georg Heinrich Feder, *On Space and Causality: An Examination of the Kantian Philosophy* (Göttingen: Dietrich, 1787), 1–64, 84*–91* 106

[Anonymous], Göttingen, Dietrich. "*On Space and Causality: An Examination of the Kantian Philosophy*, by Johann Georg Heinrich Feder. 263 pages in Octavo, 1787." *ALZ (28 January 1788): 249–54* 127

Friedrich Gottlob Born, *Investigation into the First Grounds of the Doctrine of the Senses* (Leipzig: Klaubarth, 1788), 87–92 133

Dietrich Tiedemann

On the Nature of Metaphysics: An Examination of Professor Kant's Principles – Against the Aesthetic

Since the emergence of what one calls metaphysics, disputes have prevailed about its most important tasks. Compared to the great expansion of all [other] sciences in recent times, these tasks now seem even farther from their completion. This has occasioned Professor **Kant** to ask whether the reason is to be found in the way in which one pursues this science, and whether it has not so far been taken to be something altogether different than what it should be according to its nature. [54] He has investigated [this question] with the insight and penetrating reflection that is evident in his other writings as well and found that these disputes lie beyond the limits of our understanding; that they arise with the ill-understood application of certain concepts, and, consequently, that given the way these concepts are now interpreted, they do not permit a satisfactory resolution; that reason and understanding, to the extent that we have them, may not look beyond the experience that is now possible for us; finally, that we cannot cognize what is outside of ourselves as it is in itself, but only insofar as it appears to us. This is what he presented in 1781 in the *Critique of Pure Reason*, expecting that philosophers would give it a close examination. When that did not occur, he published the *Prolegomena to Any Future Metaphysic* at the last Easter Fair with the repeated urgent request that one undertake this examination in accord with its importance and report what is found unacceptable. I have not perceived anything in Mr. **Kant's** conclusions that compels applause, and I will now present my objections in order to determine whether the fault lies entirely with me. Given that treating this material in its entirety would take up too much space, I will first examine the proofs by which he abolishes the reality of **space** and **time**, and, with that, our cognition of the objects they contain.

Mr. **Kant** argues both that it is undeniable that we have necessary, hence a priori, cognitions of **space** and **time**, and that many of them take the form of **synthetic** judgments. A **synthetic** judgment, however, cannot originate from the analysis of a given concept because it is the essence of such a judgment that a predicate, which does not already lie in the concept of a thing, is added to it. Furthermore, a **synthetic** judgment can only arise from an intuition. The ground of calling a body heavy [55] does not lie in its definition, but in experience or outer intuition, which always presents heaviness combined with extension, solidity, and figure, in conformity with the definition of **synthetic** judgments. Now, the judgments of pure mathematics are **synthetic** and concern **space** and **time**. Hence **space** and **time** are intuited a priori and are not concepts based on experience (*Prol.*, p. 49 ff).[1]

Here the main question we will have to ask is whether mathematical propositions are **synthetic**. Mr. **Kant** claims that the proposition 7 + 5 = 12 is **synthetic** because the concept twelve is far from already being thought when one thinks merely the unification of **seven** and **five**. The proposition that the straight line is the shortest [distance] between two points is similarly synthetic because the concept of what is straight does not contain magnitude, only quality (*Prol.*, p. 28f).[2]

When one analyzes a concept, one separates in thought all predicates previously thought confusedly and represents them one after the other to oneself. One separates the different interconnected acts by which one thought the concept and considers each on its own. When one divides a whole in one's thoughts, one separates the representations of the parts and thinks each on its own. There is only this difference between these two operations: in the first case the different predicates are all representations with different inner natures; in the other case, the parts often have the same inner nature and are rendered different only by being arbitrarily separated. Let us now ask whether this distinction constitutes an essential difference between the two operations. Does one not have to be called analysis as much as the other? Both, after all, consist in this: that what might be thought to be different in an object, but was previously thought confusedly, is separated in thought. It follows from this that [56] the proposition **seven** plus **five** equals **twelve** must be analytic. Among the possible parts of **twelve** we also find **seven** and **five**. Hence, in order to say that **seven** plus **five** equals **twelve**, it is not necessary that we go beyond the concept **twelve**. And that **twelve** can be accurately resolved into **seven** and **five**, is in the end the proof of the fact that **seven** plus **five** equals **twelve**. Or, to put this differently, in order to prove to myself that 7 + 5 = 12, I have to determine what I understand by **twelve**, and when I add 5 to 7, I obtain the previously determined concept. Hence, I do not need to go beyond the two given and proceed **synthetically**. [57]

From this it also follows that the propositions of geometry, where a new proposition is found by means of the division and renewed composition [58] of figures, are not **synthetic** because we do not go outside of the given concepts. [59]

Let us now consider whether the proposition that the straight line between two points is the shortest must be **synthetic**. [60] When some relation is determined between two concepts, the ground of this determination (the *fundamentum relationis*, as the scholastics put it) lies already in the concepts themselves. Understanding, which compares them, need only go from one to the other in order to make out which impressions such a transition brings forth in it. Propositions, accordingly, that designate connections or relations, are not **synthetic**. The proposition that the straight line between two points is the shortest is of this type. This line is to be the shortest; hence, more lines are given as possible. These are compared with the straight line, and the result is drawn from this. To be sure, in the bare concept of what is straight there is no thought of magnitude; however, when the straight is compared with the tacitly given crooked, the difference in magnitude is evident. [61]

In my estimation, many other mathematical principles are of the same kind: for instance, that three points always lie in one plane. Here the act by which one thinks three points is compared with that by which one represents a plane, and from this it is derived that the three points can only be thought as in one plane.[3]

This first proof would accordingly require the presentation of some mathematical propositions that are indubitably **synthetic**.

Mr. **Kant** presents another equally insightful proof: "that in which sensations can alone be ordered and placed in a certain form, cannot itself be sensation. Hence, the matter of all appearance is indeed given a posteriori, but the form must lie ready for sensations a priori in the mind, and it must accordingly be possible to consider it separately from all sensation" (*Critique*, p. 20).

Before we can say anything about this inference, we must further illuminate its content. [62] As I understand it, Mr. **Kant** envisages matters as follows: we sense impressions of certain, albeit unknown, objects, the solidity, hardness, divisibility, and so on of a body. These concern its matter. In addition, we find extension and shape in it. These concern its form. Now, the matter of intuition is that which corresponds to sensation, the form is what is responsible for the fact that the manifold of appearance is intuited as ordered in certain relations. There is still a certain vagueness in this: do color, smell, taste belong to the form of a body in intuition or not? If not, why not? After all, they make up the form of the now present body as much as extension and shape do. But if they do belong to its form, they must also be intuited a priori, at least according to Mr. **Kant**. [63]

Leaving this aside, I ask whether a special form of intuition in which the manifold of appearance is ordered in certain relations is necessary. Suppose a body consists of nothing but simple parts. In that case, the matter of intuition is the collection of them. The representation of extension and figure arises because the individual impressions of [64] the parts are not perceived singly, but as flowing together. Thus, it lies in part in the manner in which the impressions are made together, in part in the capacity of the soul to synthesize a multiplicity of single sensations into a whole. It does not lie outside of the body in a form that lies ready in the soul; nor do we need such a special thing that is distinguished from the body, in which the multiplicity of its parts would be ordered. The application to **space** existing outside of the body is in this respect not difficult.

Consequently, it remains necessary to prove that there must be a form of intuition different from its objects, in which their manifold is ordered.

Apart from these general grounds, Mr. **Kant** uses different specific reasons to show that neither **space** nor **time** are cognized a posteriori. They are presented in the following order: "first, **space** is not an **empirical** concept that has been drawn from our[4] experience. For in order that certain sensations can be related to something outside me (that is, to something that is in a different location of **space** than where I find myself), and similarly, in order that I can represent them as outside of one another, and consequently, as not merely different but as in different locations, the representation of space must already lie at the ground" (*Critique*, p. 23). The same is the case for **time**, "for simultaneity and[5] succession would not come into perception if the representation of **time** did not lie a priori at the ground" (ibid. p. 30).

Splendidly inferred! Completely worthy of the insightful man! Those things that are placed outside of one another must be in different **spaces**, so outsideness presupposes **space**. Hence, its representation did not arise with outer objects. I could not but submit to the power of the proof if only it did not occur to me to ask [65] whether difference in **space** is the first criterion of outsideness. With closed eyes, and without knowing if there is a **space** or anything outside of me, I extend my hand and encounter something that resists. After a short rest, I move it along this thing in a straight line, and again feel the same resistance. I know that what I felt first is not what I feel now because I have moved my hand; also, it is not in what was felt previously but beside and outside of it because I have perceived the same impression twice in succession, after the movement of my hand. Hence, I do not cognize outsideness through a difference of **space** because I know as yet nothing of it, but through the fact that I perceive the same impression of resistance at different moments twice in succession. Given that I am clearly conscious of the movement of my hand, I know at the same time that it does not spring from one and the same resisting object. In the same way, if I want to represent two points as outside of one another, I do not first take the representation of **space** in order to place them in it, rather, I imagine that I see the one and while I still see it in my thoughts, I imagine the other one at the same time. Hence, we first cognize that things are outside of one another by repeating a multiplicity of acts of sensation or of representations of sensation, letting each continue while we perceive the next. If the previous representation disappears altogether, the representation of outsideness does still arise, but not the representation of the fact that things are beside each other, that is, of succession. If I continue to move my hand along the resisting object, I obtain the representation of something extended, and if I move it in a straight line without sensing resistance, then [66] I arrive at the concept of **extension** and **space**.

But how? In order to be able to move the hand, **space** must already be there, hence, what is to be explained is already presupposed. To be sure, we must be able to move the hand, but, as I begin to move it, I do not know whether this is possible. Hence, I do not as yet have the representation of **space**. So even though one states correctly that things that exist outside of one another are in **different spaces**, that is not its first criterion. Nor is it a sufficient one, for now one raises a different question: which spaces are different? How does one cognize this difference? By the fact that they are outside of one another? But then we move in a circle: in order for things to be outside of us and outside of one another, we require difference of places and spaces, and in order that there are different places and spaces, we require that they are outside one another. There must, accordingly, be a different criterion of outsideness, and if that is the case, Mr. **Kant's** proof demonstrates nothing.

We find such a circle also in what Mr. **Kant** says of **time**. That which is in one time is simultaneous; that which is in different times is not simultaneous. Hence, simultaneity and nonsimultaneity cannot be perceived without the representation of time. Conversely, what is in different times is not simultaneous; what in one time is simultaneous. Hence, difference and oneness of time cannot be cognized without simultaneity and nonsimultaneity. Which of these two inferences should one trust? Is it not necessary to assume a different criterion of **simultaneity** and **nonsimultaneity** than **oneness** and **difference of time**? And must the representation of time, therefore, be excluded from the perception of **simultaneity** and **succession**? And this criterion is, as far as I understand matters, [67] nothing other but that one act of sensation, representation and thought, and so on, ceases completely when another one begins.

Second, Mr. **Kant** continues: "**space** is a necessary representation a priori which lies at the ground of all outer appearances.[6] One can never represent to oneself that there is no space, though one can quite well think that no objects are found in it" (*Critique*, p. 24). Similarly, "with respect to appearances in general one cannot remove time, even though one can quite well take the appearances out of time" (ibid., p. 31).

But have not **Leibniz's** students denied all actual space even of the world of the senses, and have not, before them, the Neoplatonists done the same with respect to the intellectual or spiritual world? Were there only one single, simple being, it would not perceive anything outside of itself. It would not be able to look around itself and say: this is me, but that, or that, is not me; it would, accordingly, know nothing of a space outside of itself. For in order to cognize this, a being must have outer perception; it must intuit objects outside of itself or at least change its place through activity directed outward. Remove touch and sight from us and see whether the least representation of space remains. It must thus be possible to think it as not existing.

And time? Who does not know that an interval of time can well be thought without succession, and is in fact often thought in this way, by a being who is not subject to change?

Of greater weight is Mr. **Kant's** third argument: [68] "the apodeictic certainty of all geometric principles and the possibility of their a priori construction are grounded on this **a priori** necessity. If this representation of **space** were a concept acquired a posteriori, taken from general outer experience, then the first principles of mathematical determination would be nothing but perceptions. Hence, they would have all the contingency of perception, and it would not be necessary that there should be only one straight line between two points; rather, experience would always teach this to be the case. What is borrowed from experience has only comparative universality, namely, through induction. One would thus only be able to say that as far as one has thus far observed, no space has been found that has more than three dimensions" (*Critique*, p. 24). The same is true of the "axioms of time in general. It has only one dimension; different times are not simultaneous but successive. These [axioms][7] cannot be drawn from experience" (ibid., p. 31).

In order to test the strength of this inference, I will ask in a preliminary manner what constitutes an a priori cognition. It is supposed not to have arisen from experience, rather, to precede experience, and to have apodeictic certainty independently of all experience. It is therefore not supposed to be a mere concept or a mere representation, for certainty exists only in judgments. Now, are a priori concepts also required in order that a judgment have complete certainty prior to experience and without all experience? When the relation and connection of concepts is understood on the basis of those concepts alone, when all experience is excluded from it, and when in all this we clearly recognize that no other combination is possible, then all conditions for an a priori cognition are met, and we do not ask further about the origin of concepts. Mr. **Kant** himself concedes, furthermore, that all **analytic propositions** must be [69] taken as knowledge a priori, even when their concepts are **empirical** (*Prol.*, p. 26).[8] Hence, insofar as geometrical principles are of a type that can be inferred out of concepts, a priori concepts cannot be demanded for their certainty. I have already noted earlier[9] that those geometrical propositions not considered by Mr. **Kant** to be analytic nevertheless follow from the component concepts themselves. The few examples that he introduces here to convince us of the opposite fail to be persuasive. That there is only one straight line between two points is something that concepts themselves teach, for it is impossible to think more than one. Any line other than a straight one deviates from the direction, hence is not straight. The reason we know that space has only three dimensions is not merely that we have found no others through the senses, but primarily that our concept of **space** does not allow more. The same is the case for the axioms of **time**. If we actually had the concepts of **space** and **time** prior to all experience, the certainty of all principles drawn from them would nevertheless not gain anything from it all. We would still not know them except through comparison and analysis of concepts, in other words, in the same way in which we do so now. Nor would something be gained if we were to understand these principles by means of a priori intuition, as Mr. **Kant's** theory specifies. If two philosophers could not agree on a point concerning these principles, each would appeal to **his** intuition, and with this the whole foundation of this certainty would be undermined.

[70] With great insight Mr. **Kant** responds, however, that the metaphysical principles, which encompass not just principles but also basic concepts, must never be taken from experience. For this cognition is

not to be physical but metaphysical, that is, it is to lie beyond experience (*Prol.*, p. 24).[10]

But it can do so even when the concepts spring first from experience, as he himself has already conceded in connection with analytic propositions. Metaphysics is not to teach anything that cannot lie either in our own experience, or in that of any thinking being, for that would be nonsense. Instead, [it teaches] what does not now occur in our experience or what does not occur completely, but what would occur under other conditions of outer intuition and does occur in the experience of other thinking beings. Now, even if concepts arise only from experience, if only their combination according to the essential principles of understanding should reveal them to contain more than the raw experience of them indicates, then they will lead us farther than experience. But if on the other hand they were to arise a priori but were to remain only what they now are, they would not teach us more, and nothing with more certainty, than what we now draw from them.

Mr. **Kant** says, fourth, that "**space** and **time** are not discursive, or, as one says, general concepts of relations of things in general, but pure intuitions. For one can represent only one space, and when one speaks of many spaces, one understands by this only **parts** of one and the same unique space. These parts, moreover, cannot precede the one all-embracing space, as [71] its component parts as it were (out of which its composition would be possible), but can only be thought in it" (*Critique*, p. 25). "Different times are only parts of one and the same time. Furthermore, the proposition that different times cannot be simultaneous cannot be derived from a general concept. It is **synthetic**, and cannot arise from concepts alone" (*Critique*, p. 32). "Similarly, all geometric principles, for instance, that two sides of a triangle are together greater than the third, are never derived from the general concepts of line and triangle, but from intuition, indeed, in an a priori fashion, with apodeictic certainty" [*Critique*, p. 25]. As far as I can make out, the conclusion says: there are no specifically different **times** and **spaces**; hence, neither concept is universal, each specific space is space in general. However, a space circumscribed by three sides is not that circumscribed by four, and neither is that limited by no sides. Out of the first, the last is formed in thought through the deletion of limits, just as, conversely, the former arises through addition of possible limits to the latter. Are these differently limited spaces not [just] general concepts narrowed by manifold differences through a procedure involving the ascent from the limited to the unlimited, or the descent from the unlimited to the limited? Is this not just what is observed in the elevation of specific to general concepts, and the determination of specific from general concepts? To be sure, particular spaces are called parts of the general space, but not as species of genus; the difference is that the parts of space can be taken as beside each other, and also each on its own, whereas species cannot be taken as independent of genus and as existing independently. Nevertheless, the procedure of going from a whole in which the parts are not determined [72] to its parts which have a determined figure, has significant agreement with that by which we go from genus to species, which is why the scholastics called the species the *partes intentionales* or *subjectivas* of the genus.[11]

However, one would not easily deem the proposition that different times cannot be simultaneous as **synthetic**. Different parts of time, a day, for instance, and an hour, can indeed be simultaneous; hence, the proposition cannot say anything other than that parts of time, which are not differentiated by virtue of an inner determination, cannot be different except through the fact that they are **not simultaneous**. Inner differences are here taken away. What remains in that case except outer ones? And these outer ones, what are they if not that one time is not when another one is? Other differences cannot be thought in the concept of time.

That in a triangle two sides together must be greater than the third, is, to be sure, demonstrated in intuition through lines and triangles, that is the shortest and most secure mode of conviction. But it does not therefore follow that it cannot be demonstrated through concepts as well. If one line of a triangle is given, then the other two must touch its outer points; otherwise, there would not be two angles. In a triangle, however, there must be two angles on each line; otherwise, no space is enclosed. But if the two other lines must have two angles, then they must lie between the same two points between which the straight line lies as well. Now, between any two points the straight line is the shortest; hence, the other two lines must be longer than the third.

The fifth and last proof seems to me to amount to much the same thing. If not, I must ask for further elucidation. [73]

In addition, in order to effect greater conviction, Mr. **Kant** bids us to consider the following: when two things are completely identical in all respects that can be cognized in each on its own, it must follow that one can in all cases and circumstances replace the other without having the switch make the least perceptible difference. Now, the image of my hand in a mirror is completely similar to my hand. And yet, the hand in the mirror cannot take the place of the actual hand. For if this is a right hand, that is a left one which can never take the place of the first. There are in this case no internal differences that any one understanding could think, and yet the differences are internal ones. Hence, the objects are not representations of things as they are in themselves, but only sensible intuitions (*Prol.*, pp. 57, 58).[12]

In the left hand, the parts have a different orientation [*Lage*] with respect to each other than they do in the right hand. This is an internal difference and one, furthermore, that is grounded in pure concepts of understanding. For even if the acts of thought and representation are identical in two cases, the manner in which they are represented after one another or together gives rise to an internal difference. A series of the same inferences ordered synthetically contains the same propositions and inferences that occur in the analytic ordering and has one and the same result in understanding; and yet they are different. Therefore, even in the operations of pure understanding, there is a distinction that springs from the order in which these operations are undertaken; we cannot say, therefore, that such a difference in the objects of sensibility does not create a difference for understanding; hence, the objects in which they occur are not objects in themselves.

So much for the proofs. It will still be necessary, for purposes of greater clarity, to consider the content of the final inference [74] more closely. Mr. **Kant** believes that he has established this much through these inferences, that the concepts of **space** and **time** do not arise from sensible impressions but precede them, which is also why he repeatedly calls them intuitions, pure intuitions a priori.

Intuition designates two things for the philosophers, as far as I have been able to note. First, it stands for present, perceived sensations, acquired and noticed through attention. In this sense, the concepts of **space** and **time** cannot without contradiction be a priori intuitions.

Second, it stands for sensations, renewed through the reproductive capacity, and now carefully considered. In this sense, as well, the concepts of space and time cannot be a priori.

It would remain to say that the soul can create representations of **space** and **time** out of itself without prior sensations, but all experience would contradict this.

Alternatively, [one could say that] sensations are indeed required in order to occasion these concepts, but sensations on their own do not constitute them. Something is added that does not come from sensation. This is the direction Mr. **Kant** seems to want to take when he says that "because the receptivity of the subject, to be affected by objects, necessarily precedes all intuitions of these objects, we can understand how the form of all appearances can be given in the mind prior to all actual perceptions, thus a priori, and how, as a pure intuition in which all objects must be determined, it can contain principles of their relations prior to all experience" (*Critique*, p. 26). [75]

In order to be able to accept this explanation with more readiness and conviction, one would gladly like to know precisely what understanding contributes to sensations in order to create the concepts of **space** and **time**. For then one could investigate the matter itself and so be convinced that one thinks more than words.

Now, something that the soul itself contributes to sensations does not seem to be present as element of the concepts of **space** and **time**, and if it is not, then the explanation fails by itself. There would have to be some such component of the concepts for were there none, the whole concept would be taken only from outer impressions. I feel something as extended when I move my hand, or another organ connected with the sense of touch, along it, and so I receive different impressions one after the other and retain the preceding in those that follow. All, therefore, that has to be added to the simple act of touch is that the preceding impression is not immediately extinguished, that there is not merely touch present, but a retention of the previous impression. In a similar manner, something is cognized to be extended by means of the sense of sight. This ability to retain impressions is admittedly a capacity of the soul; but it does not add anything new to the representation; it is only responsible for the fact that the impression is taken up as it is.

One cannot have the concept of extension except when one imagines that one touches and sees something extended; that is, that imagination renews the particular acts of touch and seeing and does not let the previous ones disappear with those that follow. So without already having touched or seen, the concept of extension is impossible. For how does one want to renew an impression one has never had? From the side of the soul nothing is added to this renewal [76] except the capacity to retain the preceding representation in the following one, and this capacity does not constitute an element of the concept of extension, it only ensures that the [following] representations are brought about in the same way the outer impressions were. So the concept of extension is completely impossible a priori and does not contain anything arising out of the soul itself apart from all experiences.

One can easily apply this to time.

From all this an important final inference emerges with respect to Mr. **Kant's** other conclusions. He teaches that **space** and **time** are merely conditions of our sensibility, hence mere ideas, and nothing real. To the extent, on the other hand, that the origin I have argued for is correct, it emerges that these ideas are not a function of the manner in which we touch and see, but that they presuppose nothing more than a capacity to perceive objects outside of ourselves as persistent. We do not have this concept of extension and space because our eyes have this construction, our touch these nerves, our organs this constitution. We have them, rather, because we can represent something outside of ourselves as persisting and continuing. Every being, accordingly, which is equipped with the same capacity, must have the same concepts of **space** and **time**.

[*Hermann Andreas Pistorius*]

Elucidations of Professor Kant's 'Critique of Pure Reason,' by Johann Schultze,[13] Prussian Court Chaplain. Königsberg: Dengel, 1784. 8, 254 Pages.

All those experts and half experts who have expressed any opinion on this matter with their complaints about the obscurity of Professor **Kant's** *Critique of Pure Reason* have conceded, it seems to me, that it is neither unnecessary nor superfluous that there be elucidations of it whereby the content of this important but difficult work should be so far revealed to readers who are lacking in leisure and patience, though not entirely in ability to study the system of the profound philosopher, as to enable them to understand its content more easily, and to engage in philosophical reflection with it. So court chaplain **Schulze** has rendered an attractive and important service to philosophy and its devotees with these *Elucidations*. They deliver a clear commentary about the most important book in metaphysics that has been written since Aristotle's times, a commentary, moreover, that has been sanctioned by Mr. **Kant**. For this he certainly deserves the gratitude of all speculative thinkers. [93]

The *Elucidations* contains a short report of the content of **Kant's** work, in which the system is presented in plain language, though Mr. **Kant's** terminology is used and explained at the same time. It also contains several hints for the closer examination of this system. There will be few readers of Mr. **Kant's** *Critique* and *Prolegomena*, I think, who will not find that these *Elucidations* illuminate many obscurities and solve many difficulties concerning Mr. **K.**'s actual meaning. The reviewer at least acknowledges that many difficulties he had with the *Prolegomena* have been clarified to the extent that he now believes he has at least understood Mr. **K.** And yet I find that the greatest difficulty, which I had with Mr. **K.**'s principles concerning space and time and the theory of appearance [*Schein*][14] and truth that is based on them, has not been resolved. I have already mentioned this difficulty in my review of the *Prolegomena* (*Allgemeine deutsche Bibliothek*, LIX, p. 345).[15] I took up these *Elucidations* with some eagerness, hoping to perhaps find a resolution of my doubts in them. However, as mentioned, I found nothing that would have explained to me how, according to the author's system, appearance [*Schein*] could be possible at all, if that through which all appearing [*scheinen*] becomes possible (which must, accordingly, be presupposed prior to all appearance [*Schein*] and cannot therefore itself be an appearance [*Schein*]) is supposed to be appearance [*Schein*]. In one word, I could not see how appearance [*Schein*] could be possible at all if representation and thought themselves are supposed to be appearance [*Schein*]. And yet that is precisely what they must be because all our thought occurs successively and in accord with the determinations of time, [because] space and time are **merely** subjective forms of our sensibility, and everything that is intuited in space and sensed and thought in accord with time determinations is nothing but appearance.

Rather than provide further information about Mr. **K.**'s principles and system by compiling a summary of these *Elucidations*, which would seem to be quite superfluous in view of this work, I will venture to follow Mr. **Schulze's** hint for the closer examination of the *Critique* as far as my powers permit. . . . [94] I will appeal equally to Mr. **K.**'s great work and the *Prolegomena*. . . . [16]

[100] . . . [O]ne would have to view the concepts of space and time, which are so important to the author, and which serve as pillars for the whole critical system, somewhat differently and specify them in a different way. That is, one would have to declare them to be relational concepts that are not merely grounded in the nature of our sensibility, and that do not merely constitute its subjective form, as Mr. **K.** argues, but that would also have to be considered as grounded in the nature of the **things in themselves** that appear in space and time. In this way a roughly Leibnizian concept of space and time would emerge. Let us see whether this concept can be defended against the author's objections. However, first I will have to further explain my understanding of these two objects, so singular in kind. In my view, the concepts of space and time are not simply empirical but can also be counted among the a priori concepts. They constitute the limit between the intelligible and the sensible world, and connect the two together, or make it possible for **things in themselves** to become appearances. This mixed nature of the concepts of space and time can somewhat explain why they are so peculiar, so singular in kind, and why it is impossible for our understanding to regard them as things, and for our imagination to regard them as relations. Because they lie between our activity and its objects as the unifying and connecting middle ground (between what is subjective and what is objective) and touch both, they also have,

as it were, something of both. Their intermediate nature is responsible for the fact that in a manner of speaking one can take them to be either, depending on whether one considers them from this or that side. Insofar as they are grounded in what is subjective, namely, as [101] I understand it, in the limitation of the human power of thought, they have the nature of a priori concepts, but insofar as they are grounded in **things in themselves** or in the objective sphere, space in the **actual** multiplicity, and time both in the multiplicity and the **actual** variability of the represented **things in themselves**,* they must have similarities with empirical representations or concepts of experience. The fact that, if we are to differentiate them from ourselves, we must place the objects of the outer senses, particularly those of sight, outside of us and that we must perceive them in space, is grounded in our limitation. In this way, it can and must seem that the concept of space is an innate concept, that it must precede all sensations and lie at the ground of all intuitions. But how are we to determine that nothing empirical is mixed up with it, and how are we to demonstrate that this does not happen? Our first perceptions through sight and touch occur at an age when we cannot be conscious whether it was the concept of space or that of the object that was first in the soul, or whether it is not perhaps rather the case, as it seems to me, that both are together in the soul. If space is a relational concept at least, then the last alternative must be true, for in that case it would have to be in the soul simultaneously with the things that stand in the relation, namely objects and our **I** (which must differentiate itself from the object by means of just this representation). We would find some insight into this obscure matter [102] if we knew precisely how persons born blind think space, particularly if we knew what sort of concept of space Saunderson, a person born blind and a profound mathematician who wrote about light and color, constructed for himself. That something empirical is intermixed with the representation of space seems to me

* In general, one could say: the multiplicity that is differentiated from ourselves (as intuited or felt in space) provides, insofar and as long as it is not differentiated within itself, the concept of extension, of constant magnitude (*quantitas continuae*); that multiplicity, however, that is differentiated not just from ourselves but also within itself provides the concept of number (*quantitas discretae*). Because it is impossible to make further separations of multiplicity in universality, one can see that the universal science of multiplicity (pure mathematics) cannot have more or other parts than pure arithmetic, or the universal science of numbers (*quantitas discretae*) and pure geometry, or the universal science of constant magnitude (*quantitas continuae*).

to be clear also from the account that is given of a person born blind who was operated on by the famous Cheselden. After he could see, it seemed to him as if all visible objects lay immediately in his eye and touched it. Hence, he knew nothing of distance, and even less of its measure, and did not have an as it were innate geometry. Do we not all learn to judge distance and the size of distant objects gradually and through experience? – But how can the author's so-called **pure intuition** be reconciled with the concepts of space as they have up to now been explained? How does the certainty and evidence of pure geometry, which is independent of all experience, accord with it? I think a reconciliation can be found. When we consider that everything that is intuited must be perceived in space, then space is indeed for us a universal concept of relations that recurs with every intuition and outer perception, no matter how different it may otherwise be. How does this preclude us from abstracting this concept in part from the objects themselves which are given in it, and in part from the specific limitations which are created by the figures and arrangements of objects in space? What prevents us from thinking it as an independent, coherent, uniform totality and in this way form, or rather devise, the concept of a general space as a receptacle in which bodies and objects can be? After we have reached this point, we can differentiate this general relation as it were into compartments, give it manifold forms or attribute all manner of limitations and modifications to space. These compartments generate the places we assign to objects; the limitations and modifications of general space generate the different figures and locations that are creations of imagination that we arbitrarily construct. What we ourselves contribute to these constructions must surely be valid of them; they [103] must be what we make them. When we find, accordingly, that an object has just the figure and location that has been constructed, that it fits itself into our compartments, then precisely to the extent that it is constructed by our imagination, what holds true of its figure and location, is exactly what holds true of the products of our imagination.

Let us go on to see what support the author's other arguments lend to the exclusive truth of his concept of space and time and against the validity of the concept I have set out. He says: "space and time are completely necessary representations, they adhere to us with complete necessity. To be sure, we can think all objects as removed from space and time, but we cannot remove space and time themselves."[17] We cannot remove the concept of time if only because all our thinking is successive, hence, takes place in time, and it is precisely this successive thinking that leads to the concept of time. However, if the concept of time, as well as that of space, is in part subjective and grounded in the nature of our spirit, specifically in our limitation, then this limitation is something essential and constant. As a consequence or as an insepara-ble accompanying circumstance, accordingly, the concepts of space and time must be necessary. The essential limitation of our power of thought renders the concepts of space and time necessary conditions of our sensibility, and the unavoidable feeling of this limitation bids us to always expect that objects along with our sensibility must stand in relations of space and time. We cannot differentiate objects either from ourselves or from one another, unless we place them in part outside of ourselves, that is, intuit them in space, and in part successively, that is, perceive them in time. But none of this precludes the possibility that the concepts of space and time can also have an objective foundation. – "All axioms of space and time are apodeictically certain, and consequently, cannot have been obtained from experience, for in that case we would only be able to say: this is what common perception instructs, but not, it must be so. Hence, they precede all experience and are propositions a priori. Examples are the principles that different spaces cannot follow each other [104] and that different times cannot be at the same time, that there is only one straight line between two points, etc." I think that exactly the same must be the case also according to my concepts of space and time, for these concepts express relations of **things in themselves** to our sensibility that are made necessary by the essential limitation of our spirit. Specifically, the concept of space expresses multiplicity irrespective of variability, that of time expresses just this multiplicity with respect to variability either of the objects themselves or their modifications. If this is the case, then one can easily understand that these different relations are not interchangeable, and hence that axioms that assert these relations cannot be transferred from one relation to the other and we cannot say: different spaces follow each other or different times are simultaneous. As far as the third axiom is concerned, it expresses a necessary relation of two objects that does not depend on their constitution, but on their actual or supposed existence. Strictly speaking, it does not say anything but that two objects are actually in the position in which they are supposed to be. Their position determines their distance, and there can be only one distance.

Nor do the grounds the author uses to demonstrate that space and time are not discursive and general concepts but intuitions affect my concept, for I do not derive these concepts through reasoning, by means of an abstraction, but from the necessary relation of **things in themselves** to our sensibility. Space and time are always perceived and intuited along with objects, so the concept of space in particular is a necessary appendage or circumstance that must be posited with every outer appearance. The proposition that whatever is, and is to be an object of our outer senses, must be somewhere or occupy a place is not a proposition we arrive at through a process of reasoning; rather, it is due to the inescapable feeling of our limitation. However, the proposition that here is a general empty space of which all spaces or places are not component parts but limitations is in part a product of imagination, in part a work of reasoning. But it is not an innate proposition that could be presented by someone without the use of sight, without instruction by someone else and without one's own exercise of [105] thought. And what is more, space and time are, in my view, grounded in part in objects, and so they are to that extent empirical, and are intuitions, not abstractions. For that reason as well I can happily accept the author's reason that, because all principles of time and space are synthetic propositions, they must be intuitions, not general concepts. – For insofar as they are grounded in the objective sphere, they are intuitions, that is, they are relations perceived along with the things that stand in the relation. If they are separated from the objects, then they are creations of imagination, namely, general empty space and infinite empty time, which are formed in the manner already indicated, as will also be confirmed in what follows. – I can also happily concede the author's following argument, insofar as the last inference he draws from it is concerned: "since we represent space as well as time as an infinite magnitude, all determinate magnitudes of its parts are possible only through limitation of infinite space and infinite time, but by no means possible through a general concept of space and time. Hence, if space and time were not intuitions but general concepts, no concept of magnitude and of the relations in space and time would be possible at all." There is only one remark I want to make regarding the genesis of the concept of magnitude and the relations in space and time that are indicated here. The author claims that what is, as it were, an innate concept of an infinite empty space and an infinite empty time lies at the ground of all concepts of determined spaces and times in such a way that one can obtain the latter only through the limitation of the former, or that they are basically nothing other than certain incisions that one makes in immeasurable space and infinite time. In my opinion the opposite is the case: the concept of limited spaces or places and of a determinate time is in the soul first and is intuited and sensed in every intuition and sensation. An immeasurable space and an infinite time are subsequently composed from these limited spaces and places through imagination. But after one has a concept of them, the philosopher can in turn use this concept as a ground and, like the author, consider all limited [106] spaces and times as just so many limitations of it. The philosophical lay person at least seems to be able to ascend to the concept of the immeasurability of space and the infinity of time only by means of imagination. He has to do this in more or less the manner in which the psalmist represents the omnipresence of god: **if I ascend to heaven, then you are there, if I make my bed in hell, then you are also there, if I took flight with the dawn of day and remained at the outermost ocean**† etc. . . . [18]

So the concepts of immeasurability and eternity do not lie a priori at the ground of all limited concepts of magnitude in space and in time; on the contrary, we arrive at them only when we extend and combine the latter to infinity, that is, extend and combine them without stopping. How many human beings can there possibly be who can think the concepts of immeasurability and eternity accurately and correctly without admixture of limits?

And what is the purpose of all this? As a matter of fact, it is not to demonstrate that my concept of space and time must be the only true one, but only to show that it is a possible concept, that it withstands Mr. **K.**'s objections, that the phenomena and correct principles that he presents with respect to space and time are just as consistent with the presupposition that these concepts are not just subjective but objective as well, and, consequently, that we are simply not forced to assume, with Mr. **K.**, [107] that space and time are only subjective forms of our sensibility and have nothing that is objective. For we could only accept the author's concept if we really had to do so, or because the impossibility and inadmissibility of every other concept of space and time could be apodeictically demonstrated. Just as the author's system can generally speaking be built only on the wreckage of every other system, so this concept in particular seems to me not to be unlike an oriental despot who can enthrone and assert himself in this position only after having murdered all his brothers. But if we can assert that another representation, for example, the one presented here, which supposes that space and time are in part grounded in objects, is at least possible, then it would, it seems to me, claim preferential approbation, in view of the following advantages.

First, the author's concepts of space and time have given rise to a theory of appearance [*Schein*] and reality that places us in the extremely unfortunate and dubious situation that I have already indicated – one encompassing even our own existence. My concept of space and time

† See also Klopstock's *Ode über die Allgegenwart Gottes.*

would free us from this situation. The actual existence of an objective intelligible world would no longer be as problematic, it would, rather, become dependable and certain. And what is even more important and interesting for us, if we could convince ourselves that representations and thoughts are true effects of a power that is homogeneous with us, namely, of a thinking power, then we would also be able to trust our inner sensation [which tells us] that we are not just logical and apparent [*scheinbar*], but **actual** individual thinking subjects or substances. In one word, we would then no longer be allowed to doubt whether there actually are **things in themselves** that constitute the substratum of our intuitions and that appear to us. And, as seems to me, we would have even less cause to doubt whether there is in actuality a thinking subject to whom **things in themselves** appear and whether the subject that we designate through our **I** is this thinking subject. In general, the theory of appearance [*Schein*] and truth would be able to attain greater correctness and the autonomy that, it seems to me, the author's theory lacks. On the author's theory, the existence of **things in themselves** is presented now as merely problematic, now as certain, the first because we [108] can know or cognize absolutely nothing of them, the latter because all **things in themselves must** after all lie at the ground of appearances that indicate their existence whether we know something of them or not. Quite independently of that fact, in view of the author's concepts of space and time, it becomes, as I will soon show more closely, if not altogether impossible, then at least quite difficult, to think **things in themselves** as the possible foundation or substratum of appearances. . . . [19]

[114] . . . Second, on the basis of our concepts of space and time, appearances and **things in themselves**, the subjective world of the senses and the objective intelligible world would be brought into an actual and true combination. Thus, we would be able to avoid the most important and, in my opinion, essential error that pervades the author's entire system, namely, that according to it an objective intelligible world and **things in themselves** are assumed, as we put it in our provincial dialect, for no reason at all [*für nichts und wieder nichts*]. If it was not the case that the author's whole unsettled system had to be given a kind of composure and foundation, we would simply not require anything at all but apparent [*scheinbare*] objects, and no other subjects but merely logical ones.‡ But this composure and this foun-

‡ The entire argument by which the author wants to present the core of the so-called paralogisms of reason amounts to an attempt to show this: the unity of consciousness leads us only to the presupposition of an apparent [*scheinbar*]

dation are themselves only apparent [*scheinbar*]. There is no real connection between the world of the senses and the intelligible world, for if there were, **things in themselves** would actually have to be objects of our sensibility, and how would we then want to intuit them but in space, how else but in time and in accord with temporal determinations? Space and time are therefore the only intermediary between **things in themselves** and our representative power, the pathway along which the communication between the two worlds travels. However, now that space and time are merely subjective forms of our sensibility and do not encompass an objective dimension, are not grounded in anything objective, hence do not relate at all to **things in themselves**, [115] all communication has been cut, and such an abyss has been established between the two worlds that **things in themselves** can no more reach our cognition than our representative capacities can reach them. The author objects to the Leibnizian system, not unjustifiably, on the ground that it attributes to the senses the disagreeable task of presenting to the soul an obscure and disguised image of the objective intelligible world. But I think that this task is not as hated as when one assigns to the senses the task of presenting an entirely wrong image and that is what the author actually does. According to Leibniz our senses are a dimmed and crudely ground glass through which our soul actually intuits **things in themselves**, although in dark and dim distance, now and then somewhat distorted, disguised, and disarrayed. But according to our author they are a glass whose exterior has an entirely foreign painting, as it were, glued to it. It does not present the objective world at all, nor an aspect thereof, but a landscape that is completely isolated from it, although beautifully illuminated, well ordered in all its parts by means of understanding and its concepts, and excellently harmonized with our organs of sight to which alone it fits, for which alone it is determined. Most of those who see through the telescope of the senses get no idea at all that what they see is not the actual true external world, or that it should not be constituted as they see it. Only some develop the suspicion that they do not, after all, perceive things completely in their proper and true form. This happens through those disguised aspects of the painting on the telescope that are misplaced and, in their opinion, do not properly fit and do not completely har-

and logical subject, that is, a subject that must be assumed for purposes of thought, but that does not allow us to infer the existence of one thinking substance. So we must assume that we need nothing more than an apparent [*scheinbares*], logical subject. If this were not the case, then one would be justified to infer the existence of the former from the latter one.

monize with their more practiced or sophistical judgment. They think that the aspects that do not harmonize are a function of the imperfect instrument and their limited power of vision. Yet another wanted to, as it were, reverse his telescope of the senses, and by means of it see not outside but inside himself because he thought that there are no outer things that can be perceived, no objective world, indeed, that there could not be. All things that were presented to him in this way would be only thought images, happening and alternating in his soul. Some of them would be represented with such admirable skill that one would have to believe them [116] to be not mere images in us but actual objects outside of us. Finally, our author arrived, and having most closely examined our telescope and power of vision, he explained that even though there actually is and must be an objective world and real things outside of us, in view of the special form of our instrument of vision, we can still neither perceive nor discover the least fact about them with it. What we believe we see are all mere appearances. They are produced and formed through our instrument itself, in view of the way in which it has been artificially ground and constructed. These appearances, meanwhile, serve us as if they were actual realities. All we have to know is how to properly order, ascribe, and connect them in a regular whole. However, all comparisons aside, we can always assert that according to the author's system, the objective intelligible world is as good as destroyed for us, for if **things in themselves** do exist, they exist completely apart from the world of the senses, in which everything remains as it is, everything proceeds in its proper, regular manner whether there is an objective world or not. Indeed, we cannot even assume that one is there for the sake of the other and that one is constructed in harmony with the other. Nor can we assume that a previously determined harmony takes place between the world of the senses and the intelligible world, for even if both worlds did belong together through this subtle thread, our sensibility and its form, the concepts of space and time, would have to have a relation to the world of understanding that is to be represented, they would have to be constructed in accord with it, or, in other words, this form of our sensibility could then no longer be merely subjective but would have to be objective and grounded in the objective sphere at the same time.

Third, if we might now also be permitted to assume that just as the concepts of space and time are not merely subjective, but also at the same time objective, so are the concepts of understanding and ideas of reason, then this would require some further limitation and correction of the overall result of the *Critique of Pure Reason*, namely, that the intrinsically completely empty concepts of understanding permit no other application than to appearances, and that they are no more to be applied dogmatically beyond the field of experience than the ideas of reason. [117] If the concepts of space and time are not merely subjective, then the concepts of understanding cannot be either, if only because they are assigned to work on the appearances given in space and time, to order them and to make them thinkable. For if these appearances themselves have an objective dimension, if their substratum, their material proper, were **things in themselves**, or if, as Mr. **K.** clearly explains in another one of his texts, the *Groundwork to a Metaphysics of Morals* (although in my view rather inconsistently with the principles of the *Critique*) **["][t]he intelligible world contains the ground of the sensible world, and consequently, of its laws,["]**[20] then the nature of understanding, and the constitution of its concepts, would have to be determined and constituted in harmony with this intelligible world of understanding and its laws in order to cohere with this objective dimension, in order to be able to work on it, in order not to introduce laws that contradict the laws of the intelligible world, or that are not appropriate to them. If there is, furthermore, in the intelligible world, an **actual** multiplicity of objects, which are **actually** variable and do change, then we also have to assume that analogical relations exist between them, specifically those of inherence, of causality, of reciprocity. This makes it highly probable that these relations lie at the ground of and conform to the relations in the world of the senses. For example, the concepts of the relations of cause and effect, and of reciprocity, should be grounded in these relations of **things in themselves** by means of which they all belong to and constitute one system of beings, and by means of which one is there for the sake of another; in one word, they should be grounded in the universal harmony of all parts of the intelligible world. The universal laws of nature: **nothing happens in a vacuum, nothing happens without cause, there are no gaps, there is no fate**, these laws, which Mr. **K.** derives from the nature of our power of thought in an a priori fashion and posits as necessary laws of thought, have been considered by all other philosophers (with the exception of those idealists who destroy the external world altogether) either as if they had been taken from reflection on nature and abstracted from constant experience, [118] or they have been presupposed as axioms that do not require proof. Mr. **K.** objects to the first account by saying that they could not then have the stamp or character of necessity that marks them in such a peculiar manner. Now, obviously, we could respond to this objection by reminding him that the pervasive constancy of these natural laws, which are repeatedly found in all experience, indeed, which lie in a sense at the ground of all experience, constitutes an indissoluble association of concepts by means of which we must consider them to be necessary even if we could not prove this necessity in a strict manner or deduce it properly. But both opinions can also be reconciled in another manner, namely, if we assume that the combination, the effects and countereffects of the parts of the intelligible world are constituted according to just those laws also prescribed to the operations of the human understanding. If, for example, the nature of our spirit requires completely connected representations, then the things that are supposed to be involved with its representations would have to be similarly put in combination, in conformity with this law.[§] Because only three cases are possible – either that the world of understanding does not have any laws at all, or that it has laws entirely distinct from the laws of the world of the senses, or that the laws of both worlds accord with each other and are, at bottom, the same – I think we must represent matters as follows. With respect to the first case, I will not even appeal to the author's curious explanation about the world of understanding and its laws from the *Groundwork of the Metaphysic of Morals* that I cited earlier, but note only that everything that exists, no matter what it is, has a form of existence or must exist in a **certain determinate** [119] way, and that just this form of existence, this manner in which the world of understanding is there, constitutes its laws. If it is to be a complete unity and a necessary one, then this complete unity and unconditioned necessity is its law. But if it consists of parts, then these parts must be together in a **certain determined** manner, and in that case this manner of being together is its law. If we assume the second case, then we would have to assert that our understanding treats **things in themselves** contrary to their nature and according to laws that conflict with their laws, hence, completely wrongly and erroneously, and then nothing other than a thoroughgoing deception could be the result, and the charge made earlier against the author's system, that according to it the intelligible world is as good as destroyed, would thereby be completely confirmed and justified. Hence, nothing remains but the third case, which has even more force behind it because on the basis of this

[§] The commentator on Hartley's *Observations on Man* has already attempted in just this way to give a psychological proof for the universal validity of the principle of sufficient reason on the basis of the nature of a human spirit that can only think connected representations, and on the basis of the harmony that exists in this respect between the objective nature of things and the nature of our power of thought. See Hartley's *Observations on Man*, Part 1, p. 62.

presupposed harmony of the laws of both worlds, of this conformity of both sides in the universality of all experience, we can explain why these laws of nature, which are at the same time the laws of human thought, must appear to us as necessary insofar as they are simultaneously these laws. We could similarly explain how and why it is possible that spirit can take them in an a priori fashion out of its nature, or, as it were, predetermine them through a synthesis according to which they have to occur in all experience. It lets us comprehend, further, how philosophers who pay more attention to and reflect on the outer world of experience than to the nature and the procedure of their spirit in its operations could regard just these laws as lying in and given through experience. . . . [21]

[122] . . . It may appear to be presumptions that the reviewer, a mere lover of speculative investigations, wants to reveal errors in the system of our first speculative thinker, a system that is itself the fruit of many years of reflections; however, if this effort serves at least to occasion a closer explanation by Mr. **K.** and the removal of the true and the imagined difficulties and problems in his system, or [123] to inspire more gifted and perspicacious examiners of it, or in general, to only afford the opportunity to bring forth and invite the examination of these extremely important topics that Mr. **K.** has treated in so original a manner from the dead silence in which they lie buried, then it would not be for nothing to have attempted this somewhat daring examination. And even if nothing of what I have said against the *Critique* and its system would stand up to an examination, I would still not have cause to rue my efforts if they were only to generate instruction about important and interesting points. But "in great things it is enough to have willed"[22] remains always as an excuse and to the profound sage who loves truth, from whom I await instruction about my doubts, any attempts, no matter how imperfect, to judge his masterwork must surely be more pleasant and welcome than the silent indifference (and even than the admiring, thoroughgoing, but uncritical applause) with which so many who should and would have been able to examine it have so far responded.

Johann Georg Heinrich Feder

On Space and Causality: An Examination of the Kantian Philosophy

I. ON THE ULTIMATE GROUNDS OF THE HUMAN COGNITION OF SPACE AND THE CORPOREAL WORLD

§ 1
Main Propositions of Kant's Doctrine of Space and the Corporeal World

The Kantian philosophy of space rests on the following main propositions:

1. Space is nothing more than the **form** or **condition** of sensible cognition, or of the intuitions of outer sense (*CPR*, pp. 22 ff). [2]
2. Hence, the representation of space must already be present in us **before** [*vor*] all particular intuitions or sensations of outer sense. The concept of space cannot be formed through abstraction from particular perceptions, rather, it must be a **pure intuition** and a priori; a cognition that we can have prior to all actual perception (ibid. and p. 42).
3. Properly speaking, accordingly, space, along with all appearances, all bodies that it contains, is something **in us**; outer sense is a property of our mind (pp. 22, 114, 366 ff).
4. In **common language** we can say, therefore, that the things that appear to our senses are **outside of us** in space. For to be outside of us, or to appear outside of us means the same as to appear or be perceived in space (pp. 370 ff).
5. But since space is the form and condition of outer intuitions and the [3] things perceived by us as outer, namely, the appearances in space, are not **things in themselves**, but only modifications of outer sense, a property of our mind, what is valid of space has to be valid of those things. (L.c. and *Prol.*, p. 60 ff).[23]

6. Thus, we can justifiably infer the **infinite divisibility of matter**, or what is real in space, from the **infinite divisibility of space**.

§ 2
Counterpropositions

I will attempt to establish the following main propositions against the former.

1. **Space** is **among our outer intuitions** or sensible cognition. It is the most abstract and emptiest part of it, **mere extension** in all direction, and does not have any other positive characteristic. [4]
2. It is not reasonable to assume that the **concept** or **representation of space** is in us prior to all sensible perceptions, even though this representation can be named a **pure intuition** insofar as it can do without all other sensible representations after it is given.
3. The proposition that space along with bodies is something **in us** cannot be justified in any way. Quite the contrary, it renders anything from which it necessarily follows objectionable.
4. No valid presuppositions can **explain how** the representations of things outside of us and of space **arise in us**. The farthest we can go in giving such an explanation is to identify the circumstances and conditions under which they arise. However, that can still not prevent us from taking it as completely established **that** the objects of sensible perception and the space in which they occur do exist outside of us. [5]
5. The representation of space is **one part** of our cognition, and the representation of the impenetrable or, in general, of what is real in space is **another**, equally well-grounded part of our cognition. Neither, accordingly, can contradict the other. But there is also no reason to transfer the predicates of the one to the other. In particular, therefore,
6. There is no reason for the inference that what is real in space is infinitely divisible, even if it were in a certain sense conceded that space is infinitely divisible.

§3
Remark Regarding the First Main Proposition and Its Counterproposition

I would not object to **Kant's** first principle if it stood alone. For it is certain that without space there cannot be any bodies, hence, that we cannot have any cognition of outer sense, and [6] cannot represent anything at all to ourselves **figuratively**, as existing outside of us. So space, it is true, is the **condition** of all **figurative**, hence of all more **determined** representations of objects of outer sense. It may even be called the **form** of this cognition, in contrast to the things in space proper, the bodies, whose general essence is designated with the name **matter**, and the figure or form of which is nothing but a certain limiting determination in space.

In addition, the proposition that space is the form or condition of intuitions of outer sense can similarly express the true and important doctrine that everything of which we do not have sensible intuitions, which does not belong under the type or form of the outer senses, is not combined with the representation of space and would have to be, as it were, transposed into it. This is a remark that can serve to prevent us from making unjustifiable assertions in questions regarding the soul and its unity with the body, its seat in any one part thereof, as [7] well as in the doctrine of God's existence and omnipresence. At the same time, the truths that are contained in this first Kantian principle are not undermined by the manner in which I have presented my first counterproposition. For that space is a part of the cognition of outer sense can easily be further specified to say that it constitutes an **essential** part that cannot be removed from it. That it is **one part** thereof, and a constant part, however, is something **Kant** also concedes by calling it **pure intuition**.

In what follows, a number of reasons will emerge that indicate why I prefer my wholly simple expression. [8]

§4
Report of Kant's Arguments for the Assertion that the Representation of Space Does Not Spring from Particular Perceptions, But Must be Present in Us Prior to All Sensation

The second principle is, properly speaking, the basis of **Kant's** entire theory of space. Hence the philosopher dwells on it in the beginning and tries to prove it by appeal to several arguments. In a certain sense, it can be inferred from the first one. For this reason I have presented it as such in §1. However, the philosopher himself presents his arguments as follows (*Critique*, pp. 23 ff).

1. In order to be able to relate our sensations to something **outside of us**, in order to be able to represent the objects that appear as **outside one another**, as in different locations, we must [9] already have the representation of space. Hence this representation cannot be taken from outer appearances, and the concept of space cannot be an empirical concept.
2. One can never represent to oneself that there is no space, even though one can quite well think that no objects are found in it. Hence the ground of this representation of space must lie more deeply in us than the appearances of the senses, and it must be independent of them. As lying at their ground, it must rather be (a priori) in us prior to all experience.
3. If the representation of space were a concept acquired (a posteriori) from experience, then there could not be the **highest certainty** of geometrical principles and of the truths that spring from the combination of concepts (synthetically) that do exist. These principles would be nothing but **perceptions**. Hence they would have all the **contingency** of perceptions, and it would [10] not be **necessary** that there should be only one straight line between two points. Rather, one would only be able to say that **as far as one has thus far observed**, this is the case and so on.
4. There is no **general concept** of space, as there are other general concepts. The latter are put together from several simple concepts or are abstracted from several similar sensations of, for example, human beings or [civil] states. There is only one object that conforms to the concept of space. There is only one space that is cognized through an a priori intuition. The representations of several spaces arise from it only through division or limitation. Hence the reverse, namely, that the concept of **space in general** arises from the latter, is not the case.
5. The representation of space also contains its **infinity**. This could not be the case if the concept of space were a concept drawn from the representations of [11] particular limited spaces. Under this presupposition, the general concept of space (which would have to be contained as much in the foot as in the yard) would not determine anything with respect to magnitude. This infinity that lies in the basic concept proves, therefore, that space is based on a pure intuition that is independent of particular sensations and for that very reason is unlimited. . . . [24]

[21] . . .

§6
Examination of Kant's First Argument for the Claim that the Representation of Space Cannot have Arisen from Sensations

The first argument through which **Kant** tries to prove that the concept of space cannot [22] originally have arisen from the sensations of outer sense is basically the same [argument] by which **Plato** already attempted to prove the existence of concepts of understanding prior to sensations.†† He says: if our soul did not already contain in itself the ideas of the beautiful, the true and the good, as well as those of other essential properties of things, then how would it be able to judge, appreciate and order sensuous appearances according to those criteria?

The answer to this question is that **at the time** when we do **judge**, **recognize**, and **distinguish** appearances outside of us in accord with these ideas in our minds, as appearances that do or do not accord with them, we must, of course, already have these ideas. However, we must ask whether these ideas could not have been formed on the basis of sensations before understanding begins to make such judgments? [23]

Is it not established as well that thousands of sensuous impressions are given to us before we proceed to make such judgments?

To be sure, it is beyond doubt in just the same way that unless we already have the representation of space in our power, we would be unable to distinguish ourselves from things outside of us, or those from each other with the clarity and the consciousness with which we are now able to do so. But since no one is in himself conscious of this distinction from the very beginning of his life and sensation, before the representation of space can be viewed as present in us prior to all sensation, we must ask whether it could not have arisen from the obscure chaos of the first sensible impressions or from the power of thought of the human spirit before we were able to make the clear distinction of bodies in space of which we are first aware after thousands of sensible impressions. [24]

And no matter how difficult it is to give a precise and indubitable account of the first beginnings of the establishment and development of human concepts, to which no consciousness extends, precisely because consciousness does not extend back that far, there is at least nothing in the experience that **Kant's** argument is based on that prevents us from taking the human representation of space to emerge

†† In the *Phaedo*

gradually when the sensations of sight and touch are unified with one another.#

For the essential content of this idea lies in the feelings that arise for human beings in their movements, and they also develop the concept of space out of each picture that appears to the eye by appeal to those feelings. [25]

In order to develop the content of the concept of space from these two types of sensuous impressions, we do, admittedly, require a power that forms concepts, that is, we require human understanding. But this is clearly different from the alternative, namely, that the representation of space does not spring from sensation and I have already declared my opposition to the confusion of the two.

Hopefully nobody will attempt to escape what has thus far been stated by interpreting **Kant's** proposition as saying that we cannot perceive **things in space** unless space were already given and perceived by us, or that it is a natural order in the **ranking of concepts** that we first perceive space and then place things in space. [26]

§7
Examination of the Second Argument; Necessity of the Representation of Space

However, our philosopher claims that the independence of the representation of space and its grounds from sensible impressions can be further proven by the fact that this representation remains when one holds back all representations of things in space, although it is not conversely possible to hold back the representation of space and still represent these things.

However, even if one were to concede this impossibility of doing without space, as is here supposed, the disputed proposition would still not follow. For there is many a thing that cannot be removed from human nature, the soul or the body, yet we nevertheless know that they were not originally in it, but were introduced from outside, through sensations, or in another manner. [27] For example, in thought we cannot do without **words**, but these are supplied from the outside. And words or other signs are for the concepts of understanding almost what space is for sensuous intuitions.

I will make some remarks appropriate to the present investigation later, about the representations that blind people and those who have been cured of their blindness have of space.

Still, the proposition itself, that we cannot do without the representation of space, that we **cannot represent that there is no space**, as our philosopher puts it, must be considered more closely.

1. Does it mean that we cannot represent the absence of space to ourselves sensibly or figuratively? If so, then it would admittedly be very true. For an image is nothing without space. But what follows from this except that space is an essential **part of sensible representation**; that it is the least that can be required for it, the simplest form thereof, empty extension? [28]
2. The proposition that even our **understanding** cannot deny the **existence** of space, though it is assumed that there are no things in space, would be just as clear. For empty space – and properly speaking that is what space is – would remain. My understanding at least does not find a reason to deny this.
3. That we cannot do without the representation of space **anywhere** in our thought, contradicts even **Kant's** philosophy, just as it contradicts experience. Space is only the form of sensible cognition, or of the representations of outer sense. It does not properly and immediately belong to the sensations of inner sense and the concepts that arise from it, namely, the concepts of truth and justice, of power and goodness, and so on.
4. Meanwhile, we do all sufficiently know from experience that these concepts of understanding combine all too easily with [29] the sensible representation of space and become absorbed in it. In this way too, they reveal their sensible origin. And even if they did not have a sensible origin, the nature of language, which is so indispensable for all our thought, would produce the connection with space. With the aid of the representations of written and verbal signs, we may arouse and retain our concepts and continually place ourselves in the representations of space by means of these signs.
5. Properly speaking, however, it is not solely the representation of **empty space** alone that accompanies all our thought and follows us everywhere. Can a living and sober individual really do entirely without the representation of things in space or without the representation of things that limit space at this or that point?

I can at times reach this point, when I tightly close both of my eyes. [30] Then I am for a time not aware of any figurative representations in myself, and hence am without the representation of space. But this **Nothing**, in which my **intuition** disappears, transforms itself as soon as possible again into a dark region, without distance. I cannot represent the **image** of empty space, without all material additions, without any color, without any focus of self-awareness, or without any limiting points here or there.

Therefore, on the basis of the fact that a representation is necessary for our thought, we cannot infer the independence of its ground from the grounds of sensation.

§8
Examination of the Third Argument. Necessity of Geometrical Truths. Development of the Main Point

The third argument is the Achilles of our philosopher. It constitutes the main support [31] of all his proofs for the possibility and actuality of a philosophy that is to ground itself and its concepts not on experience, but on **pure reason**. So it deserves a most careful consideration.

If the representation of space were the fruit of experience, then all cognition of space would in principle only be **perception** and, with that, **contingent**. The principles of geometry, accordingly, would not be apodeictically certain. This is **Kant's** argument.

Perception; therefore **contingent**? How are we to understand this?

Can I **cognize something** without **perceiving** it? So can there be **any** necessary cognition, any general truth for us when all perceptions contain only contingent truth?

But should someone like to introduce into the explanation of the **word** perception that by it we are to understand only a contingent [32] cognition, then logic teaches that the **definitions of words** cannot demonstrate anything with respect to the nature of things.

What other proof is there for the claim that all perceptions contain only contingent truths? Perhaps that perceptions refer to the perceiving **subject**, to some relation between it and the object?

I ask, accordingly:

1. Who can demonstrate that there could **not** be or actually are **no** relations between subject and object that are constant and unchanging?
2. Let us review the argument again, from the beginning. **All** cognition is a relation between the cognizing subject and the object of cognition. So if perception is to be a contingent cognition because it rests only on a relation, then all cognition, including that of geometrical principles, is contingent cognition. [33]

Or is a cognition to have a **merely subjective** ground, is it to concern only the relation of the subjective power and its own expressions in order to be universal and necessarily true for **such a subject**? Should it not be, like the cognition of sensible appearances, a function of **impressions** of things outside of the cognizing subject?

I think:

1. Given the profound insight into the grounds of idealism that **Kant's** *Critique* contains, this cannot very well be the position. Nor can it be a matter of a question of what in our sensible cognition arises from subjective, what from objective grounds (where objective is taken in the antiidealist sense). At least, I would not know how, without a petitio principii it could be claimed **that the representation of space arises from merely subjective grounds, but the representation of things in space from objective grounds**. [34]
2. No matter what one supposes in this regard, I still demand a proof for the claim that any cognition that arises equally from internal subjective and external objective grounds is and must be contingent. Surely one does not want to commit a fallacious inference: **most** of our perceptions are contingent; hence, **all** must be.

   But how can **one** perception, **one** experience, teach **universal** and **necessary** truth? It tells us what is now, and when it has occurred repeatedly in a uniform manner, what has been several times. But how can it tell us what must be **always** and **everywhere**, and that its opposite cannot be the case?

Here we arrive at the **main question** with which **Hume's** skepticism or, if one prefers, criticism, attacks the science of reason. And I am happy to have progressed this far, even though **Kant** did not raise it at this point. [35] For apart from it all my objections against **Kant's** argument might have appeared only as excuses or, at most, as ad hominem objections.

§9
Continuation. First Insight into the Ground of our Necessary Truths

The following is my final answer not just to the **specific question** of how the theorems of space can be necessary truths even though they rest merely on perceptions, but at the same time also to the **general**

Humean question of how we can arrive at the concept of necessity and the cognition of necessary relations by means of experience.

Whenever we sense that there is something we cannot do, and that is surely the case often enough, we **sense necessity**. For the opposite of what cannot be is necessary. What we cannot change, [36] we have to leave as it is, and what we cannot leave, we have to do.

I hear the objection that this is **subjective** necessity, whereas the question concerned **objective** necessity – patience, we will get there. But there is good reason to begin here.

In particular cases, this – admittedly initially merely subjective – necessity, that we sense, is only the necessity of the present state of affairs, and is **recognized as conditioned**, as soon as the condition can be changed in such a way that it ceases. However, when we can never and in no way change this condition, when we cannot remove this necessity, cannot in the least show and render intelligible just how it could be removed, what shall we call it then? Is it still a conditioned, a contingent necessity? This would be contradictory, or at least without reason. Hence it is an **absolute necessity**, at least **for us**. [37]

And if we were to find that all human beings whom we have so far known deem themselves to stand under the same necessity, **if** we did not have the least reason to suspect that it might be different for some, **indeed if** we could not at all represent to ourselves how it could be different for any human being, at least any **sensing, willing, thinking** being, could we then still object to considering this necessity that we sense and cognize as such, no matter what objective states it concerns, to be **absolute** and **universal**? Certainly not, if our judgments are to be determined by **reasons** . . . [25]

[38] Our **perceptions of space** and of that which can be located and determined in it contain necessary truths because we are unable to represent their opposite to ourselves. That which we cannot in any way think is for us **nothing**. And what we cannot think otherwise than in this way, is, for us or according to the judgment of our understanding, **necessarily so. This is the case no matter where the impossibility to think the opposite has its final ground**.

Whenever we cannot in any way think the opposite of something, it is a **necessary truth** or **manner of thought**. But whenever we have **only a strong ground**, that is, a ground appropriate to that which is considered necessary [39] and sufficient according to the **laws of correct action**, to suppose and assume something rather than its opposite, it is not an **absolutely necessary manner of thought**, but only a **probable**, perhaps **binding** manner of thought, or one that is **morally certain**.

These two principles contain the ultimate grounds of all rational thought. . . . [26]
[41]

§11
Why There Is No Apodeictic Certainty Outside of Pure Mathematics, or to What Extent We Do Find It There?

It will not be an inappropriate digression to consider the distinction between pure mathematical and philosophical cognition more closely, as well as the reason why the latter cannot deliver apodeictic proofs, whereas the former can.

It is sufficiently clear from what has gone before that I do not suppose that pure mathematical propositions are always judgments a priori and not empirical as Mr. **Kant** thinks (*Prol.*, p. 28).[27] Nor does this need to be supposed in order to explain the difference between mathematical and [42] philosophical cognition and the superior certainty and evidence of the former. This difference and this evidence rest merely in the fact that pure mathematics deals with representations that are capable of **complete clarity and determination**, which is not and cannot be the case in philosophy. For pure mathematics abstracts from all **powers** or affecting properties of things, it has to do neither with the (physical) bodies, nor with the souls that constitute the objects of philosophy. The latter are objects that must necessarily be, to some extent, **impenetrable** and **opaque** for us given that we only ever perceive them in **certain relations**. Where should proofs that are **grounded in the nature of things in accord with their complete and clear concepts** originate, the kind of proof that is grounded in the nature of a triangle or circle by means of their entirely clear concepts? [43]

When we nevertheless arrive by means of many observations at the point at which we can take certain **properties** and **relations** in the nature of things to be universal and necessary, we still do **not completely understand it**. And though we are justified to claim **it is so**, we cannot say that **it must be so**, that **we cannot think it otherwise**, and that it cannot become other than it is. Given the impenetrability and opaqueness of beings, our best insights remain **surrounded by obscurity**; **not everything is evident**.

Because these affecting properties, these powers, constitute the intrinsic nature of **actual things**, we can also say that philosophy has to do with actual things, whereas pure mathematics deals with **mere**

representations, which, admittedly, do still find sufficient application in actual nature according to our requirements. [44]

So the **difference of the respective objects**, the fact that those of pure mathematics are **mere representations** that are capable of complete clarity and determination, whereas those of philosophy are **complete actual things** though only incompletely cognized, constitutes the ground of the unequal evidence in mathematical and philosophical cognition. It is not a function of the fact that one type of representation rests only on an inner ground or is in us in an a priori fashion, whereas the others are abstracted from sensible impressions. Even if our representations of **bodies** and **souls** were, as **Plato** presented matters, memories from a previous life, or, as **Leibniz's** preestablished harmony specifies, if they emerged out of the essence of the soul without any prior external impressions, we would for all that be easily aware of the great distance between the evidence of the cognition that arises from them and that available through geometry **as long as** we were to retain the consciousness of their incompleteness, impenetrability, and opaqueness. [45] Geometry loses nothing of its evidence even if one assumes that the representations of space spring from sensible impressions (§9). That will always remain a consequence of the simplicity and, with that, of the complete clarity and determination of its basic concepts.

As soon as understanding occupies itself with and limits itself to **mere representations**, it becomes possible to synthesize even those representations that even Mr. **Kant** declares to be empirical, **without the aid of particular outer experiences**, under the guidance of imagination and understanding, and to do so in a way that would be coherent and have a certain necessary connection. Or, to put this in Kantian terms, one can **construct representations** and form **synthetic propositions** without requiring particular corresponding outer experiences to confirm them. This is what mathematics does with the representations of space. In this way [46] the creations and inventions of **music**, **painting**, and **poetry** arise. There may never have been or ever have to be a corresponding experience in the actual world, but they nevertheless rest on certain rules which are grounded in the nature of human feeling and understanding. It must at least be possible to **hear**, **see**, and **think** these representations **together**. Of course all sorts of other grounds, such as accidental inclinations, intentions, and peculiarities of taste, are intermixed in the **complete evaluation**. But this does not remove the implication that should make evident that the origin of these representations is empirical but that their relations can nevertheless be determinable independently of particular outer experiences.

It is just this that has on occasion deceived philosophers to such an extent that they believed themselves able to do without experience and to get apodeictic proofs from pure concepts of reason in the metaphysics [47] of soul and body, in moral philosophy, and in political philosophy in just the a priori fashion in which they do in geometry. They tried to do so by drawing inferences from nominal definitions and **ideas they created themselves**, which unfortunately did not correspond to the actual world – except where they drew their conclusions from **available concepts of nature**, which happened to rest on just the experiences that one sought to demonstrate on their basis in an a priori fashion.

Accordingly, I do not understand how our philosopher could take it to be such a great error or *hysteron proteron* to generally assume that the object of pure mathematics is merely **quantity** from which all **quality** has been separated and that, because of this simple content, its representations are capable of complete clarity and its proofs of the highest evidence. One should rather have said that the **form** of mathematical cognition, pure intuition, is such that it can apply only to quanta (*Critique*, p. 714, compare *Prol.*, p. 34).[28] [48] I think that one could just as well say that because mathematics limits itself to quantities, of which we have completely determinate and clear representations, it is possible for it to demonstrate everything from pure intuitions or mere representations. And as stated, this is the case also for **qualities** and their **syntheses** when we limit ourselves to **mere representations** and their **inner possibilities**. So we can synthesize for ourselves, as we please, countries in which milk and honey flow, Elysian fields and magnificent things. The only difference is that we are not certain that we can find these combinations of qualities in their totality in the actual world, whereas we do find that the simple representations of lines and figures are realized in actual things.

I find that the distinction by means of which **Kant** declares the principles of mathematics to be **synthetic** [49] but those of philosophy to be **analytic** also contains something of an arbitrary definition of words (*Prol.*, p. 27).[29] In order to remain with only one example, why should the arithmetic proposition $5 + 7 = 12$ be synthetic but not the philosophic proposition that the person who is **good** and **wise** is also **just**? Is the proposition $12 = 5 + 7$ not arithmetic as well and is it not clearly analytic?

That it is not the form of cognition or the difference of the origin of the representations that constitutes the difference between philosophical and mathematical cognition and the ground of their unequal evidence, but their different objective content, can be seen from what constitutes the main object of this chapter, the concept of space. For the philosopher is occupied with this as well. But the philosopher, unlike the mathematician, does not want to limit himself to taking it as it is or to intuit what sort of lines can be drawn in it, and how they are [50] related with respect to one another. He asks, rather, where this representation originates, what it depends on, whether space is anything other than representation, whether it is substance, accident, or relation, whether body or God's sensorium, in short, here too he asks about **actual grounds** and **affecting powers**. He wants to get farther than the **mere representation** even though the **positive** things philosophers have said about space can, for the most part, be easily **refuted** through the representation as long as one does not obscure it through words.

§12
Examination of the Fourth Argument

How does the author of the *Critique* demonstrate that the general concept of space is not composed out of perceived small spaces, that it is essentially one, that, conversely, the representations of spaces rest on the limitations of the general concept of space, which lies, accordingly, [51] at the ground of all particular intuitions? None of these propositions is obvious.

1. Suppose that there is such a general concept of space in all mature individuals and that is rests at the ground of all their determinate representations of space. Even if this were so, we could still understand how imagination could have constructed the large representation of space out of smaller representations of space. We cannot deny its capacity to combine representations, and by combining **representations of the same kind**, it expands and enlarges the images of occurring objects. But nothing could be simpler and more straightforward than the particular perceptions of space. The combination and expansion of impressions, accordingly, is easiest here and happens almost on its own.
2. If the concept of space does not arise merely **symbolically**, if one actually [52] effects the **intuition** of it in oneself, then, it seems to me, the empirical origin of this representation can still be easily recognized. It retains the marks of its birth in manifold ways. It is a picture of an earthly color that has been illuminated from the heavens, this **general picture** of space. In those born

blind, it is likely shown with completely different impressions of touch. Should we now **remove** all these heterogeneous qualities from the intuition of space **in thought**, we can still comprehend not just the possibility that this representation might have a similar origin as other representations arising from sensible impressions, but the fact of this origin. In short, the representation that the word "space" reveals is not constituted in the same way in one individual as in another, and it reveals, through the special determinations under which it appears to the one or the other in such or such a way, the empirical origin that it shares with other sensible representations. [53]

3. Suppose that only one single object corresponds to the **general concept of space** or, better, to the concept of space **in general** and taken as a whole. It can still be separated and combined out of sensible impressions. There is only one single object that corresponds to our representations of our earth, of our sun, of our universe. Does it follow, therefore, that they are not empirical concepts?

§13
Infinity of Space

As far as the infinity of space is concerned, finally, which is similarly to serve in the demonstration of its nonempirical origin, I answer:

1. That this **infinity** is not a part of intuition, hence not a function of our **positive**, actual **cognition**. All our actual intuitions have limits, whether they have been caused from the outside, or [54] internally through imagination. The only reason we assign the predicate **infinite** to space is that we cannot give it determinate limits. Where are they to originate? Where there is no reality, there is also nothing that can cease. **Where there is nothing**, where it is empty, **there is space**. In this way, we judge that space is infinite. Do we need an innate concept for this?
2. The **expansion** of our concept of space, including that filled with realities, the universe, far beyond the limits of our actual intuition, also has its ground in the fact that we experience in manifold ways that the end of our vision is not the end of nature. It is certain, however, that the representation of space as a whole is of rather different extension in the minds of different humans according to the number and extent of their experiences, and also according to the inferences they draw from observations, such as

the inferences of the natural scientists and astronomers. [55] One easily becomes aware of this from the talk of small children and other unenlightened people, when they want to indicate great distance or great circumference. The infinity of space in human understanding is, accordingly, nothing original, but is gradually added in thought, like all other aspects of actual intuition.

3. There is an ambiguity in the expression that **Kant** uses in this context: **general concept of space** or space **in general**. One can understand by this (a) space **objectively**, or the continuing emptiness in which things are or can be. We cannot determine the limits of space in this sense, it is infinite; (b) the **figurative representation** that the word "space" recalls, even if we do not have the intention to think any one specific space concretely. This is always limited and of determinate magnitude, like any image, [56] even though the limits are variable and can disappear in obscurity, as happens when we represent enormous bodies; (c) the **symbolic general concept** of space, that is, mere extension in all directions. This symbolic general concept of space does not determine anything with respect to its limits, it is neither finite nor infinite. And as such it applies to the space that is in the ell and the foot as well as to the universe. Just as the symbolic concept or the definition of body, unlike the **image of body**, fits the elephant and oak tree as well as the mite and the moss.

At this point I do not know which of the Kantian grounds remains to be answered, or why the concept of space could not, like other concepts, have arisen from sensible impressions.

[57] Nevertheless, I will always be ready to be instructed otherwise, should anyone be able to do so.

§14
On the Representation of Space Had by Someone Born Blind

The question how the representation of space of a **person born blind** is different from that of other people is one that, as far as I recall, has not been raised anywhere in **Kant's** *Critique*. And yet this question seems entirely natural and important in an investigation of the grounds of this representation.

The best observations of persons born blind clarify that before they began to see, they did not at all have the **same** representation of space that others have in mind with this expression. If this representation had been in the soul of the person born blind prior to **actual seeing**, then we could not understand why it is the case that when he does begin [58] to see, he does not immediately recognize the globe and cube felt earlier, or why the objects of sight first seem to him to touch the eyes, or why it takes so long to see distances, circumference, and position of bodies, that is, note them when seeing.

For if the **common scheme** of space and its divisions in all sorts of figures, distances and outlines lay in the soul prior to all experience, why should the representation of space of the person born blind not have the same features as the representation of the person with sight? Why does the observed extension seem to him to be so foreign and impossible to comprehend?

We do know that the person born blind does have the concepts of space, namely, in the way he can have them by means of touch, and can learn as well as teach the same geometry by means of it. The question is, however, why he [59] does not have it in its entirety in the same way in which we have it, **given that these concepts are not supposed to be empirical**?

The common and old answer of the defenders of innate concepts, that sensations are indeed necessary to **awaken** or **clarify** the representations that slumbered in the soul or were present without consciousness, but that they do not in any way create or ground these concepts, is one that admittedly might be used here. But this answer constitutes a recourse to a scholastic **occult quality**. As long as it has not yet been shown at least, that nothing is contained in the ostensibly innate representations that cannot also be explained through sensible impressions and inner feelings, it is not permitted to assume that such representations slumber in the soul prior to all sensations. For that would mean that we assume something without reason.

One or another person could perhaps arrive at some subtle, idealist theory [60] and answer as follows. The person born blind is nothing other than a human being for whom something in his **representative power** has been spoiled or is not as it is with others, a human being in whom a **property of the mind that we call outer sense**, the form and condition of which is space, is imperfect. No wonder that his representation of space differs from that had by sighted persons. On the basis of the same inner ground, his representative power is with respect to its **form** and **matter** more limited than those of others. And we can say just as easily that the blind person cannot see **objects in space** because he lacks the **pure intuition** of space as we can say, conversely, that it is missing because he cannot see.

Leaving aside the idealist element, this answer would not even be consistent with our philosopher's basic principles. For the perception of bodies in space [61] is for him empirical. And the idealist, should he want to make common cause with our philosopher, would similarly have to recognize as empirical what has the same ground and origin.

But in that case this idealist language of space and appearances of outer sense belongs to those things for which I cannot find good grounds. . . . [30'31]
[84*]

§22
Is Idealism Necessary to Prevent Contradictions of Reason? Predicates of Space Are Not for This Reason Predicates of Bodies

According to the idealist, however, absurdities and accidentally associated errors are not the only reasons that demonstrate that sensible objects are mere representations in us rather than actualities outside of us. He goes further and claims that from this assumed actuality true contradictions and a quarrel of reason with itself unavoidably arise. Our philosopher thinks the greatest advantage of his doctrine lies here. In order to avoid this quarrel of reason with itself, this **antimony**, as he calls it, he attacks **material** idealism with **formal** idealism.

But I hope to be able to demonstrate that we do not need the peculiarities of the Kantian doctrine [85*] of space for this purpose, and that we can undermine yet another idealistic premise, one that **Kant** grants and even attempts to demonstrate.

It is well known that idealists take their objections against the reality and logical justifiability of our representations of the corporeal world, among other things, particularly from applying predicates that are consistent with the idea of an empty space that does not resist any addition to real extension or things in space. In this way, they assume **infinitely many parts** in every body, because it is possible to **think** or **presuppose** an arbitrarily large number of parts in empty space. From this infinity of parts of every body, they then infer, as they deem fit, all sorts of true or apparent absurdities, for example, that parts contain as much as the whole. Alternatively, they assert that there can be no motion because [86*] every ever so small distance contains an infinite number of smaller spaces that a body could not possibly traverse in a given time.

There is no doubt that the Königsberg philosopher despises these games. But he does emphatically declare himself for the principle that what is true of space must be true also of things in space (*Prol.*, p. 59).[32] How does he prove it? In general, by the fact that the properties of what constitutes the form and necessary condition of our sensible perceptions must necessarily be true also of the perceptions, and hence of the bodies **in our cognition**, since we have only this empirical sensible cognition of them. All propositions of geometry that are true of space must therefore also be true of things in space, he says on page 60 of the *Prolegomena*.[33] Indeed, the things in space can **never** [87*] **contain anything except what geometry prescribes to them**.

Here we must consider two things:

1. Whether and to what extent all our sensible cognition of bodies is contingent on the cognition of space, as their pure form and condition.
2. And whether, insofar as the latter is a condition of the former, the properties of one object must also be properties of the other.

To be sure, I have explained earlier (§3), that I would have no objection to the Kantian principle that space is the general form and condition of sensible cognition, if it were considered on its own, and I have indicated in a more precise fashion what I take to be true of it. Meanwhile, however, I prefer the simpler and less anticipatory expression that space is a part of [88*] sensible cognition, as a foundation for further investigation.

Given our present viewpoint, however, there is much that serves to limit this principle. Specifically, though the idea of space is admittedly an indispensable substratum of the image of the **entire body**, not just in intuition proper but also in the surrounding feeling, it is not a necessary ingredient or form of **each** sensible perception of corporeal nature and its properties. It is neither an ingredient nor the form in the feeling of **impenetrability** and **collision**, in the feeling of **resistance** against the moving force, no more than of **taste**, that is, it is not a necessary ingredient in what constitutes the **original** and **proper** element of this sensible perception. Suppose a human being who is blind and enclosed [89*] in a space in which he could not move, although he would be motivated to do so through an inner force, and who, accordingly, does not have the idea of space itself. Such a being could have all these feelings, **though not as clearly and determinately as we do**. Not as clearly and determinately as we do, I say, but only according to what is proper to it and original in it. For one thing, all opposing feelings clarify each other, including those of free motion and resistance. After that, the types of sensible perceptions and the remaining sensations of touch and sight soon associate themselves with each other, according to the laws of association. And because only the sensations of touch and sight provide us with the representation of entire things and, in general, with the most determinate and clearest representations, our other sensible perceptions are more readily associated with touch and sight and registered almost as if on a firm ground and foundation.

Meanwhile, those sensible feelings of impenetrability and resistance that are in their nature independent of the idea of space are and remain [90*] precisely those that the concept of what is real in space or of corporeal nature emerges from. They are those feelings through which space is filled, and a body is differentiated from empty space.

With what justification should we now be able to infer the constitution of bodies from the constitution of space, given that the essential and differentiating properties of the former rest on perceptions that do not require the idea of space, that do not arise from space but are rather placed in it? To be sure, space must have properties that are consistent with the constitution of bodies. But given that the latter simply do not, even in our cognition, depend on the former, they can contain more or less, and in some respects different [properties]. And no matter how much representations depend on each other, no matter how much they are coordinated or subordinated, [91*] they do not for that reason have to have predicates that are identical in all respects.**

Bodies must have **extension if** and **insofar** as they are to be perceived in the form of space. But from this it does not follow – and this is what led Descartes to his fallacious inferences – that the extension of space is in all respects the same as the extension of bodies, no more than that all others, including all in some sense sensibly perceived properties of bodies must be reducible to the concept of extension.

In the same way in which **Kant** makes the perceptions of the properties of bodies too dependent on the idea of [92*] space in its totality, so by the same token, in some parts of his *Critique*, he makes the representation of space too dependent on all other sensible perceptions. Space, he says, is merely the **form** of outer intuition, but not an actual object that can be intuited externally. – Empirical intuition, accordingly, is not compounded from **appearances** and **space**, one is not the correlatum, synthesis, of the other, rather they are only com-

** It seems to me that in the present inference from form to matter the same mistake has been made that has often been made in the inference from genus to species, according to the well known *Quidquid valet de g* [i.e., whatever is valid of the genus holds of the species]. This rule of inference, which holds only for positive predicates, has been wrongly applied also to negative predicates. This is what happens here as well: in space we never arrive at a last part; hence, we cannot do so in what is real either.

bined in one and the same empirical intuition, as its matter and form (*Critique*, pp. 429, 256)

This seems to me to be contrary not just to the natural understanding of this matter but also to be inconsistent with other claims of the Kantian philosophy. According to a natural, undisturbed representation, it certainly seems to me to be possible to say that sensible cognition or empirical intuition [93*] is put together out of **space** and the **appearances in space**, and that space, or empty extension is in itself an object of our representation. A motion in which I do not feel the least resistance gives me the pure idea of space. And how should the assertions that **Kant** makes here be consistent with the first principles of space? (*Critique*, p. 23). If space is not an empirical concept, if one can very well think that no objects are found in space, but can never have the representation that there is no space, if the certainty of mathematics rests on the fact that space is a **pure intuition** a priori, and given as an infinite magnitude, has an **objectivity** a priori, indeed, if all determinations of space, all forms and figures can and must be represented a priori, how then can space not be a special object of intuition, but only [94*] be combined with the appearances of bodies in one and the same empirical intuition?

It may well appear immodest if one claims that an author, particularly an author who is as perspicacious as **Kant**, contradicts himself. Accordingly, I do not make this charge here, but I am certain, that many readers of the *Critique*, particularly those trained in thought and interpretation, will find it difficult to think that everything that appears here and on some other occasions is consistent.

[Anonymous]

Göttingen, Dietrich: *On Space and Causality: An Examination of the Kantian Philosophy*, by Johann Georg Heinrich Feder. 263 Pages in Octavo, 1787.

In the Preface the author concedes that Kant's *Critique of Pure Reason* demonstrates an unusual power of thought, both in the comprehensive vision with which the most abstract speculations of logic and metaphysics are presented and classified and in the profundity of the particular investigations. Complaints have been most widely raised about its **language**, and Mr. **F.** admits that he too does not like the great number of Greek, Latin, and German technical terms, because the many deviations from the commonly used language, taken in their totality, are certain to produce more harm than benefit for the purpose of **instruction** and the like. (This depends very much on whether useful concepts underlie the **technical terms**, and whether one could have found better technical terms for these concepts. Otherwise, the **number** of technical terms should not be a deterrence. What friend of mathematics is frightened away by its **uncommon** language? To choose only one of the more readily accessible examples, when Mr. **Kant** differentiates between **definition**, **explication**, **exposition**, and **declaration** under what is commonly called **explanations**, one would have to either contest the actual difference, or **show** that these differences already have other established names.) In spite of this, even Mr. **F.** concedes characteristic perfection to the author's language.

That the author should have undertaken to write against Mr. **K.** with such even-handedness and openness, given that he could not agree in all respects with many of the concepts and principles particular to his opponent, deserves applause and gratitude from all unbiased investigators of truth, even those, who, [250] having examined the objections he has laid out, do not find their conviction of the main basic principles of the *Critique of Pure Reason* in any way challenged. As one would at any rate expect from his well-known gentle character, Mr. **F.** has remained so far from the appearance of all personally offensive expressions that he admits to have prescribed a rule for himself for the tone of a review, the correctness or universality of which we do not concede. He says that he has made it a rule in all reviews to ask: **would you talk in this manner with the man if he were to stand before you or sit beside you on the sofa?** – and if he could doubt this, to tone down his judgment or at least its formulation. But the reviewer of a book does not in fact speak **with** the author, rather, he **reports** on the author's book to the public. So it can often be a duty to say something about the book to the public **in a manner** in which one would not say it to the author on the sofa. As long as both are justified, or at least as long as the reviewer has reasons for both, one can be more candid with praise and criticism.

So we recommend this book to all devotees of an unbiased investigation. At the same time we have to request of them not to make judgments about it until they have studied **Kant's** work itself. We cannot undertake a complete examination of it here and propose to note only some points concerning **Kant's** here contested doctrine of space.

Mr. **F.** presents the main propositions of Kant's doctrine of space as follows:

1. "Space is nothing more than the **form**, or **condition** of **sensible cognition**, or of the **intuitions of outer sense**."[34]

   Here already **Kant's** meaning has not been completely grasped. Sensible cognition and intuition of outer sense are not so close to being the same thing that they can be connected with an "or." **Kant** clearly does not say that space is the form of **sensible cognition**, which includes **inner sense** as well, but only that it is the form of all appearances of outer sense, that is, [that it is] the subjective [252] condition of sensibility, the sole condition under which outer intuition is possible for us. (*KdrV*, B 42).
2. "**Hence** (Mr. **F.** lets the philosopher continue) the representation of space must already be present in us **before** all particular intuitions or sensations of outer sense."

   The **hence** is something that Mr. **F.** has wholly imputed to **Kant**, although in good faith. For **Kant** does not present this proposition as an inference from the first but demonstrates it on its own. Mr. **F.** notes this himself on page 8 but suggests that on a certain interpretation of the words it can be inferred from the first. We do not agree at all. What can be the purpose of connecting a philosopher's propositions differently than he connects them himself, particularly in an investigation that is in its nature as subtle as this one is?

3. "Properly speaking, accordingly, space, along with all appearances, all **bodies** that it contains, is something **in us** – "

This is properly presented. Nevertheless, as can be seen in Mr. **F.**'s counterproposition, there is a misunderstanding. For **Kant** claims: the **corporeal world** is for us only **appearance**, we have absolutely no knowledge of what bodies may be in and for themselves. The representation of each body emerges from what we sense, so from what touch, taste, smell, hearing, and sight instruct. Hence it emerges from nothing but appearances and then out of the form of these appearances, space and time, together with appearances.

4. "Yet we can still say in accord with common language that the things that appear to our sense are outside of us in space."[35]

To proceed to Mr. **Feder's** counterpropositions. The first one, which he explains in §3, is not in fact a counterproposition. So we can ignore it. In §4 Mr. **F.** proceeds to **Kant's** second principle, namely, that the **representation of space does not spring from particular perceptions**. Here Mr. **F.** again needlessly changes the philosopher's words. Properly speaking, the proposition is as follows: **Space is not an empirical concept that has been drawn from outer experiences**. **Kant** demonstrates this proposition as follows: "**In order that certain sensations can be related to something outside of myself (that is, something that is at a different location in space than where I find myself), and similarly, that I can represent them as *outside of* and *beside each other*, and consequently as not merely different but as in different locations, the representation of space must already lie at the ground**."[36] Against this, Mr. **F.** adds on page 23: "**could it not** have arisen from the obscure chaos of the first sensible impressions or from the power of thought of the human spirit, before we were able to make the clear distinction of objects in space?" and so on. But what has been proven against **Kant** with this "**could it not**"? [252] The representation of space, even if only little developed, perhaps even prior to having been named, must already lie at the ground of the very first differentiation of two things as outside of one another, no matter how obscure it may be. For as soon as I am to represent two things as outside of one another, I must think at least two points that limit a **line**. Indeed, the very first representation of a body already presupposes the representation of space in which it is located. – Mr. **F.** says on page 24: "There is nothing that prevents us from taking the representation of space

> to emerge gradually when the sensations of sight and touch are unified with one another." – But the example of the person born blind whose lack of sight does not translate into the least lack of the concept of space teaches that the sense of sight does not create the concept of space. And we can admit that the representation of space is primarily developed and clarified through and by means of the impressions of the **sense of touch** [*tactum*] but not, for this reason, that it is **created** by this sense. Even if the soul is only to think that one finger is **outside** of another, that the right hand is **outside** of the left, the representation of space lies already at the ground.

Kant has said, in addition, that the status of space as a necessary representation that lies at the ground of all outer intuitions is clear also from the fact that one can **never** have the representation that there is **no space**, although one can very well think that no objects are found in it. Mr. **Feder** says against this: "The former does not follow from the latter. For there is many a thing that cannot be removed from human nature, the soul or the body, yet we nevertheless know that they were not originally in it, but were introduced from outside, through sensations, or in another manner. For example, in thought we cannot do without **words**" and so on.[37] However, the example does not fit. If Mr. **F.** could demonstrate the proposition that **we cannot have a representation of the fact that human beings do not have a language of words**, then **words** would have to lie a priori at the ground of human thought. But we can easily think that human beings in general, or this and that one, as, for example, those born mute, think without words. So the cases are not identical. The closer examination of **Kant's** proposition on pages 27 f. does not contain anything through which it would become clearer than it is on its own, and even less anything through which it would be refuted. Consider the following dual question which Mr. **F.** presents:

"Does the proposition (**one cannot represent to oneself that there is no space**) mean that we cannot represent the absence of space to ourselves sensibly or figuratively? [253] If so, then it would admittedly be very true. For an image is nothing without space. But what follows from this except that space is an essential **part of sensible representation**, that it is the least that can be required for it, the simplest form thereof, empty extension?"

The first element of this dual question is completely superfluous. When someone says that we can simply not represent [something], why then should one have to first ask whether one speaks of sensible representation? In the second element Mr. **F.** almost concedes the whole Kantian proposition with barren words. Not only does Mr. **Kant** not want to infer **anything further**, he does **not even** want to infer **as much** as Mr. **F.** infers. All **Kant** wants to establish is that space is essential for outer intuition, not that it is essential for all sensible representation; he presents it as the form of the former, not of the latter. Mr. **F.** continues on page 28: "The proposition that even our understanding cannot **deny** the **existence** of space, though it is assumed that there are no things in space, would be just as clear. For empty space – and properly speaking that is what space is – would remain."

Alright, then Mr. **F.** again agrees with Mr. **Kant**. The only difference is that the latter has expressed the proposition more clearly. One can imagine that there are neither suns nor heavenly bodies, one can, in thought, remove everything that is in space, and yet space always remains. Its representation can simply not be removed. However, Mr. **Feder** continues on page 30: "I cannot represent the image of empty space, without all material additions, without any color, without any focus of self-awareness or without any limiting points here or there."

Here many things that do not belong together are confused. **Without any color!** The person born blind thinks space without any color. And even if we, who have since childhood seen all bodies as colored, represent emptiness as colored, then, **first**, it is not **absolute emptiness** that has thus been represented, but an image of atmosphere that only appears to be empty. Second, we can nevertheless represent this image of empty space to ourselves now in this, now in that color. Nothing prevents us from imagining it as blue, black, dark, or illuminated. Thus, no one color image belongs to it. We cannot explain just what Mr. **F.** wants to say with the expression: **without a midpoint of my feeling of self**, or just how this limitation is to be applicable here.[38] Finally: **without limiting points here and there**. That is something that **Kant** will happily concede. That space has three dimensions, that we can draw lines and limit regions everywhere in it, [254] is just as necessary as the representation of space itself.[39]

Mr. **Feder** has not in the least done justice to another argument of the Königsberg philosopher. Kant reasons: because geometry determines the properties of space synthetically and yet a priori, the representation of space must originally be **intuition** so that such a cognition of it is possible. For we cannot arrive at propositions that go beyond concepts on the basis of a mere **concept**. Mr. **F.** has not even attempted to refute any of this. He merely states by the by on page 41 that it is sufficiently clear from what has gone before that he does not suppose that pure mathematical propositions are always judgments a priori and not empirical as Mr. **Kant** thinks. And elsewhere (p. 49) he states, similarly by the by: "I find that the distinction by means of which **Kant** declares the principles of mathematics to be synthetic but those of philosophy to be analytic also contains something of an arbitrary definition of words. In order to remain with one example, why should the arithmetic proposition 5 + 7 = 12 be synthetic but not the philosophic proposition that the person who is **good** and **wise** is also **just**? Is the proposition 12 = 5 + 7 not arithmetic as well and is it not clearly **analytic**?" Mr. **F.** ought to admit that such questions are not yet proofs. So if he were to demonstrate to us that the proposition **whoever is kind and wise is also just** is synthetic, and that the proposition 12= 5+7 is analytic, then we would be happy to say that he has shaken the entire Kantian system. We would be quite willing to bet at unfavorable odds against it. But how does he want to demonstrate that this philosophical proposition is not analytic but synthetic, given that there is absolutely no way to arrive at the concept of a **wise goodness** from the concept of justice as long as one does not show an identity between both. But that can clearly be effected only through analysis. And how does he want to show that the formula 12 = 5 + 7 is analytic? One can dissect the **concept** 12 into many parts, but one can never demonstrate, on the basis of mere analysis without the aid of intuition, that it consists of the sum of 5 and 7.

The argument that Kant takes from the infinity of space in order to demonstrate that it is not originally **concept** but **intuition** has, in our estimation, been up to now no more satisfactorily refuted than earlier ones. Nevertheless, we must leave it to the reader to examine it as well as the denial of the Kantian doctrine about causal connections.

Friedrich Gottlob Born

Investigation into the First Grounds of the Doctrine of the Senses

§23
THE REPRESENTATION OF SPACE OF A PERSON BORN BLIND

I have shown ... that space is a representation that originally lies in the soul prior to all experience, albeit indeterminately, [88] as a representation that is intrinsically only laid out and sketched, needing to be fully formed through the addition of outer objects, like an outline for a yet to be completed painting. If this is what it is, that is, if it is a representation that is merely laid out, not yet completed and still indeterminate, then it follows that its formation must entail appropriately different determinations and modifications in accord with the different constitution of sensible subjects. Hence, one should not first ask whether the person born blind has a representation of space, for that he must certainly have. Nor should one ask whether this representation is present in him in the same manner in which it is present in other human beings. Given that the person born blind has the same sensibility that all other human beings have, why should it not be similarly constituted? But nobody should be surprised that this general, indeterminate representation of space is determined and modified differently in the person born blind than in other human beings when objects of the senses are given to him. Because the person born blind can perceive the visible objects only through the merely one-sided sense of touch, without being supported by sight, his representation of space must receive entirely different determinations and modifications than those of the sighted person. That is, his representation of **empirical** and **relative** space is constituted altogether differently than the representation that other human beings have of it. So it [89] seems very strange to me how Mr. **Feder**†† can wonder that Mr. **Kant** has never investigated this problem. It lay entirely outside of the path the

†† See *Ueber Raum und Caussalität: zur Prüfung der Kantischen Philosophie* by Joh. Georg Heinrich Feder pp. 57–62.

Königsberg philosopher was taking and is too trivial to require consideration. But this famous philosopher's book against **Kant** happens to have uniformly misunderstood **Kant's position**, no matter how clear it is to the unprejudiced reader and that is precisely what has led him astray here as well. For he says:

> it is known from the best observations of persons born blind that before they began to see, they did not have at all the **same** representation of space that others have in mind with this expression. If this representation had been in the soul of the person born blind prior to **actual seeing**, then we could not understand why it is the case that when he does begin to see, he does not immediately recognize the globe and cube felt earlier, or why the objects of sight first seem to him to touch the eyes, or why it takes so long to see distances, circumference, and position of bodies, that is, note them when seeing. For if [90] the common **scheme** of **space** and its divisions in all sorts of **figures, distances** and **outlines** lay in the soul prior to all experience, why should the representation of space of the person born blind not have the same features as the representation of the person with sight? Why does the observed extension seem to him to be so foreign and impossible to comprehend?

So far Mr. **Feder**.

I answer that as an unformed, indeterminate representation, absolute space, that is, the **pure intuition** that lies antecedently in the soul does not contain any differentiating feature and is, therefore, an unconscious and, accordingly, entirely obscure representation that only first enters our consciousness when objects are given through which it is determined and thus acquires differentiating features. Because, however, in persons born blind, it is determined only one-sidedly through touch, whereas in other beings touch and sight combined determine it, the empirical representation of space of the one must naturally be quite different from that had by others, even though the foundation of it, the general representation of absolute empty space must be the same in the person born blind just as in the sighted person, because both have one and the same sensibility and the person born blind can no more represent bodies than the sighted person except by thinking them to be **somewhere**. But this absolute necessity [91] simply cannot be the result of experience as I have indisputably established elsewhere. It appears, accordingly, that Mr. **Feder** has not sufficiently differentiated the empirical representation of space and pure intuition.

Furthermore, Mr. **Feder** maintains:

> that the formation of the original, indeterminate, obscure basic representation of absolute empty space that [ostensibly] happens through the actual existence of outer objects constitutes a recourse to a scholastic **occult quality**. As long

as it has not yet been shown that nothing is contained in the ostensibly innate representations that cannot also be explained through sensible impressions and inner feelings, it is not permitted to assume that such representations slumber in the soul prior to all sensations. For that would mean that we assume something without reason.[40]

But here Mr. **Feder** forgets that pure intuitions is, in accord with its nature, a merely laid out, not completely determined but nevertheless true representation and, as such, could not contain what constitutes the empirical representation of space, which has been determined and completed in this or that way in virtue of the manner of experience. As a representation that is obscure, that does not have in itself a characteristic of differentiation and, consequently, is not one of which we are conscious prior to experience, it [the pure intuition of space] could not deliver a complete image. The only remaining issue is whether the Kantian [92] arguments for the original existence of a general basic representation that precedes all experience and is necessarily required for the possibility of that experience that I have presented here could be evidently refuted. But there is no need to rush to do so; these grounds, as I have previously shown, cannot be refuted.

Section III

Idealism

Johann Georg Heinrich Feder, *On Space and Causality: An Examination of the Kantian Philosophy* (Göttingen: Dietrich, 1787), 61–83*, 114–18 139

J. C. G. Schaumann, *On the Transcendental Aesthetic: A Critical Attempt* (Leipzig: Weidmann, 1789), 131–75 155

Friedrich Heinrich Jacobi, "On Transcendental Idealism," in *David Hume über den Glauben oder Idealismus und Realismus* (Breslau: Löwe, 1787), 209–30 164

Reprinted in *The Philosophy of David Hume*, Lewis White Beck, ed. (New York: Garland, 1983). [The translation and pagination are based on this reprint edition.]

[Hermann Andreas Pistorius], "*Critique of Pure Reason* by Immanuel Kant, Professor in Königsberg, member of the Royal Academy of Sciences in Berlin. Second edition, improved here and there. Riga: Hartknoch, 1788. 884 pages." *AdB*, 81/2 (1788): 343–54 176

Friedrich Gottlob Born, *Investigation into the First Gounds of the Doctrine of the Senses* (Leipzig: Klaubarth, 1788), 117–20, 141–53 183

Johann Georg Heinrich Feder

On Space and Causality: An Examination of the Kantian Philosophy

§15

Are Space and Bodies Something in the Mind or Soul? Kant's Observations About This Question

If space is nothing other than the form of our sensible intuition, and if these intuitions themselves are nothing other than varying states of a **property of our mind, outer sense**, then the inference that things in space, which we perceive, are **strictly speaking** nothing but states or modifications [62] of ourselves is correct. This is so even if we might also have a **logical, subjective** reason to assume that **something real** exists in addition to our perceptions, which would, however, be entirely different from them and entirely unknown to us.

This is where the **esoteric** explanations of our philosopher lead, although he does, as it were, **exoterically** tolerate and in a way justify ordinary language, according to which appearances in space must be considered to be actual things that exist outside of us. However, the actual principles of his **Transcendental Aesthetic** or his metaphysics of the sensible world are consistently these: that the representation of a body in intuition contains **nothing at all** that can be attributed to an object in itself (*Critique*, pp. 44 ff); that the raindrops as well as the space in which they fall **are nothing in themselves** but are mere modifications of our sensible intuition (p. 46), hence modifications [63] of a property of our mind (p. 22); and as Kant himself briefly and clearly sums up the main implication (*Prol.*, p. 62),[1] that ["]**all bodies along with the space in which they are, must be considered nothing but mere representations in us and do not exist anywhere but in our thoughts. Is this not manifest idealism**?["] He poses this question himself, expecting, no doubt, that we will say **no**, or that we will at least not identify this idealism, which is called **transcendental** or **formal idealism**, with the form that has been known so far.

Another classic passage can be found on page 376. Here the explanation of the manner in which the transcendental idealist can acknowledge the reality of the world of the senses ends as follows: "**Matter** is only a **species of representations**, which are called external, not in the sense of being in themselves related to external objects,[2] but because they relate perceptions to space in which all things are external to one another, whereas space itself is in us." Further: "external objects, bodies, are nothing but a species of my representations the objects of which are something only through these representations, but are nothing separate from them."[3]

The entire section on pages 366–88 deserves to be read should one want to become familiar with the spirit of the Kantian philosophy, and to become convinced that his *Critique*, no matter how sharply it takes issue with a **certain dogmatism**, remains much too dogmatic itself. And excessive dogmatism in metaphysics always generates skeptical disputes with the natural mode of thought.

§16
Antiidealism According to Simple and Secure Grounds of Common Sense.
Explanation of the Expressions: Objects Actually Existing Outside of U.S.

There are some things about which the philosopher must in no way seek to know or decide more [65] than can be known by anyone through common sense, for otherwise he becomes confused and loses his way, no matter how learnedly and cleverly he begins. In the dispute over idealism, both sides have often overlooked this.

I have never been an **antiidealist** of the ordinary kind, have always denied the necessity of a **demonstration** of the actuality of the world of bodies and so, **as far as the matter itself is concerned**, I agree, **in most points**, with what Mr. **Kant** says about idealism and realism.

However, I think that here as well as in the critique of theology **his expressions** needlessly distance him too far from the common and natural manner of representation. For that reason, the manner in which he wants to forge a **reconciliation** and agreement with this manner of representation cannot appear completely satisfactory. [66]

In this context he says: ["]I would like to know what my assertions would have to be in order not to entail idealism? I would without doubt have to say that the representation of space must accord completely not only with the relation that our sensibility has to objects, for that is what I have said, but that it must even be similar to the object. But that is a claim in which I can find no more meaning than in the claim that the sensation of red is similar to the property of cinnabar that gives rise to this sensation in me["] (*Prol.*, p. 64).[4]

It seems to me, however, that this, as well as any other expression of common sense, can be intelligibly explained and that it is completely unnecessary to consider body along with space to be **mere representations in us** in order to ward off all representations of the corporeal world that do not pass muster before reason. [67] By contrast, the judgment that bodies are mere representations in us, that they **do not exist anywhere except in our thought** (§15) seems to me so contrary to the nature of our understanding, that any concepts and principles that necessarily lead to it must be rejected for precisely that reason.

Accordingly, first we want to completely clarify the meaning of the common antiidealist proposition that bodies are not mere representations in us but **actual things outside of us**.

Here it is beyond all doubt that the assertion of the actual existence of bodies outside of our representation rests on the difference between sensation and its objects, on the one hand, and mere imagination and recollection, on the other, and that this assertion should call our attention to this difference. And, as everyone knows, this distinction is very real and very great, and therefore surely deserves its own name. To identify things that are as different as the [68] object of an actual outer sensation and a mere representation of it under the same name, the book that I see in front of me or that I have in my hands and the one I think of, to identify both as mere representations in me, as mere ideas, directly contravenes the basic rules of language and thought, which demand that we distinguish different things. This is even more the case when there is no scarcity whatsoever of means to effect the distinction, when completely appropriate expressions are available in ordinary language, when the omission or interchange of these expressions brings about only confusion and does not serve any purpose at all.

But this is precisely what the idealist metaphysician wants to deny. He thinks that even if common sense manages very well with ordinary language in everyday life, ordinary language is not to be used in the sciences because it either contains fundamental errors or necessarily occasions them. [69]

Let us see, then, where the error either lies or necessarily arises. Let us go through and closely examine piece by piece the entire antiidealist picture of common language and mode of thought.

First, the objects of sense are accorded an **actuality**, which is denied to mere representations. And why is this? Because the words "**actuality**," "**existence**" signify just, or at least **mainly** and **in the first**

instance, what is the case with sensations and not with mere representations. Or let anyone who knows how say what else actuality and existence can and should mean except to be sensed **or** to possess the power to cause sensations. Let someone explain and develop the concept of actuality without reference to sensation. The soul does not have any proof of its existence except this feeling. This feeling generates the difference through which it knows itself as [70] something actual and as different from its **representations** of other mental powers and states of mind.* It is only on account of the actuality, which we sense, that grounds can be generated for us to assume the present or past or future existence, which we do not sense.

And we say that these things are **outside of us** because – they are outside of us. That is, because we perceive so clearly and distinctly that they are not, like our mere representations, in us, we sense their actuality not as something that concerns us, but as something entirely distinct from us and our mere representations. Hence we would confuse concepts and language if we were to say anything other than that they are outside of us. [71]

It would, however, be a good idea to further clarify this.

Kant allows that we can say that sensible appearances are outside of us **because we perceive them in space** and that this just means that we **perceive them as external**. But this explanation does not yet contain the entire ground of the common mode of thought, indeed, it does not yet indicate any difference at all between actual things and mere imagination. As such it fits best into the idealist system. In space, more specifically, in an imagined uniform space, which really is only **in us**, which is what space in general is for **Kant**, we also perceive objects of imagination, no matter how ideal its constructions. However, these images of fantasy, along with **the** space in which they appear and act on one another, are not an actual external world for any human being of natural sound understanding, [72] rather, they are merely a world of ideas in him. This is the case in the first instance because they are not present, cannot even be seen **in the way** in which things of the actual world in space outside of us are seen or are present. Or, if sight were to leave doubts, given that illusions can occur in vision, because there is nothing that can be felt. Or, because other human beings, whose actuality and sound understanding cannot be doubted by our sound understanding, cannot see or feel anything of the mere representations

* Kant has himself noted and emphasized all of this. It is only that in this case – as on a number of occasions – he takes back with one hand what he has conceded with the other.

in us, and of other merely subjective appearances. Or, finally, perhaps also because our other, indubitable sensations and most solidly grounded concepts are so contrary to the nature of these representations, that we must ascribe the latter to peculiar subjective grounds in us rather than consider them parts of nature outside of us.

As we know, [73] these are the reflections human understanding engages in when comparing its mere representations and actual sensations. All of them ground and solidify our recognition of actual nature outside of us and our distinction of this actual nature [from our other representations], though in most cases not all of them are required together.

§17
To What Extent are the Objects of Outer Sensation Independent Things?

In the judgment about the objects of sensation, common sense, to put it in the language of life, limits itself entirely to these two predicates of **actuality** and **existence outside of us**.

The dispute with the idealists, however, has produced a further claim that is subject to the strongest attacks, and that does admittedly require some care over separation of truth and falsity. This claim is **that the things that appear to our senses also exist independently of us**. [74]

Now, were this to be interpreted as saying that **things** and their **qualities**, which I perceive through my senses, exist **independently of me, just as I perceive them**, and **insofar** as I perceive them; or, to put this even more clearly, that **my perceptions** (in the subjective sense) **exist independently of me**, then it would be such clear nonsense that this interpretation would not have the least support. For who would want to assert that **his** perceptions are something independent of **him**?

Moreover, and this is, admittedly, not something that is quite commonly known, but that is nevertheless easily discovered with some reflection, the entire **manner in which** we perceive things outside of us and their qualities conforms with the constitution of our sensible equipment, our entire nature which apprehends impressions, passes them on and is to its innermost core active in manifold ways in this respect. It conforms no less [75] with the constitution of the **mediating causes**, the air and the light. This is so obviously the case that to take this kind of cognition to be the cognition of what things **in themselves** are, or of what must appear in relation to **all sorts of other** cognitive powers, equipment and, mediating causes, would, to be sure, be a grave error.

If one were to call the assertion of **this** dependence of sensible appearances, their relativity, **idealism**, then idealism would, to be sure, be the only acceptable philosophy. But this is not the customary concept of idealism. By the same token, the assertion of the independence of our sensible perception from subjective grounds, which has in part already been refuted through the most ordinary experience, cannot be required from those who do not want to be idealists.

But what sort of independence from us, the perceiving subjects, can then be [76] accorded to the actual things outside of us? It is certain that not everyone restricts himself within the same limits, as shall later be indicated more clearly. But what can be asserted, and what makes intelligible and justifies the **independent** existence of sensible objects from perceiving subjects is the following:

1. That in our cognition of sensible objects we become aware of their dependence on **one another** to a much greater degree than on their dependence **on us**. We can find ourselves in countless relations and circumstances and not have the object that we once saw with us. In order to see it again we have to go to its location, to the other things outside of us next to which nature has placed it. No matter how much we desire to make its representation actual, we will not be able to do so in any other way. [77]
2. We know that **other human beings** do not need us in order to see the same thing, to feel it, own it and enjoy it, no more than we need them to do so.
3. We must concede that nothing in these things of the sensible world has been changed when those who have previously seen them with us die or otherwise disappear. And so we must surely concede as well that when we no longer perceive them, they do not for that reason cease to exist for others.
4. Even if we are different from other human beings in the manner in which we see and judge these things, we find ourselves forced to concede an outer existence to these things that is independent of both types of representation.
5. We know, or must reasonably believe, that many more other things than appear or have sometimes [78] occurred to us, have appeared or occurred to **other human beings**, even when we have not been able to perceive their existence. I have never been so fortunate to see Königsberg and its famous philosopher, even though I have a lively and presumably in many parts correct rep-

resentation of him. I have spoken with many persons who know him personally, who love and honor him. But who would refuse to accord him an existence independently of the representations of those who have seen him as well as of my representations?

Now, is not all of this sufficient reason to accord an independent existence **from us**, the cognizing subjects, to these things, to the sun and the moon, the animals in the forest, in oceans and rivers, some of which we have seen ourselves, some of which we have not seen? I would think that it is.

But does this main antiidealist proposition not necessarily lead to inconsistencies when it is further developed? If according [79] to what has just been said, an existence independent of **each** perceiving subject is accorded to the objects of sensible perceptions, must we then not also concede that they similarly have a continuing existence that is independent of **all** perceiving subjects **taken together**? And is it not obviously **false**, or at least groundless that what we cognize should endure even if all of us were to cease to exist!

But really? Would an affirmative answer to the question **whether animals could exist on earth were there no longer any human beings at all**, be such a shameful absurdity or would the negative answer be so reasonable? Could we answer this question differently than the question whether there could be animals in **Rome** without one human being? The undeniable assertions of common sense are never absurd; one must only not explain them incorrectly, and understand oneself correctly in what one thinks about them. [80] That suns, moons, rivers and mountains, animals, and trees would indeed exist even if no human beings did, does not mean for any human being that they would be **perceived in a human fashion** if there were no human beings. Rather (a) negatively it means that: everything that we know of these things does not allow us to say that they will not exist if we no longer did, and (b) positively it means that: (1) if human beings were to emerge again, then these things would be there for them without having to be newly created and (2) God and his world are more manifold and real than mere representations of a human being, which cease to exist when he forgets or disregards them, when he falls ill or dies. If the idealist agrees with me in this last judgment, then he must also agree with the one that has gone before. If its denial does **not** disturb him, well, then he must see how he can arrange matters [81] with humanity and himself.†

† If anyone wants to answer that when one removes the human manner of

Meanwhile, we can be undisturbed by the wisdom of the person who would render our common sense absurd or at most **indulgently** allow us to continue to play with its illusions outside the schools. It is a pity, though, that so many beautiful hours and the powers that would have been worthy of many a better application have been wasted by this scholastic wisdom! [82]

Or does the student of transcendental wisdom perhaps want to object sweetly that everything that I have said is **empirically true** but – what? That – **our human** cognition is nothing but our **human** cognition; that invisible things cannot be intuited like visible ones can, and that we cannot very well say what the objects of our cognition may be aside from what we know of them. Surely, he will not be able to tell us more about this. And admittedly, he is completely right in this. Indeed, in just this way I tried to put the idealist on the proper path, namely, by calling his attention to the fact that there cannot be a more solid cognition of actuality, and no more real reality than specifically in sensation, whereas he, contrary to the better use of language, wants to acknowledge only mere representations, as if he could create a better cognition of reality and actuality in some other way.

[83] I agree completely with Mr. **Kant** about the following points: that we can have only sensible cognition of the world of bodies and cannot either **say what the things in themselves are** (an expression that makes no sense at all when clearly illuminated)‡ or elucidate and correct or in any way perfect those sensible representations in a Leibnizian manner by means of representations of another kind, representations of mental powers and characteristics that inner sense affords.

And so I am even more amazed that he allows that which constitutes

representation, then the objects that lie at their ground, the *ontos onta*, will indeed remain, but that the appearances that originate with the human manner of representation will disappear, then this is quite acceptable. But then one would have to concede that one has expressed matters too strongly when one said that bodies are nothing but mere representations in us. And it is only this, namely, that he exaggerated what is true and expresses himself too strongly, of which we accuse the idealist.

‡ To be sure, substances must be something in themselves. However, in order to know what they are in themselves, it is required either (a) that we are in their place, that is, that we are these substances with complete and clear self-consciousness or (b) that we understand all their actual or possible relations. The latter is the cognition of omniscience. Neither of them is the case with respect to things outside of us. But we can specify what our representations of circles and triangles are in themselves because they are nothing but our representations and we can see them completely.

our **sole** cognition [84] of something to be only empirically true in this manner, that is, that he only allows it to be true in this manner outside of **science**, and that in science he declares, in agreement with the idealist, all bodies along with the space in which they exist to be nothing but **mere representations**. This is an expression that offends common sense, attacks its grounds, and cannot be justified.

§18
Primariae and Secundariae Qualitates

Though the belief in the actuality of the world of bodies outside of us has been defended as well as possibly **in general**, it nevertheless seems on occasion that it cannot be so well defended in its **particular aspects**. For how should this be possible? Should we declare **colors**, **smells**, **tastes** to be something in the things themselves, rather than merely **affections** or **modifications in us**? Should we declare colors to be properties of bodies, even though it is clear that only the different refraction and separation of the different lightbeams is what creates the different colors, [85] and experience teaches that the same thing can at the same time appear as differently colored to different human beings?

Here too it is necessary that we understand one another correctly, for then the dispute is quickly resolved. This much is admittedly soon clear, that the color in the rose itself **outside of me** is not what it is in my eye and in my representation, no more than the taste and smell of food is the same on my tongue and in my nose, and that, in turn, it is in my bodily instruments something entirely different than it is in my soul. This, it seems to me, is something that is understood on its own among people of some reflection.

However, we **may** and **must** say that colors and smells and tastes are in the bodies outside of us, insofar as we may and must say that these actual things outside of us (§16, 17) have **characteristics**, **powers**, **parts** in themselves **without** [86] **which** we would be unable to sense the colors, smells and tastes that we do sense in them, and **by means** of which they cause in all cases the same sensations **as long as** the other conditions and grounds, the mediating causes and the subjects able to have these sensations are not missing. This is our best and truest cognition of this matter which nobody will be able to dispute. But we can also not go much beyond it. For we have not particularly succeeded with the **explanation** of these characteristics, as it were, **derived** from the basic properties of bodies, extension, impenetrability, figure, and motion.

In the dispute with the idealist, however, one has often made the mistake of attempting to assert only these four characteristics as absolute, real properties of bodies independent of our cognition, and one has done so by declaring, in agreement with the idealists, [87] all others to be merely subjectively grounded semblance. But many have already noted that in this way everything is ruined. To be sure, these four properties are privileged in certain respects, which is why one can and does call them **basic properties** (*primariae qualitates*). But one cannot **exclusively** declare them to be **pure objective realities**. The privilege that they have is

1. That they are perceived not just by one sense, but by two: touch and sight,
2. Hence, that they are perceived through the two most superior senses, which ground our richest and most proven representations.
3. That they are the shared properties of all bodies, hence constitute the **general concept** or the **essence** of bodies, in accord with our concepts.
4. That these four properties and their modifications do, to **some extent**, afford the ground of all other properties. [88]

However, in spite of all these advantages, we cannot assert

1. That what **we** know of motion and mobility, impenetrability, extension and figure, must appear in the same way to **every** cognizing subject. Rather, these properties must appear otherwise even to ourselves when we use other senses. Experience has sufficiently taught us the variability of these appearances as well as their dependence on standpoint, distance, and the like.
2. On the other hand, the grounds on which the judgment that accords objective reality to colors, smells, and tastes has earlier been justified must with even more reason be recognized as valid. For we can no more take the ground of this judgment to be completely in us, [89] subjectively, than the ground of the perception of the basic properties.

§19
Main Objection of the Idealists: How Can We Cognize What is Outside of U.S.?

Everything, however, that we have so far established may nevertheless appear to collapse with the **main objection of the idealists**, that in spite of everything all our sensible perceptions are **our** perceptions or representations; hence they are **in us**. For how can our representations be outside of us? Or how can it be allowed to pretend our representations are something other than our representations, that they are things outside of us and independent of us?

This is what **Berkeley** inferred. And **Kant** infers this as well: "If we assume outer objects to be things in themselves, then it is absolutely [90] impossible to comprehend how we are to attain a cognition of their actuality outside of us by relying merely on the representation that is in us. For one cannot sense what is outside of oneself, only what is in oneself, and our entire self-consciousness, therefore, does not deliver anything **except merely our own determinations**" (*Critique*, p. 378; *Prol.*, p. 63).[5]

So the idealist demands an **explanation** of **how** there *can* be representations and perceptions in us of things outside of us. May he do so? Or is it enough to demonstrate **that** we do have objects before us in our sensible cognition, and that these objects are what one calls things outside of us, and cannot justifiably call anything else?

If our idealist is a philosopher, if he understands what an explanation is, what its purpose is and how far it can go, then he must not demand from us an explanation, a further ground of the **last grounds** of our cognition. [91]

Or can **he** explain how such representations and feelings arise **from our soul itself** in such an order, even against its desire and in the face of all its opposition? It is not my intention to use this common ground, which is equally if not more directed against the Leibnizian hypotheses of preestablished harmony, instead of a **proof** against the idealist. The idealist can always reply by appeal to **Berkeley's** hypothesis, or **Malebranche's** *Nous voyons tout en Dieu*. The only question at issue is who can insist on an explanation here. And considered from that angle, none of the idealist hypotheses will truly recommend themselves, at least on closer examination.

If explanations are to be completely omitted or must be completely omitted (even though, were it to come down to it, the influx theorist probably manages better in the end than the **Leibnizian** or the **egoistic idealist**), if the task at hand is only to present the **facts** appropriately, then we say that [92] the proposition **that sensible appearances are mere perceptions or representations in us** is ambiguous and, as used in the idealist's inference, wrong.

If we do not ignore the nature of these sensible appearances, if we do not contradict our consciousness, if we adhere to the common meaning of words, and do not give them unusual confusing meanings, in short, if we do not want to contradict nature, then in sensible appearances we must differentiate **ourselves** and what we can call **our perceptions** [*perceptiones*] and the **objects** of perceptions from one another. To be sure, these are **occasionally** included in perceptions. But this does not at all do away with the difference between the **act of perception** and the **objects of perception**.

Because, in what has been said so far, sufficient reasons have been provided to indicate that and why [93] the objects of sensible cognition are called actualities outside of us, and cannot be called mere representations in us, or **merely our own determinations**, we must remain with these propositions as the **truest and closest presentations of the fact**, whether we are able to penetrate its grounds further or can give an explanation from other cognitions or not. For to deny facts because we cannot explain them is the straightest road to the destruction of all reasonable cognition and all science. For both rest on facts, experiences, sensations, and intuitions that cannot be further explained.

§20
The Primary Imperfection of our Sensible Knowledge Does Not Provide Any Evidence for the Idealist

A closer analysis of the grounds of our sensible knowledge and the [94] concepts originating from it does indeed show that much in the impression that, for people of passably skilled understanding, contributes to the constitution of their representation and judgment was not and could not have been considered in this way in the **initial** and **simpler, basic representations of the senses**. It is undoubtedly only after much training and the unification of many perceptions of sight and the sense of touch that **distances**, **positions** and **directions**, and **corporeal extension** can be differentiated and recognized in our sight.

But neither does this have any negative implications for the actuality of visible things outside of us. For if we have to assume something in our best and most fully formed cognition, why should we be allowed to doubt it just because we did not completely perceive it in our less perfect cognition? [95]

It is in general one of the idealistic or implicitly idealistic peculiarities and paradoxes to speak of the actuality of things as if it began and ended with perception. If that were the case, there admittedly could not be anything apart from the perceiving subject.

One asks whether colors exist for the blind and answers no. From this one infers further that things and characteristics not known by any one human being do not exist for any of us and, accordingly, that those properties and relations that human beings are unable to note originally, that is, at the beginning of their sensible perception, **arise** for them only when they acquire knowledge of them with the aid of their concepts. And from here one can easily arrive with Mr. **Kant** at the inference that by introducing relations and regularities into his perceptions through understanding, the human being [96] **creates the nature itself** with which his cognition is concerned. But surely this is not the natural arrangement of our concepts.

One can say that colors do not exist for the blind person. But one can just as well say that the blind person does not have a sense for the colors that do exist. And the blind person can easily be convinced of this claim. For even though our concept of actuality **in general** grounds itself on sensations and always relates itself to them, a human being soon realizes that much can and must actually exist that he has never sensed and may never sense.

From this it clearly follows that there can be much in nature that is not perceived by any human being, for which none of us has a sense. [79][6]

And that, it seems to me, is the direct path and viewpoint of common sense. It is unnatural, by contrast, and not scientific, to turn the fact that human beings **become aware** of things into **origin** or **creation** of things. Or do we perhaps want to say that before **Herschel** discovered it the *Sidus Georgium*[7] did not exist? That this clever observer was able to create planets?

§21
Common Errors With Respect to Sensible Appearances [Do Not Provide Any Evidence for the Idealist]

Nor is any support lent to idealism or to the opinion that space along with its bodies consists in mere representations in us by the fact that in our judgment about these errors, errors that have been believed for centuries, deceptions occur that, though they can easily lead even the most sound common sense astray, are knowable to reason. [80*]

Is there anyone who will deny that all of us do often err? But does this mean that there is no truth in human cognition? Or that reason does not exist because lunatics have lost its use? We would not be able to speak of irrationality if there were no rationality, nor of error if there were no truth. So it is in general, and hence also with respect to sensible knowledge.

The errors that arise with sensible cognition can, indeed, must all be discovered and removed by another sensible cognition. Thus, the false judgment about the stick in the water must be removed or refuted either through seeing it again when it has been taken out of the water, or through touching it in water, or through prior experience and the optical knowledge that comes from it.

In this way the great and general error that the sun along with all stars [81*] moves around the earth was finally recognized through nothing other than the careful combination of manifold perceptions of this kind. The longer and more carefully the changes in the appearances and positions of the planets, the eclipses of moon and sun were observed, the less they showed themselves to agree with that false presupposition: the fact that when nature was otherwise arranged, it was so much more in accord with the law of simplicity contradicted the belief in the immobility of the earth. As well, there was sufficient opportunity to notice that a body on which we are, a ship on which we move, seemed to be at rest while other bodies, actually at rest, seemed to move.

In this way, sensible cognition purifies itself gradually of the errors that are associated with it. It alone is judge of itself. Whoever wants to show that it is in error must take the ground for this out of sensible cognition itself. To simply declare it to be empty semblance and deception, [82*] because errors do occur, is an inadmissible judgment not only because we cannot make inferences about the whole on the basis of a part of it, and even less about the essential on the basis of what is contingent, but also because no **representation** can be declared to be an empty semblance and deception unless a stronger undeniable representation **of the same kind** can be contrasted with it. For it is impossible to dispute **hearing** through the fact that **what is heard cannot be seen** and vice versa.

Sight likewise does not allow the cognition proper to it to be corrected through touch, even though we subject the **judgment** about what is visible to its examination. Why? Because errors in the judgments about what is visible consist in nothing other than in the hasty addition of the impressions provided by touch that did arise **on another occasion** connected with such an appearance. So touch as well judges only its own cognitions. And in this way each type of cognition is the highest [83*] measure in its field. But one main ground of this pretended wisdom has always been that one has attempted to **reduce** one type of cognition to another, to **explain** one through another, or, where that was not possible, to reject one for the sake of another.

In this way, the idealist wants to reduce everything to perceptions of inner sense, to **representations in us**; the materialist wants to reduce everything to representations of outer sense, the Platonist wants to judge everything according to concepts of pure understanding, and yet another, finally, wants to limit understanding and reason only to the regulation of sensible perceptions, and to rob us of the right to judge according to the analogy with what has been experienced given that analogical cognition is not a direct intuition. In this way the philosopher narrows his concepts of truth by taking everything under one point of view, or subsumes one under another more than nature has done so. . . . [8] [114]

§25
Is Kant's Idealism Better Than Other Versions?

So **Kant** is an idealist, and concedes this himself. He takes his idealism to be necessary in order to guard reason from inconsistencies and contradictions in its representation of space and sensible appearances. But he does want to see his **transcendental** or **formal** idealism differentiated from other types of idealism thus far known.

I hope to have shown here that this formal idealism is not necessary in order to prevent inconsistencies and contradictions. So we need to consider only in what respects Kantian idealism is differentiated from others and whether it is better than they are.

1. Idealism is not at all a morally harmful position. It does not bring about murder and bodily harm. [115] Nor do we need to fear an influence on the population, or on goodness and happiness from it, as we do from atheism. Considered on its own, it is an **innocent** though, to be sure, somewhat **eccentric** hypothesis, that speculative minds easily accept when they **want to know more than can be known**. The worst thing that can be said about idealism, the greatest evil that it can cause, if human understanding does not sufficiently oppose it, would be this, that it **confuses language**. And that is something that **Kant's** idealism, should it be accepted, does as well as any other form. The claim that bodies are representations in us, that space is something in us, that outer sense is a property of our mind, and so on, are these

not confusions of language? Where would it lead if it were continued in more determinate applications? To the claim that Göttingen is something in me, a mere representation or modification of myself, that the wall on which I am taking a walk is in me, that the view over meadows [116] and fields to the mountains, and the sun and moon [are in me] –. I do not desire to jest or otherwise undermine the position. But I do have trouble disputing in this way against a person whose philosophical insights I esteem highly on the whole. However, it is still necessary, in the examination of **such** doctrines, to give some attention to their **applications**. These invite **orientation**.

2. But **Kant** does not desire these applications. He does not want us to leave ordinary language, he does in fact concede the **empirical** actuality of bodies and their **empirical** existence outside of us. Indeed, but that is something that every idealist does. Outside of his study or esoteric lecture, none has dared to make himself unintelligible or ridiculous through departing from ordinary language. Not even the strongest Pyrrhonist had ever denied the **apparent**, or, if one wants, **empirical**, actuality [117] of bodies outside of us. So in this respect Mr. **Kant** does not do more. But these **distinctions**, these **additions**, namely, **empirically apparent**, destroy everything. For it always follows from this that matters are properly speaking otherwise, that we speak in this way only to serve **common** understanding, as it were, exoterically. Here too the esoteric opposite is always expressly indicated.
3. But **Kant's** idealism is not the **fantastical** idealism of a **Berkeley**. No, admittedly, it is not. But I do not see why the worst aspect of Berkeley's idealism should be that he uses it in order to refute not just materialism, which **Kant** does as well, but even atheism. And in all other respects, Berkeley's idealism is completely similar to Kant's. Nor is one **saved** from this Berkeleyan inference in Kant's idealism. For simply because **Kant** does not further consider the question [118] where the appearances of things in space originate, if they are not impressions of substances that actually exist outside of us, it does not follow that all his students will be prevented from considering this question. And then they must take all these appearances either to be effects of the representative power of the soul, according to the Leibnizian hypothesis, or to be impressions of God, with **Malebranche** and **Berkeley**, or else they must appeal to manichaeism. And of **these** three, I would, at all times, prefer the Berkeleyan hypothesis.

J. C. G. Schaumann

On the Transcendental Aesthetic: A Critical Attempt

"TO PRIVY COUNCILLOR FEDER, ABOUT TRANSCENDENTAL IDEALISM"

Your love of truth, honored Sir, and your general benevolence, have now been disclosed to the public through the pen[9] of your critical writings as well as the pen of your public investigations and friendly communications, as your kind disposition has been disclosed particularly to me. So worthy Sir, do not attribute the disturbance that this letter might create, a letter that has been composed with the confidence in your love of truth and kindness, entirely to the importunity of the author, but in part also to the treachery of your heart. [132]

According to you, Kant is an idealist, and his idealism is on the whole not significantly different from Berkeleyan idealism. This seems otherwise to me, worthy Sir, so allow me to submit the reasons for my opinion to your examination. – To be sure, I already have permission to do so, but I have another request: please forgive me should I become too loquacious. I **sought** to vindicate Kant, whom I esteem highly, in your eyes, since I admire you as much. You do know that one can easily become too verbose in such a vindication, since one has a dual interest in reaching one's end.

Kant is not an idealist in the ordinary sense: [on the contrary] Kantian idealism demonstrates the invalidity of the ordinary idealist systems. That is what I want to show, and in order to be able to do so in a more coherent fashion, [133] allow me to forget that I am writing a letter, and to transform the style of an epistle into that of a systematic treatise for the purposes of the proof.

Ordinary idealism is that doctrine according to which it is asserted that there is no matter, and that our representations of it are nothing but fancies aroused in our souls by God (Plattner's *Philosophical Aphorisms*, part 1, bk 2, div. 1, §922).[10] Hence, according to it nothing is actual except subjective representations, and matter is everywhere an impossibility. The reasons for this have been presented by the philosopher just identified in the indicated location.

This is not the case with transcendental idealism. That is the doctrine according to which space and time are taken to be necessary conditions for the possibility of sensibility. It, [134] accordingly, considers everything that is represented as contained in space and time, namely, all appearances, to be mere representations in us, not things in themselves. Things in themselves it takes to actually exist as such even without our sensibility. The system of the transcendental idealist is the following:

That the actual existence of which I can cognize without doubt must be **immediately** perceived by me. But I can only perceive immediately what is in myself, hence, nothing but **representations**. Therefore, the existence of those objects that are outside of me in the **strict** sense of the word, which are distinct from myself, can never be proven through my perception (for that is nothing but a modification of my mind). I can only infer it, as the cause of the effect that exists in me (perception). [135] But that inference is not a conclusive proof of the actual existence [of such things] outside of me given that the effect that occurs in us can arise from more than one cause. Hence I cannot directly **pass off** what I **take** to be the cause as the actually existing cause. I say, accordingly, that as soon as you claim the existence of the objects of your sensibility to be the existence of things that are truly outside of you, you substantialize a mere idea, or take something to be the cause of a perception in you that, however, you simply cannot **immediately** and **indubitably** know to be the true and sole cause.

Nevertheless, I also firmly assert that these things exist; however, I do not take them to be things in themselves, things which are outside of me in the intellectual sense (for in that case I would contradict my first [136] principle), but mere appearances. That is to say, I take them to be representations in my sensibility which, therefore, I perceive **immediately** and whose existence I do not first need to infer. I prove in the following manner that I can and must with good reason pass off everything that I sensibly perceive to be mere representation and appearance in me:

The only conditions under which we can sensibly represent anything to ourselves are space and time. Were one to remove these representations, then one would have at the same time removed the possibility of representing anything to oneself in sensibility. We have proven in the Transcendental Aesthetic that this is the case, and that space and time are the forms of intuition. However, on its own, this **form** is empty and void of all real content for cognition. Hence, if cognition [137] is to have a content, **matter** must be added, and that is delivered by **sensation**. Sensation cannot be a priori but must be given a posteriori. Because we can well imagine a sensibility without positing sensation in it, even though we cannot obtain cognition through sensibility without sensation, sensation does not belong to our sensibility as a necessary condition of its possibility. But even if we could raise this sensation to the highest degree of clarity, it would still not be able to teach us anything about the actual composition of the objects in themselves,[§] rather, [138] it can only ever represent the manner in which we intuit these objects.

But in all this we do not at all deny the existence of objects outside of our representation, quite the contrary, according to our assertions that must be necessarily assumed. We say that what is real is given and that means that our cognitive capacity did not create it out of itself (for in that case we could not say that it is given, that is, brought about through different causality), rather, there must be something outside of it which is the cause of this real [thing] that is given to us through sensation. However, this object that lies at the ground of appearance has as good as no reality for us, and the qualities of appearances, or representations, brought about in us through any one object, in itself unknown, cannot be considered as qualities of this thing in itself. [139] For given that only that is actual for us which we perceive immediately, that is, in ourselves, we could not ascribe objective reality to them.

As I sit here and reflect, a painting meets my eye, and I would surely be very dismayed were someone to prove to me that it is nothing but a play of my imagination because it reminds me of the affection of one of my best friends. No – all qualities of this painting are grounded in some object that in fact actually exists outside of me; nevertheless, they belong to the object only insofar as it relates itself to my sensibility. Not just the outline of the painting, not just that on which it is painted, but also the different colors and their shades are grounded in a transcendental object and could [140] not be perceived at all if what is real, which lies at the ground of this painting, did not have an effect on me and thus came into a sort of relation with my sensibility.

This relation disappears when one of the things that are related to one another is removed. Accordingly, when I remove the transcendental object, the ground of all appearances, the appearances themselves are removed as well. I am forced, therefore, by my own principles, to assert that actual objects exist in an intellectual sense outside of me. For I take appearances to be the only things that can have actuality for me, yet, these would entirely disappear were I to remove that through which they become possible as relations of something to my sensibility. [141]

[§] For we can only infer them as the causes of our sensations. Accordingly, they can be quite heterogeneous with our sensations.

Accordingly, one goes distinctly wrong when one confuses transcendental with empirical idealism. For the former conflicts almost entirely with the latter and removes the ground of the whole doctrine. The transcendental idealist concedes the actual existence of matter in space but does not assume anything other than immediate perception as criterion of actuality. For him all material objects are nothing but appearances or representation in him, even their inner possibility rests on sensation, on something in him. In this way, he perceives their actuality immediately and does not merely infer it. Matter is for him a species of representations which are called **external**, not because they refer to objects **in themselves** external but because they refer to **space** or because space is their necessary condition; [142] though, admittedly, even though all things are external to one another in space, it itself is in us.

Thus the transcendental idealist reasons as follows: Whatever is immediately perceived by me, that is, what is perceived in myself, is actual; I perceive material objects immediately (through sensation). Hence they are actual.

The person who takes the material or sensible world to be a universe that exists independently of sensibility can certainly not reason in this way. For who authorizes him to infer the actuality of things existing outside of his representation on the basis of the actuality of his representations? In this way, he cannot be certain that all things he takes to be actual are not just illusions of his imagination. He is not able, accordingly, to defend himself thoroughly against empirical idealism, indeed, [143] is even in danger of falling into it upon strict examination. For, after he has presupposed that the objects that are called outer exist outside of us even without being referred to our sensibility, he must surely acknowledge that all proofs of their actuality, which are based on the representation of our sensibility, are entirely unsatisfactory and less than conclusive. For he cannot possibly assume that just because he **represents** something to himself, that thing **exists** actually in the strict sense outside of him just as he represents it.

So we see clearly that the transcendental realist who takes sensible objects to be things in themselves must fall into empirical idealism, but that person who declares the things in themselves that lie at the ground of the sensible representations to be mere ideas, and [144] takes solely their appearances to be something real, is an empirical realist who attributes to the matter given through sensations actuality as appearance. We perceive this appearance immediately in us, and its actuality cannot be disputed in any way. We sensibly cognizing beings cannot at all determine what exists at its ground; that is the same in all appearances because it is equally unknown to us in all.

But could someone object to transcendental idealism as follows: given that, according to your system, you allow only that to be actual that exists in yourself as representation, you in fact obfuscate thereby the distinction between that which is **actual** and that which is merely **imagined**. What is your criterion of actual things, what of the things created by you in imagination? [145]

The transcendental idealist will reply: this objection has already been sufficiently solved in my system. The criterion of actuality is **sensation**. Where there is no sensation, where no impression of anything on your sensibility precedes your representation, there the representation does not designate anything real. If you are conscious that by means of a previous impression on your eye the representation of the horse has been created in you, in that case this appearance is an **actual** horse, but when the representation of a horse arises in you without a previous sensation, in that case you can be certain that this is a mere creature of your imagination. For example, if you say to someone that you would like to see a light brown English stallion that has four white feet and a white star on its head and so on, then this image of the English stallion is so far only [146] a mere image forged by your imagination because it has not been created through sensation. When, however, someone else says: here is such a horse, look at it, determine whether all those representations previously created by your imagination are created by it; if so, then your representation does designate something real for it is connected with sensation. Of course, without sensation, neither the actual nor the imagined [horse] is possible. In what we are to cognize as actual, we must either be conscious of our own sensation, or, and this is the same thing, we must know with certainty that another trustworthy human being has had the sensation. For the imagined [thing], we must similarly have obtained the material from sensation, given that no representation that is to deliver cognition is possible at all except through sensation, but in imagination we can [147] compose many an object out of this delivered material. Of these none may actually exist in this manner because it has itself been composed as such, has not become representation in us through sensation.

In view of this general presentation of the transcendental system, which, I flatter myself to think, grasps Kant's meaning, allow me, worthy Sir, to consider some of the objections that you have raised. Perhaps I have been fortunate enough to understand their spirit –

perhaps I will be so fortunate as to bring you and Kant into agreement with respect to some of them. I say **perhaps** for I am not conceited enough to assert with certainty ahead of time that I can do so.

You think, first and foremost, worthy Sir, that Kant, with whom you do seem to agree in most respects, [148] distances himself too much from the common manner of representation with his expressions and that he does so needlessly. For this reason, the manner in which he wants to forge a reconciliation with them cannot appear to be completely satisfactory (*On Space and Causality*, p. 65). – Now, it cannot very well be denied that Kant connects a different meaning with these ordinary expressions that he retains than do most who can be content to remain with the ordinary manner of representation because they do not think further about its grounds and are satisfied when it suffices for ordinary life. – But it seems to me that the philosopher has a more ambitious aim. He has to meticulously investigate and examine how it is that the ordinary manners of representation are satisfactory for most, and what sort of meaning must really be given to them [149] if they are to really contain truth and not to shrink from the touchstone of the hardest critique. – Mr. Kant has done this. He has shown what allows us to speak of actual things in space and outside of us as objects of cognition and how we have to represent this matter if we want to avoid the danger of sceptical objections that can mislead us in our cognition. – Even though the author of the *Critique* takes the objects of outer sense without exception to be mere representations in us, it is still not at all the case that the difference between the transcendental objects of intuition and our representations has been overthrown. All that has been asserted is that it is impossible to pinpoint the differentiating characteristic given that the former (transcendental objects) are not given to us and can [150] never be given to a sensible being. What can be given is only the manner in which they relate to our sensibility (their appearance). And when this impossibility is further strengthened, as it is with proofs, until now unrefuted, taken from the nature of our cognitive capacities themselves, then it cannot be disagreeable to a researcher that someone should attribute a different meaning to the expressions that are to be used to designate this impossibility than has ordinarily been connected with them.

Furthermore, dear Sir, you believe that the Kantian position on space abolishes the distinction between actual things and products of imagination (p. 71). It seems to me, however, that what I have already said above pertaining to this issue is enough to clarify this distinction sufficiently. Allow me to make only a few more remarks. [151]

Admittedly, we do perceive both the objects of outer sensation and of imagination in space.[§] We have to perceive the latter in space because their material is taken from previous outer sensation. One can only represent a Pegasus, Tempe, or Elysium in space, that is, as objects that, if they were actual, would have to be objects of outer sense. Nevertheless, it is still easy to differentiate them from **actual** appearances. When, in a state of sound understanding, one is aware that one has arbitrarily created representations [152] solely through one's own effort, in that case the object is not something real but a creature of imagination. But where one is aware that one has been passive, that the representation was necessitated, there it is clear that its cause lay elsewhere than in my will, and in that case the representation designates a real object.

Let me now attempt, worthy Sir, to investigate what you say in paragraph seventeen of your treatise against the transcendental idealist about the independence of sensible objects from the cognizing subject.

It seems to me to be your view that "according to the system of the transcendental idealist, the existence of sensible objects has to be [153] entirely dependent on the perceiving subject, so that the whole sensible world would have to lose its existence if there were no human beings to intuit it. – That, however, is refuted through experience, and, by contrast, the independence of the existence of sensible objects from the perceiving subject is clearly demonstrated.["][11] Prior to examining the reasons for this proof one by one, allow me only one general preliminary remark to which I will refer in the examination of the particular reasons.

When one speaks of the dependence of objects of sensible cognition on the cognizing subject, one cannot possibly mean the dependence of the **transcendental** object, but only a dependence of **appearances** of it; or, to use your own words, [154] the **dependence of the things that appear to our senses**.

This presupposed, let me investigate whether this dependence could not be demonstrated after all without denying the truth and demonstrability of the reasons that you have identified in the indicated passage. The first reason for the independence of sensible objects from the perceiving subject is the following:

Sensible objects are dependent on **one another** to a much greater degree than they are on **us**. We can find ourselves in countless relations and circumstances

[§] I would not want to identify this space, the form of outer sense, as imagined. It is supposed to be in the mind as form prior to all imagination, so identifying it as imagined, it seems to me, would be a contradiction.

and not have the object that we once saw with us. In order to see it again, we have to go to its location, to the other things outside of us next to which nature has placed it. No matter how much we desire to make its representation actual, [155] we will not be able to do so in any other way.[12]

First, it would of course be absurd to claim that the existence of sensible objects is dependent on the **single** subject who can perceive them. But that is also not what is claimed. If sensible beings like human beings did not exist at all, then the appearances that constitute the objects of **human** sensibility would also not exist. – This aside, however, it seems to me that the dependence of things on **each other** is of an entirely different nature from their dependence on the **human being**. The latter means that if there were no human sensibility, then appearances would simply not exist at all. The first means that if certain appearances were absent, then certain **relations** of these appearances with others [156] would also disappear, but not that **these** other appearances themselves would disappear. To be sure, I cannot see the tower in the valley unless I climb the mountain in front of it, but this does not mean that this tower would not exist at all if the mountain were not there. If this or that **single** subject who is behind the mountain wants to **see** the tower, he has to climb the mountain. In this respect, seeing the tower is, for this particular subject, dependent on the mountain. However, this does not mean that were I to remove the mountain, I would also remove the tower, as would be the case if one were to remove sensibility in general. I proceed to the second reason.

Other human beings do not need us in order to see the **same** thing, to feel it, own it, and enjoy it; no more than we need them to do so.[13] [157]

Admittedly, they do not need **us**, but they do need **our form of sensibility**. If they do not have it, then the appearances of their sensibility would be of an entirely different nature and could never be the same. But in that case, they would not be, as we are, intuiting beings, they would not be human beings.

3. "Nothing in these things of the sensible world has been changed when those who have previously seen them with us die or otherwise disappear. And so we must surely concede as well that when we no longer perceive them, they do not for that reason cease to exist for others."[14]

   That is certain. Who will want to assert that when I die or go away, the tree or the flower ceases to exist as well? That is surely the most absurd assertion that can be imagined. But it is not

[158] absurd to assert that when all human intuition ceases, all appearances, as its objects, cease as well since those exist only in it and are mere modifications of it.

4. "Even if we are different from other human beings in the manner in which we see and judge these things, we find ourselves forced to concede an outer existence to these things that is independent of both types of representation."[15]

This too we are happy to concede. Doing so does not in any way undermine our assertions. The small child, for instance, has a completely different representation of the sun than the astronomer. The child thinks it to be the size of a bowl, the astronomer as a body in diameter 109 times, in volume [159] 1,295,000 times greater than earth. But both concede the outer existence, the actuality of the sun. That is, both sense that something affects their senses and represents itself to them in space. This outer existence of the sun, accordingly, is not at all dependent on the different representations of its size or quality in different subjects; rather, these could not exist at all until an outer sensation is actual. But the appearance, the actual existence of which is indicated through sensation, is still dependent on the form of intuition in the intuiting subject because it is represented as existing in space but space is something in the intuiting subject. Hence, were there no space, this appearance could never become actual. [160]

5. "We know, or must reasonably believe that many other things than appear or have sometimes occurred to us, have appeared or occurred to **other** human beings, even when we have not been able to perceive their existence. Many a person has not seen Königsberg or its philosopher but has heard about him from others. Can he therefore refuse to accord him an existence independent from his representation as well as from those of others? And is all this not sufficient reason to accord an independent existence from us, the cognizing subjects, to all things that we perceive through our sensibility, the sun, the moon, the stars, the animals?"[16]

I answer this question in the same way that I answered the previous one. [161] Only the person who judges obstinately or without insight can assert that only what **he** perceives is actual. – But this is not so, rather, what is actual is what is connected with sensation, that is, **human** sensation in general, not only with that of the individual. I am as convinced of the existence of the Königsberg philosopher as I am of my own, regardless of the fact

> that I have never seen him. And where does this conviction come from? Partly from the fact that many of my friends have seen him, partly because I have his most peculiar products in my hands. The whole world is convinced that these are products of the Kantian spirit. Of course, his existence, that is, his existence as a being **in itself**, is neither contingent on the representations of those who have seen him, nor on mine. His existence as appearance, however, which is for me the [162] only meaning that his existence can have, is, like the existence of all outer appearances, only possible because I or a human being in general can represent him as existing in space.

And now I look back again to the point from which I started. – It is not the case that the transcendental objects that lie at the ground of the appearances, such as sun, moon and so forth, are dependent on the form of sensibility of the intuiting being, but that the appearances themselves are. The former can never become objects of sensibility; hence, they cannot exist in any way for a being that cognizes through sensibility.

The main thing that you seem to dislike, worthy Sir, is that, contrary to the ordinary use of language, the transcendental idealist does not recognize anything but mere representations, that he declares space, [163] along with all bodies in it, to be representation in us. However, I think that we can concede this point [to the transcendental idealist]. – Indeed, I think that the precision of his expression must even please us. After all, one does, in principle, already find the same thought among some of the best philosophers, except that one does not there find it as clearly expressed. You yourself, worthy Sir, say more than once that we can only have sensible cognition of the corporeal world and that we do not know what the things in themselves are. And if we do not know this, and can never know this, what is it then that we cognize? Surely, nothing other than the manner in which the things that we cannot know in themselves appear to us. And what are these objects of sensible cognition, body and space, or what is it that we associate with this name? They are appearances, [164] representations in us of an object in itself unknown.

An expression thus specified can surely not harm human understanding. For it is completely in agreement with its **meaning**. Of course, it must not be immediately transferred from the school of the philosopher into the ordinary use of language, for here it would surely cause confusion. In view of the fact that the meaning [of the expression] adheres only to its sign, it would be easily possible to confuse different concepts that are expressed through similar words and in this way that which is actual – actual, that is, for human beings – would soon be taken as arbitrary imagination, or that would be taken as reality. Moreover, the philosopher will be more easily understood and can give his presentation more precision if he has a specific word for each of his concepts. For this reason, he can always identify what he cognizes through sensation an actual thing. [165] It does differentiate itself sufficiently from arbitrary representations and he does know what constitutes a thing for him.

The main principle on which the transcendental idealist builds his entire system is the following: **we can indisputably cognize only that as actual which we perceive immediately**. For if we take what we perceive as an outer object to be a thing in itself that exists in this manner also outside of our representation, then it is incomprehensible, given that we only have representations, how we arrive at the cognition that it is actual also outside of our representation. After all, we cannot sense outside of us but only in us, and therefore, cannot take what we sense as anything but our own determinations.

Here you think, esteemed Sir, that the transcendental idealist demands an explanation that [166] he should not be permitted to demand – an explanation of how one can cognize that our representation can contain something that is completely adequate to a thing entirely different from us. However, in the first instance nothing further is here said except that it is incomprehensible how one can cognize something like this; it is said that we have no reason, no third thing by which we can cognize representation and thing in itself as harmonious and one. – And if that is so, if one wants to assume that our representations correspond to things in themselves, then the demand that an explanation [of how we can know things in themselves by means of our representations] be provided is not so inconsistent. For one can surely not simply assume in good faith that our representations contain the essence and nature of things that are entirely different from them, given that we can only be entirely certain of a cognition when representations [167] correspond to the represented things. But we can only cognize that that is the case when the representation is one with the represented thing since we do not otherwise have a criterion through which we can cognize their agreement.

And if this is the case, if there can be for us no certain cognition of things outside of us, other than their representation in our sensibility, why should we not then say that the entire sensible world, the totality of all things that are cognized sensibly, exists only in our thoughts[?] It seems to me that this expression is not too strong or excessive; it is only unusual and seems to be too close to the empirical-idealist [position]. However, it is nevertheless correct and precise. – Nor is it the thinker's business to be concerned with words – no matter how shocking they may be, it is irrelevant to him as long as the concepts [they convey] contain truth. [168]

For this reason, most esteemed Privy Councillor, I also do not believe that Kantian idealism confuses language. I do not want to deny that the language of **some people** who completely misunderstand it could thereby be confused, but what sort of influence will they have on language in general? One will easily become aware of their error and then be strong enough to work against it. And where is there a philosophical system, where a scientific system, that contains truth that has not been misunderstood and through this misunderstanding confused minds? Have not the simplest teachings of the book we Christians honor, been distorted and misrepresented through having been misunderstood? However, this misunderstanding has never been able to extend its negative consequences generally, there have always been human beings who knew the truth [169] and understood correctly and who were thus able to work against error. And in the same way the doctrines of the *Critique* will, admittedly, be misunderstood and many inferences will be drawn from them the grounds of which do not lie in these doctrines, but there will also always be enlightened men who, by means of the light of enlightenment and correct explanation, can dispel the shadow that misunderstanding and false interpretation throw on truth.

Kant does in fact say that bodies are representations in us, that space is something in us, that outer sense is a property of our mind – but he leaves us a sufficient criterion to differentiate bodies from that which belongs to our self. We can always apply it to specific cases as long as we do so consistently. The universal proposition will [170] present itself as correct and true also in specific and singular [propositions]. The city in which I live is a representation in me – the meadow on which I amuse myself by looking at joyful herds and playing shepherds is a representation in me; sun, moon, and all stars of heaven are representations in me. But what does this mean? Does it mean that all these things are nothing but a changed condition of me, a play of my imagination, an empty illusion, and deception of the senses? No, that is not what it means. It says only this much: of all the things that represent themselves to me in space, I cognize only what they effect in my mind, only my representations of them. I do not cognize the nature of all these things in themselves, nor the inner constitution they have without relation to my sensibility; rather, I cognize only their appearance. And [171] that appearance is what is actual; it is what I cognize through my sensibility, the only thing that no one can dispute, and everyone of sound mind and body must cognize in the same way. And for this reason, one can always accept the common expressions: body may signify not mere representations, but actual things outside of us, as long as the philosopher makes sure that one does not use these expressions to signify something impossible, but that truth lies at their ground and that deception and error do not come into cognition.

But all skeptics from Pyrrho and the Eleatics to Hume and Berkeley have maintained the common expression, no one has dared to make himself a laughingstock outside of the study through deviation from the ordinary use of language. So even if Kant remains with the ordinary use of language, [172] how does it help and by what does he differentiate himself from the other skeptics and idealists when he shows through additional distinctions that the common expression is not completely true and that the thing itself is actually different.[17]

However, Kant does the opposite. He develops and explains the expressions of the ordinary use of language and secures matters so that nobody can henceforth confuse and deceive us through empty distinctions and misleading additions. He demonstrates what truth is, and what actuality has meaning for us. He does not claim that sensible objects are properly speaking something other than what we cognize them to be, and he does not speak in this way merely to please common understanding. He says: what you cognize of bodies is actually so and let [173] Phyrronists, let Zeno and Protagoras, and whatever they may all be called, say that what you know is semblance, you can reject them all and be certain against their attacks for your representations cannot be disputed away, no matter how sophistical and critical the attempts with which one attempts to do so.

From what has been said thus far it is also clear that Kantian idealism does not lead to the Berkeleyan but stands against it. Kant himself has shown this so clearly in his *Prolegomena* (p. 205) that I need only use his words without adding a further explanation. He says: the proposition of all true idealists, from the Eleatic school to Bishop Berkeley is contained in the following formula: "all cognition through the senses and experience is nothing but semblance, and truth is only in the ideas of [174] pure understanding and reason." The principle, which guides and determines my idealism is however: "All cognition of things from mere pure understanding or pure reason is nothing but semblance, and truth is only in experience."[18]

We do not have to fear, therefore, from any philosopher of the

Kantian school, if he is a worthy student of his teacher, that is, if he has apprehended the spirit of the Kantian system and understood his teacher, that he will ask for more. For as such a student, he will comprehend that the question of the last objective grounds of appearance is unanswerable and that, in order not to fall into enthusiasm, he will have to be content with the cognition [175] that the senses provide of things, that is, with appearances.

Friedrich Heinrich Jacobi

On Transcendental Idealism

The transcendental or critical idealism that constitutes the foundation of Kant's *Critique of Pure Reason* is not, it seems to me, treated with sufficient care by several defenders of the Kantian philosophy, or, in order to say explicitly what I think: they seem to fear the general charge of idealism so much that, rather than confess to it, which could deter people, they prefer to create some confusion. Now, in itself this is hardly a reprehensible act, given that before one can shackle people's prejudices, one must usually first tame them, and even though it is generally difficult to get people to pay attention, it is virtually impossible to do so when a general prejudice interferes. But in the present case, the matter is such that the least misunderstanding [210] makes all instruction impossible, so that one simply cannot understand any longer what is being proposed. This is not something for which one can fault the *Critique of Pure Reason*. It expresses its position with sufficient clarity, and, aside from the short Transcendental Aesthetic, one need only read the Critique of the Fourth Paralogism of Transcendental Psychology (pp. 367–80) in order to understand the nature of Transcendental Idealism.

In the latter passage, Kant says (p. 370):

> [t]he transcendental idealist can be an empirical realist, thus, as he is called, a dualist. That is, he can admit the existence of matter without going beyond mere self-consciousness and assuming anything more than the certainty of the representations in me, thus the *cogito ergo sum*. Because he takes matter and even its inner possibility to be only appearance, and appearance is nothing apart from our sensibility, it [211] [matter] is for him only a species of representations (intuitions), which are called external, not **as if they stood in relation to objects in themselves external**, but because they relate perceptions to space, in which all things are external to one another **whereas space itself is in us**. – We have declared ourselves for this transcendental idealism from the start....
>
> If one regards outer appearances as representations that have been produced in us by their objects, which are things that are in themselves to be found outside us, then it is impossible to see how one could cognize the existence of these latter objects other than through an inference from effect to cause. In

such an inference it must always remain doubtful whether this cause is in us or outside of us. Now, one can in fact concede that the cause of our outer intuitions may be something that is outside of us in the transcendental sense, but this is not the object we have in mind in the [212] representations of matter and corporeal things. For these are merely appearances, that is, merely species of representation that are at all times only in us and the actuality of which rests on immediate consciousness in the same way in which the consciousness of my own thoughts does. The transcendental object is equally unknown in regard to inner and outer intuition. But we do not here speak of it, rather, we are speaking here of the empirical object, which is called an external object when it is represented as in space, and an inner object when it is only represented in a temporal relation. Space and time, however, can both be found only in us. [A372–3]

Meanwhile, the expression "outside us" is unavoidably ambiguous, referring now to something that exists as thing in itself distinct from us, now to something that belongs only to outer appearance, so in order to be certain that we are using this concept in the latter sense, which is properly speaking the sense in which the psychological question [213] about the reality of our outer intuition has to be understood, we will distinguish empirically external objects from those that are called external in the transcendental sense, by explicitly calling them [the only empirically external objects] things that are to be found in space. . . . [A373]

But there is nothing in space except what is represented in it. For space itself is nothing other than representation; hence, what is in it must be contained in representation. **Nothing at all is in space except insofar as it is actually represented in it.** The proposition, which must, admittedly, sound strange, that a thing can only exist in the representation of it, will here no longer be objectionable because the things that we are dealing with are not things in themselves, but only appearances, that is, **representations.** [A374–375n]

If we do not want to confuse ourselves in our commonest [214] assertions, we must regard all our perceptions, whether we call them inner or outer, to be only a consciousness of what is dependent on our sensibility. We must similarly regard the outer objects of these perceptions to be not things in themselves, but only representations that we can become immediately conscious of as of every other representation, but that are **called** outer because they are dependent on that sense that we call outer sense, whose intuition is space. This space, however, is itself nothing other than a kind of inner representation in which certain perceptions are connected with one another. [A378] The transcendental object that lies at the ground of outer appearances, and similarly, the one that lies at the ground of inner intuitions, is in itself neither matter nor a thinking being, it is, rather, a ground, unknown to us, of all appearances, a ground that provides the empirical concept of the first as well as the second kind. [A379–80] [215]

I will cite the following passage about the transcendental ideality of time from the Transcendental Aesthetic, to which I referred:

Against this theory, which concedes empirical reality to time, but denies that it has absolute and transcendental reality, intelligent people have raised the following objection so unanimously that I can only conclude that it will spontaneously occur to every reader who is unfamiliar with reflections of this kind. It reads as follows: Alterations are actual (this is proved by the change in our own representations, even if one wanted to deny all outer appearances along with their alterations). Now alterations are possible only in time, hence time is something actual. It is not difficult to answer this objection. I grant the entire argument. Time is in fact something actual, namely, **the actual form** of inner intuition. Hence, it has subjective reality with respect to inner experience, that is, I really have the **representation** of time and [216] of my determination in it. It is actual, accordingly, not as object but as the mode of representation of myself as object. But if I could intuit myself, or if another being could intuit me without the condition of sensibility, then just these determinations, that we now represent to ourselves as alterations, would deliver a cognition into which the representation of time, and, **consequently, that of alterations as well, would not occur at all**. . . . I can say, admittedly, that our representations follow each other, but this is to say only that we are conscious of them in a temporal sequence, namely, in accord with the form of inner sense, and so on." (*Critique of Pure Reason*, pp. 36 and 37). [A 37 note]

Hence, what we realists call actual objects, things that are independent of our representations, are only inner beings for the transcendental idealist, they are beings **that present nothing of the thing that MAY be outside of us, or to** [217] **which the appearance MAY relate, rather, they are MERELY SUBJECTIVE determinations of the mind, completely void of everything that is ACTUALLY objective**. "**Representations**" – nothing but representations – "that is what the objects# are that, whether they are represented as extended beings or **series of alterations**, do not have an existence in themselves outside of our thoughts" (p. 491). "They" – these objects that are only appearances, that simply do not present anything that is actually objective, that present everywhere only themselves – "are the mere play of our representations and in the end reduce to determinations of inner sense" (p. 101). [218]

Consequently,

even the order and regularity in appearances that we call **nature** is one that we ourselves introduce, and we would not be able to find it there, if we, or the nature of our mind, had not originally set it there (p. 125). . . . Even though

Consequently, Mr. Kant calls realists who are not **merely empirical** realists **dreaming idealists**, for they take the objects **that are merely representations** to be things in themselves.

we learn many laws through experience, they are only **particular determinations** of yet higher laws, the highest of which (**by which all others are governed**) originate a priori out of understanding itself, **and are not borrowed from experience**. Quite the contrary, they must provide the lawfulness to appearances and thus make experience possible. Understanding, accordingly, is not just a capacity to make laws on the basis of comparison, **it is itself the lawgiver of nature**. That is, without understanding there would be no nature at all, no synthetic unity of the manifold according to rules, for appearances cannot as such exist outside of us, [219] but only in our sensibility." ** [A126–7] [220]

I believe that the passages that have just been cited are sufficient to demonstrate that the Kantian philosopher deviates completely from the spirit of his system when he says of objects that they make **impressions** on the senses and thus **arouse** sensations in us, and in this way **produce** representations. For according to the Kantian doctrine, the empirical object, which is always only an appearance, cannot exist outside of us and be something other than a representation. According to this doctrine, we know nothing at all of the **transcendental object**, and it is also never referred to when we consider objects; its concept is at most problematic, and rests on the **entirely subjective form of our thought which belongs solely to the sensibility proper to us**. Experience does not deliver this transcendental object and cannot deliver it in any way at all, since what is not **appearance** can never be an object of experience. The appearance, however, and [221] the fact that this or that affection of sensibility is in me, does not at all constitute a relation of such representations to any object. It is understanding that **adds** the object to the appearance, and it does so by combining its multiplicity in one consciousness. **So we say that we cognize the object when we have GENERATED a synthetic unity in the mul-**

** One must be very careful here not to confuse Kant's claim with the claims presented in manifold ways by Leibniz, and in fine and clearly comprehensible fashion in Mendelssohn's *Phaedo*, namely, that order, harmony, every agreement of a multiplicity cannot, as such, be found in the things, but solely in the thinking being who combines the multiplicity and unifies it in one representation. For according to the latter assertion, the order – this agreement that I perceive – is not merely subjective, rather **its conditions** lie outside of me in the object, and I am required to combine its parts in this rather than that way through its constitution. Here, accordingly, the object gives laws to understanding, with respect to the concept that understanding forms of it. The concept is in all its parts and relations given through the object, and only the **comprehension itself** lies solely in me. See pages 169 and 170 of Mendelssohn's dialogue.

tiplicity of intuition, and the concept of this unity is the representation of object = x. This =**x**, however, is not the **transcendental** object, for we cannot even know that much of the transcendental object, and it is only assumed to be the intelligible cause of the appearance, in order that there be something that corresponds to sensibility as receptivity.††

Nevertheless, however contrary to the spirit of the Kantian philosophy it may be [222] to say that objects make **impressions** on the senses, and in this way produce representations, it is hard to see how the Kantian philosophy could find an entry point for itself without this presupposition, and make any kind of presentation of its doctrine. The word "sensibility" is already entirely meaningless if we do not understand it to be a distinct real medium between what is real and what is real – an actual intermediary **from** something **to** something. The concepts of externality and connection, of action and passion, of causality and dependence, ought to already be contained in the concept of sensibility, **as real and objective determinations,** in such a way that the prior presupposition of the absolute universality and necessity of these concepts is given along with the concept of sensibility. I must confess that this impasse has hampered me more than a little in my study of the Kantian philosophy, so that for several years running I [223] had to repeatedly start the *Critique of Pure Reason* from the beginning because I continued to be confused by the fact that **without** this presupposition, I could not find my way into the system, whereas **with** it I could not stay there.

To remain in the system with this presupposition is flatly impossible because it presupposes the conviction of the objective validity of our perception of objects outside of us as things in themselves, and not **merely** as subjective appearances, and it similarly presupposes the conviction of the objective validity of our representations **of the necessary relations** that these objects have with one another and of their **essential relations as objectively real determinations.** These are assertions that simply cannot cohere with the Kantian philosophy because it is thoroughly committed to proving that the objects as well as their relations are merely subjective beings, mere determinations of our own self [224] and do not in any way exist outside of us. For even if, according to it, one can **concede** that there **may** be a transcendental something, as **cause**, that corresponds to these merely subjective beings, which are only determinations of **our own being**, it remains hidden in deepest obscurity just where this cause is, and what is the

†† *Critik der reinen Vernunft*, pp. 246, 253, 254, 115, 494.

nature of its relation to the effect. In any case, we have already seen that we cannot obtain any experience of this transcendental something, whether from up close or afar, and that there is no way we can perceive the least thing about it. Quite the contrary, all objects of experience are mere appearances the matter and real content of which is throughout nothing but our own sensation. We find ourselves in total ignorance of the special determinations of this sensation, that is, of their source or, to use the language of the Kantian philosophy, of the **manner in which we are affected by objects**. And as far as the [225] inner processing or digestion of this matter is concerned, through which it receives its **form** and the sensations in us become objects for us, that rests on a **spontaneity** of our being. The principle of this spontaneity is, again, completely unknown to us. We know only that its first expression is the expression of a blind capacity to combine forward and backward, a capacity that we call imagination. Because, however, the concepts that are generated in this manner, and the judgments and propositions that emerge from these concepts do not have validity except in relation to our sensations, our entire cognition is nothing but a consciousness of combined determinations of our own selves from which no inferences can be drawn about anything else. Our universal representations, concepts, and principles express only the essential form in which every particular representation and every particular judgment must fit, in accord with the constitution of our nature, in order to be able to be taken up and combined in one universal or transcendental [226] consciousness, and, so obtain relative truth or relative objective validity. If one abstracts from the human form, however, then these laws of our intuition and thought are without all meaning and validity, and do not tell us the least thing about the laws of nature. Neither the principle of sufficient reason, nor even the principle that nothing can come from nothing, pertain to things in themselves. In short, all our cognition contains nothing, flatly nothing that would have any **truly** objective significance.

I ask: how is it possible to combine the presupposition of objects that make impressions on our senses, and in this way cause representations, with a doctrine that wants to destroy all the grounds on which this presupposition rests? Consider what has been shown at the very beginning of this essay: that according to the Kantian system space and all things in space exist in us, and not anywhere [227] else; that all alterations, even the alterations of our own inner state (which we believe ourselves to be immediately conscious of through the succession of our thoughts) are only modes of representation, that these modes of representation are not objectively actual alterations, and do not prove that there is any objectively actual succession either in us or outside of us; consider that all the principles of our understanding express only subjective conditions that are laws of our thought, but in no way laws of nature in itself – laws that are, rather, without all **truly** objective content and use; consider these points properly and reflect whether, in addition to them, one can also maintain the supposition of objects that make impressions on our senses and in this way produce representations. One cannot possibly do so, unless one assigns an alien meaning to every word and an entirely mystical meaning to their combination. For according to the general use of language, the object must signify a thing that [228] **exists outside of us in the transcendental sense,** and how would we arrive at such a thing in the Kantian philosophy? Perhaps through the fact that we feel ourselves to be passive in the representations that we call appearances? But to feel or be passive is only half of a state, **which cannot be thought solely according to this half.** – Indeed, one could expressly insist that it could not possibly be thought according to this half. Hence we would have to sense cause and effect in the transcendental sense and, by means of this sensation, we could infer things outside of us and their necessary relations to one another in the transcendental sense. But since the whole of Transcendental Idealism would be destroyed in this way, and would lose all application and purpose, its adepts must simply do without this presupposition and not even find it **probable** that things that are outside of us in the transcendental sense, exist and have relations with us, [229] **that we could be able to perceive in some way**. As soon as they find it to be as much as merely probable, or want only to **believe** it from afar, they must leave transcendental idealism or[19] end up in truly **unbelievable** contradictions. The transcendental idealist, accordingly, must have the courage to assert the strongest idealism that has ever been taught, and not even to fear the charge of speculative egoism because he cannot possibly function in his system when he wants to do as much as reject the latter charge.

Should the Kantian philosophy want to distance itself, through supposition or faith, by as much as a hair's breadth from the transcendental ignorance that transcendental idealism teaches, then it would not only instantaneously lose all coherence, but it would have to do entirely without what it takes to be its main advantage, namely to bring reason to peace with itself, for this supposition cannot have a ground other than the [230] **thoroughgoing absolute ignorance** that transcendental idealism asserts; but this thoroughgoing absolute ignorance would lose all power if any supposition would be able to rise up and make a claim for even the smallest advantage.

[Hermann Andreas Pistorius]

Critique of Pure Reason by Immanuel Kant, Professor in Königsberg, Member of the Royal Academy of Sciences in Berlin. Second Edition, Improved Here and There. Riga: Hartknoch, 1787. 884 Pages.

The reviewer admits that he began the examination of the new edition of this famous book with great eagerness. The objections that have for some time been raised against it by several famous scholars including **Feder**, **Reimarus**, and others, as well as in our [*Allgemeine deutsche*] *Bibliothek*, seemed to him to be so significant and to attack the basic pillars of the entire Kantian system so thoroughly that he could not but presume to find an answer here. However, he was completely mistaken in this expectation. For not only did he not find a refutation of the objections that were raised, or a resolution of the doubts that were submitted, he found the renewal of a certain, though the reviewer hardly likes to say so, arrogant tone that has been sadly evident in Mr. Kant and some of his disciples, when they depend solely on the evidence of their [344] claims and the apodeictic certainty of the proofs they offer and respond to all of their opponents' attacks with derision. It could only be in view of this strong confidence in the internal consistency and the unshakable solidity of his system that Mr. Kant could precipitately blurt out: "[t]here is no danger here of being refuted, the danger is not to be understood."[20] To what extent this confidence is justified and whether it has any place in the company of the thorough spirit of examination that characterizes the sort of great thinker that Mr. Kant really is (to whom any examination should be welcome, even if he believes himself already in possession of the truth), is something we do not here dare to decide. It is nevertheless undeniable that the Kantian *Critique* itself would have gained a great deal if it had also taken the occasion to answer these apparent objections (for that, namely, apparent, is all they are according to the author's judgment), and if the men whose misunderstanding led them to raise these objections had been dignified with friendly instruction. Before this happens, the *Critique* will not easily achieve the general high regard that Mr. Kant wishes for it when he says, surely too harshly, though he rightly feels and criticizes the inequity of a known prohibition:

> When governments deem it proper to concern themselves with the affairs of scholars, it would be much more appropriate for the purposes of the wise provisions they want to make for the sciences and for human beings, to foster the freedom of this sort of critique, which is the only means by which the work of reason can be placed on solid ground, than to support the ridiculous despotism of the schools, [345] which create a great clamor over the danger to the public when one tears up their cobwebs – cobwebs, however, that the public has never noticed and the loss of which, accordingly, it will never feel.[21]

Until Mr. Kant answers his critics' objections, one can at least not blame those philosophers if they continue to doubt the infallibility and undeniability of Kant's principles and do not concede that the system built on them, which Mr. Kant has yet to deliver, is a demonstrated and solidly grounded **science**. Given that this is so, we want to make some remarks, both about the author's assertions in the Preface and about the wholly new Refutation of Idealism he has added in this edition, although we may hardly expect that Mr. Kant will pay any more attention to what follows than he has paid to earlier remarks, particularly given that he has frankly declared that he can no longer involve himself in disputes.

One of the questions that is investigated in the Preface is why metaphysics, a wholly isolated speculative science, has not been fortunate enough to take the secure path of a science, although it is older than other sciences and would remain even if the others would one and all entirely disappear in the gorge of an all consuming barbarism. Mr. Kant finds the reason for this in the fact that one has so far assumed that all our cognition must conform to objects. On this presupposition, all attempts to learn something about metaphysics in an a priori fashion, [346] through concepts, had to fail. He says that one should see, therefore, whether we would not make more progress with the tasks of metaphysics if we were to assume that objects must conform to our cognition. This is no different than the first thought of Copernicus who, after failing to make satisfactory progress with the explanation of the movements of the heavenly bodies as long as he assumed that the entire starry host revolved around the observer, tried to see whether he might not be more successful if he allowed the observers to revolve but left the stars at rest. In metaphysics, one can take a similar approach with respect to the intuition of objects. This succeeds splendidly and promises to place metaphysics on the sure path of science. For according to this change in the mode of thought, one can very well explain the possibility of a priori cognition, and, what is more, one can provide satisfactory proofs of the laws that lie a priori at the ground of nature, as the sum of objects of experience, neither of which was possible according to previous modes of experience.[22] It cannot be disputed that this way of treating metaphysics, which is peculiar to Mr. Kant and which he adopts from the scientists, has its great and important benefits. For not only does it call an end to proud dogmatism and to the harmful mania for definitions, which has so far reigned in this science to its great disadvantage, but it also shows us what must be the proper and first object of all speculative investigation: knowledge of the human spirit and its powers and the laws in accord with which it operates. In addition, many appearances [347] can only be explained on the supposition that the objects of our intuition must conform to our manner of representation. Nevertheless, on the negative side, one must concede, in turn, that this assertion, as it is here stated and as it is applied in the *Critique of Pure Reason*, is much exaggerated. It cannot possibly be maintained in its complete breadth when one makes any assumption of the existence of a real, self-subsisting actual external world independently of our representations. For if one admits the real existence of actual objects outside of us, and if one wants to take the external world to be something other than a mere world of ideas, it also follows necessarily that these external things must exist in a determinate manner, that is, in accord with certain rules and an order that is essentially grounded in the things themselves and their relations to one another and that understanding, therefore, cannot first have prescribed to them. This order would exist among them even if they were not represented by any spirit because without it no existence could be thought at all. Therefore, we cannot simply say that objects conform to our cognition or that understanding first prescribes its laws to nature. Admittedly, they suffer many changes through the human power of representation, are often transformed into completely different figures from the ones they actually had outside of our representation through our specific organization and the determinate rules of our sensation and thought. But they are not for that reason so passive and indifferent as to allow us to make anything out of them and be [348] subsumed under all the other notions of a representing being. Quite the contrary, the notions must often conform to the objects if they are to correspond with them. These notions are not such absolute masters over the objects that they would never have to fear insubordination from them. To be sure, the moving air, for example, must suffer manifold modifications in its passage through our organs of hearing before it becomes what we call a sound, however, it is nevertheless not up to us in each particular case whether we hear a deeper or a higher sound, a louder or a softer one; rather, that is solely a function of the slowness or speed of the vibration in the parts of air that hit our auditory nerves. Admittedly, light matter is transformed into very many different colors by our organs of sight, but it is not up to us whether we see an object as blue or red or green; rather, the colors of objects are determined by their properties and the manner in which light is refracted by them. By the same token, we would not be able to intuit things in space and time, unless there were properties and relations in them through which our determinate manner of intuition would be made possible. Nor would we be able to prescribe the general laws of nature to them if they were not themselves ordered according to those laws, or at least according to laws that correspond to the laws of our understanding. For otherwise they would either have to be an entirely raw undifferentiated mass that would take every form that one might like to give it, or, if we were to treat them according to the rules of our rational thought, we would very often clash with them and not see eye to eye with them. [349] The first is unthinkable, and the second is contradicted by our constant experience. One sees, accordingly, that the claim that objects follow our cognition cannot be maintained, at least not in the sense in which Mr. Kant understands it.

For these reasons, the Refutation of Idealism added on page 275 (which must be considered the only real addition to this new edition) also seems to be completely incompatible with the Kantian system. For the author seeks here to prove that the mere, albeit empirically determined, consciousness of our own existence presupposes the existence of the objects in space outside of us; but everyone who knows the Kantian system well, knows that according to it the actual existence of external objects is merely problematic. For according to the first rule of the *Critique*, we are not allowed to apply the concepts of understanding to things in themselves and can therefore not say whether they are possible, actual, or necessary. The proof itself runs as follows:

I am conscious of my own existence as determined in time. All time determination presupposes something persistent in perception. This persistent thing, however, cannot be an intuition in me. For all determining grounds of my existence which can be found in me are representations. As such, they themselves require something persistent distinct from them with respect to which their change, and consequently, my existence in the time, in which they change, can be determined. Hence, perception of this [350] persistent thing is possible only through a thing outside of me, and not through the mere representation of a thing outside of me. Consequently, the determination of my existence in time is possible only through the existence of actual things which

> I perceive outside of me. Now, consciousness in time is necessarily bound up with consciousness of the possibility of this time determination; hence, it is also necessarily bound up with the existence of things outside of me as condition of time determination. That is to say, the consciousness of my own existence is at the same time an immediate consciousness of the existence of other things outside of me.[23]

There is only one question I would like Mr. Kant to answer about this proof. Throughout this proof, are we to understand by "the existence of outer objects" an actual self-subsisting existence of things, or a merely logical, apparent existence, in the sense that for the purposes of proper thought and in order to be able to have inner appearances, we have to have outer appearances as well? One cannot be too careful to avoid such equivocal expressions in Kant's writings. If the first alternative is true, then it is not only the case that the entire theory of space and time, which Mr. Kant has set up, is null and void, but he himself also violates the main critical law. For according to this Refutation of Idealism, the concept of time has an objective foundation in actual external things, consciousness of our own existence in time is possible only through the intuition of external things, and the idea of persistence can be created in us only through actually existing external objects. However, how [351] does this accord with Kant's Transcendental Aesthetic where it is shown extensively and with many reasons that the concept of time is a merely subjective form of sensibility, that it is not grounded in the properties of things in themselves and cannot be abstracted from them? Here it is claimed that there must be actual external things because we could not otherwise have a consciousness of persistence in us, there it is assumed that all our concepts of change in time, of alteration, and hence also of persistence are only subjective and arise from the essential constitution of human representative power. That requires that we intuit everything in terms of time determinations without being in the least justified for that reason to consider time to be something that belongs to things in themselves or corresponds to them. Moreover, had Mr. Kant completely forgotten, when he wrote this, that he designates reason's consciousness of persistence in ourselves, of our own individual existence as empty semblance? If it is semblance, if our own person does not have certainty, then the idea of persistence in external objects will be all the more so, given that we can, after all, only have a mediate experience of them. This contradiction is quite striking in my estimation and cannot emerge from a mere misunderstanding. But perhaps only the logical existence of things, an existence in appearance, is at issue here. But in that case the entire Refutation of Idealism is a mere word play, and is an affirmation [352] rather than a refutation of idealism. Mr. Kant adds in the note to this proof:

> One can see from this that the game that idealism played has been turned back on itself with greater justice. Idealism assumed that the only immediate experience is inner experience and that one can only infer outer things from it, but, as always when one proceeds from given effects to determinate causes, one cannot make this assumption dependably, because the cause of the representations that we ascribe, perhaps wrongly, to outer things, can also lie in ourselves. But here it is proven that outer experience is really immediate, and that inner experience, not, admittedly, the consciousness of our own existence but its determination in time, is possible only by means of it [outer experience].[24]

However, I do not understand how he can claim this, given that in the remainder of his system he derives the possibility of experience only from the subjective forms of our thought and the laws in accord with which it operates. Human understanding first creates nature for itself, to use Mr. Kant's own expression, it produces experience for itself by applying its concepts and rules to objects. And how then can I prove anything about the actual existence of objects from the constitution of outer experience, given that the entire manner in which we represent these objects to ourselves and in which we experience them, is not grounded in the things themselves but in the original constitution of our spirit? How little does the [353] proposition assumed here, that it is outer experience that is really immediate and that first makes inner experience possible, really agree with these assertions, which I could document through many passages in the *Critique*? It [outer experience] is after all only our own self-created product, and how can we infer anything from this about the objective reality of outer things? Does Mr. Kant not know a great deal more of outer things than he could know of them if he wanted to remain consistent and true to his system? Indeed, he does continue:

> ... all the employment of our cognitive power in experience in the determination of time, is also entirely in accord with this [proof]. Besides the fact that all time determination can only be undertaken through reference to the change of external relations (motion) relative to what persists in space, for instance, the movement of the sun relative to the objects on the earth, we do not even have anything persistent that could function as ground for the concept of substance as intuition other than matter.

But that is surely inconsistent. For according to the Kantian theory of space and time, all time determination is only subjective, and all change in outer relations springs only from the determinate form of our sensibility which makes the representation of variability in intuited things necessary. But it does not at all follow from this that things in themselves may actually change, nor that there is any real persistence in them. One would almost believe that Mr. Kant himself begins to realize the untenability of his theory, which clearly shows many weak aspects. In spite of this, however, in this edition as well, it, like everything else, has remained completely unchanged, apart from some elucidations. [354] The author has not found it necessary to change anything in the propositions themselves, or in the manner of proof. Admittedly, in a few passages, clarity has been improved through abbreviations or additions, and the survey has been made easier through more frequent headings. But essentially this edition has remained completely identical with the first.

Friedrich Gottlob Born

Investigation into the First Grounds of the Doctrine of the Senses

§36

ON IDEALISM

The grounds on which the Kantian theory of sensibility is based are of such tangible force, such illuminating clarity and truth, that they should demand acceptance and approval from everyone who is not blinded by obsolete prejudices. For this reason, no one has yet been found who could mount a direct attack capable of disarming and destroying these grounds. Much has certainly been said and written against them, but nothing has been presented that really gets to the point. For the most part, the premises have been accepted, or at least left uncontested, but the conclusion has been disputed, even though it follows from the premises by necessary inference. Kant's critics have accepted‡‡ that sensibility does not conform to objects, but that objects conform to sensibility, but they have refused to allow themselves to be convinced that the representation of a body in [118] intuition can contain nothing that would have to belong to an object in itself. They have conceded that we are not beings who can penetrate the inner nature of things,[§§] but have not been able to see that raindrops as well as the space in which they fall are mere modifications of our sensibility, rather than things in themselves. They have admitted** that phenomena and *ontos onta* are altogether distinct things, that appearances have their ground merely in the manner of representation, and that the things in themselves that lie at their ground have a completely independent existence from appearances, but have found it shocking that all bodies along with the space in which they are, are to be considered nothing but mere representations in us, things that do not exist anywhere but in our representations.[##] It is as if someone were to take

‡‡ Feder, *Ueber Raum und Caussalität*, p. 74.

§§ ibid., pp. 94, 83.

** ibid., p. 81.

ibid., p. 63.

water to be water, wet fluid, but yet not be able to accept that for this reason it gets us wet. Kant has been accused of **idealism**. – But how could this accusation be asserted with the least semblance of truth? The idealist says: there are no beings other than thinking beings. Kant, by [119] contrast, says: things are given to us as objects of our senses existing outside of us. The idealist says: there are no sensible objects outside of our representation, and the things we believe to perceive in intuition are by no means effects that we obtain from things outside of us, they are mere representations and no external object corresponds to them. Kant, by contrast, claims: actual objects outside of us do exist, but their effects are neither absolute nor essential effects that modify all types of sensibility equally. They are not effects that allow us to cognize things as they exist in themselves and independently of our representation; rather, they are relative effects that correspond to the specific nature of our sensibility. As such they can only arouse representations of the manner in which we are affected by things. Because the constitution of our sensibility is entirely contingent and arbitrary, and could be otherwise than it actually is, our representations of the objects of sense would be entirely different if our sensibility and representative capacity had obtained a different constitution. The idealist says: there is no world of sense at all, rather, everything is semblance and deception. Kant, by contrast, says: the world of the senses is surely something actual; nothing is for us more real than that world, and everything that we believe to find **outside** of it [120] is mere **illusion**. The objects and the truth in the world of the senses are determined, for us, according to necessary laws. It must be our first task to investigate these rules and to come to know them more and more. Nor do the senses ever deceive us, for they do not judge, and hence they do not err. Cognition arises solely through the judging **understanding**. So cognition always contains truth insofar as the understanding remains faithful to the laws prescribed to it. And judgments of experience are always certain when perceptions are combined according to logical laws and are related merely to our sensible world. By contrast, nothing in empirical cognition could be shown a priori to be certain unless we think the sensible objects as determined through pure intuition a priori. Appearances and the sensible world are entirely innocent of **illusion**, that is, of tempting us into the error of empirical realism, viz. that the sensible world exists outside of our representation just as our intuition presents it. . . . [141]

§41
REPLY TO SOME QUESTIONS PRESENTED BY A REVIEWER IN THE *ALLGEMEINE DEUTSCHE BIBLIOTHEK*

I had just completed this investigation, when I received the second part of the eighty-first volume of the *Allgemeine deutsche Bibliothek*. On pages 343–54 I found a review of the second edition of Kant's *Critique of Pure Reason*.

The learned author of this evaluation, whom I do not know, thinks the assertion that objects conform to our cognition too extreme and believes that it cannot possibly be maintained in its complete breadth when one assumes the real, self-subsistent existence of an actual external world independently of our representation. For if this real existence of actual objects outside of us is conceded, it follows necessarily (according to the author) that these outer objects must exist in a determinate manner or according to certain rules and an order that is essentially grounded in the things themselves and their relations to one another, and that understanding, therefore, cannot first have prescribed to them. This order would exist among them even if they [142] were not represented by any spirit, because without it one cannot think an existence at all. One cannot simply say, therefore, that objects conform to our cognition. – Second, the Refutation of Idealism that has been added in the new edition of the *Critique of Pure Reason* on page 275 does not seem to him to fit into the Kantian system at all. For (the author claims) Kant there attempts to prove that the mere, albeit empirically determined consciousness of our own existence presupposes the existence of objects in space, and yet the existence of outer things is merely problematic in his system. – Here he submits the following question to Mr. Kant: ["]Throughout this proof, are we to understand by the existence of outer objects an actual, self-subsistent existence of things, or a merely logical, apparent existence? [. . .] If the first alternative is true, then it is not only the case that the entire theory of space and time is null and void, but also the main critical law["] that in order for us to order our thought and have inner appearances, we must also have outer appearances. ["]For according to this Refutation of Idealism, the concept of time does have an objective foundation in actual external things, the consciousness of our own existence in time is possible only through the intuition of external things, and the idea of persistence could be created in us only through actually existing external objects.["] [143] But this is said to contradict the Kantian concept of time as a merely subjective form of sensibility. – But if the issue is one of a logical existence of things, of an existence in appearance, then the entire Refutation of Idealism is said to be a mere word play and serves as an affirmation rather than as a refutation of idealism. This is what the Berlin reviewer states.

Because this insightful scholar wishes to obtain a solution to these difficulties from Mr. Kant, but he is too occupied with frequent official duties and literary work and will scarcely have sufficient time to undertake this task himself, I consider it my duty to take his place and to make an attempt to answer these doubts.

Let us grant that actual things exist outside of us – for given that we sense their effects, that cannot be doubted; let us grant that these external things are altogether independent of our representation and exist in a determinate manner and in certain original relations to one another that our understanding cannot prescribe to them. In this respect, they are absolute beings. However, they are not given to us as such, that is, as things in themselves, and in this respect they cannot at all conform to our cognition, for [144] we have no cognition of them. Rather, as transcendental objects they are for us = x. We cognize only their effects on our sensibility. But who can demonstrate that these effects on us, these modifications of our sensibility, are **absolute** effects of things in themselves that do in fact belong to the things independently of our representation in the manner in which we supply them to the things in appearance, and that each thinking being would have to cognize in the same way in which we represent them? No, these effects are only relative, that is, they accord with the constitution and receptivity of our sensible and cognitive powers. This organization of our sensibility, this constitution of our cognitive capacity is not necessary, but is a contingent and arbitrary disposition, as I have shown earlier (§1–3, 5–8).[25] In accord with the specific or individual constitution of our organs, the impressions of sensible objects on them occur in this or that way, and our representations of these impressions are determined in this or that manner. So how we are affected by sensible objects, and how we represent these modifications of our sensibility does not in the least depend on our will. Nor has **Kant** ever claimed this. Rather, our sensibility cannot be otherwise affected by external objects than according to the specific constitution of the sense [145] organs and the receptivity of our cognitive capacity that was originally bestowed on it by the highest wisdom. This, and not more, is what **Kant** wants to say when he asserts that things conform to our cognition. We are not able to represent sensible objects otherwise than in space and time. But does it follow from this that transcendental objects themselves must have properties and relations through which we are required to intuit appearances in space and time? Not at all. The receptivity of our cognitive capacities does not permit us to do anything but represent appearances only under these forms. And it is only in this respect that we say that our cognition prescribes universal laws of nature to the sensible world. Nor does it follow from this that the transcendental objects that lie at the ground of appearances are a raw undifferentiated mass that takes whatever form one wants to give to it. For I have only just shown that the cognition of the objects as appearances does not depend at all on our will, rather, we must be content with what the senses can report of them, and, because our sensibility is not all able to deliver it, we do not know the absolute constitution of things. Our consistent experience confirms, rather, that space and time are the two laws of [146] human sensibility in accord with which all appearances must be ordered and intuited.

From this it also follows that the Refutation of Idealism that has been added in the new edition of the *Critique of Pure Reason* fits very well into the Kantian system. For when **Kant** says that the mere, albeit empirically determined consciousness of our own existence presupposes the existence of **objects in space** outside of us, then this philosopher does not mean to say, as everyone who is familiar with this system must know, that what is presupposed is the existence of transcendental objects **outside of us** (that is, outside of our representation) insofar as they exist **in space**. He wants to say, rather, that there is something at the ground of the objects that we perceive **in space**, that is, of appearances, and that what is at their ground actually exists **outside of us**, that is, not merely in our representation. This is already very clear from the wording. For it does not say: the existence of objects **outside of us in space** [das Daseyn der Gegenstände ***außer uns im Raume***], but rather, the existence of objects **in space outside of us** [das Daseyn der Gegenstände ***im Raume außer uns***]. The "**outside of**" modifies **existence**, and the "**in space**" modifies **object**. If I exchange these adjectives, then this does create a significant difference by which understanding is completely misdirected. As is his habit, [147] here as everywhere Kant expresses himself with great precision and is entirely innocent of the many equivocal expressions the Berlin reviewer believes to find in his system – which one can supposedly not be too careful to avoid. **No**, as **Pope** says, Homer does not slumber, we are the ones who dream.

However, if the objects that we perceive in space, that is, appearances, do have something at their ground that actually exists outside of us, that is, outside of our representation, does it follow from this that the things in themselves that lie at the ground of appearances, or the transcendental objects, must also be in space, or, as the reviewer puts matters, that the representation of time and space must have an objective foundation in actual external things? Has Kant not rather demonstrated the opposite? Has he not proven that space and time are neither something that exists independently, nor an accident or other determination of the things themselves, nor yet a concept drawn from them or from general concepts, nor anything else that could in some way be grounded in the transcendental objects? And has he not shown all of this to be the case through reasons that no one has yet been able to raise a significant and pertinent objection to? . . . Kant's theory of space and time remains unshaken. Consequently, all the other inconsistencies that the learned reviewer wants to infer from this proof concerning idealism also disappear on their own. . . . [26]

On the basis of all of this, it is clear, accordingly, that, like every other refutation that has thus far appeared against Kant, these ostensible objections only serve to give greater support to the claim that "there is no danger here of being refuted, the danger is not to be understood." **Kant** did not write this claim down precipitately, as the Berlin reviewer precipitately enough declares. He said it on the basis of quite sufficient reflection. He built and perfected this system over more than 20 years, and that has entirely secured him from the danger of being refuted, no matter how special the insight. Though many have tried, has there so far been anyone who has been able to remove the support of the Kantian system? How many have written against **Kant**? And who has really managed to actually touch these supports? Who has been able to damage them? Any number of misinterpretations, confusions, [149] hated inconsistencies have appeared, but nothing that actually attacks the matter itself. Such examinations cannot be pleasant for any author, and Kant's *Critique* cannot gain anything through such absurdities. If you sages cannot shake the foundations of this system, if you cannot refute it through direct reasons, you act very inconsistently when, in spite of this, you continue to doubt the truth and irrefutability of the principles that you cannot refute, even if other reviewers would not take this amiss. Does it honor a philosopher to judge, doubt, declare war on, and proclaim a system to be inconsistent, if he has been unable, in spite of having had seven long years of his life, to understand this system, and familiarize himself with it from the different parts and relations on up to a precise survey of the whole? What is one to say about the reviewer who after this considerable time says, with almost singular confidence, that **Kant** assumes that transcendental [150] objects **exist in space** where everyone who is closely familiar with the Kantian system knows that according to it the **actual existence of outer things** is merely **problematic**? Who has scales on his eyes? **Kant** and his school? Or a reviewer who has been so little able to grasp the terminology of the Königsberg philosopher or even to determine what he means on the basis of grammatical rules? Every concept that does not contain a contradiction and that, as a limit of given concepts is connected with other cognitions, but the **objective reality** of which cannot be in any way known, Kant identifies as **problematic**, an entirely appropriate term. Because the absolute beings, the transcendental beings that lie at the ground of appearances, are not given in their **objective reality**, and, accordingly, cannot be cognized by us **as they are in themselves**, they must also be **problematic concepts**. Can a contradiction be found here? Can we assert that a being whose existence we must assume as ground of appearance, but that is for us **in itself** [151] =x, is not a problem for us, that is, that we comprehend its objective existence and constitution quite independently of this? What could be more contradictory, what more absurd and meaningless?

When **Kant** asserts that actual outer things must exist because we could not otherwise have the consciousness of persistence in us, then this assertion in no way contradicts the claim that all our concepts of change in time, of alteration, and hence also of persistence are merely subjective and arise from the human representative power, which necessitates that we must intuit everything as determined by time – without, however, being allowed to assume that time is something that belongs to things in themselves. – For persistence, that is, existence at all times without creation and destruction, is one way in which we represent the existence of appearances. It is the condition under which something can be subsumed under the concept of substance in the sensible world: it cannot be demonstrated from the concept of substance as a thing in itself, but can only be demonstrated for the purposes of [152] experience, as has been clearly shown on pages 224–32 of the *Critique of Pure Reason*. Nor does it contradict what **Kant** asserts elsewhere, that the consciousness of persistence in ourselves, our own personality, is an empty semblance. For the proposition that the soul is conscious of always being the same substance; consequently, a person already presupposes its objective persistence. This objective persistence, however, is indemonstrable, for the reason indicated. Who does not understand at this point that a judge of a system who knows it so little cannot accuse **Kant** and his school of arrogance just because they depend solely on the evidence of their claims and the apodeictic certainty of the available proofs and rightly respond to their opponents' attacks with derision without bringing this complaint up against himself. If **Kant** is incorrect, then one should attack his error at its root. One must show with clearly indicated reasons and a priori that the principles on which the entire philosophy of the critical system rests are wrong. If one can destroy a single one of the principles on which it rests, [153] then one has also destroyed the whole edifice. **Kant** has either been correct in nothing, or in everything. But if one cannot deny his premises, then what holds one to particular, misunderstood, confused assertions? It is foolishness to attempt to stem a current when one cannot plug up its source. It is similarly foolishness to question immediate inferences, if one cannot do away with their principles, the premises from which they follow necessarily.

Section IV

The Categories

C. G. Selle, "Attempt at a Proof That There Are No Pure Concepts of Reason That Are Independent of Experience," *Berlinische Monatsschrift* (1784): 565–75. **193**
Reprinted in Hausius, *Materialien*, vol.1, 98–106

Dietrich Tiedemann, "Continuation of the Examination of Professor Kant's Thoughts About the Nature of Metaphysics – Against the Analytic," *Hessische Beyträge zur Gelehrsamkeit und Kunst* 1 (1785), 233–48. **199**
Reprinted in Hausius, *Materialien*, vol. 2, 77–92 [The translation and pagination are based on this reprint edition.]

[Johann Schultz], Jena, Cröker: "*Institutiones Logicae et Metaphysicae* by Jo. Aug. Henr. Ulrich 1785, gr. 8, 426 and 153 pages without preface and index," *ALZ* (13 December 1785): 297–9. **210**
Reprinted in Landau, *Rezensionen*, 243–48

Gottlob August Tittel, *On Kantian Forms of Thought or Categories* (Frankfurt am Main: Gebhard, 1787), 3–41, 103–111. **215**

C. G. Selle

Attempt at a Proof That There Are No Pure Concepts of Reason That Are Independent of Experience

In the minds of many people, metaphysics is to everyday affairs just what chess is to social gatherings: a pastime for reflective minds. Now, I certainly do not want to presume to claim that the majority of metaphysical speculations from Chaldean times to the present are anything more. Nevertheless, it seems to me, it follows also from the nature of metaphysics that what has just been said does not exhaustively present its nature. Quite the contrary, we must attribute our true happiness to its genuine practice, and it is properly speaking through metaphysics and [566] nothing else that we can effect the greatest improvement of our powers. Without metaphysics, our most sacred concepts are dubious, and only through it can we become acquainted with and learn to appreciate our true destiny. To be sure, it often fails to attain this noble purpose. It does so because there is no mathematical evidence for intrinsically philosophical truths, and nothing affords as much opportunity for misunderstanding and mistaken application as what has only physical certainty, and hence, only ever probability, even if it does have the highest degree thereof. – In the meantime, this difficulty would have much less negative influence if people had not persistently, by their reliance on certain principles, smothered the precise sense requisite for those probabilities that have the closest relation to authentic truth.

I count among these principles primarily the proposition that there are **certain concepts of reason that are independent of all experience**. People did not want to be content with probabilities, but found them unworthy of genuine philosophy. And so they turned to universal and necessary principles, reasoned on their basis, and thus created a system of – words.

There are only two sources of our cognitive capacity: **sensibility** and **reason**. **Sensibility** is the capacity to have sensations [567] and representations. **Reason** is the capacity to form concepts and judgments.

Through **sensibility**, we are conscious only of the existence of things. Through **reason**, we cognize their relation to each other. We cognize this relation in two ways. Either the predicate belongs to the subject concept, so that one is already contained in the other, which needs only to be analyzed in order [for the relation] to be cognized as true. In this case our cognition is called an **analytic judgment**. Alternatively, the concepts of a judgment are independent of one other, and another type of proof is required [to determine] their natural connection. Such a cognition is called a **synthetic judgment**.

Analytic judgments always consist of identical concepts. When we say that all bodies are extended, then we say nothing other than: all extended beings are extended. They are universal and necessary also because it would be contradictory if extended beings could also be unextended.

The truth of analytic judgments is in all cases grounded only on the cognition of the laws of our power of thought. So when one asks about the sources of analytic cognition, then one must first investigate the origin of the concepts of the laws of our power of thought, and here one must consider whether we take this cognition of the [568] truth of the laws of our power of thought from reason or from experience.

Here many philosophers appeal to inner conviction. But this particular subjective conviction cannot possibly vouch for universal objective truth. Do not many human beings take errors to be truths with the greatest conviction? What particular individual is justified in presenting his feeling as the correct one, as belonging to the consciousness of real truth, only on the basis of his feeling? Is not many an insane person convinced, with the greatest certainty, that he lives in a palace, in which he is the undisputed authority, in spite of all the humiliations which he suffers? We know that the fabric that is colored in a certain way, that we call scarlet, causes in our instrument of sight the sensation of the color red. We also know that it is the nature of our instrument of sight to see scarlet as red and not differently. If there are human beings in whom this fabric causes the sensation of the color yellow, then we claim that these human beings are ill, that they have a corrupt organ. In just the same way we say of the insane person that his inner sense is corrupt, that he does not judge according to the natural laws of the power of thought. But what gives us the right to consider ourselves to be healthy, and them to be ill, to take the laws in accord with which we judge to be natural, and the laws according [569] to which they judge to be unnatural, to cognize our judgments as true, their judgments as false?

There can be only two reasons for this. Either we infer their correctness and natural constitution from the widespread generality of the laws according to which we judge, and the incorrectness and unnaturalness of the laws of those who think and see differently from their rarity, or we must demonstrate, on the basis of the nature of the soul and our instrument of sight, that a healthy soul and a healthy eye could not possibly think and see differently, that it would be contrary to nature if a healthy soul and eye could think and see differently.

And this is a proof that no mortal human being on earth can provide. Whatever he could say about this matter would surely only be empty foolishness.

Therefore, nothing remains but experience. It teaches us that the great majority of human beings think and see according to certain laws, and that only a very small portion deviates from this. On the basis of this, we infer the legitimacy and truth of these laws of thought and use them to demonstrate the truth of analytic judgments. Induction, accordingly, is and remains the only guarantee of the truth of the laws of our power of thought, just as experience is the only source for their [570] cognition. But one must take care here not to confuse concepts. Experience cannot make a proposition universal and necessary, but it can acquaint us with a universal and necessary proposition. If these universal and necessary propositions concern objects outside of us, then considered for us and subjectively, they can never become universal and necessary, or rather, we can never cognize their universality and necessity. But if the laws of thought themselves constitute the proposition, then nothing is more certain and natural than that we cognize them as universal and necessary along with the experiential cognition they afford. It is impossible for us to think according to laws other than those that we cognize in ourselves through experience. But that is not a proof that mere reason has arrived at this knowledge independently of experience.

The objective truth of the laws of thought, accordingly, can only be taken from experience and can only be demonstrated through it. In and for itself subjective conviction proves nothing because there is no sign anywhere on the basis of which one could judge with certainty whether that of which this or that person thinks himself convinced is actually objectively true. Only the richest induction, the experience human beings have had through so many centuries, [571] can deliver the proofs of the legitimacy of the laws of thought.

Let me turn now to synthetic judgments. In these judgments, the relation of concepts cannot be cognized on the basis of the concepts themselves, rather, we require other proofs that cannot be developed from the concepts themselves that the judgment contains.

In the case of particular propositions, it is experience that delivers the proof of a synthetic judgment. And because experience can never be universal, because it can never capture objects completely, it follows also that those synthetic propositions, that are not about our own laws of thought, can never be cognized as universal and necessary on the basis of experience. Experience teaches us only that whenever it has appeared to us the subject has always been combined with the predicate. Experience cannot teach us that and whether it belongs to the subject necessarily. We must ask, therefore: are there synthetic judgments that we cognize as universal and necessary? If there are such judgments, then this synthesis cannot happen through experience, and there must be a synthesis of pure reason, and hence pure concepts of reason. If such judgments do not exist, then there also are no pure concepts of reason, and a concept cannot have an origin except experience. [572]

Now, some philosophers assert that there really are synthetic judgments the truth of which we cognize as universal and necessary. Among these, they count the **principle of sufficient reason**. The designation of this proposition as purely synthetic has long seemed to me to be suspicious and I believed, therefore, that it is of mixed nature, that what is actually synthesized in it is given by experience only, and what makes it a universal and necessary proposition is analysis. After a great deal of reflection with some of our best minds, I found my proofs of this claim very difficult, and I began, therefore, to attempt to view it as analytic – and behold! I believe I have found that the principle of sufficient reason is a pure analytic proposition. For our cognition of its universal and necessary truth, we require only the principle of noncontradiction.

The most difficult aspect in the examination of this proposition is the determination of what we call the sufficient reason. Do we think of it as something that is self-subsistent and independent of that which it grounds? In that case, the principle would read: everything has its sufficient reason outside of itself. And that can be demonstrated neither from the principle of noncontradiction nor from experience. If we take sufficient reason to be something that inheres in what it grounds and belongs to its essence, then [573] this would imply that all things have their sufficient reason in themselves, and this contradicts experience. Nor do we perceive the necessity of this. Nothing remains, therefore, but a third case, namely that what we call sufficient reason belongs to the form of our thought and inheres in the **concept** of what is grounded. The concept of sufficient reason, therefore, must already be contained in the concept of everything. Otherwise, the principle is not universal and necessary, and there could be things without sufficient reason.

In other words, the principle reads as follows: nothing can exist without being sufficiently grounded. And that is the same as: that which belongs to the existence of a thing must also exist. Or, in short, the thing which exists must exist. Now, the existence of a thing requires either only the thing itself, in which case we call it independent, unchangeable, infinite, necessary, and grounded in itself, or something external is required for the existence of a thing. In that case, the thing is finite and contingent and has its sufficient reason outside of itself. This should make very clear and obvious, I think, that the principle of sufficient reason is not a synthetic proposition. It also follows immediately that propositions, such as for example, that an independent, unchangeable, infinite, [574] necessary thing has its sufficient reason in itself, are neither more nor less than analytic propositions. I will remain satisfied that there are no universal and necessary synthetic propositions until I have been convinced of the opposite.

As fruitless as this discussion may appear to be, it is nevertheless certain that this more precise analysis is of the greatest importance. If matters are as I have tried to demonstrate, it would show at the same time that there is no other philosophy of pure reason than analysis of identical propositions, and that doing philosophy on the basis of such propositions may contribute to the intelligibility of just these propositions, but that the acquisition of other items of knowledge that do not lie in the propositions themselves is a fruitless and useless enterprise. The closer analysis would lead philosophers to a correct standpoint, and it would teach them that even the most clever and sophistical considerations of such propositions are nothing but collections of identical words, and that experience is the only route that leads to the cognition of truth.

When, apart from this, it cannot be the case that everything in our knowledge is an immediate result of experience, and there certainly are synthetic propositions, the physical certainty of which is not denied by anyone, even though they go beyond our immediate experience, then we must ask: what in our knowledge is experience, what reasoning? According to my firm conviction, the latter is nothing but the application of the experience of causal connections. Experience delivers the proposition that same causes have same [575] effects, and similar causes have appropriately similar effects. All inferences that go from what has been experienced to what has not been experienced are grounded on the proper application of these propositions, as is, consequently, our entire reasoning.

Incidentally, as correct as propositions of experience may be, they can never be universal and necessary for us. All reasoning that employs synthetic concepts, therefore, is not capable of mathematical certainty, but only of physical certainty. And even if propositions of this kind were to have their perfect objective correctness, we cannot ever attain complete certainty of them. A subjective gap remains, and this is one that we can perhaps close only in the next life.

Dietrich Tiedemann

Continuation of the Examination of Professor Kant's Thoughts About the Nature of Metaphysics – Against the Analytic

Like the traveller who thinks a familiar region unknown when he is led into it from a new side, and cannot find his way until he has compared the new appearance with the old one, so the philosopher, who finds otherwise known concepts foreign when they are placed in new arrangements, must first relate these connections back to his previously familiar manner of thought. Similarly, when, having investigated the concepts of **space** and **time**, Mr. **Kant** proceeds to the higher concepts of understanding: **cause** and **effect**, **substance** and **accident**, and other related ones, he considers them from such a peculiar perspective, in a language so removed from its ordinary usage, that it is difficult to discover his meaning. Should I not have always understood him correctly, therefore, I will be the more readily excused because others have been similarly misdirected as well, and for the same reason. Furthermore, tracing these concepts back to the familiar ones is not among the easiest tasks. He begins with the claim that we have a priori principles concerning the **causal relation**, concerning **substance** and **accidents**, and so on. Because these cannot be **analytically** inferred from the concepts themselves, he concludes that insofar as they are laws of **our** power of thought, they have their seat only in **our** understanding and that, accordingly, their application [78] to objects that we cannot experience is impossible. It will be best to first examine the proof of the main proposition and then the inference.

Kant states that the universal laws of nature – for example, everything that happens has a cause; all substances stand in thoroughgoing community; substance persists, only the accidents change, and so on – cannot be cognized a priori because they are not **analytic**. They do not determine what is contained in the concept, but what is added to the thing itself in its existence apart from the concept. Our understanding and the conditions under which alone it can connect the determinations of things in their existence, does not prescribe any rule to the things themselves; they do not conform to our understanding, rather, understanding must conform to them. These universal natural laws also are not a posteriori, for experience does not teach that something must necessarily be in this way and not otherwise (*Prol.*, p. 71 etc).[1]

The second element of the dilemma is an irrevocable fact, but is the first? Is the principle of a causal connection, to consider just this one, in fact **synthetic**? It admittedly seems to be, for in order to say of a thing that it has a cause one does have to go outside its concept to that of another thing, one has to bring two things together that are separate in themselves, one of which is not a part of the other either in **intuition** or **conceptually**. **Hume** already presented matters in this way. And because the attempts to demonstrate the principles of sufficient reason and sufficient cause on the basis of the principle of contradiction have so far failed, it seems presumptuous, according to the almost unanimous judgment of insightful philosophers, to so much as doubt that it belongs among the **synthetic** [principles]. [79]

Nevertheless, I dare to doubt [it] and to present my reasons to the experts, hoping at least to obtain the acknowledgment that my doubts are not without cause. Propositions expressing relations bring together two things that are otherwise separate, and not connected as parts as far as their concepts are concerned. Such propositions can be cognized a priori as soon as the extremes are given. Hence, not all propositions in which concepts are conjoined without an analysis through which one is found in the other are **synthetic**. Or else, should they absolutely have to be called **synthetic**, it is not the case that no **synthetic** propositions can be cognized a priori. At least we cannot automatically infer this from the underlying concept of a **synthetic** proposition, and, consequently, the first proof[2] cannot be irrefutable. Further, the principle of sufficient reason, or that of sufficient cause, expresses a relation; hence, it is surely obvious that more is required for the conclusion than is already contained in the premises. Should it be further observed that this principle along with its supplements has not yet been demonstrated in an a priori fashion that would indeed establish a favorable prejudice, but not a strong proof, and a strong proof is surely required in a matter of this significance. Should the lack of a satisfactory proof not perhaps be supposed a function of the fact that no one has yet sought it in the right manner? At least nobody has yet shown it to be impossible, for in view of what has just been shown, what **Hume** and **Kant** have said in this regard is not sufficient.

Because it is still possible to attempt it, I will do so here. To be sure, this material will be somewhat dry, given that everything that concerns our highest and most abstract concepts cannot be other than dry. However, readers, who consider that [80] the most important investigations about the reality and certainty of our knowledge and, consequently, also the satisfaction of our reason about a future state ultimately follow from such dry subtleties, will not be deterred by this. In order to avoid all unnecessary rambling, I will limit myself to the principle of sufficient reason, from which that of sufficient cause can be easily derived, even though they are different. Further, I will not consider whether everything does or must without exception have a sufficient reason but only try to demonstrate that everything that is contingent has a sufficient reason.

That is contingent that can be otherwise than it is, that is, the essence or concept of which is not contradicted when it is differently constituted, when it has other predicates than it does have. A ground is that thing from which a certain constitution follows in another thing, from which that constitution can be comprehended or derived, with which it is posited.

It does not contradict the concept or essence of a contingent thing to have different predicates than it has. However, one contradiction is not greater than the other; contradiction is something unchangeable and does not take on variable quantities. Hence the contingent thing, considered in itself, can be "a" just as easily as it can be "not-a", the wax can be square as well as not-square, one is as possible for it as the other. Even when I specify that the contingent [thing] is now "a", I can specify just as well that it is now "not-a"; I can as easily say of the wax that it is now square as I can say it is now not square.

It is clear, furthermore, that when two predicates belong to a thing independently, they must also be attributed to it simultaneously, since, where the single parts are, their aggregate or sum is also. If one can say [81] Socrates is wise and Socrates is poor, it is also permitted to say that Socrates is poor and wise. So if we can posit of the contingent [thing] that it is "a" and that it is "not-a", then it must also be possible to say it is "a" and "not-a"; if the essence of wax permits us to posit it is square and it is not-square, it must also be possible to say of it that it is square and not-square.

However, something cannot be "a" and "not-a" at the same time; hence, there must be something that determines, from which it follows, that the contingent [thing] is "a" but not "not-a"; that is, when the wax is square there must be **a reason** why it is [not] not-square.

Second, it is no more contradictory for the contingent [thing] to be "a" than "not-a". If I posit it is "a", I can posit with equal justification that it is "not-a". If there is nothing that makes it more "a" than "not-a", then it must either be "a" and "not-a" simultaneously or neither "a" nor "not-a". Only the following three cases are possible: that it is either "a" or "not-a", or "a" and "not-a" simultaneously, or neither. The first case cannot be assumed because, as soon as one wants to posit "a", "not-a" appears as a possibility that can be posited with equal right. The other two cases are likewise impossible; hence, the only possibility that remains is that when "a" is posited, there must be some reason why it is more "a" than "not-a". That is, there must be a sufficient reason for what is contingent.

Third, when the contingent [thing] is given a predicate that it did not have before, it is determined. The predicate or the characteristic is the determination. Apart from this, however, there is either something else by virtue of which it obtains the determination, with or by virtue of which this determination is posited of it, or no such thing is given. In the latter case, either Nothing gives it the determination or the contingent [thing] is not determined at all. The first alternative, that [82] Nothing affords the determination, is absurd because Nothing cannot have positive predicates. The second alternative contradicts the first assumption, namely, that it is determined. The proposition that the contingent [thing] that is now determined has not been determined by anything can only have these two senses, namely, that it is not determined at all or that Nothing affords its determination. Both are absurd; hence, it remains that something affords its determination, that is, that it has a sufficient determining reason.

This[3] is the proof for Mr. **Kant's** main proposition, and after its refutation one could believe the matter to be settled. However, Mr. **Kant** supports these inferences with many reasons that are so seemingly obvious and clever that they gain an air of truth quite independent of proof, and require special investigation. A disputant who is armed with all possible weapons and who, in addition to natural strength, has experience in their usage does not fall with the first stroke. The most natural inference, springing from two lines of proof, is: "there are no a priori principles whatsoever that apply to objects of experience." However, given that the general agreement of the philosophical world and the particular evidence for propositions like that of sufficient reason, contradicts this claim too clearly, Mr. **Kant** takes another path. He concedes that such principles do exist but denies that they have objective validity and leaves them no status other than to be laws of **our** understanding. Of course, one could immediately respond that if they were also laws of **every** understanding, would they then not have more than subjective validity with respect to **our** understanding? Concepts and principles of understanding, whether they are drawn from experience [83] or intuition, or formed prior to all experience, as we represent the concept of the highest being, do always apply to something that can be intuited or experienced. So what cannot be thought by any understanding, also cannot be outside any thinking being, that is, it cannot be at all. Insofar, then, as principles of understanding are laws of every thinking power, they have objective validity along with subjective validity. In order to avoid this, Mr. **Kant** claims that we do not know an intuition other than our own. Nor do we know whether there is another intuition; hence, we do not know if our laws of understanding extend farther than to ourselves (*Critique*, p. 277 ff).

And yet we do know that there are different kinds of intuition in us, that is, we know that it is one thing to see an object, another to feel it, and yet another to sense it internally. We can draw a universal concept from this and in this way arrive at the concept of intuition in general. Furthermore, we know the limitations and weaknesses of our understanding and can derive from this the concepts of higher powers of understanding and thus arrive at a universal concept. In this way, we can similarly obtain the insight that no understanding can affirm or deny something without sufficient reason. This is the case because we comprehend clearly that judgment always takes its cue from given concepts, and so, in those cases where there is nothing in the given concepts that requires affirmation or denial, neither affirmation or denial follow. If one wanted to say that it is nevertheless in our power to make judgments and form propositions independently of concepts, or to deny what better insight says must be affirmed, I would reply that such a judgment would not be the work of understanding but that it would instead be an arbitrary synthesis of words or else intentional pretence, both of which are detrimental to the essential laws of understanding. [84] Suffice it to say that where understanding proceeds as understanding without hindrance according to its own nature, there it must conform to the insight of the representations it is given and the principle of sufficient reason must be a law of every understanding. This is the case because an understanding that determines the relation of representations without finding the reason for this in the representations themselves is not an understanding at all. Suppose, then, that the principle of sufficient reason, along with other similar ones, is only a subjective law of thought but also a universal law of every understanding. If that were so, it would nevertheless have objective validity.

But this explanation, too, is one Mr. **Kant** does not allow. Admittedly, he does not rule it out explicitly because he never mentions it in this form, but he does so implicitly by positing something as an inference from his principles that serves to undermine it. The pure concepts and principles of understanding, he says, are meaningless in themselves and independent of any possible experience. They represent only logical functions of judgment; hence, on the basis of them alone and independent of all experience nothing can be inferred or determined (*Prol.*, p. 106 f).[4] The pure concepts of understanding are completely heterogeneous from sensible intuitions and experience and can never be found in any intuition. Nobody will say that causality, for instance, can be intuited through the senses and is contained in experience. Hence, even experiences cannot be subsumed under it (*Critique*, p. 137 ff). When the condition of time is deleted, the pure concept of understanding of cause does not contain anything except that there is something from which we can infer the existence of something else. That of substance does not contain anything but the logical representation of the subject, from which we cannot draw any inferences because no object at all is determined through the use of this concept and [85] one does not know if it means anything at all (*Critique*, p. 242 ff).

Mr. **Kant** seems to me at his most obscure here. I do not see any other option but to clarify his meaning in my own way and then to examine it. Should I not have grasped his meaning entirely, then an elucidation on his part will lead me to the correct path. Two sources lead us to the pure concepts of understanding: **outer sensations** and **inner feelings of relation**. So the concept of substance is partially drawn from inner experience, which teaches that we think certain things as the subjects of others without in turn making them predicates, and partially from outer sensation, which lets us be acquainted with many things on their own without the help of other things. Both of these elements are rather different from one another so that the content of the former does not provide us with any insight into the content of the latter. Solely from the fact that a substance appears in inner perception as a special subject, without again being a predicate, it does not follow that in outer sensation as well it must occur on its own, without dependence on another thing. No more does it follow that human beings in general must be cognized as substances in intuition just because they are thought as such in understanding. Now, Mr. **Kant** takes the pure concepts of understanding, which he also calls **categories**, merely from the operations of the power of thought. For this reason they are, for him, nothing but functions of judgment. Hence, he has the right to assert that they cannot be immediately applied to intuitions.

Does it follow, however, that the concepts of understanding cannot be at all applied to intuitions? According to their definition, they are to have the greatest possible universality, to extend not just to inner, but [86] also to outer perceptions. The concept of substance is one-sided if it affirms only how it appears to understanding, just as it is faulty if it is merely drawn from outer sensations. Its correctness essentially requires that it conforms to all our perceptions, which is to say, that it contains what outer and inner sensations or intuitions have in common. If it does contain this commonality, then it is also applicable on its own to our intuitions precisely by virtue of it.

Mr. **Kant** responds that nothing is gained by this, however; for as soon as something is added from outer intuition, it follows that the concept is applied not to things in themselves, but only to intuitions, that is, that its validity does not go beyond the limits of possible experience. – But what is possible experience? Is it what we have only in our present state, and our present circumstance, or is it what we can have in general, whatever circumstance we are in, as long as we retain the capacity for outer sensation and inner thought? The first alternative can scarcely be assumed, for when our universal concepts are grounded in our entire capacity of sensation and thought, and so are in complete conformity with the laws of our entire nature, then they could hardly be altered without a change of the entire nature. In that case, we would surely have sufficient certainty that appearances that do . . . [5] accord with them, would conform to them in every circumstance. Furthermore, if the ground of the universal concept of understanding is not the act of a particular power of thought, but of every one, if it is not outer intuition by means of particular organs, but intuition in general, with or without organs, then one is surely sufficiently justified in attributing universality and objective validity to them.[6] [87]

But what if, **for us**, only representations exist? In that case the universal principles can be taken from anywhere; they still do not determine anything except how we have to connect representations in understanding. This is a further argument that Mr. **Kant** appeals to. Nature, he says, is nothing but a sum total of appearances, consequently, not a thing in itself, but merely a collection of representations of the mind (*Critique*, p. 114). This is precisely what the idealists, who knew how to coat this assertion with a strong color of truth, said; even if, when considered more closely, all that remained was the coating. **Representations** and **sensations** are essentially different, a **sensation** of displeasure is surely something completely different from a **representation** of it. If the claim is that nature is nothing but a collection of such images or imprints on the mind, which we can call up or remove from consciousness as we please, then it affirms something that contradicts all experience. But if it is to affirm that beside the images, which we can arbitrarily call up, there are also impressions, perceptions that we cannot create for ourselves as we please, that are not at all subsumed under **our** power, that we only apprehend through affection, then what

Mr. **Kant** infers does not follow. We cannot conclude that since the representations over which we have control are subsumed under the laws of the power of thought, those over which we do not have control must similarly be so subsumed.

Mr. **Kant** also arrives at this result, which does, after all, lie on his path and seeks to show, with the expenditure of more than a little ingenuity, that understanding does not take its laws from nature but prescribes them to it. He concedes that this sounds strange, but [claims] that it is not, for that reason, any less certain. I have not been able to find that satisfaction, or at least that clarity, that I [88] would hope for, and so it will not be taken amiss, I hope, should I not have grasped Mr. **Kant's** entire meaning. What I have been able to understand of what he has said follows. ["]First, all **our judgments** are first only judgments of perception, they are valid only for us, that is, for our subject, and we give them a new relation only subsequently, namely to an **object**. We want it to be valid for us at every time and in the same way for everyone, for when a judgment agrees with an object, then all judgments about the same object must agree with one another. The **objective** validity of judgments of experience, accordingly, does not mean anything but its necessary universality. And conversely, when we have reason to take a judgment to be necessary and universally valid, then we must also take it to be **objective**, that is, take it as not just expressing a relation of perception to the subject but also a characteristic of the object. For there would be no reason why other judgments must necessarily agree with mine if they do not relate to the unity of the object["] (*Prol.*, p. 78 f).[7]

A judgment is **subjective** if it only affirms that we sense in this or that way and represent something in this or that way; it is **objective** when these sensations or representation[s] are related to an object outside of them to which the sensed or represented constitution is attributed. When I say "the sugar is sweet" in the **subjective** sense, this means only: whenever I sense what is white, soluble in moisture, and yet hard, I sense it at the same time as sweet; in the **objective** sense, by contrast, it means: something that is outside of my sensation, which is white and the like, is also at the same time sweet. This [89] relation of a sensation to an object, the assumption that such an object is actually present, does not spring from the universality of the judgment, considered as what is merely conditioned with respect to objects. The universal and necessary propositions do not say whether the things named in them actually exist; they merely assure us that if they are present, they must be constituted as specified. It follows from this that, according to Mr. **Kant's** principles, all our cognition is merely **subjec-**

tive, if we do not know anything of objects, not even whether such things exist, and if everything is merely appearance for us, the necessity and universality of propositions cannot make them objective. To understand that we and others must always experience them in this way does not signify anything but the cognition that such and such sensations must follow each other and accompany each other at all times. But through this it is not by any means posited that there is or must also be something outside of us to which such sensations are related.

Leaving this aside, it is only explained here how merely **subjective** cognition can become **objective**, and that is by no means the main difficulty. That has to do, rather, with how understanding prescribes laws to experience, why experience or intuition must necessarily be subsumed under laws of understanding? In order to illuminate this, Mr. **Kant** says, secondly: it is necessary for thought that regularity be observed in the succession of representations. Without this, certain representations do not consistently arouse each other, and so could not even constitute a series of ideas. It is necessary, furthermore, that we are aware that what has previously been represented is still the same, without which no judgment can be made. Accordingly, if we are to have understanding, and do have it, we must find regularity, solidity, and order in our representations and, consequently, also [90] in appearances through the senses, that is, in sensations. Furthermore, appearances are nothing but the play of representations, not things in themselves, hence experiences, and since their sum total constitutes nature, nature itself, must conform to the laws of our understanding (*Critique*, p. 100 ff).

In my estimation, it follows irrefutably that if understanding is to be employed, there must be regularity in the succession of representations, and stability in each representation itself, that is, that each must in each instant be uniform with itself. If it were not the case that certain representations are regularly found to accompany each other, then no solid irrefutable propositions would be possible, and if no representation were the same from one moment to the next, then none could be compared with another, hence, there could be no judgment. Does it follow from this, however, that it must be the same in outer sensations as well? Suppose that what I now see as triangle appears in the next instance as a square, and in every other instant as something different. In that case my understanding would not be able to occupy itself with this thing as appearance, but it would nevertheless be able, insofar as it is the understanding, to draw concepts of triangle and square from representations, and from these and related ones discover a geometry that is as good as the one we now have. The connection and combination of representations in the inner sphere is our own accomplishment, the work of our understanding. As long as we only have control over our own representations, as well as memory and the power of thought, understanding can still be used, no matter how things are in sensation. Consequently, the existence of understanding does not by any means presuppose regularity in the outer appearances.

But are appearances anything other than a play of **our** representations? – If that is the case, then Mr. **Kant** is admittedly completely correct, but that it is the case is something that neither he [91] nor any other idealist has been able to demonstrate satisfactorily. Granted, that we should represent sugar as sweet in its absence, is a play of representation: we could represent it just as well as sour or bitter. After all, we see no more connection between the representations of this hardness, this whiteness, and so on and of sweetness than we see between the former and those of sourness or bitterness. But it is no play of representations that without our knowledge and intentions we notice the impression of sweetness along with those of hardness and this whiteness. Because it is not up to us at this time to simultaneously sense another state, we are forced to experience it in this way and not in another. If this were nothing but a play of representations, why would we not be able, just as easily, to sense sugar as bitter as we can represent it?

This much is clear, that between the combination and succession in representations, properly so called, and those in sensations, there is an essential difference and that one type does not necessarily conform to the other. So Mr. **Kant** must still demonstrate that if understanding is to play a role, the latter must necessarily conform to the former.

Even more so, the use of understanding requires nothing more than a constitution in the inner sphere of the thinking being by means of which an impression once made remains the same in the succeeding moment, by means of which a constant connection and regular succession is cognized between such impressions. Independent of this constitution, outer sensations can always change and need not be subjected to laws of successions. After I have had the impression of a triangle, and this impression remains the same through several instances, this is [92] enough to form the concept of a triangle and then to base judgments on it. In the outer sphere, meanwhile, the triangle can change, be transformed into every other figure, indeed, become a color or even have an odor, but my concept of triangle is not for that reason any less certain. However, we do not find such constancy and regularity only in the inner sphere, we find them also in outer intuitions. Where does this come from? One does not determine the other. This is something

Mr. **Kant** wanted or should have explained, but he did not do so and would find it difficult to do so. From the fact that the concept of triangle in understanding has to remain unchanged in order to be used as foundation of a judgment, it does not follow that outer intuition does and must also remain the same.

[Johann Schultz]

Jena, Cröker: *Institutiones Logicae et Metaphysicae* by Jo. Aug. Henr. Ulrich 1785, gr. 8, 426 and 153 Pages Without Preface and Index.

We review this completely revised textbook with pleasure. In addition to being suitably organized, it makes many useful contributions for the correction of philosophical concepts. The author's thorough presentation and his insightful division and differentiation of concepts are too well known already to require further praise. The most important contribution distinguishing this textbook is its constant consideration of the **Kantian** system and the perspicacious manner in which the author tries to integrate the latter, to the extent that he agrees with it, into his own system. The Kantian system is in all regards eminently worthy of examination and this textbook is up to this point one of a kind in its consideration of it. Being himself a teacher, the author's impartial love of truth leads him to neither consider it to be disgraceful to give up long-held convictions in view of someone else's instruction, nor hesitate to indicate what in the Kantian principles seems to him unproven or even incorrect, and this both honors this worthy man and deserves imitation.

It would be a useless exercise to follow the outline of a whole textbook in a review. But it seems to us to be all the more appropriate and useful to familiarize our reader with its **specific characteristics** and to emphasize what science itself actually seems to have gained through it.

The author has actually already adopted a great many of Kant's claims, in our estimation with good reason. Among these are the following: that there is **pure** reason; that there are not just analytic but also synthetic judgments a priori; that there is a difference between mathematical and philosophical cognition, and between sensibility and understanding as two different original sources of our cognition; that the concepts of space and time, which have proven so fruitful in the Kantian system, are the forms of our sensibility; that the categories are the original forms of our thought; that everything empirical must be separated from metaphysics, and so forth. . . . [8]

However, the degree to which the author agrees with Kant's *Critique* up to the Table of Categories, reflects the degree to which he departs from it beyond that. He believes (§176) that just as in mathematical [judgments a priori] one must in the end appeal to the nature and form of our sensibility, so all philosophical judgments a priori must in the end be derived from the **nature** and **original form** of our **understanding** and our **reason**. He is not satisfied with the manner in which **Kant** seeks to demonstrate the synthetic principles of pure reason (§177). He claims that he cannot possibly be convinced that, [298] outside of the field of mathematics, no other synthetic principles are to have a priori objective reality except those without which even the **possibility of experience** would disappear. For, as he argues, the principle of **causality**, according to which everything that **happens** or **begins** to exist presupposes something else from which it follows in accord with a rule, is much too narrow. It is already contained in the general principle of **sufficient reason** because we would not bother to look for a cause of what **happens** if it were not the case that the essential form of our understanding necessitates that we ask about the cause of everything that **is** and can nevertheless be **otherwise**. Professor **Kant** himself presupposes this, as the author notes on page 309, when he says in his *Critique* (p. 193): "I will, accordingly, have to derive the **subjective** sequence of apprehension from the **objective** sequence of appearances, since the former is otherwise entirely undetermined and does not differentiate one appearance from another." For what is this **derivation** to signify if not the need to ask for a **sufficient reason** that must be sought in the objective sequence because it does not lie in the subjective one? The **experience** or **perception** of successive things is possible in itself without presupposing something from which something else follows in accord with a rule. For example, one can successfully **perceive** the sequence of three tones, C, D, E, without thinking of their cause. To be sure, everyone sees that no **judgments of experience** would be possible without the principle of causality, that is, that without it we could never infer that B must **always** and **necessarily** follow A. However, [he continues,] this proposition is almost **identical** and much too scanty. It could not be **Kant's** intention to demonstrate nothing more than this. As far as the principle of persistence is concerned, in the strictest sense **appearances** are neither **substances** nor something **persistent** (§316, 317). Because appearances considered as such are only representations in us, there is, with respect to them, a constant disappearance and reappearance. Consequently, there must be some cause that always presents them anew and that, accordingly, is itself **persistent** and **lasting** and for that very reason not itself appearance but an *ontos on* or a **thing in itself**. To be sure, [he admits] it appears contradictory to ascribe **persistence** to **things in themselves** because persistence is an existence in **time**, and time, in turn, signifies only the form of inner **sensibility** and does not pertain, therefore, to **things in themselves**. However, one cannot separate the concept of time from the concept of existence (§236). in fact, one cannot but express time through an **existing** [thing]. Time, therefore, cannot be a **merely subjective** form of intuition but must be an objective property of **things in themselves** as well. The author says (§238, 239) that no one will ever convince him that the **transcendental consciousness** is a mere appearance and not rather a **thing in itself**. For appearances are nothing other than certain representations unified in a **consciousness**; hence, without a consciousness to which they appear, they are nothing. Our **consciousness**, however, could not itself appear to another consciousness; it could not be a phenomenon. Hence it must be a **thing in itself**. Because there is nevertheless in the activity of our consciousness an actual succession, it follows from this anew that in the **things in themselves** as well there is a true succession, and that even the most perfect understanding must **intuit** the successive activities of our consciousness as **successive things**. Moreover, even the synthetic principles of **pure reason** must have necessary objective validity, not just those of pure understanding. For instance (§177), the proposition that, when something **conditioned** is given, there must also be something that is **absolute** is a principle that lies in the nature of our reason itself, without which it would not be content. Hence, the categories as well are applicable not just to appearances, but similarly to **things in themselves**. Accordingly, they have not only an **immanent** but also a transcendent use. **Kant**, who denies this, nevertheless predicates them in many places of things in themselves. And for the same reason, the so-called **ideas** of pure reason, for example, the idea of the absolute, are not merely **ideas**; rather, they are **real** concepts of reason.

The reviewer must admit that he found his own doubts reflected in many of the author's doubts. This agreement is, of course, not a presumption of their correctness, but perhaps only a mere consequence of a long familiar mode of thought. Nevertheless, it is at least certain that these doubts, which no impartial person can take as entirely insignificant, directly concern the main foundation of the entire Kantian doctrine and that the latter, no matter how much it contains of what is excellent, important, and indubitably certain, does not yet carry the sort of apodeictic conviction that would be necessary to an **unrestricted** acceptance of what is really its main purpose. At the same time, the doubts I have mentioned do not have such a degree of evidence that one could take them to be a complete refutation of the Kantian system. Many, much deeper insights into the entire totality of the system would be necessary for that to occur. The main element of **Kant's** system, on which the true limitation of pure reason depends, rests primarily on the **deduction** of the pure concepts of understanding, which the *Critique of Pure Reason* sets out on pages 84–147. It is regrettable, therefore, that the author has not in the first instance examined **it**. But perhaps it was only its obscurity that prevented him from doing so, an obscurity that occurs primarily here, in this part of the *Critique* that should be the clearest, if the Kantian system [299] is to afford complete conviction.

It would be useless to undertake an extensive examination of these obscure matters at the end of a review. Still, we cannot avoid taking this opportunity to at least set down some thoughts for further investigation. **Kant** deduces the objective reality of the categories or synthetic concepts from the fact that without them **experience** would not be possible. Now, he takes experience alternatively in the sense of mere **judgments of perception**, that is, those empirical judgments that are merely **subjectively** valid for me, and in the sense of **judgments of experience**, that is, those that are **objective** and hence universally valid for everyone (*Prol.*, p. 78).[9] Accordingly, in the first sense of the word, the meaning of the deduction would be as follows: without the objective reality of the categories, no **judgments of perception** are possible. He does actually take the proposition in this sense in many places, but particularly in the proofs of the three principles of the analogies of experience (p. 182 ff).[10] Here the central point is that, given that our **apprehension** of the manifold of experience is always **successive, it could not itself tell us** what is **simultaneous** and what is **successive**, if there were not the sort of objective connection in appearances themselves that determines their temporal relations. However, if I cannot perceive anything without first bringing my empirical representations under an objectively valid category, does this not say: in order to be able to judge **empirically**, I must first judge a priori and, more specifically, synthetically? For example, would I have to know that the sunlight is the **cause** of the warmth of the stone in order to be able to say: when the sun shines, the stone grows warm? But even aside from this worry, Kant would contradict himself were he to make this claim about judgments of perception given that he says explicitly (*Prol.*, p. 78):[11] judgments of perception do not require **any pure concepts of understanding**; they require only the **logical** connection of perceptions in a thinking subject. If, by contrast, we understand experience to be a **judgment of experience**, then the Kantian deduction would have the following meaning: without the objective reality of the categories no **judgment of experience** is possible. This seems to be its true meaning, given that Kant always emphasizes that if the categories did not have a necessary relation to appearances, all our perceptions would be a disorderly mass from which nothing would come together in cognition. However, unless we are mistaken, the preceding proposition says nothing other than the following: if the categories did not have a necessary relation to appearances, that is, if they did not have **objective** validity in them, then we would never be able to make a priori, that is, universally and **objectively valid** judgments about appearances. We would not be able to say, for example, that warmth follows always and **necessarily** upon sunshine. However, is this proposition not, as Privy Councillor [Ulrich] already notes, in fact **identical**? Was it not precisely Hume's claim that we can never say a priori that B must **necessarily** follow A? And did not the excellent Kant want to **convince** us that such general judgments of experience are **in fact legitimate**? One does not, meanwhile, have to be a sceptical Hume in order to doubt this. Suppose that appearances were in fact a disorderly mass, a mere accumulation of **simultaneous** and **successive** [events], that appear to us as regular only because their existence in accord with the relations of space and time, has been **preestablished** through the will of the creator in a most wise way so that certain appearances (which are, after all, nothing other than representations in us or certain modifications of our consciousness) are always followed by certain other ones in the most orderly fashion, without there being the least **real** connection between them. If that were the case, then the categories of **causality** and **reciprocity** would not be at all applicable to the appearances of nature. Moreover, in that case, our understanding would not prescribe the laws to nature, rather, it would only learn its merely apparent lawfulness from it a posteriori through perception. But these thoughts are here presented only for further examination.

Philosophy would gain much if more of our famous sages would decide to undertake a close examination of the Kantian system with the impartiality of Privy Councillor Ulrich.

Gottlob August Tittel

On Kantian Forms of Thought or Categories

The **categories** (predicaments) are an old, exhausted, long forgotten, and degraded piece of the Aristotelian philosophy. . . . [12] [8] Mr. **Kant** has sought out this despised and obsolete doctrine; revised, repositioned, and adorned it; changed its composition and color; and proceeded to solemnly present his **categories** with a much higher rank and honor than they have ever had before. Indeed, he has sought to use them and even to turn them into things they were never intended to be.

Compare these **new** (Kantian) categories with the **old** (Aristotelian) ones to see what **Kant** has done for them.

1. He has increased their **number** from 10 to 12. They are now presented as follows (p. 106 of the *Critique**): [9]
   Unity, Multiplicity, Totality
   (constitute the first class: **quantity**)
   Reality, Negation, Limitation
   (constitute the second class: **quality**)
   Inherence and **subsistence** (substance and accidents), **causality** and **dependence** (cause and effect), **community** (reciprocity between agent and patient)
   (constitute the third class: **relation**)
   Possibility – impossibility, existence – nonexistence, necessity – contingency
   (constitute the fourth class: **modality**)
   Kant calls the first two classes **mathematical** and the last two **dynamical**. The subordinate concepts of, for example, **power, action, passivity**, which have been derived from the category of causality, he identifies as **predicabiles** (also an Aristotelian term).
2. K. has changed their **position** and **expression** somewhat, and, as it suited him, has added or removed things here and there. **Substance, quantity, quality**, and **relation** have been [10] com-

* I note, once and for all, that the pagination is that of the new, 1787 edition of the Kantian *Critique*.

pletely retained from the Aristotelian table; but each of the three latter concepts has immediately been further divided into three special moments. K. designates **modality** as itself a main concept, whereas according to Aristotle the last nine categories are all placed together under the concept of **accident** or **mode. Time** and **space** (according to Aristotle only a subsidiary concept of the predicament of quantity) have been removed from the categories (as forms of thought) but have instead been designated forms of **sensibility** and the like.

3. K. has significantly raised the **rank** and **designation** of the categories. After all, according to **Aristotle** the categories were to be only an index or register of certain main concepts occurring in existing knowledge which, thus compiled and ordered, could be more easily examined and surveyed and which could facilitate the direction of understanding to the more important moments of cognition for each given object. But **Aristotle** did not in the least think that the **origin** of these concepts is independent of experience or, for that matter, that they bracket and encircle all human insights. According to **Kant**, these categories [11] are supposed to be so many products of understanding that originally inhere in it, and that are **pure** and independent of all prior experience. What is more – they are supposed to be the absolute measure of understanding so that "by means of them the understanding is **completely specified** and its capacity is **exhaustively measured**" (*Critique*, p. 105). In point of fact, this is surely the most audacious thought that has ever occurred to a human soul, to [enumerate] not just the actual store of the **cognitions of understanding**, but to go as far as to completely encompass the entire **capacity of understanding** roundly and nicely through a dozen categories, that is, through concepts ostensively given (a priori) to the mind. I will return to this topic later.

Having presented and ordered everything in this way, Mr. **Kant** looks at his work not differently than he would had this table been immediately drawn in this way by nature. He believes to find material here for many **systematic** reflections. He deems it to be **systematic** that the table has four divisions; that each division has three moments, that in the first two classes [12] the moments, for example, **unity**, **reality** and the like, are isolated, and that in the two other ones each moment, for example, **substance** and **accidents**, **necessity** and **contingency**, and so on, has a correlate. It seems to him equally **systematic** that the third category of each class always emerges out of the combination of the second with the first, as in **totality** (multiplicity considered as unity), **limitation** (negation mixed with reality), **necessity** (existence determined through possibility), and so on. (*Critique*, §11, p. 109 ff).

Is it **nature** who is leading here or is it **Kant**? Everything surely depends on how these concepts have first been arranged and ordered by him. Of course one must be able to find what one has placed in it. If I divide a deck of **cards** into four equal piles, each of which contains ten cards, and if I place king and queen **together** in two of these piles, in one of the others the king **alone**, in the other one the queen **alone**, and if I place in each one the 7 at the top and below it 6 and 1 and below that 5 and 2, and then 4 and 3 and in this way obtain at all times 7 through the combination of the two previous numbers, is this surprising? I would only have to [13] change something in the arrangement itself and the supposed **system** would disappear. If I were to place **unity** and **plurality** (and as such partial and total plurality), **reality** and **deficiency** (positive and negative lack including limitation which, considered **as such**, is only a lack) and so on into the Table of Categories, the arrangement would immediately be different. "That person,["] says Mr. Feder imitating **Kant** himself, ["]who first wrote the syllogism in three rows, one of which is on top of another, looked at it as if it were a chess set and sought to determine what emerged from altering the position of the middle concept, was just as surprised by the fact that a meaningful sense emerged as is the person who finds an anagram in a name. It would be just as childish to be delighted about the one as about the other, particularly since one forgets that one has found nothing new with respect to clarity, only an increase in obscurity" (Feder's *Logik*, 1774, p. 105 f†). [14]

To turn more closely to the matter itself. I have the following remarks about the Kantian categories:

I. Every impartial person must immediately see that this entire business is merely a certain arrangement of certain concepts already familiar from speculative cognition. Ordering ideas is in principle always a useful undertaking. However, in my opinion, an ordering of ideas that designate the **source** of human understanding, and that is supposed to contain only the first **original concepts** of real cognition, ought to collect only those **simple** and **positive** fundamental concepts to which all human cogni-

† The table of syllogistic figures was worth at least as much as the Kantian table of nothing on p. 348 of the *Critique*.

tion can be traced. Among these are unity, reality, existence, and the like. **Multiplicity** and **totality**, by contrast, originate from unity; **negation** and **limitation**, as such, are not positive concepts, they designate an absence of reality. **Necessity** and **contingency** are merely two modes of existence. Indeed, **Kant** himself also differentiates here between the higher foundational concepts of reason and the derivative ones. These two types, therefore, should not, as actually happens here, [15] be intermixed. And for this reason the Kantian Table of Categories may already appear to many to contain errors.

II. Whatever determinate point of view **Kant** may have taken for his arrangement, it would surely be the most extreme hybris to imagine that this is by all means the only correct and the **only necessary** order of ideas and that no one else would be at all able to produce a similar classification of concepts from another arbitrary point of view. To be sure, **Kant** does not want to accept the charge that he has proceeded **arbitrarily**. He places the superiority of his classification precisely in the fact that it is "systematic and produced from a firm[13] principle, namely, the capacity to judge (which, is for him the same as the capacity to think)" (*Critique*, p. 106). According to him, the great **Aristotle** proceeded in a rhapsodic fashion; he had no principle, picked up his **categories** wherever they occurred to him, without ever being able to be convinced of their completion, and also included many derivative concepts, for instance, *actio* and *passio* (which belong already under the category of causality) [16] in the original concepts (*Critique*, p. 107). But investigate this Kantian **principle** from which the entire order is supposed to have emerged with all diligence and earnestness. K. grounds the determinate number of his **categories** on the possible **functions** of understanding (of judgment or thought). "There arise just as many pure concepts of understanding, as there were logical functions of all possible judgments in the preceding table. For those functions have **completely specified** understanding, its capacity is **exhaustively measured** through them" (*Critique*, p. 105). Everything, accordingly, depends on the table of the functions of understanding. And this table is available to everyone on page 95 of the *Critique*. And what do I find there? Nothing more and nothing less but that all judgments can be considered in accord with a certain form, in a fourfold respect, and that with respect to **quantity** there are universal, particular, and singular [judgments or propositions], with respect to **qual-**

ity there are affirmative, negative, and infinite [judgments or propositions] (*propositia infinita*, for example, "Adam was able not to sin"[14] in contrast to "Adam was not able to sin."[15] See Reusch, *Systema Logic*, 1750, §365, 366, 371 f). [17] With respect to **relation**, there are categorical, hypothetical, and disjunctive [judgments or propositions] (one can see on pages 98 and 99 of the *Critique* just how forced the application of this well-known differentiation to relation is, particularly since it can ordinarily be easily attributed to **composition**), and with respect to **modality**, there are problematic, assertoric, and apodeictic judgments or propositions.

One is indeed stopped in one's tracks here. – These entirely trivial things, which even the mere beginner of the least logic knows, are to disclose the entire economy of understanding? And K. thinks he has completely specified the entire operation of understanding with this? And these (not even completely presented) ways of considering propositions, in accord with this or that form, are supposed to contain the great and indubitable principle that measures the scope and mass of our concepts of understanding in their entirety? And furthermore, this principle is one that the great **Aristotle**, from whose philosophy the quantity and quality and relation and the like have been taken, is supposed to have missed? – All this is fully incomprehensible to me. And it is altogether impossible for me to find here a certain and [18] firm foundation of the Kantian Table of Categories.

III. But what does **Kant** want his categories, these pure concepts of understanding, to be? They are supposed to be forms of pure thought, mere **forms of understanding**; in themselves they are to be without content and meaning – **empty** forms; they are to be without any determinate object – only forms for objects **in general**. They are to be only applicable to the objects first given in experience. Though not of empirical origin, they are only to have an **empirical use**. They are **pure** products of understanding, completely independent of all experience, yet necessary **conditions** of experience that first becomes possible through them. They are self-thought **first** a priori principles, elements of all cognition, and as **formal** [conditions] of this cognition, [they are] connected with the elements of sensibility, with what is given as **matter** for cognition in intuition. Their objective **reality** is necessarily limited to the objects of intuition as schemata; without them [they are] a mere play of understanding.

> And for this reason, whenever separated from sensibility, [19] [they are] not capable of an explanation of reality. [They are] merely concepts, the determinate form under which the objects given in experience can be subsumed. . . . [16] [24]

1. "**The categories are only forms**" – But now I must ask: what sorts of things are these forms to be? To be sure, they are to be forms of understanding, forms of thought. But what is a mere **form of thought**?

It could possibly be some modification, an **inner subjective constitution** of my power of understanding, to become aware of, comprehend and order certain impressions in a determinate manner, [25] that is, it could be a certain **law of thought** that harmonizes with the objects that appear in nature, arising from an original **capacity** and **receptivity** given by the creator of things to the being capable of thought, all sorts of possible **types of representation** of possible objects. – I can in fact think of the **forms** of understanding in this way. But this is precisely what the **Kantian** forms are not to be. Consider how **Kant** himself expressly contradicts this explanation. "Were someone to want to take a middle path between the two just named, namely that they (the categories) are neither **self-thought** first principles a priori of our cognition, nor drawn from experience, but subjective predispositions of thought, implanted in us along with our existence, which have been ordered by our creator in such a way that their employment would precisely harmonize with the laws of nature in accord with which experience proceeds (a kind of **preformation system** of pure reason), then, apart from the fact that on this hypothesis one cannot set a limit to how far **predetermined** dispositions [26] would direct future judgments (but is this not also a problem with the presupposition of self-thought **concepts created** in the mind a priori?), it would be decisive against the suggested middle path that if this were the case, the categories would lack the **necessity** that essentially belongs to their concept (but how could one demonstrate this necessity should it be denied?)" *Critique*, p. 167.[17]

I could possibly think certain **abstractions** as forms under which the objects we encounter can be subsumed. For example, **tree**, **human being** (in general) would be the, as it were, general form, under which many particular things of the respective kind could be subsumed: the **plane** is a **tree**, **Alexander** was a **human being**, and so on. But an abstraction cannot be thought without something from which it abstracts. All our **abstractions**, these general conceptual forms, had to first be derived from particular things as these are given in inner and outer experience (sensation or reflection) by means of prior comparison of certain common marks. They then [27] had to be made applicable to a multiplicity of things in view of just such a **commonality** of characteristics and a certain name. A person, who has never known or seen an **actual** tree and **particular** human beings, would also never be able to have a general concept of tree, human being, and so on. Even the simplest concept of **unity** itself (unity in general) could not possibly have come into the soul if actual things had not first presented themselves in experience in their own existence **separately** from all other existence. To be sure, imagination can, by means of arbitrary addition (combination), create certain forms, for which no original exists in experience. I can think of **castles in the air**. But even here, in fiction itself, at least the ingredients must already have been given in experience. I would already have to know **air** and **castle**, each on its own, from experience before I can think both in this unity. Even each representation of ourselves that may not have occurred in experience, and of things that we do not know through our own experience, is only ever possible by being traced back [28] to some other experience that we have already had and to a certain similarity with other things already known through experience. But if this is the case, then **forms of thought** (abstractions) would all be only of empirical origin, would all have been produced and woven from experience. According to **Kant**, however, all these **forms of thought** and **sense** do not "arise" from experience, but "from the inner source of pure intuition and thought" and are to be applied only when some **matter** (object) is given in experience. Everything that we seem to find in experience for their empirical generation, is to serve only for purposes of **illustration**, but not their **deduction**. And "to attempt their empirical deduction, would be entirely futile work." Even "the famous **Locke**, for want of this consideration (the distinction between **illustration** and **deduction**), because he found pure concepts of understanding in experience, also (erroneously) derived them from experience" (*Critique*, p. 118, 126 f). – But if the Kantian **categories** or forms of understanding are neither [29] certain **laws of thought**, as subjective determinations and directions of our power of understanding, nor certain general concepts (**abstractions**) drawn from experience, what then may these forms be?

2. "Taken independently of the conditions of sensibility, **they are empty forms**, and extended beyond the limits of possible experience, they are **without meaning and sense**." – Now, that I do understand. Pure concepts of understanding, **Kant** says, do not extend beyond the field of sensibility; the forms of pure understanding cannot be made appropriate to any other objects than those that are given or that are possible in experience. I also already understand the overall result of the Kantian philosophy to which all of this points: pure understanding (understanding purified by critique) must never venture to achieve a cognition of **God**, **freedom**, and **immortality**, because the objects of this cognition cannot be given in experience. I should like to ask here, by the by, whether objects must always be given in experience with complete immediacy? Can [30] data for such cognitions lie **mediately** in experience? But I do not here speak of application. I first want to know what the forms of understanding are **in themselves**, that is, what they are prior to experience and as yet independent of it, as yet without application, **what they are** when they lie in the mind and "spring from the inner pure source of thought." To be sure, I can also think any other material form, whether a **printing form**, a **pastry mold**, and so on as empty, I can think them without the canvas and paper and things of that sort, and without actual pastries. But I cannot possibly think an **empty form of thought** – not merely as a capacity for a concept, but **as** an actual **concept**, a concept, accordingly, without something that has been comprehended, an idea without content – a form that contains and means nothing. And they would have to be **general** concepts because their object has to be something **in general**, not something particular and determinate. But where do these forms sit? Surely, not in the **name** – **reality**, **causality**, **substance**, and so on. These names cannot, after all, have been placed in the mind a priori. There are thousands and thousands of human beings who do not learn [31] them in their entire life. So how are they to become noticeable and memorable to the mind. – These **empty** forms, are they empty of content, or empty in name? Surely, one will not object that I do not properly understand **Kant**. "The view is not that these **forms** lie already in the mind prior to and earlier than experience, rather that both **form** and **matter** (object) come together in experience from entirely different sources." So the issue here is **coming together**. To be sure, the **knower** (subject) and **what is to be known** (object), that **which can be perceived** and the **perceiver**,

do come together in every experience. And one does say that the elements of such an experience come together from two different sources: the **inner** source of the capacity to understand (knowing power) and the **outer** source of the knowable objects of nature. One separates these different contributions from each other and calls the manner of thought the **form**, and the known object the **matter**. One does not need more than these two conditions for any [32] experience. If **Kant** does not have anything else in mind, then I do not have the least objection. But these are the most ordinary and best known things in the world. So **Kant** would only have to speak in this manner, and he would be understood by the whole world. Nobody has ever claimed that experience would be possible without a **capacity to know**. Nobody has ever denied that understanding is determined through certain original and natural **laws of perception**.

But these natural **determinations of understanding** (laws of thought) are no more the **Kantian forms** (categories), than the **abstractions** collected in experience in accord with them are the categories. They are not the **pure** concepts of understanding which Mr. **Kant** attributes only to the inner pure source of thought, which spring from it independently of all experience, and which he presents as already actually formed **concepts** that first meet in experience itself with the given object. So when we speak of the **coming together** of these Kantian forms with the objects given in experience, then we will be permitted to pose the altogether simple question: were these forms ostensively already lying in the mind [33] something **in themselves** prior to all experience? Or were they nothing? – If they were **nothing** in themselves, then it is clear that these forms (no matter how one interprets them) did obtain their birth certificate only from experience, not from the ostensive higher source (a priori) as was first supposed. **They were something in themselves**! Then I may pose the further question: **What**?

3. "**They are forms for objects in general**." – Strictly speaking this is not yet an answer to the question of what these forms are **in themselves**. But what is more, their use and applicability are also made further suspect thereby. For what does "**for objects in general**" mean? Do we understand **objects in general** to be objects of all possible kinds as they can be given in experience, or those of a certain and specific kind? In either case, every impartial person must immediately see this complete inconceivability: how can a thing that first attains sense and meaning only

through objects nevertheless rest at the ground of objects as **regulative principle**? [34]

If such a form of thought were to be something like a **measuring stick** by means of which I determine a multitude of magnitudes and relations, then it could be comprehended. For here the already known homogeneity between the measurable magnitude and the measuring stick cannot lead me astray, because I determine the content of the one by means of the already determined content of the other. But everyone must find it incomprehensible how an **empty form of thought**, a form of thought without determinate content and reality, both of which it can only first obtain through objects, a form of thought that is such that I simply cannot know what cases and what objects can be accommodated to it, can become a **regulative principle** for objects. So for example, I approach the world of sense with my category of **causality** and ask: what appearances will I encounter that I can lay at the ground of my form as **matter**? I note that after the appearance of a **comet** a **bloody war** begins, that an **earthquake** follows a **calm**, that a ball A **is hit** by a ball B and **begins to move**, and so on. Which of these is appropriate to my category? [35] Where do I properly apply it? With respect to this question, my category cannot decide anything. The examination of the constitution of the given cases must first itself lead me to the idea of either a causal connection, or a merely accidental succession. So according to the first origin of the concept, **causality** was not by any means a prior (anticipated) form of understanding but rather the sound result of many observations that have been compared and examined. Only now, after the concept of causality has been found in this manner, can it serve as **form** (if one wants to call it that) to make sense of a number of other cases, insofar as they are similar to those from which the abstraction was originally formed. And the same is the case with all the other categories which, as prior empty forms not found in and verified through experience, would not have the least use for the correction, measurement, and extension of our cognition, because **in** and **for themselves** they entirely lack determination, content, reality, and meaning. [36]

Objects **in general** cannot be thought in any way at all except through a combination (collection) of previously known or given objects. It is impossible to think "**human being**" in general, that is, the commonality of a multiplicity of human beings, or "**things**" in general, that is, the commonality of a multiplicity of things, without presupposing that **particular** human beings, **particular** things are already known in the concept. And without this presupposed familiarity, all these "**objects in general**" are a pure **nothing** for our concept. And the relation of any empty form of thought to objects **in general** is similarly **nothing**. And the entire task of determining **how such forms of thought**, or the concepts lying in the mind a priori **can relate to objects** also leads to nothing.

4. "They are to be **concepts originally independent** of experience, lying a priori in the mind, and **self-thought** principles purified by understanding." – **Locke**, the deep thinker, had traced the source of human concepts from the lowest root, [had traced back] the totality of our knowledge [37] to its smallest elements. He analysed our **simplest** concepts and pursued them to their origin and first emergence from their experiential sources (sensation and reflection) with the strictest precision. His deduction has been compellingly provided with irrefutable evidence from human history! In this way he has taken the certain path of truth, has presented the imagined, dreamed ownership of original **intelligence** and **axioms** as so much nothingness and poverty and removed the rotten branch of many deceptions and fantasies.‡ One would have expected that everyone who would even venture to assert that in addition to the sources indicated by **Locke**, there are original concepts and principles completely independent of all (inner and outer) experience, would first make at least an attempt to refute and destroy Locke's proofs. But Mr. **Kant** has been careful not to do so. [38] "**Locke** has sought pure concepts of understanding in an inappropriate manner. His procedure, moreover, is inconsistent. His deduction is only empirical. And there is, and cannot be, an empirical deduction of pure concepts of understanding!"[18] That is everything **Kant** has to say by way of refutation.

Just listen to him! "We must thank the famous **Locke** for first opening the way to this (the investigation of the origin of human concepts). However, a deduction of pure a priori concepts can never be achieved in this way, for it does not lie on this road" (*Critique*, p. 119). And again: "the famous **Locke**, for want of this consideration, and because he found pure concepts of understanding in experience, also derived them from experience, yet

‡ I refer the readers of my philosophical treatises to my presentation of Locke's theory, *Logic*, p. 175–85.

proceeded so inconsistently that he attempted with their aid to obtain cognitions that far exceed all limits of experience" (*Critique*, p. 127).

Locke did not seek pure concepts of understanding, rather, he sought the origin of human concepts in general and found, in the end, that those **pure** concepts of understanding [39] which were believed to have been obtained outside of experience and independently of it, were nothing but chimera. His procedure remained entirely consistent, insofar as he held that, quite independently of the first origin of human concepts in experience, human understanding might progress to a certain cognition of other objects not **immediately** given in experience, for example, the cognition of **God**. He did not, as **Kant** did, exclude and remove these objects entirely from human cognition. Admittedly, **Locke's** deduction was entirely **empirical**, and was supposed to be, because in view of undeniable facts and human history, he found it to be the only proven one. There cannot be a deduction of **pure** concepts of understanding that are entirely independent of experience. But **Locke** also denies that **pure** concepts and cognitions exist a priori in this sense, and declares all presumed intelligences and principles to be chimeras and dreams.

The Kantian view of the origin of our concepts is an intermediary between the Lockean view [40] and its opposite. **Kant** is, as it were, split between them: half for, half against the empirical origin of concepts. He allows only the **formal** principles of cognition of be **pure** and to emerge from understanding, the **material** principles (objects), by contrast, he wants to be given **so narrowly** in experience that one cannot go beyond the limits of possible experience with these pure forms of understanding. These, however, are the incomprehensible forms which no **Aristotle**, no **Hume**, no **Locke**, has ever thought in the Kantian sense, and which even now so many reflective men **cannot** think and do not **want** to believe. **Locke** referred all **formal** principles, even the principle of noncontradiction, in its primitive formation, to the field of **experience** and **sensible evidence**.[§] **Locke** did not take this and all other axioms as anything but abstraction taken from **particular** evidence and summarized under one expression. But **Kant** wants to see his categories and the [41] principles that follow from them as primitive, as not taken from experience at any point, but as forms and principles originating

[§] See my *Logic*, pp. 339–42.

in pure understanding. And for just this reason neither he nor anyone else can clearly say what his forms are. . . . [19]

. . . [103]

V. With respect to the question of the **origin of human concepts**, the following comparison of the **Lockean** and the **Kantian** philosophy will clarify the difference between them and will be welcomed, I hope, by many a reader.

Locke believes that he finds the **generation** of all human concepts in experience. **Kant** takes everything that experience can deliver to be merely an **illustration** of the concepts already given in the mind, of the self-thought concepts that are forged in it.

According to **Locke**, understanding follows nature, it collects and takes from nature, it forms **in accord** with it. According to **Kant** understanding precedes nature, works out of itself, and **pre**-forms.

For **Locke** all our concepts of understanding are only **copies** of nature. For **Kant** they are [104] **forms** for nature (for the objects that occur in nature).

Locke says that in the final analysis all our concepts **resolve** themselves in experience, they are woven from experience. **Kant** says: "they are **pure** products of understanding and are merely transferred and **applied** to experience."

According to **Locke**, **abstraction** is the only way through which to arrive at concepts of understanding. **Kant** says that **anticipation** is the proper task of understanding.

Locke states that **sensibility** transfers its materials to the fabric of **understanding** in order to arouse it to activity. All operations of understanding are first made possible through prior experience. The task of understanding is solely the further development of the given material. – Not so, says **Kant**. Understanding only transfers its **own** product, its prepared forms, **into** the world of the senses in order to realize them through intuitable objects. They contain the ground of all possible experience. According to **Kant**, I must already have, for instance, the pure [105] concept of understanding of a mathematical **circle** in order to be able to think the roundness of the **sun**, as an intuitable object. According to **Locke**, I have first been led to the general concept of a **round** figure through a multiplicity of perceptions of such a figure. According to **Kant**, I would not even be able to think the totality of the fingers of my hand without the prior concept of understanding of **number** in general. According to **Locke**, by contrast, it is the multiplicity of any given unity that nature presents to me, for instance, **finger**, that first creates the concept of number in me.

Locke says that experience (inner and outer sense) is the **final** and **sole** source of our cognition. Even understanding begins with experience. It cannot work without material. Sensibility receives raw matter from nature, understanding processes it, clarifies, raises, develops, and expands sensible representations. Understanding and sensibility are two **interconnected** capacities that closely correspond to one another. – Not so, says **Kant**. Sensibility [106] and understanding are two entirely **separate** sources of cognition. Understanding has its own work room, it forges its forms **purely** out of itself, without any help from experience. It is only when it is to realize its products that it proceeds into the field of experience where intuitive objects are given for this purpose.

According to **Locke**, general concepts are only the **result** of previously collected experiences. **Kant**, however, grounds experience on the previously formed concepts of understanding, which function as **regulative** principles.

According to **Locke**, understanding and imagination are not able to create and produce any one original, **simple** concept (for example, of a **tone**, a **taste**, a **color**) out of themselves that has not already been brought to them via the large canal of experience. – According to **Kant**, originally independent concepts lie in understanding prior to all experience. "Pure understanding separates itself not merely from everything that is empirical, but even completely from all sensibility. It is a unity that is [107] self-subsistent, self-sufficient, and not to be augmented through any external additions." (*Critique*, pp. 89, 90).

According to **Locke**, the formation of ideas requires nothing more than intuitive **objects** and the formative power of a being **capable of concepts**. – **Kant** adds a **third** [thing], as condition, between those, a pure form already prewoven in the mind.

According to **Locke**, all axioms are valid only for the sum of factors, of single experiences, and observations from which they have been drawn. Their necessity and universality is a function of sensible evidence or the agreement with possible experience. – According to **Kant**, the principles of thought are spun from

pure concepts of understanding, carry an **inner** necessity and universality, and affirm their complete independence from experience precisely in virtue of their necessity and universality.

Locke derives all human cognition, beginning with its first elements, from experience but, through further development as well as through data only **mediately** given in experience, [108] he leads it **up** to objects not **immediately** given in experience (for example the cognition of God). – And **Kant** believes to find in the former the source of **scepticism** (because according to him there would then be no necessary and universal truths); in the latter a source for **enthusiasm** (because reason would become too arrogant if one were to give it the right to the cognition of such objects *Critique*, p. 128). According to him, the **genesis** of our cognition is only empirical qua **matter** (according to objects), but it is transcendental qua **form** (according to concepts). Their **application**, however, is not transcendental, but only empirical.

VI. Final **result** of the entire investigation.

Because **Kant** has the entire **human history** on which **Locke** grounds his theory of the origin of human concepts so indisputably against him, [it is not surprising that] he (**Kant**) does not dare to attempt a refutation of it. The fact he lists as support, namely the existence of the cognitions of pure mathematics that are entirely independent of experience, [109] is an **incorrect** position. The Kantian assertion that all experience (experiential cognition) first becomes possible through the categories (pure concepts of understanding) rests on **arbitrary** explanations and suppositions (for example, that all thinking is already judging, that intuition does not deliver thought about a thing). The possibility of creating universal concepts (like the categories) in understanding without borrowing at least the initial **simple** material for this from experience, **cannot in any way** be demonstrated. The Kantian **forms**, these concepts woven in the mind are **in themselves** (as **Kant** himself concedes) without sense and meaning and not capable of a real explanation. Sound human understanding is thoroughly opposed to the notion that, for instance, I do not gradually proceed from the intuited round figure of the **sun** to the mathematical concepts of a **circle** in general, but that I transfer this concept to the sun in order to be able to think its figure. The criteria of pure cognition of understanding that **Kant** himself sets out, **necessity** [110] and **universality**, must in the final analysis conform to sensible evidence and the agreement with possible experience. The development and growth of all sciences (including mathematics) confirm undeniably that to the degree to which one has collected a multiplicity of experiences and observations scientific **concepts** also increase. The Kantian **categories** do not contain anything that could not have been drawn from long prior experiences and would thus carry the mark of an empirical origin. The strong suspicion that **Kant** has misunderstood the natural order of things, has mistakenly taken what comes **later** for what comes **first**, and has placed the concepts that properly speaking are taken from experience prior to experience, is so far confirmed at least until **Kant** presents only one original, pure form of thought of not yet known but nevertheless possible experiences. Finally the charges of **scepticism** and **enthusiasm** leveled against the **Lockean** theory do not hold, and are, in fact, more appropriately [111] referred back to the **Kantian** philosophy. – Given all this, the decision must fall against **Kant** and his system, and the final result of everything cannot be otherwise than that the Kantian pure concepts of understanding or categories, in the Kantian sense, and what is to be further developed from them, must be counted among the number of nonentities.

Section V

Empiricism versus Purism

Carl Christian Erhard Schmid, "Some Remarks About Empiricism and Purism in Philosophy Occasioned by Selle's *Principles of Pure Philosophy*," Appendix to the *Dictionary for Easier Use of Kant's Writings*, 4th edition (Jena: Cröker, 1798), 619–68. 233

[Hermann Andreas Pistorius], "On Carl Christian Erhard Schmid's Essay About Kant's Purism and Selle's Empiricism. Appendix to *Outline of the Critique of Pure Reason*," *AdB* 88/1 (1789): 104 –22. 255

Reprinted in Hausius, *Materialien*, vol. 1, 200–17.

Carl Christian Erhard Schmid

Dictionary for the Easier Use of Kant's Writings

APPENDIX

Some Remarks about Empiricism and Purism in Philosophy Occasioned by Selle's *Principles of Pure Philosophy*[1]

If insightful and truth-loving individuals read a philosophical text by a recognizedly clear and intelligent author, and this text contains more than a small number of acute observations, precise developments of concepts and original new connections of thoughts, and the entire design and appearance of the text creates at least the appearance of thoroughness of proof and interconnectedness of the entire system; and if these individuals read the text with respect for the author, with attention to the matter at hand, with an open mind to all reasons, and without at all attempting to belittle the author or the text, [620] or trying to please some party – and then assure us that they have nonetheless run into indeterminate concepts and propositions, or contradictions and inconsistencies – and one furthermore finds, without prejudice for the anonymous person of such a judge, or for a learned and now traditionally accepted system, that their critique of such a text is at least in part a well-founded one, then one becomes suspicious that the fault lies more with the essential deficiencies of the presented doctrine, than with the mistaken presentation of its expositors and defenders, and one then feels not only aptly rewarded for the effort that the study of such a text has cost, but also indebted to its author for his examination and presentation. This seems to me to be the case with respect: to the newest fruit from the philosophical research of Mr. **Selle**; to some rather strict judges of it (for instance, in the *Allgemeine Literatur-Zeitung*, 2/6 [1788]); and, as far as the last point is concerned, to myself.

What I want to do here is draw a critical parallel between two opposed philosophical modes of thought, namely, general empiricism and purism in philosophy, the first of which has been [621] presented in Selle's text, the latter in all of Kant's critical writings, where each has been presented from its strongest side, and proven so far as is now possible. This enterprise is best and most instructively undertaken with a brief presentation of Selle's system, a comparison of it with the Kantian position and some remarks designed to examine the first. Friends of philosophy will find my enterprise to be worthwhile, at least as far as its purpose is concerned. Moreover, given his whole manner of thought as well as his express assertion that he is in the first instance concerned with serious and truthful investigations, I will not have to fear at all that the worthy **Selle** will disapprove of my purpose. After all, I am concerned only with the knowledge and evaluation of empiricism, and do not belittle the service he has done us as author, which I can only honor and admire in the philosophical field.

In every investigation about the grounds, the possibility, and the limits of metaphysical cognition (which is what one must understand the principles of pure philosophy to be [concerned with]), everything depends on the concepts of the nature and operation of the human cognitive capacities. Assuming [622] that a philosophical author knows to avoid **gross** inconsistencies (for a thoroughgoing consistency in the system of a philosopher is just as much a mere ideal as is the complete isomorphism of laws with human action), then one knows the spirit of his philosophy when one has familiarized oneself with his thoughts on this issue. Accordingly, everything that is proper to Selle's empiricism, and by virtue of which it is differentiated from Kant's purism, can be captured through the following questions:

(1) According to both doctrines, what is sensibility? (2) What is understanding? (3) What is reason? (4) How are these cognitive capacities related to one another? (5) How are they related to objects? (6) What can be cognized? (7) To what form and to what degree of certainty can human cognition be raised?

The answers each of the defenders of the two systems gives to these questions will be considered separately. [623]

I.
Sensibility

In Selle's empiricism, sensibility is the capacity to receive sensations, a capacity to be affected by things, to be changed through them, that is, the capacity to receive impressions from them. The constitution of these impressions is determined in part by the nature of the mind itself and its sensing equipment, in part by the nature of things. The immediate and first impression of things on sensibility is called sensation in the narrow sense, **immediate sensation**; the consciousness of former sensations is called **representation**. All sensations and the (sensible) representations that correspond to them have something in common. However, in neither the case of this common element nor that of the remaining particular sensations is it possible to draw a determinate boundary between what originates **from the capacity** to sense, and what, in contrast, originates from the **things** that affect this capacity. The cause of this impossibility is nothing other than that our awareness of both arises in entirely the same manner, namely as an alteration of the mind. The objects of sensibility are called **appearances**. Whatever is found in all sensations is also found in all their objects, the [624] appearances. The laws of sensibility, accordingly, are identical with the laws of objects, as appearances. Nevertheless, one cannot derive the latter exclusively from the former, or take the sensible constitution of objects to follow exclusively from the original nature of the capacity to sense; rather, one can and must derive the laws and the constitution of objects just as much from the things themselves that are their source. So even if there must be a priori laws, that is, original forms of the sensible capacity of cognition, these can nevertheless not be cognized as such by us, because we become aware of them in inseparable connection with the laws of things in a gradual and contingent manner.

If the consciousness of alterations in our cognitive capacities, as mere **alterations**, is generally called experience, then one can understand **sensible experience** to be the consciousness of the alterations of our sensibility, that is, of sensations and representations, insofar as they are considered to be only alterations in general. Sensible experience is therefore experience of appearances as such, without regard to the connections in which they stand, for sensibility does not contain or deliver connections. [625]

An aggregate of the manifold of representations, that is, of sensations, that have been consciously renewed, is a **sensible concept**, say, of a tree. We obtain these concepts only contingently, and in our sensible cognition there is no absolute universality and necessity, only a comparative one, grounded on the induction from perceptions.

There is, accordingly, no **pure sensibility**, which we could cognize as such independently from its empirical components, that is, from those of its components that originate from the objects outside of the cognitive capacities. To be sure, there is something in the totality of experience that does arise a priori, however, there is no characteristic feature that differentiates this something from what is objective, that is, from what originates from objects.

I think this is as far as the general features, which can be found in every merely empirical doctrine about sensibility, reach. The identification of anything that is peculiar to, perhaps even faulty in Selle's presentation of it, is better presented after a general comparison with what Kantian rationalism or **purism** has to say about this subject. [626]

According to the latter, **sensibility** is the entire passive capacity of the mind, the capacity to be altered through objects. (The empiricists, by contrast, as will become clearer later, also consider understanding to be passive in the production of its cognition.) To be sure, sensibility delivers only particular impressions, but these occur in certain original and necessary relations that depend solely on the nature of the subject, namely the soul itself, not the organs of sense (which must be considered to be sensible objects, not necessary conditions of the sensible capacity), and certainly not on things in themselves. What these relations have in common, namely, that we intuit everything in space and time, is, therefore, only the subjective condition of appearances, and a sensible representation a priori, that is, a representation that lies solely in the **intuitive capacity**. As such it can be known and differentiated from the sensations given in a representation, although only by applying this capacity in connection with the given sensations. One can call this **pure sensibility**, a priori sensibility, or the pure law of sensibility. It contains the sole and exclusive condition of everything that is perceived as common to sensible representations and appearances. Its universality and [627] necessity is therefore absolute, that is, we are conscious of the fact that all sensible representations and their objects must be appropriate to these forms, without so much as one possible exception.

This Kantian purism is **irrefutable** supposing it is in principle impossible to intuit the object in itself and make comprehensible how representations arise from its influence on sensibility. Nevertheless, one would have to consider Kant's purism to be **groundless**, and its assertion to be an arbitrary dogmatism, if the proofs of its truth did not also demonstrate the impossibility of rationally deriving what is common to all appearances from something that belongs to the objects themselves. Otherwise to draw this, or any other particular boundary between representations that arise a priori and those that arise empirically, to ascribe everything that is **without present exception** universal in sensibility to the constitution of its own capacity, and thereby to represent these universal elements as absolute, that is, as just as necessary as our subjective capacity itself would have to be considered nothing more than an acceptable, but only contingent hypothesis. [628]

It seems noteworthy that **Selle** (p. 29) calls space a condition of sensibility, but does not want to ascribe it solely to sensibility itself. However, one can hardly understand his use of the expression **condi-**

tion in Kant's sense, namely, as related merely to the subject; rather, Selle uses it to indicate only an essential, that is, generally perceived element of sensible representations, and does not make any claims about its origin. And who would want to deny him the right to this use of this expression simply because some readers of his text, who are used to the Kantian manner of speaking, would initially misinterpret Selle's meaning?[2]

A different part of Selle's theory of sensibility, does, however, seem to require closer examination, given the short, indeterminate, and obscure assertions that one finds about it. This occurs primarily on pages 20–30 where Selle consistently speaks of sensibility in such a way that one can only think of **outer** sensibility, which is changed by objects outside of the cognitive capacities and the common element of which is space, as is explicitly claimed. No mention at all is made of those alterations that the subject itself, as an active capacity, [629] occasions in itself (as a passive capacity) through the alterations that are received from outside and that Kant calls **inner sensations**. Indeed, time, which, according to Kant, is the common element and form of these sensations (p. 40), is here presented as the common element of all perceptions that understanding has of combinations. On page 109 Selle counts sensations among noumena. However, the context in which this expression is used does not seem to allow us to think of these as sensations of inner sense, for Selle there also mentions representations, that earlier had been explicitly ascribed to a further class, along with outer sensations. The author refers to inner sensations for the first and only time on page 149, where he identifies them as **mental** or mediate sensations (which is an expression that had been used earlier, on page 27, to refer to something entirely different, namely representations, that is, renewed sensations).[3] He declares them to be alterations that have been occasioned by means of comparison, abstraction, and a new combination of representations and sensuous concepts in sensibility, but derives their existence from outer sensations. No doubt many readers would wish for a clear [630] answer here to the question of how and to what extent space, the common element that had originally (pp. 29, 134) been attributed to all sensations without restriction, is to be found in **these** sensuous representations, and whether it is not perhaps actually time, which rests in the first instance at the ground of all inner sensations, that belongs there. Moreover, because every outer sensation stimulates the activity of the cognitive capacity and every such activity occasions a proportionally strong alteration in the passive part of the mind, time can also be found as part of all sensations in general and must be considered their form.

When Selle further objects to the claim (pp. 30, 40) that the representation of space must be present even if no sensuous cognition exists, then he actually agrees with the purists on one point. However, his inference that space is not a pure representation, that is, a representation that is not in its existence grounded in any perception, even though time is a representation that is dependent on the consciousness of inner sense, does not seem to follow. Quite the contrary, the objective nothingness of empty space is much more appropriately comprehended on the basis of precisely this [purity]. For if this representation did not solely originate with the subject of [631] cognition, then it would have to be produced from its objects in themselves, and then it would have to be a component of their empirical representation. However, according to the agreement of empiricists and purists, a **necessary** connection between the manifold empirical representations cannot be known. Granted, the possibility would remain that space would also be perceived as empty space, that is, as separated from all other perceptions.

If space is an empirical representation, and if every empirical representation objectively designates a component of appearances, then space itself is something that appears, something physical, and every connection in space is a physical combination (p. 36). But how could one then deny that so-called pure geometry, which concerns itself with the investigation of relations in space, has application to reality with respect to actual things, as nonetheless happens on page 167 and in several other places?[4]

If we do in fact arrive at the representation of space only by means of perceptions, why then do we relate all places to one space, and why do we represent it as infinite? Does this not demonstrate a deeper [632] origin of our representation of space than the mere empirical one? – Not one syllable of Selle's argument has touched this heretofore completely unshaken foundation of the Kantian theory of space.

It is, incidentally, a rather obvious sophism to describe a representation from the very outset as a revived sensation, and then, from this stipulative definition to infer, quite correctly, that there is no a priori representation. For either one would have to presuppose the general empiricism of all representations, in order to be able to introduce it at the outset into the very definition of a representation, which is something the purists would not allow, or, if the explanation is not to be arbitrary, one would have to understand an a priori representation to be one that could be noticed in the mind quite independently of sensations. But the Kantian philosopher could not be accused of invoking that sort of concept of an a priori representation without obvious injustice. [633]

II.
What is Understanding?

For the empiricists, **understanding** is a capacity of the mind to be altered and to become conscious of its alterations, just like sensibility. The difference is only that the objects of the alterations that understanding suffers are not the appearances themselves, but their connections. Nor are these alterations themselves sensations; rather, they are representations of relations. Understanding does not itself connect, it only perceives connections of things, namely of appearances. These affect it and alter it; it becomes conscious of these alterations and in this way a thought arises.

If one understands sensibility in a broader sense as the entire capacity of the receptivity of the mind or the cognitive capacity in general, insofar as it passively receives representations, then understanding, as explained by the empiricists, is only a branch of sensibility, that which is affected by the connections of things. Sensibility in the narrow sense, by contrast, receives alterations of its consciousness from appearances considered apart from their connections. [634]

To be sure, there must be certain basic features of understanding, just as there is an original constitution of sensibility, however, the status of the possible knowledge of them is the same as the status of the knowledge of the basic determinations of sensibility. Each expression of understanding is the result of understanding itself, that is, of the knowing subject insofar as it experiences connections, and of the connections that belong to the things in themselves. But there is no certain means by which to differentiate the determinate contribution that the cognitive capacity makes from that which the cognized object makes to this representation. This is the case because we gradually become conscious of both of them in much the same way.

Granted, there is something that belongs to every exercise of understanding equally. There are, however, no good reasons to attribute this to a pure origin from understanding, or to an empirical origin from certain relations that belong to all things equally. So if one identifies each product of understanding as **concept**, then a **pure concept**, if it is to be a pure concept a priori, is something that cannot ever be realized through a particular reference to individual cases. But one can also call the finest and most general abstractions of combined concepts [635] **pure concepts**. In that case their existence in understanding is undeniable, but their origin remains problematic.

The proper product of understanding, that is, what it characteristically receives as understanding, is a **thought**, that is, a representation of a relation or a connection. The thought is first abstracted from **sensible concepts**, that is, from the manifold of sensations, representations, and appearances, insofar as they are thought. In part such a concept contains sensible representations and belongs, in this respect, to sensibility; in part it contains a representation of a connection, that is, a thought, and belongs in that respect to understanding. So, for example, a causal connection represented concretely is a sensuous concept; represented abstractly, it is a thought. The thought, in turn, contains a manifold the parts of which stand in a certain relation to each other. This manifold constitutes a **concept of understanding** insofar as one considers this multiplicity. In the previous example of causality, the manifold consists of cause and effect.

Now, if one further represents the relation of the manifold in a thought [636] separately from the manifold content, then a thought of a thought arises, that is, a **general** thought. One can call the particular parts of a thought **derived** thoughts.

The manifold that is connected into a sensible concept by means of a single thought is called **physically connected** and is, in turn, either **really connected**, when what is connected is at the same time present as one appearance, or **causally connected**, when it exists successively at different times in different appearances. The manifold of thoughts, which is connected through a general thought in a concept of understanding, is called **logically connected**.

So we are conscious of physical connections (real and causal combinations) through sensible concepts, and of logical connections through concepts of understanding. But the latter only exist in understanding to the extent that physical connections, which provide their matter, precede them.

According to Kantian **purism** [in contrast], understanding is active in its own right; it does not receive connections, rather, it connects. Moreover, [637] it exercises this activity in such a way and according to such laws as can be considered apart from their concrete products. One already finds such an, as it were, chemical separation of what is pure, what is originally in understanding, and what is empirical, what is added to it, in **logic**, where the object of investigation is the form of judgments considered apart from their matter. The forms of judgment are, with respect to their essence, isomorphic with the essence of the

concepts, which are likewise **undeveloped judgments**. Because, as immediate consciousness teaches, we **ourselves** judge and obtain only the material for judgments from other things, the same must be the case for these concepts.

The separated consciousness of these forms of our judgments and concepts likewise accords with our concrete concepts and judgments, because we first become conscious of our cognizing subject through the act of cognition. This, however, always presupposes objects that affect the capacity for thought. These impressions, however, do not determine the formal manner of connection; rather, they are only the material condition of our combining anything in general and this thing in particular. [638]

The concepts in themselves, considered apart from all sensible material, indeed, even from the manner (form of sensibility) in which this material is given in the first place, are called **pure** a priori **concepts**. An example of this is the representation of the relation between the ground and what is grounded in an object. The same concept, separated, admittedly, from all really given material, but yet modified and more closely determined by the manner in which we receive this material through our sensible intuitive capacity, is the general concept of understanding made sensible in a pure manner, the **schema**. An example of this is the representation of a sensible ground, of a cause, which works in time. These modifications, accordingly, are contingent on pure sensibility, that is, on time and space. Finally, the concept connected with its real sensible material is a **concrete**, **empirical concept**. This would be, for example, the concept of an actual cause. By means of the separation of the components of such concrete concepts, for instance, of gold, **abstract concepts** arise, for instance, of the color yellow. By means of the combination of a multiplicity of pure or even abstract concepts **synthesized concepts** arise. In the first case, they are **pure**, in the second **empirical** and general. The merely subjective comparison of concepts with one another generates **comparative concepts**, the comparison of objects [639] with one another **reflective concepts** and so on.

Because cognition requires material in addition to thought, we can go as far with our thought as the original store of all pure concepts and the possibility of its pure connection extends, but we can **cognize** only sensible objects, which deliver material for cognition through sensibility.

The connection of pure concepts without sensible material is a merely logical connection; the synthesis of sensible sensations, by contrast, is a **real** or physical connection.

The concepts in themselves, accordingly, are just as necessary and universal as understanding, and they are valid as laws in the entire field of its objects. According to empiricism, by contrast, they are valid only of the objects that have thus far been actually cognized, and they can only be transferred to similar objects to be cognized in the future on the basis of an analogy that must always remain uncertain.

A necessary implication of the empiricism of understanding is, accordingly, scepticism with respect to even the most general laws of nature. [640] Purism, by contrast, entails an absolute necessity of the laws of cognition and of knowable objects. Empiricism has two points against it: first, our consciousness that we do judge ourselves, and do not experience any external coercion in this action of understanding, and, second, the whole of the entire formal and unchanging logic. Purism has both points in its favor.

III.
What is Reason?

According to empiricism, it is only at this point that the independent exercise of the cognitive capacity begins. Reason produces two effects, which are, however, subordinated to one another as means to an end. It cognizes laws, and it draws inferences or it makes discoveries.

First, it cognizes laws, that is, general connections. Understanding delivers the connections themselves, as far as the material element is concerned, and it does so in part with respect to appearances, in part with respect to thoughts. Reason compares these connections and identifies those that have been confirmed through every experience made so far, and that have had no known exceptions, [641] to be **universal** and objective.

When physical connections are represented as universal, they give us **laws of appearances** or **sensibility**; when logical connections are represented generally, **laws of thought**. Both together are called (by Selle) **laws of the cognitive capacities**, even though, according to the empirical theory of sensibility and understanding, they could just as well be called laws of objects. After all, they are grounded in the latter just as much as in the former.

For the representation of this universality, nothing is required except that one knows historically that a thing appears to each human being (as far as is known), and that each human being thinks a thought in just the same way as every individual is conscious of an appearance and this thought as alteration of his mind. Hence, one cognizes these laws through the union of immediate and historical experience, and their universality and necessity is therefore merely comparative.

Second, reason **draws inferences** on the basis of these laws, that is, it applies them to cases [642] where we have not perceived the connection they express. This act is called **reasoning**, inference, or also (by Selle) judgment. In relation to the inferred cognition, the law is called its **sufficient reason**. From this reason cognizes something different, something that neither understanding nor sensibility has received.

The following elements are therefore required for each rational inference:

1. A cognized connection (major premise). This is delivered by understanding and is
   a. Either a logical connection. In this case the **reasoning** (for instance, mathematical reasoning) is similarly called **logical** and rests on the principle of identity: identical things have identical connections
   b. or a physical connection. In this case the **reasoning** built on this connection is physical and rests on the principle of analogy: similar things have similar connections. If one draws further inferences from such physical reasoning, thus generating other cognitions, [643] then these are **metaphysical**.
2. A thing that is given, either a sensible thing or a thought (minor premise). On the basis of these premises one cognizes
3. A different thing (appearance or thought) that is connected to what is given (no. 2) in accord with a universal experience (no. 1).

One can draw inferences on the basis of connections that are given immediately through understanding, or from those that are themselves inferences, but in all cases the most remote premises lie either in sensibility or in understanding.

In this manner we also infer the existence of things in themselves, because we are led from the final grounds in appearances and thoughts to their sufficient reason.

There is, accordingly (pp. 64, 90, 170), no such thing as **pure reason**, for the use of this capacity always depends on sensibility and understanding, hence, rests on actual experience. [644] To be sure, reason does have its own laws (forms), just as things have them independently of all experience. However, the cognition of the laws of reason must in part be first abstracted from concrete inferences of reason; hence, it presupposes experience and has the same certainty that they have. In part the law of cognition is so similar to that of things that a mental separation of this mix into its component parts is impossible, and no critique is capable of determining those proper to each.

It follows that the Kantian synthesis of pure reason is an impossibility.

(Kantian) **purism** lets all those (Sellean) explanations stand that deal with **empirical reason**, that is, with the capacity of reason in its concrete application to sensibly given objects. But he does not give up the claim that a pure reason exists. To be sure, logicians have abstracted the forms of rational inference, which conform to certain ideas of reason, from concrete inferences; however, they would not have been able to do so if reason had not first set them into these concrete inferences. Because there is nothing in objects, as the material of inferences, that is similar to a rational inference, [645] the forms of rational inference could not have come to the soul from them. Because, furthermore, we are immediately conscious of our own activity in reasoning, they belong to reason itself in an a priori fashion, and, given that the logician does in fact cognize them, they are cognized a priori. Pure reason does, accordingly, have its synthesis which consists in drawing inferences. However, given that the materials for these inferences must always come from sensibility and understanding, its connections considered **on their own**, as pure synthesis, do not have objective reality. It is the essence of the Kantian critique of reason to deliver the proof of this last assertion, namely, that a pure synthesis of reason cannot, considered merely speculatively, deliver a real cognition of actual objects. Selle's reasoning (pp. 112 ff), insofar as it is directed against the result of the critique of reason, seems to have missed the real point of the controversy.

Selle's treatise does not take a determinate position on whether reason actually has the right to make the cognized laws of experience applicable to those things of which no experience is possible (in Kant's language this would be called an objectively valid synthesis of pure reason). But when Selle tries to cognize the existence and nature of God through rational inferences [646] (pp. 155 ff), he does in fact help himself to this supposed right, without having even seemingly deduced its validity. So he is the one who presupposes the synthesis of pure reason and its objectivity by way of his transcendental application of laws of experience, not Kant. Kant, by contrast, denies the objectivity of such speculative rational inferences that go beyond experience (see the seventh question).

Reason uses the laws of appearances in order to draw inferences about what has not been experienced. This is a fact of human reason, the historical truth of which is equally conceded by both empiricists and purists. The legitimacy of this procedure, however, must be demonstrated and deduced. Purists do so by representing these laws as subjective conditions of experience, and by representing everything that is inferred from them as valid for all objects of experience. The restriction of the validity of these inferences to what can be experienced and the exclusion of things in themselves is admittedly a necessary consequence of this. Empiricists, by contrast, cannot present even a semblance of a proper ground and must accordingly borrow it from the fact that experience always successfully confirms these inferences. However, this [647] success cannot properly speaking deliver any objective certainty prior to experience because, according to their doctrines, this experience is only contingent. If those who deny all cognition by pure reason extend their own inferences so far as to the existence and the constitution of things in themselves, then this only possible ground of confirmation falls out of reach, and everything becomes arbitrary. This weak side of empiricism also shows itself rather obviously through the incoherent nature of the reasoning with which Selle wants to establish the existence of God, reasoning moreover, that does not properly cohere with other assertions he makes. On page 55, for instance, he himself presents the maxim: "an inference that teaches us of the existence of things that have neither identity nor similarity with the things known through experience, is without all ground and hence false." Is this not exactly what occurs, however, in each judgment about the existence and constitution of substantial powers in appearances, and even more so, about infinite substance? At the same time, an application of that principle is not made here, rather, the most disanalogous things are inferred from one another, as appearances and objects in themselves. According to page 36, "logical connections are valid only to the extent to which they are applicable to physical connections of objects." Yet the entire proof for the existence of God (p. 163) rests [648] on the very connections of thought that, since God cannot be sensibly perceived, lack given material and so cannot be provided with a physical ground. Under these presuppositions, accordingly, such a procedure cannot be taken as consistent.

IV.
How Are Sensibility, Understanding, and Reason Related to One Another?

According to **empiricism**, sensibility first delivers objects, understanding perceives their relations, and reason applies the relations cognized by understanding to things that understanding has not yet experienced. All material for cognition comes into the mind through sensibility and understanding; all form of cognition is determined by reason. In sensibility, just as in understanding, everything is mere perception, the former perceives appearances, the latter the connection of appearances, as well as the thoughts thus created. It is only as reason that the [649] cognitive capacity is spontaneously active; as sensibility and understanding the capacity remains passive. Moreover, all these differently named cognitive capacities are only different perspectives, from which one sees the same [things]. Hence they are always employed at the same time, although not always equally noted.

According to **purism**, sensibility receives impressions from objects, and understanding thinks their relations, that is, it spontaneously creates them in accord with its own laws, but only as far as the material given through the senses extends. All material for cognition comes into the mind through sensibility, understanding originally creates all forms of thought and all connections in accord with its own laws and the laws of sensibility. By means of rational inferences and ideas, reason provides systematic unity to that which understanding has cognized.

Purists also concede the unity of all cognitive capacities in one subject. They do not do so with the hope of reaching complete satisfaction by explaining all expressions of the soul from one principle but because such a presupposition is most appropriate to the rational idea of a systematic unity of all that is manifold. [650]

V.
How Are These Cognitive Capacities Related to Objects?

According to the **empiricist** doctrine, sensibility and understanding relate in the first instance to appearances, the former to their sensible nature, the latter to their connections, but both do so only passively. Everything that occurs in the cognitive capacities, including the relations in which we intuit things and the manner in which we think their relation, is grounded in objects as things in themselves. The entire manner in which the cognitive capacity expresses itself, in which sensibility receives, understanding combines, reason forms laws and draws inferences on their basis, is prescribed to it through the nature of things in themselves and their connection. All laws of nature proceed from the things into the mind and **there** they become laws of cognition.

According to the system of the **purist**, by contrast, all cognitive capacities are themselves determined and, furthermore, determine the manner in which we represent objects to ourselves. Sensibility determines the manner and relations of the intuition of objects, understanding the thought of them, that is, their connections. The form [651] and the laws of the objects, which we represent, depend, accordingly, primarily on the cognitive capacities. The (immanent) laws of nature lie in pure understanding, their closer modification in pure sensibility, their most determinate applications in empirical sensibility or sensible impressions. Reason does not determine anything in the objects of cognition. Nor is it determined by them. Rather, it only brings system into the cognitions of understanding, and, through its ideas, gives it instruction for the most extensive use of its own principles. Its (transcendent) laws of nature are ideal, hence neither learned from nature and abstracted from it, nor placed into nature in order to give its diverse manifold some connection; rather, they are only prescribed to understanding as rules in order to prevent it from giving arbitrary limits to its application. In accord with reason, the investigations of understanding do not know any limits other than those of the possibility of intuiting objects. [652]

VI.
What Can be Cognized Through These Capacities?

What **objects** and what **predicates** of objects [are cognized through these capacities]?

According to (Selle's) empiricism, the following things can be cognized:

1. **Appearances**, sensible things, that is, objects that we are conscious of through sensation by means of sensibility. Mr. Selle has not precisely specified in his treatise whether this includes only outer experiences or inner ones as well.
2. Physical **connections of appearances**, that is, their simultaneity or succession (real or causal connections), of which we are conscious as synthetical propositions through understanding.

   Reason cognizes those physical connections, which universal experience confirms as constant and regular, as **laws of appearances**, as universal synthetic propositions. [653]
3. Things in us or **noumena**, that is, sensations, representations, thoughts, concepts, judgments, inferences, desires, and the like considered as something merely **subjective** that belongs to the mind. These are perceived immediately through understanding.
4. Logical **connections of noumena**. These we cognize analytically through understanding.

We cognize constant and universal logical connections, **laws of noumena** and **thoughts** through reason.

5. We cognize the **existence of things in themselves** or, as Selle calls them, **of substances**, as condition of the possibility of cognition in general. For we cannot derive the data of cognition from the mere capacity of sensibility, understanding and reason, precisely because they are mere **capacities** (formal conditions) for cognition. Even if noumena are grounded in appearances,* [654] these along with their relations must still be grounded in something other and its connections, something that exists independently of our cognition, which would exist and continue to exist even if there were no cognition. This something must be in part **cognitive capacity**, in part **object** of cognition. Whether these things must be different substrata can actually no more be determined from the principles of empiricism than from any other noncritical doctrine because everything that one requires for the explanation only leads to something as the sufficient reason of cognition.† Selle, however, makes a decision in favor of dualism but leaves indeterminate what and how much each of these two different substances contributes to the possibility and constitution of appearances. He would have been as little false to his other principles, if he had derived everything solely from the nature of the cognitive [655] capacity, however much this assertion seems to have in common with purism.
6. The **laws** and constitutions of **substances in themselves**, insofar as they are the substrata of appearances. For the laws of appearances must be grounded in these **substrata**, as their powers, and are, therefore, at the same time laws of things, though perceived in a sensible way (p. 162).

   Each appearance presupposes a different one, so the final and sufficient ground does not lie in the appearances themselves. This is also true of the substances that ground the appearances, that is, of things in themselves. These too presuppose something other as sufficient reason for their existence. That is, they are **finite** and limited just as appearances are, so Selle argues (p. 163).

* There are two remarks that I cannot make consistent. One is that noumena are grounded in **phenomena**; the other that there is something substantial that rests at the ground of logical connections (that is, the connections of noumena) **in the cognitive capacity**. Both are on p. 154 of Selle's *Grundsätze der reinen Philosophie*.

† One must only not assume any other than inner sensations.

But is this not perhaps an inference from entirely dissimilar things to other entirely dissimilar things, one that is shown to be inadmissible on the basis of a maxim Mr. Selle himself recommends (p. 55)?[5] Is it not an attempt to determinately cognize what substance is in itself, which is not something of which we can possibly have a representation (p. 159) – an attempt that [656] must necessarily fail if this principle is to be true and valid?

The same holds with respect to the knowledge of the supersensible. The empiricists (and dogmatic philosophers in general) are incapable of providing the foundation for a natural cognition of God while preserving the validity of their proofs and an agreement of this enterprise with their own principles. For Selle counts among what is cognizable also.

7. The **existence** of an infinite substance, of **God**.

If there are finite substances, that do not contain the sufficient ground of their existence in themselves, then there must also be an infinite substance, that is, one that is not dependent on anything else for its existence.

However, is this not tantamount to taking a merely logical connection between what is grounded and its ground, for a physical one, even though we lack the sensibly given material, the perception of God? Moreover, a surreptitiously obtained and unproven presupposition may be hidden here concerning the identity of the concepts of something that is **independent** in its existence (as the [657] infinite is explained) and that which is **unlimited** in its predicates and perfections (which is usually called infinite). Given that this connection cannot be traced back to an identity through analysis of concepts, this connection would have to be especially demonstrated (but how would this be possible?).

8. **Predicates** of the Godhead, in addition to its infinity.

The Godhead is differentiated from the substrate of appearances, for they are finite.

In this proof two things are arbitrarily assumed: **first**, that substrata have similar predicates to their appearances and are, accordingly, finite, that is, dependent; **second**, that what is dependent is necessarily limited, and only the independent has limitless perfection.

Spinozism, accordingly, can hardly be successfully refuted by anything other than critical idealism, which prohibits us from identifying appearances (which include extension) with things in themselves. It can certainly not be successfully refuted with the use of such dogmatic weapons. [658]

The Godhead is **immaterial**, for (p. 175) all appearing substances have the representation of space and impenetrability, that is, are material.

All substances of appearances are finite, the Godhead, as an infinite substance is not similar to finite substances, hence must be immaterial.

Here again the necessity of an infinite substance in addition to the substrate of phenomena is presupposed without sufficient justification, because an infinite regress of appearances would be sufficient for understanding, and reason does not, in this case, feel a compelling need to explain everything. Apart from this, the inference is false even in its form, unless one presupposes a **necessary** connection between finitude and materiality, and between infinity and immateriality. And by what means is the necessity of such a necessary synthesis to be demonstrated? And how is it thereby to be demonstrated that what is material **must** be finite? How is the possibility that an infinite substance could not also appear as matter to be set aside? Universal experience certainly could not possibly exclude the unexperienced cases. [659]

The Godhead is **freely acting cause** of the laws of appearances as well as of those of the cognitive capacities and of free actions for the former can no more be explained from the substrate of appearances than the latter are explainable from the substate of the mind. Hence, the sufficient reason of their determination must lie outside of them in the infinite substance, God.

However, if **we** cannot explain the laws of outer and inner appearances on the basis of the substrate, then this may be a function of the absolute insufficiency of these substrates to determine these laws, but it can just as well be the fault of **our** unfamiliarity with their essence in itself, and of the subjective inability to explain something from what is entirely unknown. If the substrata of appearances are unknown to us, then we may not explain anything from them. But is not the essence of an infinite substance at least just as foreign, and must the last grounds of things and their laws be **discoverable** by us because reason drives us to look for them? [660]

The last case arises only when an **absolutely necessary need** drives us to the assumption of an insufficiently objectively grounded presupposition, which is not sufficiently grounded objectively. The merely speculative interest in providing an explanation produces an only contingent need that does not absolutely require satisfaction. For what should make it necessary that we explain everything, given that our experiential knowledge [and its development], which we require for the needs of life, arises independently and endlessly even without any determinate explanation of what has been experienced from its final grounds? We can be satisfied with a **merely thought** unity of all experiences among one another, even if that is not determinately cognized.

Only a **practical** need that rests on an apodeictic law of reason can have absolute necessity when, according to the essential constitution of our nature, this demand of reason cannot be satisfied by us without a certain presupposition. But philosophy knows nothing of such an absolutely necessary command of reason, especially a philosophy that recognizes only empirical principles, and derives even the moral commands from no other sources than experience that can never deliver absolute necessity. Accordingly, it can no more [661] deliver a conclusive proof of the theoretical or practical cognition of God and a firm foundation for religion than can any other merely dogmatic philosophy.

9. We have cognition of all things as well as their laws to the extent that they affect us, consequently of their necessity with respect to us, but not of an absolute necessity.

According to **purism** in philosophy, we cognize inner as well as outer appearances, through sensibility and through the (empirical) understanding that is applied to it. We similarly cognize their connections through perception, and, insofar as these connections are necessary (laws), we cognize them as absolutely necessary laws because they depend on the invariable nature of our mind. We know things in themselves only to the extent that we are required to presuppose their existence as conditions of the existence of appearances, but we do so without any determinable predicate because we can only relate sensible determinations to appearances. We can only think of the Godhead, but speculative grounds are insufficient to demonstrate the existence or nonexistence of an object that corresponds to this thought outside of understanding. [662] That is, we cannot objectively demonstrate its existence, or determine its predicates in themselves. So for mere speculation the presupposition of the Godhead as originator of the world is an acceptable, but by no means necessary hypothesis. We do recognize, however – and this is something we would have to do without in a thoroughly executed empiricism – an absolutely necessary law of reason for our free actions, and we are immediately conscious of an unlimited respect for this law and of the subjection of the will to it. However, because of our connection with sensibility, we are not able to grasp the whole decision to follow this law and its agreement with the complete nature of our faculty of desire, if we do not presuppose the existence of God as a moral and at the same time infinite being, as regent of the world and as condition of the possible harmony of the objects of this sensible faculty and our pure faculty of desire. This highest need for the agreement of our entire nature and its purpose irresistibly forces us to recognize the validity of the proofs for the existence of God, which, even though they are insufficient for theoretical knowledge in themselves, still do not contradict any theoretical insight. Our subjective need takes the place of objective certainty in supplying our conviction and fills out our belief with what would always be missing from any objective certainty. [663] For the same reason, we believe that we have to ascribe all those properties to the Godhead without which it would not be the indispensable pillar for subjective morality for us that we want it to be.

Only the purist, accordingly, knows a **pure morality**, religion, and a **pure moral theology**. One cannot expect any of those things from empiricism. It, rather, leaves the speculative as well as, much more importantly, the invincible practical needs and demands of human reason unsatisfied. In order to proceed consistently, it denies human beings their personal independence and freedom and with this, at the same time, the possibility of attaining a pure independent morality, which is the object of their innermost desire, and the condition of their highest personal honor and dignity; finally, it also denies them the one and only means by use of which, given that they are sensibly affected, they could be put into a position to assume this honor even so far as they can come to be acquainted with it, as the highest goal of their efforts.

This reasoning, in which the warmth of our passion is excused through the overwhelming interest of the object, is confirmed [664] through the consideration of every merely empirical moral philosophy and would show itself in Selle's principles, if the author had deemed it appropriate to provide an extensive treatment of this object in his text.

The purist can now ask the empiricist what are the useful and worthy convictions (p. 4) that Kant is supposed to have stolen from us through his efforts to provide apodeictic certainty of things?

VII.
What Form and What Degree of Certainty Can Human Cognition Reach?

As an **empiricist**, Mr. Selle has answered this question as follows:

All our cognitions are either themselves experiences, or reasoning that rests on premises, the truth of which we experience through understanding and sensibility.

What sensibility and understanding cognize is, in both cases, **experience**. In this way, we experience [665] immediately (**intuitively**) through sensibility, for instance, that scarlet is red and of this we have a subjective, **physical certainty**. We experience immediately (intuitively) through understanding certain alterations in the relation of things, for instance, the thought $2 \times 2 = 4$. This gives us a subjective **demonstrative** mathematical **certainty** of logical connections. In contrast to physical certainty, this mathematical certainty has the advantage of entitling the person who has this intuition to complete certainty without requiring confirmation through witnessing the consistent experience of other human beings.

When we do not perceive something ourselves, but the accounts of others bring about representations and concepts of it in us, for example, that something appears in a certain way to other human beings, this thing is experienced mediately (**historically**), and our **certainty** is **historical**. We experience mediately through understanding (**empirically**) that other human beings think a thought in a certain way. The **certainty** available here is similarly **subjectively historic**. Of all these cognitions through mere experience (of understanding or sensibility, and in both cases either immediately or mediately) we possess only **subjective certainty**, faith. [666] We are not convinced of the absolute impossibility of the opposite.

When we compare the immediate and mediate cognitions of experience through reason, and abstract what they have in common from it, then we cognize **laws** that have a comparative universality and a necessity that lies in the collected experiences themselves; laws of experience as well as laws of thought. These ground themselves in the final instance on intuitive and historical experiences of which we can properly speaking have only a subjective certainty. For this reason, we do not have any other or greater certainty than those data from which they are abstracted.

Now, when we, already knowing these laws, experience something else, whether immediately or mediately, which conforms to the already known laws of nature and the cognitive capacities, then we attain a greater conviction of the correctness of these experiences. This is called

evidence and is connected with the impossibility of thinking the opposite as possible. However, even this type of impossibility is only subjective and not absolute, since it is **still** dependent only on contingent experiences. [667]

Therefore, neither understanding, nor sensibility, nor yet reason can deliver an absolute, universal, and necessary cognition, nor any other certainty than one that is comparatively universal for the subject and **therefore called objective**.

The **purist**, by contrast, must according to his own principles take all particular perceptions to be contingent, but take the existence of experience in itself, or, and this is the same thing, nature and its laws, to be just as universal and necessary as the cognitive capacity. Each particular application of a universal law to an individual object leaves the possibility of error, but the law itself contains its certainty which, to be sure, is only subjective, but which is absolutely universal and therefore objective.

Objective certainty springs from another source as well, namely, from practical reason insofar as it provides us with practical laws that do not allow for any exception.

In addition to this apodeictic certainty of universal natural and moral laws, there is also a subjectively necessary conviction or a **faith** that is in part **contingent**, in part also **absolutely necessary**. The first is the case with the merely theoretical **hypotheses** that one assumes on the basis of the merely speculative intention to bring unity into cognition, the other with respect to practical **postulates**, that is, those presuppositions [668] with respect to which what is at issue is the production of something that is practically objectively necessary, that is, the satisfaction of the demands of the apodeictic laws of morality. So we believe merely contingently (pragmatically) that there is a God, since we can think and comprehend a purposive world unity only under this presupposition. But we believe the same thing necessarily as well, because it is only under this presupposition that we think ourselves able to unify the supreme purpose, which we must think as rational beings, with the sum of all our other purposes and direct our activity to the attainment of it, which is something that the consciousness of our high honor as rational beings demands.

This brief comparison of strict empiricism and purism in philosophy by way of the main problems of a critique of reason contains perhaps the most important resources for the answer to the question, not unimportant in general, and particularly not in our time, of which of these two essentially different doctrines is in its principles better grounded, in its unity more compelling, and in its final implications more appropriate to the interest of human reason.

[Hermann Andreas Pistorius]

On Carl Christian Erhard Schmid's Essay About Kant's Purism and Selle's Empiricism. Appendix to *Outline of the Critique of Pure Reason* . . . [6]

This essay contains a comparison of Kant's purism with Selle's empiricism. This is what Mr. Schmid names the opposed doctrines of Mr. Kant and Mr. Selle. [Selle presents the latter] in his *Principles of Pure Philosophy*. Here he specifies that the first assumes pure sensibility, pure understanding, and pure reason, whereas the second denies all of this and derives all our cognition without exception from experience. The author assumes correctly that this comparison and examination of both doctrines is best conducted through the following seven questions: (1) What is sensibility according to both systems? (2) What is understanding? (3) What is reason? (4) How are these cognitive capacities related to one another? (5) How are they related to objects? (6) What can be cognized? (7) To what form and to what degree of certainty can human cognition be raised? In this essay I will present only as much of these contrasts as is requisite in order to understand and evaluate the author's preference for Kantian purism as well as my possible objections.

With respect to the first question, the difference between both systems seems to consist only in the fact that purism assumes a so-called pure sensibility, and empiricism denies it. The concept of space constitutes this pure sensibility (for even though time belongs here as well, it is not mentioned in this comparison because it is properly and primarily the form of inner sense and Mr. Selle has hardly, if at all, discussed inner sense in the *Principles of Pure Philosophy*). Space is ostensibly only the subjective form of outer sensibility; it does not have an objective component and is not grounded in anything objective. [105] According to Selle's empiricism, by contrast, space has not just a subjective, but also an objective ground. – K.'s purism seems to Schmid irrefutable because, according to the nature of things, it is impossible to cognize the object in itself and to make comprehensible the origin of these representations (of space and time) as a function of its influence on sensibility. However, purism does not seem to me to be irrefutable, at least not for this reason. For if purism is generally valid, then there is no empirical sensibility at all, but only a pure sensibility. For of what sensation could it be made in any way evident how it arose or had to arise from the influence of objects on sensibility? The representations of space and time would in this respect be no different from all other sensations, rather, they would share this indeterminacy in common with them and so would not demonstrate anything regarding their subjectivity that they did not also demonstrate for the subjectivity of all sensations in general. However, this is something the author seems to concede when he adds: "[n]evertheless, one would have to consider it (Kant's purism) to be groundless, and its assertion to be an arbitrary dogmatism, if the proofs of its truth did not also demonstrate the impossibility of rationally deriving what is common to all appearances from something that belongs to the objects themselves."[7] As far as I know the proofs that have been presented for K's purism, they are all designed only to refute and exclude the precisely opposite case, namely, that space and time are merely objective or representations solely grounded in objects. But they do not address the middle hypothesis, assumed by all reasonable empiricists, among them Mr. Selle, namely that these representations are grounded equally in the subjective and the objective sphere. The same is the case with what the author presents as further proof of K's purism. How does he propose to obtain proofs to demonstrate that what is common to the appearances of a particular thing could not possibly [106] arise from something common to the object in itself? Perhaps from the fact that he concedes, and even dares to demonstrate, that he does not and cannot know a single property of things in themselves, and accordingly, no property they have in common? But does it follow from his ignorance that these objects do not actually have properties, and, moreover, that they do not actually have properties in common? I think rather, that the opposite is undeniable, as soon as one concedes that they actually exist as real things in themselves. How can our subjective inability to indicate this commonality and to derive it to the complete satisfaction of reason from the commonality of all things in themselves, constitute a proof of the absolute impossibility to provide such a demonstration? Moreover, as just indicated, we cannot provide such a rational derivation of any single particular property of appearances from the particularity of objects in themselves, nor indicate any particular aspect of these objects. So if this way of drawing the inference were to be conclusive, everything that can be observed in appearances would be without exception subjective and there would be no such thing as an empirical sensibility, there would only be pure sensibility.

II. WHAT IS UNDERSTANDING?

According to the empiricists, understanding is, like sensibility, a capacity of the mind to be altered and become conscious of its alterations. The only difference is that the objects of these alterations, which understanding experiences, are not particular things, but their connections and relations. Understanding does not itself connect, rather, it perceives the connections of appearances or things, these affect it, alter it, and it becomes conscious of these alterations. In this way, a thought first emerges. According to this doctrine, understanding is only a branch of sensibility and is, like it, merely passive. To be sure, certain basic determinations of understanding must be present, however, the status of our cognition of them is the same as the status of the basic determinations of sensibility. That is, there is no certain means [107] to differentiate the contribution that the cognizing subject makes to thoughts from the one that the things themselves make. – According to purism, the understanding is active when it forms thoughts and concepts, or when it judges, objects that are in themselves active affect it only to the extent that they provide the material or matter that it processes in accord with the merely subjective concepts and principles proper to it. This happens in such a way that the formal element can not only be very easily differentiated from the material, but that even the objects or their connections and laws do not provide a determining ground for its judgments. Nor does understanding consider anything objective in its judgments. – Here is the result that the author draws from this comparison and that, as one might think, turns out to be entirely to the advantage of purism. In the first instance, our undeniable consciousness is supposed to convince us that understanding is active in making judgments. – But here we might remember that though the concepts of **activity** and **passivity** might easily be differentiated when abstractly considered, this is not so on the concrete level. When, for example, one is to determine to what extent two things that affect each other are active and passive, respectively, this difficulty arises, given that, in principle, each can be at the same time both active and passive, considered from different perspectives. If activity is to signify nothing other than grounding some alteration (be the alteration one that takes place in the thing itself or in something else), whereas passivity signifies undergoing some alteration the ground of which lies in another thing, or undergoing this alteration insofar as the ground lies in some other thing, then Selle's empiricism no more excludes all activity of understanding from judgment than Kant's purism excludes all passivity from it. S.'s empiricism does not exclude all activity of understanding because it concedes basic determinations of understanding and therefore a contribution of them to thought. So understanding is active to the extent that its thoughts are in part grounded on these [basic determinations], even though it cannot create the relations and connections [108] that it processes and knows but must take them as they are given. The calculating understanding is bound to its forms, rules, or types of calculation, but it cannot apply them to the data that it is to calculate without regard to their constitution, it cannot group them in threes when they all belong together. But for this reason no one will deny its activity in calculation. But no more does the K. purism conclude (when we understand it as the author presents it) that all passivity in judgment is excluded. The author concedes explicitly "that cognition always presupposes objects that affect the capacity for thought. These impressions, however, do not determine the formal manner of connection; rather, they are only the material condition of our combining anything in general and this thing in particular."[8] Where there is an impression, there is passivity. So all difference between purism and empiricism with respect to understanding ends up depending on the degree of passivity or activity [that is ascribed to this faculty]. It depends, that is, on whether the effects of objects on the understanding only give and can only give the matter with which and out of which the understanding, using its forms, that is, its basic concepts and principles, can make what it wants, without being in the least constrained by the constitution of these materials either in the application of its basic concepts or categories, or in its decisions concerning which of its basic principles it is to use to process the material. That is, to remain with our example, it depends on whether the calculating understanding, without being determined by the constitution of the presented task, takes the grounds determining which of its different types of calculation is to be applied to the present task solely out of itself. If this is the case, then purism is correct, but if the opposite is the case, then empiricism is indisputably the correct doctrine. At any rate, how can one claim that whether the understanding cognizes just this (and hence no other) object is grounded on the impressions of objects, and then deny [109] that this difference of objects, which is entirely independent from the cognizing understanding, has any influence on the manner in which understanding connects or treats just those objects? If the objects are not different in and for themselves, or if these differences are immaterial for cognizing and judging understanding, then the understanding must be able to make everything from everything, just as, according to the Jewish fable, the Israelite in the desert makes now bread, now fish, now meat from its manna, depending on whether or not he wants to eat bread, or fish, or meat. – Furthermore, empiricism is supposed to be opposed by the entirety of formal and unchanging logic, insofar as it asserts that the formal element of judgments cannot be separated from the material element. – However, in order to separate the formal element that logic contains from the material element, nothing is required except to note the common elements that are found in all judgments, in all operations of understanding, and then to order them scientifically. This is what logic does, and this can happen according to empiricism just as much as it can happen according to purism. And logic can do this without having to determine anything about the origin of these common elements – about, that is, whether they are grounded solely in understanding or also in a universal common constitution of all objects of understanding whereby something is determined. In this way the universal rules of arithmetic which occur in each task without exception as well as the particular rules, which are common to certain cases, can be noted and ordered scientifically without it being necessary to decide the question whether and to what extent these rules are grounded in the understanding of the thinker or in the data. – Finally, empiricism is accused of leading to scepticism. – For according to purism, the concepts are supposed to count as laws in the entire field of their application to objects since they are just as necessary and universal as human understanding. According to empiricism, in contrast, they are supposed to be valid only of the objects actually known thus far and are to be transferred, on the basis of an analogy that must always remain uncertain, to objects yet to be cognized. [110] A necessary implication of empiricism, accordingly, is scepticism with respect to the most universal laws of nature. Purism, by contrast, is said to lead to a necessity of the laws of cognition and the objects that are to be cognized. – This objection to empiricism presupposes that according to it our knowledge depends only on objects, their relations, their connections and laws, in such a way that the constitution of objects, impressed on our understanding as a blank tablet, is our entire cognition. For it is only under such a presupposition that a case could be envisioned where entirely different objects standing in entirely different relations and connections according to entirely heterogeneous laws, would impress an entirely different cognition upon the understanding from anything it had previously experienced. As long as this does not happen, however, we can be certain even with this presupposition that our cognition has objective validity and real truth, for it is all that the strongest realist could wish for by way of ensuring that validity of our cognition: the unfalsified imprint of objects and their constitution. Scepticism, it seems to me, is not a danger until such time as there are objects that falsify our universal concepts and principles of thought, objects that would require that we, say, give up the principle of contradiction or of sufficient reason. Before this happens we would be certain in our objectively grounded cognition. However, this presupposition is false. According to empiricism our cognition is not just objectively, but subjectively grounded, that is, based not just in the objects and their different constitutions, but also in the basic determinations of understanding. The objects that have thus far occurred to it can be known and judged according to these basic determinations and the universal concepts and principles that are at least in part grounded in them. They at least do not contain anything through which understanding would be required to give up its previous logical manner of procedure. – If [111] something like this were to happen, then understanding would not process them, because they do not fit into its basic determination, and we would then actually have the sorts of objects in which the orthodox theologian locates the mysteries of his religion, objects beyond understanding, or even against reason. The empirical philosopher, however, need not suppose or fear such objects, for they would have to be given in some sensible experience. And it is necessary of entirely heterogeneous things, or those that even contradict our understanding, that they are beyond or against sensibility. So in all cases the threatened scepticism is not a danger.

III. WHAT IS REASON?

According to empiricism, there is no pure[9] reason, and hence there are no ideas of this pure reason, nor a synthesis of it, whereas purism affirms all of these things. – In order to examine these contrasts, one must first agree on what pure reason is and what belongs to it. If it is to consist merely of the laws of inference, or what one calls syllogism, then even empiricism can admit such a pure reason, that is, with respect to the universality and without regard to the origin of these laws. If nothing else belonged to it, then pure reason would be nothing other than empty reason. However, the following question is more critical, namely whether pure reason includes also the three known ideas of reason which Mr. Kant calls psychological, cosmological, and theological, and which, as he puts matters, are to be grounded merely in reason itself or the principles and forms of inference. In this case there would indeed be a synthesis of pure reason, when it processes its merely subjective ideas and puts them together in appropriate ways.

But then this synthesis would be a mere dissimulation, which would lead to nothing real or objectively valid. This would no more satisfy our spirit's hunger for real cognition than any movement of a hungry or empty stomach that, lacking [112] edible food attacks its own innards, is sufficient to nourish a body. But how is this hunger to be satisfied? If these ideas are not merely subjective, but also objective, if they are to relate to actual bodies that correspond to them and are to be grounded in them, as empiricism affirms, then their synthesis would not be a mere dissimulation, but would, rather, lead to actual knowledge. Which position is correct is not something that can here be determined, we note only the results of our author. The most important of these is the following:

When laws of appearance are used by reason in order to draw inferences about what has not been experienced, purism deduces and demonstrates the legitimacy of this procedure by representing these laws as subjective conditions of experience, and by representing everything that is inferred from them as valid for all objects of experience. The restriction of the validity of these inferences to what can be experienced and the exclusion of things in themselves, is admittedly a necessary consequence of this. Empiricism, by contrast, cannot present even a semblance of a proper ground and must accordingly borrow it from the fact that experience always successfully confirms these inferences. However, this success cannot properly speaking deliver any objective certainty prior to experience, since, according to their doctrines, this experience is only contingent. If those who deny all cognition by pure reason extend their own inferences so far as to the existence and the constitution of things in themselves, then this only possible ground of confirmation falls out of reach, and everything becomes arbitrary.[10]

The following reply can be made to this. Even though experience is contingent for me, this contingency does not preclude the certainty of analogical inferences grounded on constant experience. – Even though I may not be able to understand or explain the necessity of why fire burns, the sun rises every morning, and all bread has a nourishing power, I nevertheless expect with a certainty that could not be strengthened through any demonstration that the fire that will occur in the future will burn, that [113] the sun will rise tomorrow, and that the bread that I will eat in the future will have just that nourishing power that it has had so far. Moreover, even if I did not know anything of the nature of things and could or would not be able to take it into consideration, I would still expect this without doubt given an original constitution of my soul that forces me to expect that, in identical circumstances, the same appearances will have the same effects, and that in similar circumstances, similar appearances will have similar effects. This is sufficient to legitimate such inferences. Nor can I understand how such inferences are to be more dependable and more necessary given the assertion of a pure reason. (According to purism) they cannot be necessary unless the human cognitive capacity is not only unchangeable for each subject, but is one and the same also for other different subjects. According to empiricism, by contrast, the unchangeability of the nature of objects is presupposed. The certainty and dependability of inferences is here grounded with just as much necessity as it is grounded according to purism in the unchangeability and identity of the cognitive capacity. But what entitles the empiricist to draw inferences about objects that have not been experienced, about things in themselves, indeed, even about God? Nothing other than the doctrine that all concepts of understanding and principles, as well as all ideas of reason, are grounded not just in what is subjective, but also in the objective, relate to actual things, and hence are not merely, as Kant sees it, regulative, but are to be used at the same time constitutively. So when the empiricist proceeds from appearances and their laws in order to draw inferences about things in themselves and God, then he at least acts in accordance with his doctrine. [Schmid], however, accuses Mr. Selle of an inconsistency because he [Selle] asserts this maxim: "an inference that teaches us of the existence of things that have neither identity nor similarity with the things known through experience, is without all ground and hence false."[11] Because according to [Schmid's] procedure, things in themselves and particularly the infinite being, have neither identity nor similarity with appearances that can be experienced, it would be inappropriate to infer the former from the latter. – To be sure, it would be a [114] contradiction, if Mr. Selle were to concede, and would have to concede as an empiricist, that appearances do not have not the least commonality and similarity with things in themselves and the Godhead. But this he will not concede and ought not to concede with respect to things in themselves. For, according to empiricism, appearances are in principle nothing but things in themselves, insofar as they have been modified and altered through sensibility by their passage through it. These modifications and alterations, however, no matter how important one takes them to be, cannot possibly effect such a complete transformation of the things in themselves into objects that would not have the least aspect of what they were in themselves, and would not retain the least identity and similarity with them. If that were the case, the so-called sensible world would be an entirely new creation, which would take the place of the world of understanding that has been destroyed for us. – No, this is not something the empiricist assumes; he cannot and may not assume it, for he knows that things in themselves exist, that they are a manifold of actually different and, hence, finite things (because a manifold of actually different things cannot be thought as infinite), and that they stand in a causal relation with the appearances and among themselves. Indeed, even God, no matter how infinite he is and how finite we are and everything that can be sensed is, must still have some similarity with our real being, and with what purism takes to belong to us as things in themselves, for otherwise God would not be an object that could be thought by us, to do so would be an impossibility. It follows from all of this, that empiricism does not altogether lack a justification for its inferences from appearances to inexperienced things.

IV. HOW ARE SENSIBILITY, UNDERSTANDING, AND REASON RELATED TO ONE ANOTHER?

When the author notes here that purists also concede the unity of all cognitive capacities in one subject, he adds, "not with the hope of reaching complete satisfaction by explaining all expressions of the soul from one principle but because such presupposition is most appropriate to the rational idea of a systematic unity of all that is manifold.[12] In fact, purism does here seem to have a weak side, given the sharp separation of the active and passive principles of the human soul, [115] the latter of which belongs merely to sensibility, the former only to understanding and reason. According to this, the assumed unity of the different capacities of the soul is more an expedient and a subjective need than something that rests on true grounds of proof, even more so since the cognizing subject is taken to be a completely unknown something. Consequently, as far as we know, the subject could just as well be a conglomerate of many things, even nonthinking ones, as a true thinking unity, just as it could be something that always changes as well as something that is constant. According to purism, finally, it supposedly does make an important difference according to which of these divisions of the cognitive capacity an object is considered. With respect to the unity of the cognitive capacities, empiricism, by contrast, has an undeniable advantage, given that it presents this unity much more clearly and precisely, and all divisions appear as merely subjective and mere expedients for our limited power of comprehension, but not as actual parts of our own cognitive capacities. Nor does Mr. Selle forget to object to purism's sharp separation between the different capacities of the soul, which come close to an actual disintegration of the human spirit, and to take this as evidence against it.

V. HOW ARE THESE COGNITIVE CAPACITIES RELATED TO OBJECTS?

I note here that according to the author's account of how empiricism deals with this question, it may seem as if the cognitive capacity does not have its own basic determination, form, or comportment. – This hypothesis, however, would be just as unacceptable as the opposite, namely, that things in themselves or objects do not have their own proper determinations, mode of existence, or laws. Empiricism, properly understood, assumes both but asserts that things in themselves along with their connections and laws lie at the ground of appearances and their connections and laws, that both types of connections correspond to one another, and that the laws of things lie at the ground of the laws of appearances. Accordingly, they harmonize with each other and cannot be essentially different but [116] must, in the **main**, be the same. In all this, empiricism can always assert its **main proposition**, namely, that for us and with respect to our cognition, there is no certain ground, and no dependable source of our knowledge of what can be known except experience. – In the answer the author has purism give to this question, there is much that is vague and ambiguous, as is generally the case with the doctrine of appearances of the Kantian school. For instance, sensibility is said to determine the manner and the relations of its intuitions! What does this mean? Does it alone determine them without any influence on the part of the different determinations of the objects on the representations of the relations? So if it makes one appearance larger, the other smaller, alters one, leaves the other unchanged, presents one at rest, the other in motion, is this something that only sensibility or understanding determines, or does the object contribute something to the differences between appearances through the manner in which it is actually differentiated from other things? What does it mean that understanding determines the thought of objects? Is it contingent only on the laws of thought or also at the same time on the constitution of objects that understanding thinks them now in this, now in that relation, now connected, and now separated, thinks them now as cause and effect, now as substance and accident? When the author adds: "the form and the laws of the objects, which we represent, depend, accordingly, **primarily** on the cognitive capacity"[13] then this **primarily** is noteworthy. According to the usual, and almost universally endorsed assertions of the Kantian school, everything depends here on understanding. It prescribes laws to objects or nature, treats them as if they do not themselves have a form, no mode of existence, but obtain them first through it, and are such an inactive phlegmatic mass that we could construe anything from them. By this **primarily**, however, [Schmid] importantly concedes that the objects also do something, and consequently brings Kantian purism much closer to empiricism, and everything depends on the degree of the contribution which the objects or the cognitive capacities are supposed to make to representations. I think that when a possible contribution on the part of the objects is first conceded, one will come much closer [to empiricism] with time. [117] The author's following words seem to confirm this approach. "The (immanent) laws of nature lie in pure understanding, their closer modification in pure sensibility, their **most determinate** application in **empirical** sensibility or sensible impressions."[14]

VI. WHAT CAN BE COGNIZED THROUGH THESE CAPACITIES?

According to empiricism this includes (1) appearances; (2) physical connections of appearances; (3) things in us which Mr. Selle calls, somewhat clumsily it seems to us, noumena, that is, sensations, representations, thoughts, concepts, judgments, inferences, desires, and so on, as something merely subjective that belongs to the mind; (4) logical connections of these noumena, which we cognize analytically through understanding. Constant and universal logical connections, and laws of noumena and thought are cognized through reason; (5) the existence of things in and for themselves or, as Mr. Selle calls them, of substances. We cognize this as the condition of the possibility of cognition in general. – (On this occasion the author mentions two propositions of Mr. Selle that seem to him inconsistent, although I do not take them to be so. The apparent contradiction of these propositions could be avoided in the following way. The first proposition: "[n]oumena are grounded in phenomena" says nothing but that our representations, thoughts, and judgments refer in the first instance to phenomena, that is to the appearances[15] of the objects as our senses always represent and deliver them. The other proposition that ostensibly contradicts this one is "[s]omething substantial in the cognitive capacities rests at the ground of logical connections."[16] This says that no connections, no unity of representations, thoughts, and concepts would be possible if there was not in our cognitive capacities one unifying, connecting, true unity, or if no true substantial power were to take place. – And in this way both propositions would, according to empiricism, be close to one another and consistent.) (6) The laws and constitution of the substances in themselves, insofar as they are **substrata** of appearances, for the laws of appearances must be grounded in these **substrates** as their power, and are therefore laws of things in themselves, perceived in a sensible manner. – [118] The objections that the author raises against this presupposition have already been sufficiently discussed earlier. (7) The existence of an infinite substance, of the Godhead. If there are finite substances, which do not contain the sufficient ground of their existence in themselves, then there must also be an infinite substance, that is, one that is not dependent on anything else. I do not dwell on the objections that the author has raised against this inference in accord with his system. (8) Predicates of the Godhead in addition to its infinity. It is differentiated from the substrata of appearances, for those are finite. The objections that the author raises against this are in part the ordinary ones that the Kantian school has raised with respect to all speculative proofs for the existence and the characteristics of the Godhead, in part they relate to Mr. Selle's particular presentation of these proofs. I must leave all this aside here and present what can be known according to the Kantian purism. This is, in the first instance, appearances, their relations, connections, and laws. The latter are nothing but the necessary laws of the cognitive capacities and, in addition, sensibility and its two subjective forms, space and time, understanding (which purism imagines it has exhaustively described) with its entire peculiar stock, the concepts of understanding and their principles, reason with its ideas of cognition, and finally, the law of morality, as a product of pure practical reason. According to purism, these are the proper objects of cognition or they are what can be known in accord with grounds of truth. In addition, Kantian purism defends a rational belief, that is, it acknowledges a Godhead and a future state of grace, not as if it could actually know both or could demonstrate them with the proper proofs, but on the basis of a **moral need**, or because human beings cannot, as the K. purism sees morality, be moral and happy unless they believe in a higher creator of the world, a regent of it and a future life. So when the Kantian purist can only think of the Godhead, but takes speculative, that is, actual cognition or grounds of truth to be insufficient in order to demonstrate the existence or nonexistence of an object that conforms to these thoughts outside of understanding, [119] that is to demonstrate it objectively or even to determine its predicates on their own, then purism's pure morality and moral theology is supposed to more than make up for it. And since the empiricist does not have either and cannot have either, purism claims an important advantage over **empiricism**. – Here I refer to what has been extensively noted against pure morality in the review of Kant's *Foundation of the Metaphysic of Morals* in volume 66 of the *AdB*[17] and against moral theology in the review of Jacob's *Examination of Mendelssohn's Morgenstunden* in volume 82 of the *AdB*.[18]

VII. WHAT FORM AND WHAT DEGREE OF CERTAINTY CAN THE HUMAN SOUL REACH?

The result of the author's answer to this question is the following:

> according to empiricism neither understanding, nor sensibility, nor yet reason can deliver an absolute, universal and necessary cognition, nor any other certainty than one that is comparatively universal for the subject and therefore called objective. According to purism, by contrast, all particular perceptions must be taken to be contingent, but the existence of experience in itself, or, and this is the same thing, nature and its laws, must be taken to be just as universal and necessary as the cognitive capacity. Each particular application of universal laws to an individual object leaves the possibility of error, but the law itself contains its certainty that, to be sure, is only subjective, but which is absolutely universal and therefore objective. Objective certainty springs from another source as well, namely, from practical reason insofar as it provides us with practical laws that do not allow for any exception. In addition to this apodeictic certainty of universal natural and moral laws, there is also a subjectively necessary conviction or a faith that is in part contingent, in part also absolutely necessary.[19]

On first encounter, one may think that according to this presentation, Kantian purism, even though it might be accused, certainly not without reason, of an unlimited scepticism, or a complete subjectivity, would rather be able to accuse its empiricist opponent of all these things, and would assert an important preference with respect to it. [120] But we must consider this matter more closely. In the first instance, as far as contingent truth and experiential propositions are concerned, the question raised to both parties is: of what form, to what degree, and why they are certain of these truths, for instance, of the proposition that tomorrow the sun will rise at a certain time, that the bread that, according to the testament of all our senses, presents itself as bread even down to having a nourishing power, is bread and so on. The empiricist would answer: I trust my senses, as such, which, when healthy, adequately present objects in accord with their properties, in part because I take their nature to be just as dependably determined, to be as constant as the nature of outer things, and believe in a uniform, constant course of things, in part because my cognitive capacity is so constituted that I cannot resist the expectation of identical or similar cases, whether I want to or not, even less so because this expectation has, given the appropriate conditions, not deceived me or any other human beings. Whether one calls my certainty of these sorts of cases subjective or objective, or even only comparatively universal, is the same to me. Whatever it is called, it can ascend to the highest degree [of certainty], so that I would vouch my life that, for instance, the sun will rise tomorrow. – And what will the Kantian purist answer? I count on the necessity of the laws of my cognitive capacity – and particularly insofar as the preceding cases are concerned, on the unchangeability of the forms of my sensibility – without concerning myself in the least with the nature and powers of objects, or counting in the least on them because I know nothing of them. In addition, I also expect of identical and similar outcomes for identical and similar appearances, as a law of my cognitive capacities. – So on the one hand, the certainty is a function of the unchangeability of the nature of things and the cognitive capacity and the laws of both; on the other, it is a belief merely in the unchangeability of the nature of the human cognitive capacities and its laws. – So the certainty of the empiricist rests equally on subjective and objective grounds, but that of the purist rests only on subjective ground. – As far, finally, as the so-called eternal truths, for instance, the propositions [121] of pure geometry, of universal nature and laws of reason are concerned, the empiricist will answer the question of the extent to which and the reason why he takes them to be certain more or less as follows: I take them to be indubitably certain because they are analytical propositions, that is, those that constitute a logical connection and that are certain precisely because either the subject or the predicate are merely different expressions of one and the same thought or concept, or because both are indivisible parts of one and the same thought. This is the case when I say, for instance, that no mountains are possible without valleys, or, if there are mountains there are valleys, or two times two equals four. In the first case, the concepts of mountain and valley are inseparable parts of one thought, namely of the variability of the surface, and in the other case four is obviously only another expression for two times two. With respect to geometrical truths, the purist would answer the question of how he is certain never to encounter a triangle the angles of which are more or less than two right angles in the following way: because the triangle is so constructed that its three angles must always be equal to two right angles. As far as the necessary laws of nature are concerned, the purist would again appeal to the unchangeable firm nature of his laws of thought. The empiricist, by contrast, would as previously, appeal in part to the unchangeability of the basic determinations of his cognitive capacities, in part to the constancy of the nature of things and the uniformity of his laws. – The purist would not have a greater certainty for the so-called apodeictical certainty of his moral laws than he has for the laws of nature for the same reason: in both cases his entire certainty is merely subjective. That is, the natural and moral laws are valid or correct only for the sort of sensible rational beings that human beings are, whether or not there are thinking beings for whom that which is certain for us is uncertain and for whom our truths are untruths and vice versa. The empiricist, by contrast, for whom the cognition and its certainty rests to a large extent on the true reality of objects and for whom thought is not a semblance, but a substantial power, which is and must be similar in all higher beings, has for the certainty and solidity of his knowledge as much security [122] as a being as limited as human beings are can probably have.

Incidentally, I agree with the author that, as he himself is pleased to concede, the comparison of mere empiricism and purism with respect to the main problems of philosophy, that he has conducted with so much philosophical insight, contains perhaps the best overview for answering the question which of these two essentially different doctrines is in its entirety more conclusive and, in the final analysis, most appropriate to the total interests of human reason – a question that is generally not unimportant and particularly relevant in our time. It is just that entirely opposed answers can be given to the questions that are asked in this context, and those acquainted with the issues will have to decide about their value.

Appendix A

About the Authors

The short sketches in this and the next section are based on the following sources: *Allgemeine deutsche Biographie*; Beiser, *The Fate of Reason*; Erdmann, *Kants Kriticismus*; deVleeschauwer, *La Déduction Transcendentale*.

Born, Friedrich Gottlob (1743–1807)
From 1782 to 1802 Born was Professor of Philosophy in Leipzig. He was one of Kant's early defenders and, in that function, published two books: *Versuch über die ersten des Sinnen Lehre* (1788), parts of which are included in this collection, and *Versuch über die ursprünglichen Grundlagen des menschlichen Denkens und die davon abhängigen Schranken unserer Erkenntnis* (1789 and 1791). As early as 1786 he proposed to translate Kant's texts into classical Latin, but the translations were only published, in four volumes, between 1796 and 1798. In 1802 Born resigned his position in Leipzig and took on the post of court chaplain in Pirna (Eastern Germany).

Feder, Johann Georg Heinrich (1740–1821)
From 1768 Feder was Professor of Philosophy in Göttingen, a position he retained until his resignation in 1797. The resignation was likely prompted by his ill-fated role in early Kant criticism. Although best known to contemporary Kant scholars as the author of the Göttingen review, Feder had a central role in Philosophy prior to that. His first publication was a treatise on education (*Der neue Emil oder von der Erziehung nach bewährten Grundsätzen*, 1768), and he then quickly turned to publishing on logic and metaphysics with a number of widely used textbooks (*Lehrbuch der Logik und Metaphysik*, 1769, which went through eight editions; *Lehrbuch der praktischen Philosophy*, 1770). His final major work was a four-volume treatise on the will that took as its model Locke's *Essay on Human Understanding*: *Untersuchungen über den menschlichen Willen* (1779–93). In addition, he functioned as editor of the *Göttingische gelehrte Anzeigen* and contributed widely to other journals. In Kant studies, he published, in addition to the Göttin-

gen review, his reply to Kant's *Prolegomena* response to the review, *Ueber Raum and Caussalität*, 1787, the first part of which is included in this collection, and, with Christoph Meiners, produced four volumes of a journal, which was to be the "standing army" against the Kantians, the *Philosophische Bibliothek*.

Garve, Christian (1742–98)

Garve was, like Feder, one of the *Popularphilosophen*, claiming Locke's influence and a desire to be the "German Hume." He held a professorship in Leipzig for some four years (1768–72) but resigned his position for reasons of health. Although, again like Feder, best known to contemporary Kant scholars as one of the authors of the Göttingen review, his primary philosophical interests lay in aesthetics and moral philosophy. After he resigned his position in Leizig, he returned to his hometown of Breslau (now in Poland) where he was active as a translator and author. He translated English (Ferguson, Home, Burke, Gerard, Smith), Latin (Cicero), and Greek (Aristotle) texts. He was similarly responsible for a number of reviews, particularly of German authors, notably Herder and Lessing. In addition, he published several texts in moral philosophy: *Abhandlung über die Verbindung der Moral mit der Politik* (1788) and *Einige Betrachtungen über die allgemeinsten Grundsätze der Sittenlehre: Ein Anhang zu der Uebersicht der verschiedenen Moralsysteme* (1798). His final work, entitled *Uebersicht der vohrnemsten Principien der Sittenlehre*, a translation of Aristotle's *Ethics* with a text by Garve (1798), is dedicated to Kant.

Jacobi, Friedrich Heinrich (1743–1829)

A businessman in Düsseldorf, Jacobi was a representative of the counter-Enlightenment. His philosophical development was influenced by the writings of Spinoza, Pascal, and Rousseau, and in 1785, with his *Briefe über die Lehre von Spinoza*, he challenged the Enlightenment faith in reason. The challenge to the Enlightenment came to a head in his controversy with Mendelssohn over the nature and implications (for the Enlightenment) of Lessing's ostensive Spinozism or pantheism. His contribution to the critique of Kant can be found in the here included short essay on transcendental idealism. It is a radical version of the idealism objection also articulated by the early empiricist critics, but it is no less important for that reason.

Pistorius, Hermann Andreas (1730–98)

The pastor of Pöserzitz on the Island of Rügen in the Baltic Sea, Pistorius did not produce original work of his own. He was a prolific translator of British philosophy, notably Hume and Hartley, however, and an even more prolific reviewer for the *Allgemeine deutsche Bibliothek*. Under the initials "Rk," "Sg," "Wo," and "Zk," the *AdB* published his reviews of works in theology and philosophy. Here he is chiefly responsible for a majority of the *AdB*'s reviews of Kant's texts in theoretical and moral philosophy, and those of both critics and defenders. In the presentation and critique of the Kantian philosophy, he took a moderate empiricist stance, which allowed him to produce reflective and often insightful reviews that were at times positively assessed even by Kant. The selections included in this collection give just the barest hint of the extent of his contribution to early Kant studies.

Schaumann, Johann Christian Gottlob (1768–1821)

Schaumann began his career in the late 1780s as a teacher at a school in Halle, quickly became lecturer (*Privatdozent*) at the university there, and by 1794 became Professor of Philosophy in Gießen. First Kant's, then Fichte's disciple, Schaumann's first publication was a short book on the Transcendental Aesthetic to which he appended the here included (in part) letter to Feder designed to defend the critical philosophy against Feder's attack in *Ueber Raum und Caussalität*. This seems to have been his only book on Kant. Subsequent publications span a variety of fields including psychology (*Psyche oder Unterhaltungen über die Seele*, 1791; *Ideen zu einer Criminalpsychologie*, 1792), logic/metaphysics (*Elemente der allgemeinen Logic und kurzer Abriß der Metaphysic*, 1795), and Fichte (*Erklärung über Fichte's Appelation und über die Anklagen gegen die Philosophie*, 1799).

Schmid, Carl Christian Erhard (1761–1812)

Schmid was Professor of Philosophy at Jena and one of Kant's early defenders, offering a course on the *Critique* in 1785, much to the dismay of his colleague Ulrich. His major contribution to Kant studies was the *Wörterbuch zum leichteren Gebrauch der Kantischen Schriften* to which the comparison between empiricism and purism included in this selection was appended, though he also published a commentary on the *Critique*, the *Critik der reinen Vernunft im Grundrisse* (1788). Both texts went through several editions. In addition, he wrote on moral philosophy (*Versuch einer Moralphilosophie*, 2 volumes, which also went through several editions with the final, fourth, edition appearing in 1802), and political philosophy (*Grundriß des Naturrechts*, 1795)

Schultz, Johann (also written as **Schulze**) (1739–1805)

Schultz, court chaplain and, as of 1786, Professor of Mathematics in Königsberg, was Kant's friend and colleague. He was among the first members of the academic establishment to take on the defense of the critical philosophy and is likely best known as the author of the first paraphrase of the *Critique*, the *Erläuterungen über des Herrn Prof. Kant Critik der reinen Vernunft* (1784). In 1789 and 1792 he published a two-volume examination of the *Critique* and the objections raised against it by both empiricist and rationalist critics, the *Prüfung der kantischen Critik der reinen Vernunft*. In addition, he wrote on issues in theology and mathematics.

Selle, Christian Gottlieb (1748–1800)

Selle studied medicine and had a successful career as a physician to, among others, Friedrich Wilhelm II. In medicine he was both well respected and widely published. His *Handbuch der medizinischen Praxis* (1781), for instance, based on his clinical experience as physician of the Charité hospital in Berlin, was translated into French and Latin and went through eight editions. In 1786 he became a member of the Berlin Academy of Sciences. His publications were not limited to medicine, however; he was also known as the author of numerous philosophical texts. These include *Philosophische Gespräche* published in two parts in Berlin in 1780 and, more importantly, the work pertaining to the critical philosophy, which takes a strong empiricist stance against Kant, his *Grundsätze der reinen Philosophie* (1788), and several shorter essays published for the most part in the *Berlinische Monatsschrift*. Here it is particularly the short "Attempt at a Proof That There Are No Pure Concepts of Reason That Are Independent of Experience" (1784) included in this volume that stands out.

Tiedemann, Dietrich (1748–1803)

Part of the Göttingen empiricist group – he studied philosophy, theology, and classical languages at Göttingen – Tiedemann became, in 1776, Professor of Latin and Greek in Kassel and in 1786, Professor of Philosophy in Marburg. In 1771, he contributed to the debate on the origin of language with a piece that was severely criticized by Hamann. In Kant criticism, Tiedemann was the first to write an in-depth examination and critique of the *Critique*, "Ueber die Natur der Metaphysik: Zur Prüfung von Herrn Professor Kants Grundsätzen," here included (in part), which he published in three parts in the *Hessische Beyträge der Gelehrsamkeit und Kunst* and presented as responding to Kant's *Prolegomena* invitation that one undertake just such an examination. In addition, along with Pistorius, Tiedemann functioned as a faithful reviewer for the *Allgemeine deutsche Bibliothek* for more than 25 years. Throughout his career, he continued to write on the history of philosophy (*System der Stoischen Philosophie*, 3 parts, 1776; *Griechenlands erste Philosophen*, 1780; *Theätet oder über das menschliche Willen, ein Beytrag zur Vernunftkritik*, 1794; *Geist der spekulativen Philosophie*, 6 volumes, 1791–7).

Tittel, Gottlob August (1739–1816)

One of Kant's empiricist critics and very much an adherent of Locke's philosophy, Tittel was lecturer (*Privatdozent*) in Jena from 1760 to 1764 and then Professor of Philosophy in Karlsruhe. He published books on logic (*Logik*, 1783), metaphysics (*Metaphysik*, 1784), and practical philosophy (*Allgemeine praktische Philosophie*, 1785). In Kant studies he is particularly known for two books. The first of these, *Ueber Herrn Kants Moralreform* (1786), so troubled Kant that he thought for a time he might publish a reply to it in the *Berlinische Monatsschrift*, a plan he abandoned in favor of a footnote in the Preface of the *Critique of Practical Reason*. The second is the here included (in part) *Kantische Denkformen oder Kategorien* (1788), which raises serious objections to the Metaphysical and Transcendental Deductions of the categories.

Appendix B

Biographical Sketches of Figures in Early Kant Reception

Beck, Jakob Sigismund (1761–1840)
Beck was for a time one of Kant's disciples, but he eventually came to be rejected by Kant over his interpretation of the *Critique*, in *Einzig möglicher Standpunkt aus welchem die kritische Philsophie beurteilt werden muß* (1793).

Bering, Johann (1748–1825)
One of Kant's defenders, Bering was a Professor of Logic and Metaphysics. His 1785 dissertation "*Dissertation philosophica de regressu successivo*" was critical of Tiedemann and found favor with Kant.

Bertuch, Heinrich Friedrich Christian (1771–1828)
Bertuch was a civil servant in Berlin, and his work brought him into contact with the academic and artistic circles of the time. He was one of the founders of the *ALZ*.

Biester, Johann Erich (1749–1816)
Biester was the private secretary of Baron von Zedlitz (1731–93), then Minister of Justice (to whom Kant dedicated the *Critique*). He also functioned as librarian of the *Staatsbibliothek* in Berlin, contributed to the *AdB*, and was one of the founders (with Gedicke) of the *Berlinische Monatsschrift*.

Bohn, Karl Ernst (1749–1827)
A bookseller in Hamburg, Bohn also owned the university bookstore in Kiel. From 1792 to 1800 Bohn took over the editorship of the *AdB* under the name *Neue Allgemeine Deutsche Bibliothek*, likely in order to ensure the freedom of the press that had been curtailed in Prussia under the reign of Friedrich Wilhelm II. (Kiel, under the protectorate of Denmark, was not subject to the then new restrictions.)

Eberhard, Johann August (1739–1809)
From 1778 Eberhard was Professor of Philosophy in Halle and founder/editor of the vehicle of the rationalist critique of Kant,

the *Philosophisches Magazin* against which Kant's *Entdeckung* was directed.

Fries, Jakob Friedrich (1773–1843)

Although an adherent of the critical philosophy, Fries proposed a reinterpretation of it along psychological lines in his three-volume *Neue oder anthropologische Kritik der Vernunft* (1828–31).

Gedicke, Friedrich (1754–1803)

Director of a high school (*Gymnasium*) in Berlin, Gedicke was responsible for numerous reforms in the school system. He was, with Biester, founder of the *Berlinische Monatsschrift*.

Hamann, Johann Georg (1730–88)

Kant's friend and neighbor and a member of the counter-Enlightenment, Hamann was the author of an obscure short essay, the "*Metakritik über den Purismus der Vernunft*," a critique of Kant's a priorism that is based on his philosophy of language, and of *Aesthetica in nuce* (1762), which proved immensely influential on the development of the movement of *Sturm und Drang* and German Romanticism.

Helmholtz, Hermann Ludwig von (1821–94)

Considered a founder of the philosophy of science, Helmholtz, a physiologist and physicist, took an empiricist stance in philosophical matters and brought his position on the physiology of sensation to bear on his reading of the critical philosophy.

Herder, Johann Gottfried (1744–1803)

Herder, an ordained minister and preacher, was, like Hamann and Jacobi, a member of the counter-Enlightenment. Though at one time Kant's student, he was more influenced by Hamann. In 1784 he published his two part *Ideen zur Philosophie der Geschichte*, which was negatively reviewed by Kant. He was involved in the pantheism debate as well, siding with Mendelssohn and Lessing against Jacobi in *Gott: einige Gespräche* (1787).

Jakob, Ludwig Heinrich (1759–1827)

Professor of Philosophy in Halle and one of Kant's defenders. He was widely published at the time and, in 1795, founded a "journal," *Annalen der Philosophie*, which he saw as dedicated to Kant's philosophy, and in which he fought vehemently against Fichte and Schelling. The journal folded in 1797, after three issues.

Lambert, Johann Heinrich (1728–77)

Lambert was a scientist (mathematician, physicist, astronomer, and philosopher), whose two major works – the *Neue Organon oder Gedanken über die Erforschung und Bezeichnung des Wahren und dessen Unterscheidung von Irrtum und Schein* (1764), an attempt to reform Wolffian logic, and the *Neue Anlage zur Architektonik, oder Theorie des Einfachen und Ersten in der philosophischen und mathematischen Erkenntnis* (1771) – are primarily noteworthy for the influence they had on Kant.

Lotze, Rudolf Hermann (1817–81)
A physiologist and philosopher, Lotze was a neo-Kantian who, in his *Mikrokosmos* (1856–64) and later *Logik* (1874), endorsed Kant's position regarding the ideality of space and the synthetic a priori status of geometrical knowledge.

Maaß, Johann Gebhard Ehrenreich (1766–1823)
Professor of Philosophy in Halle and participant in Eberhard's *Philosophische Magazin*, he published numerous essays that were critical of Kant's philosophy.

Maimon, Salomon (1754–1800)
Author of the *Versuch über die Transcendentalphilosophie*, which raised serious questions about the Transcendental Deduction, Maimon likely played a central role in the transition from critical idealism to speculative idealism, from Kant, to Fichte, Schelling, and Hegel.

Meiners, Christoph (1747–1810)
Professor of Philosophy at Göttingen, Meiners was one of the Göttingen empiricists and edited, with Feder, the *Philosophische Bibliothek*, to which he also made numerous contributions.

Mendelssohn, Moses (1729–86)
A quintessential Enlightenment philosopher, Mendelssohn, a businessman in Berlin, was a member of the Berlin philosophical establishment, an honorary member of the *Mitwochsgesellschaft*, and a participant in the *AdB*. In 1767 his treatise on metaphysics, the *Phaedo*, appeared, and in 1785 he published his *Morgenstunden: oder, Vorlesungen über das Daseyn Gottes*, which was to be the decisive statement on the question of Lessing's pantheism. Mendelssohn was thought by Kant to be one of the few people who could undertake a serious evaluation of the critical philosophy.

Nicolai, Friedrich (1733–1811)
A publisher and bookseller in Berlin, Nicolai was the founder and longstanding publisher/editor of the *AdB*.

Reinhold, Karl Leonhard (1758–1823)
Professor of Philosophy at Jena and subsequenly at Kiel, Reinhold was initially a critic, became for a time Kant's most successful defender, and contributed significantly to popularizing the critical philosophy in the mid 1780s both with his *Briefe über die Kantische Philosophie* and his participation in the pro-Kantian *ALZ*. By the

late 1780s, he became, in Kant's eyes, one of the apostates, thinking that the critical philosophy, though fundamentally on the right track, lacked a foundation, which he set out to provide with his *Elementarphilosophie*. That can be found in a series of books devoted to the articulation to the first foundational principle and the deduction of all parts of the critical philosophy from it.

Schulze, Gottlob Ernst (1761–1806)

Professor in Helmstedt and Göttingen, Schulze wrote *Aenesidemus oder über die Fundamente der von dem Herrn Professor Reinhold in Jena gelieferten Elementarphilosophie* (1792), a skeptical attack on Reinhold and Kant.

Schütz, Christian Gottfried (1747–1832)

Professor of Rhethoric and Poetry in Jena, and, as of 1803, in Halle, Schütz was one of Kant's defenders, as well as cofounder and longstanding editor of the *ALZ*.

Schwab, Johann Christoph (1743–1821)

Schwab was Professor at a school in Stuttgart, one of Kant's rationalist critics, and contributor to the *Philosophisches Magazin*.

Tetens, Johann Nikolaus (1736–1807)

From 1776 to 1789 Tetens was Professor of Philosophy at Kiel and, subsequently, a high-ranking civil servant with the Danish government. While at Kiel, he published two influential books: *Ueber die allgemeine speculativische Philosophie* (1775) and the two volume *Philosophische Versuche über die menschliche Natur und ihre Entwicklung* (1777–78). He was responsible for the introduction of a three faculty psychology.

Ulrich, Johann August Heinrich (1744–1807)

Ulrich was Professor of Philosophy in Jena. His stance on the critical philosophy may initially have been ambiguous, but by the mid 1780s he had become a decided critic. He was the author of the *Institutiones Logicae et Metaphysicae* that received a largely positive review from Kant's disciple Schultz.

Weishaupt, Adam (1748–1830)

One of Kant's empiricist critics, Weishaupt founded and led a secret society committed to the *Aufklärung* – the *Illuminati*. He published, in 1788, three polemical treatises that were critical of Kant: *Kantische Anschauungen und Erscheinungen*, *Gründe und Gewissheit des menschlichen Erkennens: Zur Prüfung der Kantischen Critik der reinen Vernunft*, and *Zweifel über die Kantischen Begriffe von Raum und Zeit*.

Notes

Introduction

1 In a letter to Marcus Herz dated 11 May 1781 (*Briefwechsel*, 196), Kant states explicitly that Mendelssohn and Tetens would be the best reviewers, along with Marcus Herz himself. Interestingly, Mendelssohn and Tetens are always mentioned as the most suitable reviewers, but the third name depends on who the letter is addressed to. Thus, in his reply to Grave's letter clarifying his role in the Feder/Garve review (7 August 1783, *Briefwechsel*, 230), the third person is Garve, and in a letter to Bernoulli (16 November 1781, *Briefwechsel*, 203), Kant states that Lambert would have been most able to "assess and appreciate the propositions presented in the *Critique of Pure Reason*, and . . . to combine his efforts with mine in order to achieve the completion" of metaphysics.

2 Kant notes this with some regret in the first letter he wrote to Herz after the publication of the *Critique* (11 May 1781, *Briefwechsel*, 196). For Mendelssohn's own report of his inability to read the *Critique*, see his letter to Kant (10 April 1783, *Briefwechsel*, 212–13). Note that, as far as we know, this is his first letter to Kant after the publication of the *Critique*. It is in the first instance a letter of recommendation.

3 These announcements appeared in the *Frankfurter gelehrte Anzeige*, 17 and 20 July 1781, 456–61 (reprinted in Landau, *Rezensionen zur Kantischen Philosophie, 1781–87*, 3–6); and in the *Neueste Critische Nachrichten*, 3 November 1781, 345–346 (reprinted in Landau, *Rezensionen*, 6–9). The *Gothaische gelehrte Anzeige* published a brief announcement on 25 July 1781 (reprinted in Landau, *Rezensionen*, 6) and a longer summary on 24 August 1782, 560–3 (reprinted in Landau, *Rezensionen*, 17–23; tr. in Johann Schultz, *Exposition of Kant's Critique of Pure Reason*, 201–4). Note that Kant comments favorably on the Gotha review in the Appendix to the *Prolegomena* (Ak. IV, 380).

4 The review was originally written by Christian Garve, but radically shortened by Johann Feder and published anonymously (which, although not an unusual practice at the time, did upset Kant) in the *Zugabe zu den Göttingischen Anzeigen von gelehrten Sachen*, 19 January 1782, 40–8 (reprinted in Immanuel Kant, *Prolegomena*, 167–74; Landau, *Rezensionen*, 10–17; tr. in R. C. S. Walker, *The Real in the Ideal*, xv–xxiv, and in Schultz, *Exposition*, 171–7).

5 On 3 August 1781, Kant sent Schultz a copy of the *Critique*. In the accompanying note he reminded Schultz that he had already written an, as Kant put it, insightful review of the Inaugural Dissertation and requested an examination of the *Critique* (*Briefwechsel*, 201).

6 Kant's 16 August 1783 letter to Mendelssohn (*Briefwechsel*, 235) contained his request that Mendelssohn supervise and guide an examination of the *Critique*, and a plan for a proper evaluation. The examination is to be of (1) the analytic/synthetic distinction and the notion of synthetic a priori judgments; (2) the claim that a priori judgments can pertain only to the formal conditions of a possible experience and (3) the claim that speculative a priori judgments cannot extend further than to objects of a possible experience.

7 For an account of the roles the *Allgemeine deutsche Bibliothek* and the *Allgemeine Literatur-Zeitung* played in early Kant reception, see *KEC*, 42–8.

8 FGr, 42, *KEC*.

9 Unlike the *Critique*, the *Prolegomena* was widely reviewed immediately upon its publication. A brief summary appeared in the *Altonaischer Gelehrte Mercurius*, 31 July 1783 (reprinted in Landau, *Rezensionen*, 30–1), and longer reviews were published in the major review journals and publications in 1783 and 1784. These include the *Gothaische gelehrte Zeitungen*, 25 October 1783, 705–18 (reprinted in Landau, *Rezensionen*, 55–63); Loßius's *Uebersicht der neuesten Philosophischen Litteratur*, Spring 1784, 51–70 (reprinted in Landau, *Rezensionen*, 64–76); and the *AdB* 59/2, 1784, 322–56 (reprinted in Landau, *Rezensionen*, 85–108).

10 For an account of Reinhold's role in the acceptance of Kant's philosophy, see Beiser, *The Fate of Reason*, 232–5.

11 The *Elementarphilosophie* consists of a series of books (*Versuch einer neuen Theorie des menschlichen Vorstellungsvermögens*; *Beyträge zur Berichtigung bisheriger Missverständnisse der Philosophen* [1790–94]; and *Ueber das Fundament des philosophischen Wissens* [1791]) devoted to the formulation of a first principle, the principle of consciousness, which Reinhold thought the critical philosophy lacked, and the deduction of its various aspects from that first principle.

12 See Beiser, *The Fate of Reason*, chapters 8 and 9. See also di Giovanni, "The Facts of Consciousness."

13 *Ueber eine Entdeckung, nach der alle neue Kritik der reinen Vernunft durch eine ältere entbehrlich gemacht werden soll*, Ak VIII, 185–252. A translation and commentary are available in Allison, *The Kant-Eberhard Controversy*.

14 One such contemporary was G. E. Schulze whose *Aenesidemus oder über die Fundamente der von dem Herrn Professor Reinhold in Jena gelieferten Elementarphilosophie: Nebst einer Vertheidigung des Skepticismus gegen die Anmassungen der Vernunftkritik* (1792) was a critique of Reinhold, who is taken to be a Kantian, and Kant. On Schulze's critique of Reinhold (and Kant) see Beiser, *The Fate of Reason*, chapter 9, and Breazeale, "Between Kant and Fichte: Karl Leonhard Reinhold's 'Elementary Philosophy.' "

15 On this point see Breazeale, "Fichte's *Aenesidemus* Review and the Transformation of German Idealism."

16 On Maimon and Beck, see di Giovanni, "The Facts of Consciousness" and Beiser, *The Fate of Reason*, chapter 10.

17 On this point, see de Vleeschauwer, *The Development of Kantian Thought*,

173–4. Note that in the course of a Declaration against Fichte's *Wissenschaftslehre* in the Intelligenzblatt of the *Allgemeine Literatur-Zeitung* in 1799 (5/109: 876), Kant went so far as to introduce the following saying: "God protect us only from our friends, we will take care of our enemies ourselves." It is not hard to imagine who the "friends" are. Kant's assessment of his critics is particularly interesting in view of the disagreements he had with Schultz over the review of Ulrich. The review is included in this volume. See *KEC*, 308–15.

18 "Metakritik über den Purismus der Vernunft," in Hamann, *Sämmtliche Werke*, vol. 3, 276–80.

19 On the "*Metakritik*" and its role in early Kant reception, see Beiser, *The Fate of Reason*, 37–43.

20 Kant's review of the first part of Herder's *Ideen* appeared in the *ALZ* on 6 January 1785 (1/4: 17–22), his review of the second part appeared on 15 November 1785 (4/271: 153–6).

21 Kant's contribution to the controversy was his 1786 essay "Was heißt sich im Denken orientieren?" (Ak VIII, 131–47). An account of this debate and Kant's role in it, can be found in Beiser, *The Fate of Reason*, 113–18.

22 Beiser, *The Fate of Reason*, 45, 232–5.

23 The first two issues of the *Philosophische Magazin* appeared in the fall of 1788.

24 Feder's (and Meiners's) *Philosophische Bibliothek*, for instance, was published from 1788 to 1791. On the *Philosophische Bibliothek*, see *KEC*, 42–8.

25 Given this focus, I have not included early criticisms of his moral philosophy, or of texts that focus on the dialectic. Aside from a few remarks Garve made about the Third and Fourth Antinomies, other comments on those portions of the *Critique* are particularly noticeable by their absence. Pistorius's devastating assessment of the Third and Fourth Antinomies, for instance, could not be included here (but see note 49).

26 See note 4.

27 "Probe eines Urteils über die Kritik, das vor der Untersuchung vorhergeht," *Prolegomena*, Ak. IV, 372–80.

28 *Prolegomena*, Ak. IV, 373, 376.

29 In his response to the challenge Kant issued in the *Prolegomena* that the anonymous author of the FGr identify himself, Garve explained in some detail that even though he was the original author of the review, he was not responsible for the final product. He recounted how he labored over the review, fashioning it from the 12 *Bogen* (roughly 100 pages) of notes he had taken, and producing a review that was, at 25 pages, much too long. Garve admitted that he had hoped that the *Göttinger gelehrte Anzeige* would publish it in its entirety in view of the "greatness and importance of the work" or, failing that, that the editor would be able at least to shorten it appropriately, which he thought himself unable to do. He is quite vehement in expressing his dismay at the outcome to Kant, claiming that less than a tenth of his version of the review was in the published

version and less than one third of the *Göttingen* review was actually his. A comparison revels that this is actually not true, that most of what is in the FGr is also in Garve's version. Particularly interesting in this context is the request Garve claimed to have made of Nicolai, the publisher of the *Allgemeine deutsche Bibliothek*, to "change the wording that the *Göttingen* review had retained." Still, given that he invited Kant to compare the two reviews, Garve must have believed that his contribution to the FGr was relatively minor. And it is true that, given the differences in tone and thoroughness, the impressions left by the two versions of the review are quite different. See Garve to Kant, 13 July 1783, *Briefwechsel*, 219–24, particularly 221–2. It is an interesting footnote to this episode that Garve still maintains this stance some fifteen years later. In his dedication of his *Uebersicht der vornehmsten Principien der Sittenlehre von dem Zeitalter des Aristoteles an bis auf unsere Zeiten* (1–3), Garve conceded that the original review was a "miserable" work, but reiterates that he had only a small part in this review. No mention is made of his original longer review. On Garve and his role in the FGr, see Beiser, *The Fate of Reason*, 172–7 and Kant, *Prolegomena zu einer jeden künftigen Metaphysik, die als Wissenschaft wird auftreten können*, Karl Vorländer, ed., xi–xiv.

30 These concern particularly the difficulties created by Kant's new terminology and presentation, and the obscurity of much of the Analytic. Garve to Kant, *Briefwechsel*, 223–4.

31 Kant to Garve, 7 August 1783, *Briefwechsel*, 225–32.

32 FGr, 42–3, *KEC*, 65; Garve, 860, *KEC*, 76.

33 FGr, 45, *KEC* 86; Garve, 850, *KEC*, 68.

34 Hamann to Herder, 8 December 1783 (Hamann, *Briefwechsel*, vol. 5, 107).

35 FGr, 41, *KEC*, 54.

36 FGr, 41, *KEC*, 54.

37 FGr, 42–3, *KEC*, 54–5.

38 *Prolegomena*, Ak. IV, 375.

39 On Kant's stance in relation to Berkeley's, see Walker, *The Real in the Ideal*.

40 FGr, 47, *KEC*, 37.

41 This objection appeared repeatedly in the texts of Kant's early empiricist critics. It is perhaps most forcefully articulated by Pistorius (translated in *KEC*, 177–9).

42 In his autobiography, Feder conceded that the comparison with Berkeley was his contribution to the review, but claimed that although he regretted his role in the initial stages of early Kant reception, he regretted the equation of Kant's idealism with Berkeley's least. For Feder's account of his role in the FGr, see Feder, *Leben, Natur und Grundsätze*, 119.

43 Garve, 859–60, *KEC*, 75–6.

44 Not surprisingly, this concern was raised by virtually all Kant's empiricist critics. The issue is taken up in some detail in the final section in this volume.

45 Garve makes this point repeatedly. See, for instance, Garve 841, *KEC*, 61.

The point is reiterated by other early critics. Pistorius, for instance, charges that the Refutation of Idealism hinges on the ambiguity of the notion of appearance. See *KEC*, 267.

46 Garve, 858, *KEC*, 74.

47 See *KEC*, 17, and notes 78–80.

48 Again, this is a point more explicitly made by other critics. See the selection from Tittel included here (*KEC*, 215–39, particularly, 217).

49 Garve, 852, *KEC*, 69–70. Discontent with the solution of the Third Antinomy was widespread. In a discussion that has for reasons of brevity not been included here, Pistorius articulated his inability to accept the solution on Kantian grounds. He did not understand, he claimed, what would permit Kant to make a claim about things in themselves, more specifically, what would allow him to bring the concept of causality and time determination to bear on things in themselves. Quite apart from this problem, however, Pistorius argued that this "solution" brought Kant much closer to Leibniz's stance than he acknowledged or would like. For if we know actions/events as necessary even though they are in themselves free, then we know them as "other then they are," as "obscured and disguised by the fog of sensibility." See Pistorius, *Erläuterungen über des Herrn Professor Kant Critik der reinen Vernunft von Johann Schultze*, particularly, 108–15.

50 This charge, which was also raised by other contemporaries, for instance, Maaß "Ueber die Transcendentale Aesthetic" 124–5), has since become a standard objection to the argument of the First Exposition. For recent instances of discussions of this point, see Guyer, *Kant and the Claims of Knowledge*, 345–7; Falkenstein, *Kant's Intuitionism: A Commentary on the Transcendental Aesthetic*, 160–85.

51 For Jacobi's formulation of the problem of affection see *KEC*, 169–75.

52 See Vaihinger, *Kommentar zu Kants Kritik der reinen Vernunft*, vol. 2, 134–51. Note that even though Vaihinger explored the neglected alternative by way of Trendelenburg's dispute with Kuno Fisher, he did trace the origin of the argument to Pistorius.

53 Both Lambert's and Mendelssohn's comments appeared in their correspondence with Kant. See Lambert to Kant, 13 October 1770, *Briefwechsel*, 75–85; Mendelssohn to Kant, 25 December 1770, *Briefwechsel*, 87–90. Schultz published a review of the dissertation in the *Königsbergische Gelehrte und Politische Zeitungen*, 22 and 25 November 1771, reprinted in Reinhard Brandt, "Materialien zur Entstehung der *Kritik der reinen Vernunft*," in Heidemann and Ritzel, *Beiträge zur Kritik der reinen Vernunft 1781–1981*, 37–68; tr. in Schultz, *Exposition*, 163–70.

54 Tiedemann, "Ueber die Natur die Metaphysik . . . Gegen die Aesthetik," 54–61, *KEC*, 81–3. Tiedemann's examination ("Ueber die Natur die Metaphysik: Zur Prüfung von Herrn Professor Kants Grundsätzen") as a whole appeared in three parts, addressed, respectively, to the Aesthetic, Analytic, and Dialectic, in the *Hessische Beyträge zur Gelehrsamkeit und Kunst* 1 (1785): 113–30, 233–48, 464–74. Reprinted in Hausius, *Materialien zur Geschichte der Critischen Philosophie*, Vol. 2, 53–76, 77–92, 92–103.

The question of the status of mathematical judgments has been widely discussed in the contemporary literature, for instance, by Strawson (*The Bounds of Sense* 277–92), Walker (*Kant*, 60–73), and Harper ("Kant on Space, Empirical Realism and the Foundations of Geometry").

55 David Hume, *An Enquiry Concerning Human Understanding*, Section IV. The *Enquiry* was translated as *Philosophische Versuche über die Menschliche Erkenntniß* in 1755.

56 Tiedemann, "Ueber die Natur die Metaphysik . . . Gegen die Aesthetik," 68, *KEC*, 86–7.

57 Tiedemann, " Ueber die Natur die Metaphysik . . . Gegen die Aesthetik," 69, *KEC*, 87.

58 *Prolegomena*, §10–12, Ak. IV, 283–5. See also *Critique*, B40–1.

59 *Prolegomena*, Ak. IV, 350.

60 A 1787 review still referred approvingly to Tiedemann's argument that arithmetical judgments are analytic, not, as Kant claims, synthetic. Cited in Hausius, *Materialien*, vol. 2, 56, note.

61 Reviews in the *Allgemeine Literatur-Zeitung* referred to the first part of Tiedemann's essay on two occasions. A complete review appeared in 1788 (1/64: 691–94), as part of a review of the issue of the *Hessische Beyträge der Gelehrsamkeit und Kunst* in which Tiedemann's essay appeared. Though it is presented as a review of the entire issue, it is largely devoted to a critique of the first part of Tiedemann's essay. The reviewer charged that Tiedemann has misunderstood Kant; nevertheless, he praised him for having undertaken this investigation because it "has helped to arouse the spirit of examination from inglorious slumber." In the first of a five part review of Schultz's *Erläuterungen* in 1785 (3/162: 43, reprinted in Landau, *Rezensionen*, 154–5), Tiedemann's essay also came under attack.

62 Kant to Bering, 7 April 1786, *Briefwechsel*, p. 291. Kant also left a handwritten note headed "Tiedemann," but this pertained to the second part of the essay, not the first. Reflexion 5649 is dated to 1785–9 (*Handschriftlicher Nachlaß*, Ak XVIII, 296–8).

63 In the final section of the book, entitled "An Attempt to Give Several Hints for the Closer Examination of the *Critique*," Schultz delineated and examined what he considered to be the five main tasks and questions of the *Critique of Pure Reason*: the nature of sensibility, in particular its differentiation from understanding; the identification of the pure concepts of understanding; the question of the objective reality of the pure concepts; the determination of the limits of human reason; and the answer to the question of why human reason is driven to speculation about matters that go beyond these limits. See Schultz, *Erläuterungen über des Herrn Professor Kant Critik der reinen Vernunft*, 188–254; *Exposition*, 107–41.

64 Pistorius, "*Erläuterungen*," 108–15. See also note 49.

65 Pistorius, "*Erläuterungen*," 116, *KEC*, 102.

66 See note 52.

67 Pistorius, "*Erläuterungen*," 100–3, *KEC*, 94–6.

68 Pistorius makes this point in his review of the second edition of the *Critique*. See *KEC*, 177–9.

69 See [Gustav C. F. Parthey], *Die Mitarbeiter an Friedrich Nicolai's Allgemeiner deutschen Bibliothek nach ihren Namen und Zeichen in zwei Register geordnet*.

70 As far as is known, Pistorius did not produce original work of his own. He translated several English texts (by Hume, Hartley, and Priestley, among others), and was responsible for a large number of sometimes original reviews of virtually all Kant's major works along with those of Kant's critics and defenders. Indeed, according to Erdmann, who seems to consider Pistorius the only respectable early critic of Kant's philosophy, he reviewed more than 1000 books in the 33 years during which he functioned as a reviewer of theological and philosophical texts for the *AdB*. See Erdmann, *Kants Kriticismus in der ersten und in der zweiten Auflage der Kritik der reinen Vernunft*, 99–112, particularly 105–7.

71 In the *Opus Postumum* (Ak. XXI, 416), there is an uncharacteristically positive reference to the author of a review in the *AdB* whose "careful judgment, . . . true love of truth and with this also love of thoroughness clearly emerges out of the lively critique." The reference to the *AdB* and the subject matter of the criticism (the Third Antinomy) suggest that the reviewer is Pistorius even though he is not directly named. On Kant's respect for Pistorius, see also Beiser, *The Fate of Reason*, 188.

72 On this point, see Beiser, *The Fate of Reason*, 180–1.

73 In 1787 reviews appeared in the *Göttingische Anzeigen von gelehrten Sachen* ([March 1787]: 369–74, reprinted in Laudau, *Rezensionen*, 509–12), the *Gothaische gelehrte Zeitungen* ([21 and 25 April 1787]: 267–71 and 273–77, reprinted in Landau, *Rezensionen*, 564–71), the *Jenaische gelehrte Anzeigen* ([23 and 30 April 1787]: 258–62 and 277–80, reprinted in Landau, *Rezensionen*, 572–76), the *Tübingische gelehrte Anzeigen* ([August 1787]: 554–8, reprinted in Landau, *Rezensionen*, 655–7), the *Würzburger gelehrten Anzeigen* ([17–24 October 1787]: 814–41, reprinted in Landau, *Rezensionen*, 681–700), and the *Neue Leipziger Gelehrte Zeitungen* ([30 Oct and 1 November 1787]: 2039–45 and 2054–61, reprinted in Landau, *Rezensionen*, 712–22). The *ALZ* review included in this volume appeared in the following year (1/24 [28 January 1788]: 249–54, translated *KEC*, 127–32).

74 Perhaps the most obvious attempt to effect the conversion of Feder to the critical philosophy can be found in Schaumann's text included in this volume. Schaumann went so far as to state that he wanted to "vindicate Kant . . . in [Feder's] eyes." See *KEC*, 155.

75 Biester, one of the editors of the *Berlinische Monatsschrift* and one of Kant's frequent correspondents, refers to this plan, which he does not encourage, in a letter to Kant (11 June 1786, *Briefwechsel*, 304).

76 Feder, *Ueber Raum und Caussalität*, 21–5, *KEC*, 110–1.

77 The debate about whether Kant is to be interpreted as a nativist, and, if so, in what sense, continues today. For a recent statement, see Falkenstein, "Was Kant a Nativist?"

78 For an account of the psychological reading of Kant and a survey of contemporary critiques see Kitcher, *Kant's Transcendental Psychology*, chapter 1.

79 See Hatfield, *The Natural and the Normative: Theories of Spatial Perception from Kant to Helmholtz*, particularly chapters 4 and 5.

80 Kitcher, *Kant's Transcendental Psychology;* Hatfield, *The Natural and the Normative;* and Falkenstein, *Kant's Intuitionism*. The standard logical-epistemic reading can be found, for instance, in Strawson, *The Bounds of Sense* and Guyer, *Kant and the Claims of Knowledge*. On these debates and the implications of each approach see Allison, "On Naturalizing Kant's Transcendental Psychology."

81 See *KEC*, 127–32.

82 For a history of the question, see Michael Morgan, *Molyneux's Question*, particularly chapter 1. Feder's treatment of the question can be found on pp. 57–61 of *Ueber Raum und Caussalität* (*KEC*, 121–3), Born's response to Feder is on pp. 88–91 of his *Versuch über die ersten Gründe der Sinnenlehre* (*KEC*, 133–5). The issues surrounding the Molyneux question are also briefly introduced by Pistorius. See his "*Erläuterungen über des Herrn Professor Kant Critik der reinen Vernunft* von Johann Schultze," 102 (*KEC*, 95–6).

83 The reviewer appealed to the representation and abilities of blind and deaf people to attack specific features of Feder's own position, such as his claim that our concept of space is developed from a coordination of visual and tangible data, or his claim that color is necessary to represent space or words are necessary for thought ("*Ueber Raum und Caussalität* von Johann Feder," 253, *KEC*, 131).

84 Feder, *Ueber Raum und Caussalität*, 85*–91*, *KEC*, 123–6.

85 Feder, *Ueber Raum und Caussalität*, 92*–94*, *KEC*, 126.

86 Even Feder stepped back from his original equation of Kant's idealism with Berkeley's, though only to some extent, claiming that except for Berkeley's use of his position to refute atheism, "Berkeley's idealism is completely similar to Kant's." Feder, *Ueber Raum und Caussalität*, 117, *KEC*, 154.

87 *Prolegomena*, Ak. IV, 293, *KdrV* B275.

88 The published responses appear in the *Prolegomena*, Remarks II and III following §13 (Ak. IV, 288–94), Appendix (Ak. IV, 372–6). In the second edition of the *Critique*, there is the Refutation of Idealism (B274–9) and the elucidation of that argument in the Preface (Bxxxix–xli, note). There are also a number of handwritten notes: R5642 (Ak. XVIII, 279–82), R5653–54, (Ak. XVIII, 305–13), R6312–16 (Ak. XVXXX, 612–23), and a recently found discussion available in Brandt, "Eine neu aufgefundene Reflexion Kants 'Vom innern Sinne' (Loses Blatt Leningrad)."

89 Kant's contemporaries seem to have taken these as equivalent terms. It did not help matters that in the A-edition Kant did so as well. See the argument of the Fourth Paralogism (in A), particularly A 369, A372, A377, A382. The equation is still made in the *Prolegomena* (Ak. IV, 288, 289,

292, 341, 342), and to a lesser extent in the B-edition, although Kant was more careful here, and the equation appears only in those passages that he retained from the first edition (for instance, A490–1/B518–19, A494/B520, A493/B521, A494/B523).

90 Feder, *Ueber Raum und Caussalität*, 74–5, *KEC*, 143.

91 Feder, *Ueber Raum und Caussalität*, 83, *KEC*, 146.

92 Feder, *Ueber Raum und Caussalität*, 67, *KEC*, 141.

93 For instance, in the chapter on Phenomena and Noumena in the *Critique* at A251–3; B307–9.

94 Feder, *Ueber Raum und Caussalität*, 117–18, *KEC*, 154.

95 Feder, *Ueber Raum und Caussalität*, 84–9, *KEC*, 147–8.

96 Feder, *Ueber Raum und Caussalität*, 92, *KEC*, 149–50.

97 Reid, *An Inquiry into the Human Mind*, Sections 2.8; 5.8; 6.4–6. On Reid's influence on the empiricist critics, see Kuehn, "The Early Reception of Reid, Oswald and Beattie in Germany 1768–1800," and *Scottish Common Sense in Germany: A Contribution to the History of Critical Philosophy*, chapter x.

98 Feder, *Ueber Raum und Caussalität*, 115–16, *KEC*, 154.

99 Vaihinger, *Kommentar*, vol. 2, 36.

100 There is no evidence that either Kant or his contemporaries took notice of Schaumann's book. Feder, to whom the "letter" is addressed, responded in some detail in his *Philosophische Bibliothek* (3 [1790]: 121–42) and in the *Göttingische gelehrte Anzeigen* 109 (1790). By this point, however, interest in Feder and the empiricist reception of Kant had largely dissipated.

101 Schaumann, *Transcendentale Aesthetic*, 132, *KEC*, 155.

102 Schaumann, *Transcendentale Aesthetic*, 134–6, *KEC*, 156.

103 *Prolegomena*, Ak. IV, 374–5.

104 Schaumann made this point repeatedly. See, for instance, *Transcendentale Aesthetic*, 144–7, *KEC*, 158–9.

105 Although Kant did not depend on this argument, he did refer to it on several occasions, for instance, *Prolegomena*, §13 Remark II, Ak. IV, 314–15; *Entdeckung*, VIII, 215. This argument and the question of its legitimacy has been widely discussed in the literature, beginning with Jacobi (see *KEC*, 169–75) down to this century. See, for instance, Allison, *Transcendental Idealism*, 237–54; Falkenstein, *Kant's Intuitionism*, 310–33; Robinson, "Two Perspectives on Kant's Appearances and Things in Themselves," 411–41, particularly 432–35.

106 Schaumann, *Transcendentale Aesthetic*, 138, *KEC*, 157.

107 We may wonder whether Kant himself thought his arguments satisfactory and might well suspect that given the frequency with which he returned to this issue in his published writings and unpublished notes (see note 88), he did not. The issue of idealism and the viability of Kant's arguments is as widely discussed in the contemporary literature as it was by Kant's contemporaries. Today we find treatments that place the arguments into their historical context (for instance, Brandt, "Eine neu

aufgefundene Reflexion" Föster, "Kant's Refutation of Idealism"; Kuehn, "Kant and the Refutation of Idealism in the Eighteenth Century") and treatments that focus only or primarily on Kant's texts (for instance, Allison, *Transcendental Idealism*, 14–43, 237–54, 294–309; Guyer, *Kant and the Claims of Knowledge*, 279–329; Brook, "Realism in the Refutation of Idealism").

108 See Beiser, *The Fate of Reason*, 44–7.

109 Jacobi, "Transcendentaler Idealismus," 223, *KEC*, 173.

110 Pistorius, "*Critik der reinen Vernunft* von Immanuel Kant," 345–9, *KEC*, 177–9.

111 Pistorius, "*Critik der reinen Vernunft* von Immanuel Kant," 349–53, *KEC*, 179–82.

112 For instance, FGr, 42–3, *KEC*, 54–5 57–9. See *KEC*, 12, 14.

113 Such a reading would require a careful assessment of the ontological status of these "appearances in space," which Pistorius did not provide. For some recent treatments of this question see Brook, "Realism in the Refutation of Idealism" and Robinson, "Two Perspectives on Kant's Appearances and Things in Themselves."

114 Pistorius, "*Critik der reinen Vernunft* von Immanuel Kant," 350, *KEC*, 180.

115 Pistorius, "*Critik der reinen Vernunft* von Immanuel Kant," 351–2, *KEC*, 180–1.

116 See note 88.

117 As I have argued elsewhere, although R5653 is not strictly speaking dated to the period immediately following the publication of the second edition of the *Critique*, there are reasons to think that it should be so dated. See Sassen, "Critical Idealism in the Eyes of Kant's Contemporaries: 447."

118 For a detailed account of the "determinability" argument, as I have identified it, see Sassen, "Critical Idealism in the Eyes of Kant's Contemporaries," 447–52.

119 Born edited, with J. H. Abicht, a journal dedicated to the defense of the critical philosophy, the *Neues philosophisches Magazin*. The journal first appeared in 1789 and folded in 1791. In addition, he translated Kant's texts into classical Latin.

120 The three texts in question are *Kantische Anschauungen und Erscheinungen*, *Gründe und Gewissheit des menschlichen Erkennens: Zur Prüfung der Kantischen Critik der reinen Vernunft*, and *Zweifel über die Kantische Begriffe von Zeit und Raum*. In 1787 Weishaupt also published a more general statement of his stance regarding idealism: *Ueber Materialismus und Idealismus*. Born's text addresses itself to Weishaupt's *Zweifel*.

121 Born, *Versuch über die ersten Gründe der Sinnenlehre*, 141, *KEC*, 185.

122 Born, *Versuch über die ersten Gründe der Sinnenlehre*, 117–18, *KEC*, 183–4.

123 Born, *Versuch über die ersten Gründe der Sinnenlehre*, 119, *KEC*, 184.

124 Born, *Versuch über die ersten Gründe der Sinnenlehre*, 119–120, *KEC*, 184.

125 Reid, *An Inquiry into the Human Mind*, Section 6.20, particularly 167–8; Section 2.4.

126 See, for instance, Aquila, *Representational Mind* and *Matter in Mind.*
127 Born, *Versuch über die ersten Gründe der Sinnenlehre*, 143, *KEC*, 186.
128 Born, *Versuch über die ersten Gründe der Sinnenlehre*, 144–6, *KEC*, 186–7.
129 Born, *Versuch über die ersten Gründe der Sinnenlehre*, 146, *KEC*, 187.
130 As far as I have been able to determine, the identification of Kant's philosophy as "purist" was first made by Hamann (see note 18). It is difficult to know, of course, whether his use influenced early Kant criticism, since the "*Metakritik*" was not published until 1800. At the latest, however, the term was introduced into early Kant reception with Schmid's comparison of empiricism and purism included below (341–75).
131 *KdrV* A137–47, B176–87.
132 Selle, "Versuch eines Beweises, dass es keine reine von der Erfahrung unabhängige Vernunftbegriffe gebe," 566, *KEC*, 193.
133 Selle, *Grundsätze der reinen Philosophie*.
134 An *ALZ* review (3/212b [Sept. 1788]: 606–16), for instance, evaluates Selle's position in relation to Kant. It was likely written by Schmid, the author of the comparison of Selle's empiricism and Kant's purism included in the final section of this collection.
135 see note 54.
136 Schmid, *Wörterbuch zum leichteren Gebrauch der Kantischen Schriften nebst einer Abhandlung*.
137 Selle, "Versuch eines Beweises, dass es keine reine von der Erfahrung unabhängige Vernunftbegriffe gebe," 568–9, *KEC*, 194–5.
138 Selle, "Versuch eines Beweises, dass es keine reine von der Erfahrung unabhängige Vernunftbegriffe gebe," 572, *KEC*, 196.
139 Selle, "Versuch eines Beweises, dass es keine reine von der Erfahrung unabhängige Vernunftbegriffe gebe," 573, *KEC*, 197.
140 *KdrV* A189.
141 Selle, "Versuch eines Beweises, dass es keine reine von der Erfahrung unabhängige Vernunftbegriffe gebe," 572, *KEC*, 196.
142 Selle, "Versuch eines Beweises, dass es keine reine von der Erfahrung unabhängige Vernunftbegriffe gebe," 574, *KEC*, 197.
143 Tiedemann, "Ueber die Natur der Metaphysik . . . Gegen die Analytik," 81, *KEC*, 201–2.
144 Tiedemann, "Ueber die Natur der Metaphysik . . . Gegen die Analytik," 82, *KEC*, 202.
145 Tiedemann, "Ueber die Natur der Metaphysik . . . Gegen die Analytik," 89–92, *KEC*, 205–7.
146 Pistorius, "Critik der reinen Vernunft von Immanual Kant," 345–9, *KEC*, 177–9.
147 See note 63.
148 On Ulrich, his role in early Kant reception, and his possible motives, see Beiser, *The Fate of Reason*, 203–6.
149 The history of the review is interesting. Ulrich had sent Kant a copy of the *Institutiones* with a request that Kant review it for the *Allgemeine*

Literatur-Zeitung (21 April 1785, *Briefwechsel*, 263–4). Its editor, Schütz, reiterated this request some time later, and suggests that if Kant did not want to take on the review, Schultz might be willing and able to do it (13 November 1785, *Briefwechsel*, 274). In light of the pressure both Ulrich and Schütz brought to bear on Kant, it must have been doubly troubling for him that Schultz would write a positive review. Reports of Kant's reaction are conveyed by Hamann in his correspondence with Jacobi and Herder. He wrote, rather gleefully, that Kant was quite dismayed by the review, a case of "just desserts," he thought, given Kant's rather negative review of Herder's *Ideen* (Hamann to Jacobi, 25 February 1786, Hamann's *Briefwechsel*, vol. 6, 286–7). In further letters he reiterated this point (Hamann to Herder, 2 April 86, Hamann's *Briefwechsel*, vol. 6, 338) and related that Schultz went to visit Kant, that they had a long conversation, and that Kant was content with the outcome (Hamann to Jacobi, 9 April 1786, Hamann's *Briefwechsel*, vol. 6, 349).

150 For a brief account of the *ALZ*'s commitment to the critical philosophy see *KEC*, 42–8.

151 Schultz, "*Institutiones*," 298, *KEC*, 221.

152 See note 53.

153 Schultz's discomfort with the categories appeared as early as 1783 when he wrote to Kant with the request that he assess a review of the *Critique* that Schultz has just written (the later *Erläuterungen)*. At this point the question was a relatively minor one. Schultz wondered whether the third category in each of the four classes is not already derived from the first two. See Schultz to Kant, 21 August 1783, *Briefwechsel*, 237–8.

154 In his reply to the review, Kant conceded that the Deduction was obscure, though with the proviso that the obscurity is only a matter of the manner of presentation, not of the soundness of the argument. He indicated that he would rewrite it at his earliest opportunity. As we know, that is in the second edition of the *Critique* (B129–69). See *Metaphysische Anfangsgründe der Naturwissenschaft*, Ak. IV, 474 note.

155 *Prolegomena*, Ak. IV, 298. Schultz made this point in the review of Ulrich, *Institutiones*, 299, *KEC*, 213.

The distinction between judgments of perception and judgments of experience, though widely deemed "notorious" today (Guyer, *Kant and the Claims of Knowledge*, 100), was not questioned by Kant's contemporaries. Kant introduced it in the *Prolegomena* to make the Transcendental Deduction more easily accessible, and at least for his contemporaries it seems to have served this purpose quite well. Both Schultz and Tittel used it to present and explore Kant's argument, and they did so without questioning the legitimacy of the distinction or the viability of a merely subjective judgment, as contemporary interpreters do. The standard view now is that the distinction is inconsistent with the argument of the Transcendental Deduction, and, if mentioned at all, it is quickly set aside.

See, for instance, Guyer, *Kant and the Claims of Knowledge*, 100–2, 117–19; Allison, *Kant's Transcendental Idealism*, 148–54). In recent years, however, there have also been more detailed reinterpretations of the distinction itself and of the notion of a judgment of perception. See Prauss, *Erscheinung bei Kant: Ein Problem der Kritik der reinen Vernunft*, 139–253; Beck, "Did the Sage of Königsberg Have No Dreams?"; Longuenesse, "Kant et les jugements empiriques: Jugements de perception et jugements d'experience." A revised version of this paper appears (in translation) as chapter 7 of her *Kant and the Capacity to Judge*, 167–97.

156 Schultz, "*Institutiones*," 298, *KEC*, 211.

157 Schultz, "*Institutiones*," 299; *KEC*, 213.

158 Kant *Metaphysische Anfangsgründe der Naturwissenschaft*, Ak. IV, 474 note.

159 They are willing to accept the "sensibility of all our intuition," he charged, and the claim that the categories are merely "logical functions of judgment." That entails, Kant went on to argue, *that* the categories have a use only with "respect to objects of possible experience," a point he deemed of far greater importance for the purposes of the soundness of the critical philosophy than the question of *how* they make experience possible. By implication, the reviewer's claim that the failure of the Deduction entails a failure of the critical philosophy must be rejected, even on the supposition, which Kant did not grant, that the Deduction has failed to establish its point.

160 *KdrV* B167–8. For some contemporary comments on the preformation passage see, for instance, de Vleeschauwer, *La Déduction Transcendentale dans L'Oeuvre de Kant*, 271–3; Guyer, *Kant and the Claims of Knowledge*, 368–9, 381–3.

161 *Ueber Herrn Kant's Moralreform*.

162 *Kantische Denkformen oder Kategorien*.

163 11 June 1786, *Briefwechsel*, 304.

164 17 July 1786, *Briefwechsel*, 308.

165 On this point see Beiser, *The Fate of Reason*, 184–5.

166 It must be noted that Kant's reaction was chiefly to Tittel's first book, *Ueber Herrn Kants Moralreform*. It is difficult to determine whether he was similarly impressed with Tittel's second book. By the time *Kantische Denkformen oder Kategorien* was published, however, Kant had already published the second edition of the *Critique* and might have thought any further reply to the empiricist criticisms unnecessary.

167 In contemporary Kant scholarship, the Deduction is perhaps the most discussed aspect of the critical philosophy. For a sketch of the historical and contemporary literature see Guyer, "The Transcendental Deduction of the Categories," 155–6, note 2.

168 Tittel, *Kantische Denkformen oder Kategorien*, 12–13, *KEC*, 217.

169 Tittel, *Kantische Denkformen oder Kategorien*, 15–18, *KEC*, 218–9. On the question of the completeness of the Table of Categories see also Reich, *The Completeness of Kant's Table of Judgments*. Recently there has been a

revival of interest in the Metaphysical Deduction. See Brandt, *The Table of Judgments: Critique of Pure Reason A 67–76; B92–101* and Wolff, *Die Vollständigkeit der Kantischen Urteilstafel.*

170 Tittel, *Kantische Denkformen oder Kategorien*, 17, *KEC*, 219.
171 Tittel, *Kantische Denkformen oder Kategorien*, 24, *KEC*, 220.
172 Tittel, *Kantische Denkformen oder Kategorien*, 24–5, *KEC*, 220.
173 Tittel, *Kantische Denkformen oder Kategorien*, 26–8, *KEC*, 220–1.
174 Tittel, *Kantische Denkformen oder Kategorien*, 25–26, *KEC*, 220; *KdrV* B167–8.
175 Tittel, *Kantische Denkformen oder Kategorien*, 28, *KEC*, 220.
176 Tittel, *Kantische Denkformen oder Kategorien*, 29, *KEC*, 222.
177 Tittel, *Kantische Denkformen oder Kategorien*, 34, *KEC*, 224.
178 Tittel, *Kantische Denkformen oder Kategorien* 34–5, *KEC*, 224.
179 See Beck, "Six Short Pieces on the Second Analogy of Experience."
180 Tittel, *Kantische Denkformen oder Kategorien*, 111, *KEC*, 230.
181 For a recent account of the empiricist elements in the critical philosophy see Lorne Falkenstein, "Kant's Empiricism."
182 On Weishaupt see note 120.
183 Selle's *Grundsätze* was published in 1788, the year Schmid published his comparison.
184 Although not made directly, this point is repeatedly implied. See, for instance, Schmid's treatment of Selle's account of space. Schmid, "Wörterbuch zum leichteren Gebrauch der Kantischen Schriften nebst einer Abhandlung," 628–32, *KEC*, 237–9.
185 This is a point that Schmid makes repeatedly throughout the essay. See, for instance, "Wörterbuch zum leichteren Gebrauch der Kantischen Schriften nebst einer Abhandlung," 639, *KEC*, 241–2.
186 Schmid, "Wörterbuch zum leichteren Gebrauch der Kantischen Schriften nebst einer Abhandlung," 639, *KEC*, 242.
187 Schmid, "Wörterbuch zum leichteren Gebrauch der Kantischen Schriften nebst einer Abhandlung," 657–64, *KEC*, 249–52.
188 Schmid, "Wörterbuch zum leichteren Gebrauch der Kantischen Schriften nebst einer Abhandlung," 626, *KEC*, 236.
189 Pistorius, "Ueber die Abhandlung," 113, *KEC*, 261–2.
190 Pistorius, "*Critik der reinen Vernunft* von Immanuel Kant," 347–9; *KEC*, 178–9; "Ueber die Abhandlung," 116, *KEC*, 264.
191 Pistorius, "Ueber die Abhandlung," 108, *KEC*, 258.
192 Pistorius, "Ueber die Abhandlung," 116, *KEC*, 265.
193 Pistorius, "Ueber die Abhandlung," 122; *KEC*, 269.
194 For a list of eighteenth century philosophical periodicals see Joachim Kirchner, *Die Zeitschriften des Deutschen Sprachgebietes von den Anfängen bis 1830*, 32–6.
195 Feder, *Leben*, 123.
196 A number of reviews appeared in the *ALZ* where Kant's disciples, taking their cue from the *Entdeckung*, took over the task of defending the critical

philosophy against the rationalist attack. See *ALZ*, 90 (1789) [Intelligenzblatt]; 174–6 (1790); 384–5 (1790).

197 From 1739 to 1752, it was published as *Göttingische Zeitungen von gelehrten Sachen*, and from 1753 to 1801, it appeared as *Göttingische Anzeigen von gelehrten Sachen*.

198 They were not, however, the only journals to do so. Others included the *Hessische Beyträge der Gelehrsamkeit und Kunst* where Tiedemann's three-part examination of the critical philosophy appeared in 1785.

199 The *Teutsche Merkur* also published the initial announcement of the *ALZ* (*Teutsche Merkur* 1784, *Anzeiger*, cxxxi–cxliii, reprinted in *Wielands Gesammelte Schriften* vol. 23, 32–40).

200 But see here Hinske's contrary suggestion that the *Berlinische Monatsschrift* was a partisan publication. However, he made this claim only with respect to one of the editor's (Johann Erich Biester) stand on Secret Societies which was, he argued, not an Enlightenment fight against Secret Societies in general, but a partisan fight only against some of these societies. Biester himself was a member of the so-called Mitwochsgesellschaft, which also included Mendelssohn, Schmid, and Nicolai among others. See Norbert Hinske with Michael Albrecht, eds., *Was ist Aufklärung: Beiträge aus der Berlinischen Montsschrift*, LXVII–LXIX.

201 See notes 49–50.

202 In the Preface to the first volume, the editors claim that a "devotion to truth, desire for the dissemination of useful enlightenment and for the banishment of pernicious errors" on the part of authors and editors would make this a good and useful journal. See *Berlinishe Monatsschrift*, vol. 1, Vorrede.

203 See note 53.

204 This is particularly the case for the *AdB*. See Schneider, *Friedrich Nicolais Allgemeine Deutsche Bibliothek als Integrationsmedium der Gelehrtenrepublik*, 102–4.

205 Both publications sought to cover areas such as Theology, Law, Pharmacy, Science, Fine Art, Philosophy, Mathematics, Natural Science, Natural History, Philology, Economy, Novels, History, Home Economics, and Finance. The *ALZ* also covered Freemasonry, Children's Literature, and Popular Writing.

206 Bohn was a bookseller in Hamburg and also owned the university bookstore in Kiel. The stated reason for the transfer was Nicolai's advanced age, but his motivation for transferring the reins may well have been political, specifically the increasing restriction of freedom of the press under the reign of Frederick Wilhelm II. Kiel, which was at that time under the protection of Denmark, was not subject to those restrictions. On this point see Ost, *Friedrich Nicolais "Allgemeine Deutsche Bibliothek,"* 66–74, 87–90.

Note that the *AdB* was not the only journal affected by this political change. Friedrich Gedicke, for instance, resigned from his editorial role of the *Berlinische Monatsschrift* in 1791, and in 1792 the remaining editor, Biester, decided to have the paper printed outside of Prussia. See Hinske and Albrecht, *Was ist Aufklärung*, XXXII–XXXVI.

207 See Wistoff, "Die *Allgemeine Literatur-Zeitung*: Gründung – Ziele – Die ersten zehn Jahre." *Die Deutsche Romantik in der öffentlichen Literatur*, 30–2.

208 The daily issues were ultimately collected in four yearly volumes; the *Intelligenzblatt* appeared less frequently and made up the fifth volume each year. Note that before long it came to be used as a forum for the expression of contrary critical views. Against a fee, authors could express their opinion or dismay about an earlier review, an opportunity some used for ad hominem attacks. On this point see Carlsson, *Die deutsche Buchkritik*, 115–16.

209 From the start, the *AdB* was not properly set up to review the totality of the new publications and found itself publishing numerous supplementary volumes. The original four volumes soon became five, and eventually even sixteen. A list is available in Schneider, *Integrationsmedium*, 359. See also Ost, *Nicolais*, 18–20.

210 Ost, *Nicolais*, 65–6.

211 Nicolai tried a similar policy but found his reviewers often unwilling to follow his request for brevity. See Schneider, *Integrationsmedium*, 105.

212 See *AdB*, I/1 (1765), Vorbericht.

213 *ALZ*, 1/1 (1785): 2.

214 One of the worst offenders seems to have been Hamann whose extensive correspondence gives ample evidence of his tendency to "tell all." Recall the glee with which he recounted the disagreement between Kant and Schultz over the latter's review of Ulrich.

215 After Kant's (anonymous) reviews of Herder's *Ideen* appeared (see note 20), Herder vowed never to participate in the paper, or, for that matter, to let it into his house. On this point see Wistoff, *Romantik*, 41. See also Carlsson, *Buchkritik*, 90–1.

216 Ost, *Nicolais*, 24, 107–8. See also Schneider, *Integrationsmedium*, 10–11.

217 In the Preface to the first edition, Schütz indicated that the announcement had generated a great deal of interest in the journal. It began with a circulation of 600 which was raised to 1100 by the end of the first year, and to 2000 by 1787. See Wistoff, *Romantik*, 40; Schneider, *Integrationsmedium*, 337.

218 An account of the increasing specialization of periodical publication can be found in Kronick, *A History of Scientific and Technical Periodicals: The Origin and Development of the Technical Press 1665–1790*. See also Schneider, *Integrationsmedium*, 314–36.

219 Schneider, *Integrationsmedium*, 338–9.

220 This choice was not uncontroversial. In the Preface to the first issue Schütz defended it by appeal to accessibility: foreign readers as well as female reader might have greater trouble with the old type. See *ALZ*, 1/

1(1785), *Vorbericht*: 3. On this point see also Schneider, *Integrationsmedium*, 339.

221 This was likely due to the fact that, when the *AdB* began publication in 1765, there was no strictly speaking national German literature. Matters only began to change in the 1770s with the movement of Storm and Stress, hardly the sort of literature that would have positively impressed a rationalist. Indeed, in 1775 Nicolai published a satirical spoof on Goethe's 1774 novel *Die Leiden des jungen Werther* which he called *Die Freuden des jungen Werther. Leiden und Freuden von Werther, dem Mann. Zuerst und zuletzt eine Unterhaltung*. Given his attitude toward the literature of the time, it is not surprising that Nicolai would not have placed a great deal of emphasis on having literary works reviewed. On his relation to the literary community, see Schneider, *Integrationsmedium*, 61–4.

222 See Ost, *Nicolais*, 99–102, 110.

223 Schneider, *Integrationsmedium*, 49–51.

224 Cited in Schneider, *Integrationsmedium*, 51.

225 Here it must be noted that, by the 1780s, the journal had become increasingly sloppy, backlogged, and slow. On this point, see Schneider, *Integrationsmedium*, 292–5, 337.

226 See Wistoff, *Romantik*, 41.

227 Schütz's invitation of the leading figures in a given field is not limited to the Kantians. In literature, for instance, Schiller was a reviewer for a time. On this point see Wistoff, *Romantik*, 42.

228 10 July 1784, *Briefwechsel*, 254–7; 23 August 1784, *Briefwechsel*, 258–9; 18 February 1785, *Briefwechsel*, 260–2; 20 Sept. 1785, *Briefwechsel*, 266–9; 13 Nov. 1785, *Briefwechsel*, 273–6; February 1786, *Briefwechsel*, 282–3; 23 June 1788, *Briefwechsel*, 348–50.

229 See *KEC*, 2 and note 13.

230 See "*Critik der reinen Vernunft* von Immanuel Kant," 839, 841, *KEC*, 59–60. See also p. 61.

231 See, for instance, his "Ueber die Abhandlung," 113, *KEC*, 261.

232 See *KEC*, 81–92, 199–209.

233 The review that stands out most here is Schultz's review of Ulrich *Institutiones*, which Kant thought conceded too much to Ulrich. See *KEC*, 210–4.

234 On this point see Carlsson, *Buchkritik*, 90–117.

235 There the *ALZ* continued publication until 1748. Schütz served as editor until his death in 1832.

236 Carlsson, *Buchkritik*, 90–1, 117–18.

237 Praising the contribution of the *ALZ* in the *Intelligenzblatt* of 1800, Schütz put it as follows: "The blessed Hartknoch, publisher of the *Critique of Pure Reason*, has said to me that if the *Allgemeine Literatur-Zeitung* had not in the years 1786 and 1787 popularised the Kantian philosophy through its reviews, then this work which is so brilliant on its own and which has eventually become so famous would most likely have become

waste paper." Schütz, "Verteidigung gegen Herrn Professor Schelling sehr unlautbare ErlSuterungen über die *ALZ*."

Notes to Part I: Feder/Garve and Garve

1 Though Garve says *Grundsätze* (principles), he is referring to what Kant calls *Urteile* (judgments). It may be that he is getting his terminology from Kant's section titles, "Analytic of Concepts" and "Analytic of Principles."

2 Garve seems to be confusing two distinct principles, the principle that all change involves a continuous alteration of the previous state into the changed state over the time it takes for the change to occur, and the principle that everything that happens is preceded by something else, upon which it follows in accord with a rule.

3 There is a closing bracket inserted here, but the essay does not have an opening bracket.

4 Garve here reverses the roles reason and understanding are supposed to play in the antinomy. According to Kant (*KdrV*, A485–90), reason seeks completion to the series, and understanding finds any stopping point incomprehensible without a more remote antecedent.

Notes to Part II: The Transcendental Aesthetic

1 *Prolegomena*, Ak. IV, 280 ff.

2 *Prolegomena*, Ak. IV, 268 f.

3 Although Tiedemann offers these proofs as a criticism of Kant, they seem rather to concede Kant's main point: that the truth of these geometrical principles is revealed by considering how the objects, a straight and a crooked line between two points or three points and a plane, can be presented in intuition.

4 Tiedemann put "*unsern*" rather than "*äußeren*."

5 Tiedemann put "*und*" rather than "*oder*."

6 Tiedemann put "*Erscheinungen*" rather than "*Anschauungen*."

7 Kant's text specifies "*Grundsätze*" at this point. Given that Tiedemann left the terms out, the grammatical constructions suggests that "axioms" be inserted here.

8 *Prolegomena*, Ak. IV, 267.

9 "Ueber die Natur die Metaphysik – Gegen die Aesthetic," 59–60, *KEC*, 83.

10 *Prolegomena*, Ak. IV, 265.

11 Tiedemann's terms for genus [*Geschlecht*] and species [Gattung] are confused. According to the standard usage at the time, *Gattung* designated genus and *Art* designates specied. This is also Kant's usage. See the Jäsche *Logik*, §10, Ak. IX, 96–7. Thanks to Darcy Otto and Murray Miles for their assistance with the translation of these terms.

12 *Prolegomena*, Ak. IV, 285–6.

13 Johann Schultz's name is variably spelled as Schultze, Schultz, and Schulze in the context of this review and in general. He seems to have preferred Schultz.

14 Although Pistorius generally has a fairly good grasp of Kant's philosophy and terminology, he uses "*Schein*" and "*Erscheinung*" interchangeably throughout this review. Needless to say, this creates a great deal of confusion for Pistorius as well as for today's readers. Among other things, it makes finding the appropriate translation difficult. Clearly, rendering "*Schein*" as "illusion" would be too literal a translation because he often uses the term in Kant's sense of "*Erscheinung*." By the same token, "appearance" would be too interpretive because Pistorius does not seem to have entirely grasped the Kantian sense of *Erscheinung*. To capture the ambiguity of his use of the term, I translate "*Schein*" and its cognates as "appearance" but add the German term in brackets.

15 The review as a whole appeared in *AdB* 59 (1784): 322–56; reprinted in Landau, *Rezensionen*, 85–108. In the course of what is largely a summary of the *Prolegomena*, he noted the incongruity, in his eyes, of a position according to which everything, including the Self to whom things appear, is reduced to appearances. We might note here that Pistorius was not by any means the only critic who was uncomfortable with the conception of the Self as an appearance, not a thing in itself. Perhaps surprisingly, this is even a point raised in the piece by Schultz (see *KEC*, 210–4).

16 What follows is a discussion of what Pistorius took to be the implications of Kant's view that everything, including the Self, is only appearance (*Schein*).

17 Although this, as well as the other proofs, are presented here as citations, Pistorius did not provide a source. These passages are, however, fairly close paraphrases of the text of Schultz's *Erläuterungen* (22–4), itself a close paraphrase of the *Critique*.

18 Pistorius proceeded to cite some verses that he took to be indicative of a similar attitude on the part of the poet who seeks a concept of eternity.

19 Pistorius here turned to discuss the untenability of Kant's position on moral ideas, remarking in particular on the proof of the Third Antinomy, which he admitted himself unable to follow and attacked forcefully. For a summary of his argument, see Introduction, note 49.

20 *Grundlegung zur Metaphysik der Sitten*, Ak. IV, 453.

21 What follows is an additional remark on the distinction between "real" sensations and dreams/illusion. Pistorius thought that there was nothing in the *Critique* that allowed for the distinction, ultimately because, according to what he took to be Kant's position, nothing "real" grounds our sensation.

22 *in magnis voluisse sat est*. Thanks to Brian Hendrix for his help with the translation.

23 *Prolegomena*, Ak. IV, 287 f.

24 §5 is entitled: "Preliminary Remark on the Controversy over the Origin of Concepts." In this section Feder discussed the dispute over innate ideas.

He distinguished the view that we possess innate capacities or abilities from the view that we possess innate representations that are merely awakened on the occasion of experience but that are not delivered through experience. Those who had the former view, among whom he included the Kant of the Introduction of the *Critique* and A679, are said to differ only verbally from those, such as Locke, who denied innate ideas, and to have expressed themselves less precisely. This sort of "nativism," Feder observed can be granted without admitting, thereby, that space is represented before any sensation or that it is a condition of any other sensation – any more than other representations are conditions of it. Accordingly, Kant's specific proofs for the a priori status of space need to be more closely examined to see if they do not contain some special reason for his position.

25 Feder here digressed to remark that what he had just established will be relevant for his following chapter on causality.

26 §10 is entitled: "Comparison of Cartesian with Humean Doubt." Feder here digressed to comment on the Cartesian position on the creation of eternal verities by God.

27 *Prolegomena*, Ak. IV, 268.

28 *Prolegomena*, Ak. IV, 272–3.

29 *Prolegomena*, Ak. IV, 268.

30 Paragraphs 15–21 and 25 deal with the problem of idealism and appear in the next section. In paragraph 22, however, Feder returned to attacking Kant's views on space and it has for that reason been included here.

31 After page 96 the pagination was transposed so that what should have been 97 became 79. The pagination continued consecutively after that. The transposed page numbers are identified by an *.

32 *Prolegomena*, Ak. IV, 287.

33 *Prolegomena*, Ak. IV, 287.

34 This and the next three numbered propositions are citations from *Ueber Raum und Caussalität*, 1–2, *KEC*, 106.

35 Feder's sentence (*Ueber Raum und Caussalität*, 2, *KEC*, 106) reads as follows: "In common language we can say, therefore, that the things that appear to our senses are outside of us in space." The change was effected by replacing "*demnach*" with "*dennoch*."

36 *KdrV*, B38.

37 *Ueber Raum und Caussalität*, 26, *KEC*, 111.

38 Feder probably intended to refer to the focal point of vision.

39 Whereas Feder was probably thinking of limits that set the boundaries or edges of the visual and tangible fields, the reviewer was imagining limits that define the dimensions in space.

40 The first part of this passage is not a citation of Feder's text. Born picks up the text (*Ueber Raum und Caussalität*, 59, *KEC*, 122) with "recourse to a scholastic. . . ."

Notes to Part III: Idealism

1 *Prolegomena*, Ak. IV, 288.
2 Kant's text reads "*auf an sich selbst äußere Gegenstände bezögen*" (related to objects that are in themselves external), whereas Feder puts "*an sich selbst auf äußere Gegenstände bezögen*" (in themselves related to external objects). Feder's reference to p. 376 is also wrong, but this could have been due to the printer mistranscribing his "0" as a "6."
3 This passage also comes from A370.
4 *Prolegomena*, Ak. IV, 289–90.
5 *Prolegomena*, Ak. IV, 289.
6 Here the pagination was transposed so that what should have been 97 becomes 79. Pagination continued consecutively. The transposed numbers are identified with an *.
7 Uranus. William Herschel discovered Uranus, the first new planet to be discovered in historic time, in 1781, while working on a star survey in Bath, England. King George III awarded Herschel a pension, and Herschel reciprocated by calling the planet *Georgium Sidus*. Clearly, by the time Feder wrote *Ueber Raum und Caussalität*, the name "Uranus," which came to be used elsewhere in Europe, had not yet been universally adopted. Thanks to Howard Plotkin for providing this explanation.
8 In §22 Feder returned to his criticism of Kant's concept of space. It was, accordingly, included in the previous section. See *KEC*, 123–6.
9 *Feder*. Schaumann doubtless intended a (bad) play on words here.
10 Platner was a quite well-respected historian of Philosophy at the time, so it is not surprising that Schaumann turns to the *Aphorismen* for a definition, even though Platner came to be one of Kant's critics. For details on Platner see Beiser, *The Fate of Reason*, 214–17, and Alexander Košenina, *Ernst Platners Athropologie und Philosophie: Der "philosophische Arzt" und seine Wirkung auf Johann Karl Wezel und Jean Paul*.
11 There are beginning quotes here, but there are no closing quotes. Although the last sentence is an approximation of a statement Feder made on page 76 of *Ueber Raum und Caussalität* (*KEC*, 144), the passage as a whole does not have an equivalent (or close approximation) in Feder's text. I took it to be Schaumann's articulation of Feder's argument.
12 Feder, *Raum und Caussalität*, 76, *KEC*, 144. Like others at the time, Schaumann is not careful with his citations. Accordingly, they often deviate from Feder's text, though generally without changing his meaning.
13 Feder, *Ueber Raum und Caussalität*, 77, *KEC*, 144.
14 Feder, *Ueber Raum und Caussalität*, 77, *KEC*, 144.
15 Feder, *Ueber Raum und Caussalität*, 77, *KEC*, 144.
16 Feder, *Ueber Raum und Caussalität*, 77, *KEC*, 144.
17 This passage does not have an original in Feder's text. Here, as in the passage discussed in note 11, Schaumann may be imagining what Feder would say.

18 *Prolegomena*, Ak. IV, 374.
19 Reading "*oder*" instead of "*und*"
20 *KdrV*, Bxliii.
21 *KdrV*, Bxxxv.
22 There were closing quotes inserted here, even though there were no opening or continuing quotes.
23 Pistorius here cited the argument with the change specified in the B-Preface (*KdrV*, Bxxxix note).
24 *KdrV*, B276–7.
25 In the first set of passages, Born dealt with the nature of sensibility and the variability of sensuous intuitions. In the second set of passages, he discussed the reality of sensuous cognition (which involves the distinction between appearances and things in themselves) and the receptivity of sensibility (which leads to a brief discussion of space).
26 In the first omitted passage, Born referred back to his earlier discussion of Kant's reasons for these claims, notably §§12–20, 22, 24–31, 33, 35; in the second omitted passage, he referred to his earlier §§36 and 5. §36 is included here. See *KEC*, 183–4.

Notes to Part IV: The Categories

1 *Prolegomena*, Ak. IV, 294.
2 It is not clear what proof Tiedemann referred to here.
3 It is not clear what proof Tiedemann referred to here.
4 *Prolegomena*, Ak. IV, 316–17.
5 Tiedemann actually wrote, "that do not accord with them"; however, this makes no sense.
6 *ihnen*. The referent of Tiedemann's pronoun is unclear. The grammar of the sentence will not allow it to be "the universal concept of the understanding" or its ground.
7 *Prolegomena*, Ak. IV, 298.
8 What follows is a brief summary of Ulrich's claim that the Table of Categories is incomplete and Schultz's response to this charge. What is at issue here is the question of what can count as a category.
9 *Prolegomena*, Ak. IV, 298.
10 This reference is to the A-edition of the *Critique*.
11 *Prolegomena*, Ak. IV, 298.
12 Here Tittel inserted a long citation from Arnauld and Nicole's *La logique ou L'Art de Penser* and a list of the Aristotelian categories in order to support this claim. See Jill Vance Buroker, ed and tr., *Logic or the Art of Thinking*, 33–4.
13 Tittel said "*festen Princip*" not, as Kant did, "*gemeinschaftlichen Prinzip*."
14 *Adamus potuit non peccare.*
15 *Adamus non potuit peccare.*
16 To justify the claims he just made, Tittel here inserted several pages of

citations from the *Critique*, ranging from B118 to B194, and from B297 to B309.

17 Note that this citation is Kant's response to Schultz's objection that the categories might be a function of a preestablished harmony (see Schultz's review of Ulrich, *KEC*, 210–4).

18 Although presented as a citation, this passage does not have an equivalent in Kant's text. Tittel was probably paraphrasing.

19 In section IV, Tittel asked how Kant came to assert the "existence of such peculiar forms" and proceeded to a summary of the main features of Kant's philosophy, focussing on the identity of cognition and judgment; the difference between sensibility and understanding, and that between a priori and a posteriori judgments; the claim that we have synthetic a priori judgments; and, in particular, on a critique of the spatiotemporal forms of sense as represented by Kant.

Notes to Part V: Empiricism versus Purism

1 Selle, *Grundsätze der reinen Philosophie*.

2 Schmid was perhaps having some fun here with the popular complaint that Kant perverted the ordinary meaning of words and used them in ways his readers were not used to understanding them.

3 Selle's remarks on sensations on pages 148 and 149 of *Grundsätze der reinen Philosophie* read as follows:

> *Sensation* is the first result of the impression of appearances on our cognitive capacity.
>
> This sensation can be produced not only immediately through appearances, but also through their representations and concepts.
>
> Representations are images and copies of the alterations of our sensibility, through the consciousness of which a previously had sensation can be renewed, even though the immediate sensation relates to the mediate as original relates to a weak copy.
>
> In addition, alterations can also be produced through the comparison, abstraction, and new combination of representations and sensible concepts. [149] The consciousness of these alterations is sensible just like the immediate experience of appearances. Almost all mental sensations belong here. Nevertheless, these mediate sensations would not exist without prior and given immediate sensations, just as those would not exist without all appearance.

In the earlier *Grundsätze der reinen Philosophie* (p. 27) passage, he said:

> Insofar as the cognitive capacity can be conscious of things through **sensation**, it is called **sensibility**.
>
> We call the things of which we are conscious through sensation, **appearances**.
>
> We sense either **immediately** or **mediately**. The first is the case when consciousness of appearances follows immediately upon their impression of the cognitive capacity. Mediate **sensation** occurs with the aid of **representations**.

4 In a lengthy section entitled "God" to which Schmid referred here, Selle had the following to say about pure mathematics and pure philosophy:

"What pure mathematics is to application, pure philosophy must be in the search for objective truths. And just as the products of pure mathematics are never real things that exist outside of reason, so what actually exists objectively cannot be found through merely logical reasoning. In both cases, it is only to the extent that sensible material is processed that the products can have objective existence, just as in both cases, they lack that precision, necessity and certainty that can only be found in reason, but not outside of it. With respect to the determination of the **quantities** of sensible objects, strict mathematical precision is impossible, just as in philosophy the determination of **qualities** must always be imperfect. In the first case, we lack the means to find the precise *sameness*, and in the other case, the means to find the precise **similarity** of appearances. In both cases, the outer senses are indispensable means, and they are, unfortunately, extremely limited with respect to power and range. This is an imperfection that is as much a part of human nature, as it is the futile attempt to make up for this lack through **entia rationis.**"

5 The maxim in question is that analogy, which Selle claimed is "much more important and indispensable than one has believed" (*Grundsätze der reinen Philosophie*, p. 55), is not applicable to things that are dissimilar to the things we already know through experience. Selle, incidentally, was quite interested in the analogical method and contributed two papers on the subject to the *Berlinische Monatsschrift* in 1784: "Von der analogischen Schlußart" (185–7) and "Nähere Bestimmung der analogischen Schlußart" (334–7).

6 Although in its original publication this reflection on Schmid's essay appeared as part of Pistorius's review of his *Critik der reinen Vernunft im Grundrisse* and *Wörterbuch zum leichteren Gebrauch der Kantischen Schriften* to which the essay was appended, only one page of the twenty-one-page review pertains to these books. In this single page, Pistorius did little more than provide factual information about both publications and note his approval of the *Wörterbuch* (though not of *Critik der reinen Vernunft im Grundrisse*). The discussion of Schmid's essay may have been occasioned by the task of reviewing these books, but it is also a freestanding work and was reprinted as such by Hausius in the first volume of the *Materialien* (200–17). The title was chosen by Hausius, though the pagination of the translation is that of the original *AdB* publication.

Note that this essay is a commentary on the second edition of the *Outline*, my translation is of the essay as appended to the fourth edition. I have no reason to suspect, however, that these versions differ.

7 Schmid, *Wörterbuch zum leichteren Gebrauch der Kantischen Schriften nebst einer Abhandlung*, 627, *KEC*, 236.

8 Schmid, *Wörterbuch zum leichteren Gebrauch der Kantischen Schriften nebst einer Abhandlung*, 637, *KEC*, 241.

9 Reading "*eigene*" as "*reine*."

10 Schmid, *Wörterbuch zum leichteren Gebrauch der Kantischen Schriften nebst einer Abhandlung*, 646–47, *KEC*, 244–5.

11 Schmid, *Wörterbuch zum leichteren Gebrauch der Kantischen Schriften nebst einer Abhandlung*, 647, *KEC*, 245.

12 Schmid, *Wörterbuch zum leichteren Gebrauch der Kantischen Schriften nebst einer Abhandlung*, 649, *KEC*, 246.

13 Schmid, *Wörterbuch zum leichteren Gebrauch der Kantischen Schriften nebst einer Abhandlung*, 650–1, *KEC*, 247.
14 Schmid, *Wörterbuch zum leichteren Gebrauch der Kantischen Schriften nebst einer Abhandlung*, 651, *KEC*, 247.
15 Reading "*Dinge*" as "*Erscheinungen*"
16 Schmid, *Wörterbuch zum leichteren Gebrauch der Kantischen Schriften nebst einer Abhandlung*, 653 note, *KEC*, 248 note *.
17 The review in question, which was signed Sg, is likely by Pistorius (*AdB* 66/2 [1786]: 447–63).
18 Again, he was probably thinking of one of his own reviews. Signed Sg, Pistorius's initials at the time, it appeared in *AdB* 82/2 (1788): 427–70.
19 Schmid, *Wörterbuch zum leichteren Gebrauch der Kantischen Schriften nebst einer Abhandlung*, 667, *KEC*, 254

Glossary

German–English

Abfolge	succession
abhängig	dependent
ableiten	derive
absondern	separate
abstammen	descend
abstrahieren	to abstract
allgemein	general, universal
Allgemeingültigkeit	objective validity
Allheit	totality
an sich	in itself
analytisch	analytic
Anfang	beginning
angeboren	innate
anhängend	dependent
Anlass	occasion
anschauen	intuit
anschaulich	intuitive
Anschauung	intuition
Anwendung	application
Art	species, kind, type
Aufgabe	problem, task
aufheben	abolish
aufhören	cease
Ausdehnung	extension
Ausdruck	expression
ausführlich	exhaustive
außer	outer, external
Äußeres	external (thing)
äußerlich	external
bedeuten	signify
Bedeutung	significance, meaning
Bedingung	condition
begreifen	comprehend

Begriff	concept
beharren	persist
Beharrlichkeit	persistence
behaupten	assert
Beobachtung	observation
berechtigen	entitle
berichtigen	correct
Beschaffenheit	constitution
besondere	particular, special
beständig	constant
bestimmen	determine, designate
Bestimmung	determination
beurteilen	judge
Beurteilung	judgment
Bewegung	motion
Beweis	proof
Bewußtsein	consciousness
Beziehung	relation
Bild	image
bleibend	abiding, lasting, persisting
Blendwerk	semblance
bloß	mere, merely
darstellen	exhibit, present
Dasein	existence
Dauer	duration
Demonstration	demonstration
denken	think
deutlich	distinct, clear
Ding	thing
dunkel	obscure
Dunkelheit	obscurity
durchgängig	thorough(going)
Eigenschaft	property
eigentümlich	peculiar
eigentlich	actual(ly), real(ly), proper(ly)
Einbildungskraft	imagination
Eindruck	impression
Einerleiheit	identity
einfach	simple
Einfluß	influence

Einheit	unity
Einrichtung	disposition
einsehen	understand
einschränken	limit
Einstimmung	agreement
Einteilung	division
Empfänglichkeit	receptivity
Empfindung	sensation
Empfindungswerkzeug	sensory equipment
empirisch	empirical
endlich	finite
entdecken	discover
Entgegensetzung	opposition
entlehnen	borrow
entstehen	arise
Erfahrung	experience
Erinnerung	remark
erkennen	cognize, recognize
Erkenntnis	cognition
Erklärung	explanation, definition
Erscheinung	appearance
Erweiterung	amplification; expansion
erzeugen	produce, generate
Existence	existence
Fähigkeit	capacity
fassen	comprehend, grasp
figürlich	figurative
Folge	sequence, sequel
folgen	follow
folgern	conclude
Form	form
Fortgang	progression
Fortschritt	progress
Fortsetzung	continuation
gänzlich	entirely
Gattung	genus
Gebrauch	use
Gedankending	thought-entity
Gefühl	feeling, [sense of] touch
Gegenstand	object

Geist	mind, spirit
gemein	common
Gemeinschaft	community
Gemüt	mind
Gesetz	law
Gesetzgebung	legislation
Gesetzmäßigkeit	lawfulness
Gesinnung	disposition
Gestalt	shape
Gewohnheit	habit; custom
Glaube	belief; faith
gleichartig	homogenous
Glied	member
Glückseligkeit	happiness
Grad	degree
Grenze	boundary
Größe	magnitude
Grund	ground, basis
Grundsatz	principle
gültig	valid
herkommen	originate
herleiten	derive
hervorbringen	produce
hinzusetzen	add
Idealismus	idealism
Idee	idea
Kennen	know
Kenntnis	knowledge
Körper	body
körperlich	corporeal
Kraft	force, power
Lage	position, location
Lehre	doctrine
mannigfaltig	manifold
Mannigfaltigkeit	manifold
Materie	matter
Meinung	opinion

Menge	multitude, multiplicity
Merkmal	mark
möglich	possible
nach	according to, in accordance with
Nacheinandersein	succession
nachdenken	reflect
nachfolgen	succeed
nähern	approximate
Natur	nature
notwendig	necessary
notwendigerwise	necessarily
Nutzen	utility, usefulness
nützlich	useful
Obersatz	major premise
Object	object
Ort	place, location
Perception	perception
Phantasie	imagination
Quelle	source
Raum	space
Realismus	realism
Realität	reality
Reihe	series
Reihenfolge	succession
rein	pure
Relation	relation
Rückgang	regress
Ruhe	rest
Sache	thing
Satz	proposition, principle
Schein	illusion, semblance
scheinen	seem
schließen	infer
Schluß	inference
Schwärmerei	enthusiasm

schwer	heavy
Seele	soul
selbständig	self-sufficient, independent
Selbstbewußtsein	self-consciousness
setzen	posit, place, put
Sinn	sense, meaning
sinnlich	sensible
Sinnlichkeit	sensibility
Stoff	material
Streitfrage	dispute
synthetisch	synthetic
Teil	part
teilbar	divisible
Teilung	division
Tiefsinn	profundity
Trugschluß	fallacy
Übergang	transition
übergehen	pass (into)
überhaupt	in general
überlegen	reflect
überreden	persuade
überzeugen	convince
unbeständig	inconstant
Undurchdringlich	impenetrability
unendlich	infinite
ungereimt	absurd
unmittelbar	immediate
Untersatz	minor premise
unterscheiden	distinguish
Unterscheidung	distinction
Unterschied	difference
Ursache	cause
ursprünglich	original
Urteil	judgment
Urteilskraft	judgment
Urwesen	original being
Veränderlichkeit	variability
Veränderung	alteration

veranlassen	occasion
Verbindung	combination
Vereinigung	unification
Verhältnis	relation
Verknüpfung	connection
Vermögen	capacity
Vernunft	reason
Vernunftschluß	syllogism
Verschiedenheit	difference
Verstand	understanding
verstehen	understand
verwandeln	transform
Verwandtschaft	affinity
verweisen	refer
Vielheit	plurality
vollkommen	perfect
vollständig	complete
Voraussetzung	presupposition
vorherbestimmt	preestablished
vorhergehen	precede
vorstellen	represent
Vorstellung	representation
Wahrnehmung	perception
Wahrscheinlichkeit	probability
Wechsel	change
wechselseitig	reciprocal
Wechselwirkung	interaction
wegfallen	disappear
Welt	world
Weltweisheit	philosophy
Wesen	being, essence
Widerlegung	refutation
Widerspruch	contradiction
Widerstand	resistance
Widerstreit	conflict; opposition
Wiederholung	repetition
Wirken	effect
Wirklichkeit	actuality
Wirkung	effect
Wissen	knowledge
Wissenschaft	science

Zeit	time
Zeitfolge	temporal sequence
Zergliederung	analysis
zufällig	contingent
zugleich	simultaneous, at the same time
Zugleichsein	simultaneity
zureichend	sufficient
Zusammengesetztes	composite
Zusammenhang	connection
Zusammensetzung	composition
Zustand	state, condition
Zweck	end, purpose
zweckmäßig	purposive, suitable

English–German

absolutely	*absolut, schlechthin*
abstract	*abstrahieren*
absurd	*ungereimt, absurd*
actual	*wirklich*
affinity	*Affinität, Verwandschaft*
alteration	*Veränderung*
amplification	*Erweiterung*
analysis	*Analyse, Zergliederung*
analytic	*analytisch*
appearance	*Erscheinung*
approximate	*nähern*
arise	*entstehen, entspringen*
articulated	*gegliedert*
ascribe	*beilegen*
assume	*annehmen*
beginning	*Anfang*
being	*Sein, Wesen*
belong	*gehören*
body	*Körper*
capacity	*Fähigkeit, Vermögen*
cause	*Ursache*
cease	*aufhören*
change	*Wechsel*
clarification	*Erläuterung*

clear	*klar, deutlich*
cognition	*Erkenntnis*
cognize	*erkennen*
combination	*Verbindung*
common	*gemein*
community	*Gemeinschaft*
comparison	*Vergleichung*
complete	*vollständig*
composition	*Zusammensetzung*
comprehend	*begreifen*
conceive	*denken*
concept	*Begriff*
conclude	*folgern*
conclusion	*Schluß*
condition	*Bedingung, Zustand*
conditioned	*bedingt*
conflict	*Widerstreit*
connection	*Verknüpfung, Zusammenhang*
consciousness	*Bewußtsein*
consider	*betrachten, erwägen*
constant	*beständig*
constitute	*ausmachen*
constitution	*Beschaffenheit, Verfassung*
contain	*enthalten*
content	*Inhalt, Gehalt*
contingent	*zufällig*
continuation	*Fortsetzung*
contradiction	*Widerspruch*
conviction	*Überzeugung*
corporeal	*körperlich*
cosmology	*Kosmologie, Weltwissenschaft*
countereffect	*Gegenwirkung*
criterion	*Kriterium*

decision	*Entschließung*
definition	*Definition, Erklärung*
degree	*Grad*
delusion	*Wahn*
demonstrate	*demonstrieren, dartun, darlegeln*
demonstration	*Demonstration*
dependent	*abhängig, anhängend*

derive	*ableiten, herleiten*
determination	*Bestimmung*
determine	*bestimmen*
difference	*Unterschied, Verschiedenheit, Differenz*
disappear	*wegfallen*
dismiss	*abweisen*
distinct	*deutlich*
distinction	*Unterscheidung*
divisible	*teilbar*
division	*Teilung, Einteilung*
doctrine	*Lehre*
duration	*Dauer*
effect	*Wirkung*
elucidation	*Erläuterung*
empirical	*empirisch*
end	*Zweck*
endure	*bleiben, dauern*
enthusiasm	*Schwärmerei*
entirely	*gänzlich*
essence	*Wesen*
estimation	*Beurteilung*
event	*Ereignis*
exhaustive	*ausführlich*
exhibit	*darstellen*
existence	*Dasein, Existenz*
expansion	*Erweiterung*
experience	*Erfahrung*
explanation	*Erklärung*
exposition	*Erörterung, Exposition*
expression	*Ausdruck*
extension	*Ausdehnung, Erweiterung*
external (thing)	*äußerlich, Äußeres*
feeling	*Gefühl*
figurative	*figürlich*
finite	*endlich*
follow	*folgen*
force	*Kraft*
form	*Form*
fundamental power	*Grundkraft*

general	*allgemein*
genus	*Gattung*
gravitational force	*Schwerkraft*
gravity	*Schwere*
ground	*Grund*
guiding thread	*Leitfaden*
habit	*Gewohnheit*
happen	*geschehen*
happiness	*Glückseligkeit*
heavenly body	*Weltkörper*
heavy	*schwer*
homogeneous	*gleichartig; homogen*
human being	*Mensch*
idea	*Idee*
identity	*Identität, Einerleiheit*
illusion	*Schein, Illusion*
image	*Bild*
imagination	*Einbildung, Einbildungskraft*
imagine	*einbilden, sich vorstellen*
immediate(ly)	*unmittelbar*
impenetrability	*Undurchdringlichkeit*
impression	*Eindruck*
in itself	*an sich (selbst)*
indemonstrable	*unerweislich*
independent	*selbständig, unabhängig*
infer	*schließen*
inference	*Schluß*
infinite	*unendlich*
influence	*Einfluß*
inscrutable	*unerforschlich*
institute	*anstellen*
intention	*Absicht*
interaction	*Wechselwirkung*
interconnection	*Zusammenhang*
intuit	*anschauen*
intuitable	*anschaubar, anschaulich*
intuition	*Anschauung*
intuitive	*anschaulich*

judge	*urteilen*
judgment	*Urteil, Urteilskraft*
know	*wissen*
knowledge	*Wissen, Kenntnis*
lapse	*Ablauf*
lasting	*bleibend*
law	*Gesetz*
limit(ation)	*einschränken, Einschränkung, Schranke*
magnitude	*Größe*
major premise	*Obersatz*
manifold (adj)	*manigfaltige*
manifold (n)	*Mannigfaltige, Mannigfaltigkeit*
mark	*Merkmal*
material	*Stoff*
matter	*Materie*
meaning	*Sinn, Bedeutung*
member	*Glied*
mere(ly)	*bloß*
mind	*Gemüt, Geist*
minor premise	*Untersatz*
mirage	*Blendwerk*
motion	*Bewegung*
multiplicity	*Menge*
multitude	*Menge*
necessarily	*notwendigerweise*
necessary	*notwendig*
need	*Bedürfnis*
negate	*verneinen*
number	*Zahl*
object	*Gegenstand, Object*
observation	*Beobachtung*
occasion	*veranlassen*
occurrence	*Begebenheit*
opinion	*Meinung*
opposition	*Entgegensetzung, Opposition, Widerstreit*
original	*ursprünglich*

original being	*Urwesen*
outer	*außer, äußerlich*
outside	*außer*
part	*Teil*
particular	*besonder*
peculiar	*eigentümlich*
perception	*Wahrnehmung*
perfect	*vollkommen*
perfection	*Vollkommenheit*
persist	*beharren, bleiben*
persistence	*Beharrlichkeit*
persuasion	*Überredung*
philosophy	*Philosophie, Weltweisheit*
place	*Ort*
plurality	*Vielheit*
posit	*setzen*
position	*Lage, Position, Setzung*
possible	*möglich*
power	*Kraft, Macht*
precede	*vorhergehen*
preestablished	*vorherbestimmt*
present	*darstellen*
presupposition	*Voraussetzung*
principle	*Grundsatz, Prinzip, Satz*
probability	*Wahrscheinlichkeit*
produce	*erzeugen; wirken*
progress	*Fortschritt, Fortgang*
proof	*Beweis*
property	*Eigenschaft, Beschaffenheit*
proposition	*Satz*
pure	*rein*
purpose	*Zweck*
purposive	*zweckmäßig*
rationalize	*vernünfteln*
real	*real*
reality	*Realität*
reason	*Vernunft*
reciprocal	*wechselseitig, wechselweise*
refer	*verweisen*
refutation	*Widerlegung*

regress	*Rückgang, Regressus*
relation	*Beziehung, Verhältnis, Relation*
remain	*bleiben*
represent	*vorstellen*
representation	*Vorstellung*
rest	*Ruhe*
science	*Wissenschaft*
self-activity	*Selbstätigkeit*
self-consciousness	*Selbstbewußtsein*
self-sufficient	*selbständig*
semblance	*Blendwerk*
sensation	*Empfindung*
sense (n.)	*Sinn*
sensibility	*Sinnlichkeit*
sensible	*sinnlich*
sentence	*Satz*
separate	*absondern*
sequence	*Folge*
series	*Reihe*
shape	*Gestalt*
significance	*Bedeutung*
signify	*bedeuten*
simple	*einfach*
simultaneity	*zugleichsein*
simultaneous	*zugleich*
solely	*lediglich*
solution	*Auflösung*
sophistical	*venünftelnd*
source	*Quelle*
space	*Raum*
species	*Art, Species*
state	*Zustand*
subsist	*bestehen*
succeed	*nachfolgen*
succession	*Abfolge, Nacheinandersein*
sufficient	*zureichend*
sum	*Summe*
surface	*Fläche*
syllogism	*Vernunftschluß*
synthetic	*synthetisch*

temporal sequence	*Zeitfolge*
terrain	*Boden*
theorem	*Lehrsatz, Lehrspruch*
thing	*Ding, Sache*
thorough	*gründlich*
thorough(going)	*durchgängig*
thought-entity	*Gedankending*
through	*durch*
time	*Zeit*
totality	*Totalität, Allheit*
[sense of] touch	*Gefühl*
transform	*verwandeln*
transition	*Übergang*
understand	*verstehen*
understanding	*Verstand*
unity	*Einheit*
universal	*allgemein*
use (n.)	*Gebrauch*
use (v.)	*brauchen*
useful	*nützlich*
utility	*Nutzen*
valid	*gültig*
vanish	*verschwinden*
weight	*Gewicht*
well-grounded	*gründlich*
whole	*Ganze*
world	*Welt*
world-series	*Weltreihe*
world-whole	*Weltganze, Weltall*

Bibliography

Primary Sources

Unless otherwise noted, work by Kant's contemporaries that was published in monograph or "journal" format (*Philosophische Bibliothek*, *Philosophisches Magazin*) at the time has been reprinted in facsimile form in the *Aetas Kantiana* series. Brussels: Culture et Civilization, 1968.

[ANONYMOUS]. "*Prolegomena zu einer jeden künftigen Metaphysik, die als Wissenschaft wird auftreten können*, von Immanuel Kant." *Gothaische gelehrte Zeitungen* (25 Oktober 1783): 705–18. Reprinted in Landau, *Rezensionen*, 55–63. [Review]

[ANONYMOUS]. "*Prolegomena zu einer jeden künftigen Metaphysik, die als Wissenschaft wird auftreten können*, von Immanuel Kant." In Johann Christian Loβius, *Uebersicht der neuesten Litteratur der Philosophie* 1/1 (1784): 51–70. Reprinted in Landau, *Rezensionen*, 64–76. [Review]

[ANONYMOUS]. "*Erläuterungen über des Herrn Professor Kant Critik der reinen Vernunft* von Johann Schulze." *ALZ* 3/162, 3/164, 3/178, 3/179, Beylage (1785): 41–4, 53–6, 117–18, 121–4, 125–8. Reprinted in Landau, *Rezensionen*, 147–82. [Review]

[ANONYMOUS]. "*Hessische Beyträge zur Gelehrsamkeit und Kunst*." *ALZ* 1/64 (1788): 691–4. [Review]

[ANONYMOUS]. "*Ueber Raum und Caussalität* von Johann Feder." *ALZ* (28 January 1788): 249–54. [Review]

BORN, FRIEDRICH GOTTLOB. *Versuch über die ersten Gründe der Sinnenlehre: zur Prüfung verschiedener, vornämlich der Weishauptischen Zweifel nber die Kantischen Begriffe von Raum und Zeit*. Leipzig: Klaubarth, 1788.

Versuch nber die ursprünglichen Grundlagen des menschlichen Denkens und die davon abhängigen Schranken unserer Erkenntnis. Leipzig: Barth, 1791.

BRANDT, REINHARD. "Eine neu aufgefundene Reflexion Kants 'Vom innern Sinne' (Loses Blatt Leningrad)." In Reinhard Brandt and Werner Stark, eds., *Neue Autographen und Dokumente zu Kants Leben, Schriften und Vorlesungen*, 1–30. Hamburg: Felix Meiner Verlag, 1987. Hoke Robinson, tr. "A New Fragment of Immanuel Kant: 'On Inner Sense'." *International Philosophical Quarterly* 29/3 (1989): 252–61.

BUROKER, JILL VANCE. *Logic and the Art of Thinking*. New York: Cambridge University Press, 1996.

[FEDER, JOHANN CHRISTIAN HEINRICH, AND CHRISTIAN GARVE]. "*Critik der reinen Vernunft* von Immanuel Kant." *Zugabe zu den Göttingischen Anzeigen von gelehrten Sachen* (19 January 1782): 40–8. Reprinted in Immanuel Kant, *Prolegomena*, Karl Vorländer, ed. Hamburg: Felix Meiner Verlag, 1976, 167–74; Landau, *Rezensionen*, 10–17; translated in R. C. S. Walker, *The Real in the Ideal* [New York: Garland, 1989], xv–xxiv; Schultz, *Exposition*, 171–7). [Review]

FEDER, JOHANN GEORG HEINRICH. *Ueber Raum und Caussalität: zur Prüfung der Kantischen Philosophie*. Göttingen: Dietrich, 1787.

"*Ueber die transcendentale Aesthetik* von J. C. G. Schaumann." *Philosophische Bibliothek* 3 (1790): 121–42. [Review]

J. G. H. Feders Leben, Natur und Grundsätze. Leipzig: Schwickert, 1825.

GARVE, CHRISTIAN. "*Kritik der reinen Vernunft*, von Immanuel Kant." *AdB* 37–53 Supplement (1783): 838–62. Reprinted in Landau, *Rezensionen*, 34–55. [Review]

Uebersicht der vornehmsten Principien der Sittenlehre von dem Zeitalter des Aristoteles an bis auf unsere Zeiten. Breslau: Wilhelm Gottlieb Korn, 1798.

di GIOVANNI, GEORGE, AND H.S. HARRIS, TRS. *Between Kant and Hegel: Texts in the Development of Post-Kantian Idealism*. Albany: State University of New York Press, 1985.

HAMANN, JOHANN GEORG. *Sämmtliche Werke*, Josef Nadler, ed. Wien: Verlag Herder, 1949–57.

Briefwechsel, Walther Ziesemer and Arthur Henkel, eds. Wiesbaden: Insel Verlag, 1955–76.

HAUSIUS, K. GOTTLOB, *Materialien zur Geschichte der Critischen Philosophie*. 3 vols. Leipzig: J. G. J. Breitkopf und Comp, 1793.

HEIDEMANN, INGEBORG, AND WOLFGANG RITZEL, EDS.*Beiträge zur Kritik der reinen Vernunft 1781–1981*. Berlin: de Gruyter, 1981.

HUME, DAVID. *An Enquiry Concerning Human Understanding*, Eric Steinberg, ed. Indianapolis: Hackett, 1977.

JACOBI, FRIEDRICH HEINRICH. *David Hume über den Glauben oder Idealismus und Realismus*. Breslau: Löwe, 1785. Reprinted in Lewis White Beck, ed., *The Philosophy of David Hume*. New York: Garland, 1983.

[KANT, IMMANUEL]."*Ideen zur Philosophie der Geschichte der Menschheit* von *Johann Gottfried Herder*. Erster Theil." *ALZ* 1/4 und Beylage (1785): 17–23. Reprinted in Ak. VIII, 45–55. [Review]

"*Ideen zur Philosophie der Geschichte der Menschheit* von *Johann Gottfried Herder*. Zweyter Theil." *ALZ* 4/271 (1785): 153–6. Reprinted in Ak. VIII, 58–66. [Review]

[KANT, IMMANUEL]. *Grundlegung zur Metaphysik der Sitten*. Ak. IV, 385–463.

Metaphysische Anfangsgründe der Naturwissenschaft. Ak. IV, 466–565.

"Was heißt sich im Denken orientieren?" Ak. VIII, 131–47.

Ueber eine Entdeckung, nach der alle neue Kritik der reinen Vernunft durch eine ältere entbehrlich gemacht werden soll. Ak. VIII, 185–252.

Logik: Ein Handbuch zu Vorlesungen, Gottlob Benjamin Jäsche, ed. Ak. IX, 1–150.

Opus Postumum. Ak. XXI–XXII.

Prolegomena zu einer jeden künftigen Metaphysik, die als Wissenschaft wird auftreten können, Karl Vorländer, ed. Hamburg: Felix Meiner Verlag, 1976.

LANDAU, ALBERT. *Rezensionen zur Kantischen Philosophie 1781–87*. Bebra: Albert Landau Verlag, 1991.

MAAß, J. G. E. "Ueber die Transcendentale Aesthetic." *Philosophisches Magazin* I/2 (1788): 117–49.

[PARTHEY, GUSTAV C. F.] *Die Mitarbeiter an Friedrich Nicolai's Allgemeiner deutschen Bibliothek nach ihren Namen und Zeichen in zwei Register geordnet*. Berlin: In der Nicolaischen Buchhandlung, 1842. Reprint, Hildesheim: Verlag Dr. H. A. Gerstenberg, 1973.

[PISTORIUS, HERMANN ANDREAS.] "*Prolegomena zu einer jeden künftigen Metaphysik, die als Wissenschaft wird auftreten können*. Von Immanuel Kant." *AdB* 59/2 (1784): 322–56. Reprinted in Landau, *Rezensionen*, 85–108. [Review]

"*Erläuterungen über des Herrn Professor Kant Critik der reinen Vernunft* von Johann Schultze." *AdB* 66/1 (1786): 92–123. Reprinted in Landau, *Rezensionen*, 326–52. [Review]

"*Grundlegung zur Metaphysik der Sitten* von Immanuel Kant." *AdB* 66/2 (1786): 447–62. Reprinted in Landau, *Rezensionen*, 354–67. [Review]

"*Critik der reinen Vernunft* von Immanuel Kant. Zweyte Auflage." *AdB* 81/2 (1788): 343–54. [Review]

"*Prüfung der Mendelssohnischen Morgenstunden* von Ludwig Heinrich Jakob." *AdB* 82/2 (1788): 427–70. [Review]

"*Critik der reinen Vernunft im Grundrisse* von M. Carl Christian Erhard Schmid; *Wörterbuch zum leichteren Gebrauch der kantischen Schriften, nebst einer Abhandlung* von M. Carl Christian Erhard Schmid." *AdB* 88/1 (1789): 103–22. Reprinted as "Ueber die Abhandlung von Carl Christian Erhard Schmid, über den Kantischen Purismus und den Sellischen Empirismus" in Hausius, *Materialien*, vol.1, 200–17. [Review]

PLATNER, ERNST. *Philosophische Aphorismen: nebst einigen Anleitungen zur philosophischen Geschichte*, vol 1. Leipzig: Schwickert, 1776.

REID, THOMAS. *An Inquiry into the Human Mind*, Derek R. Brooks, ed. University Park: The Pennsylvania State University Press, 1997.

REINHOLD, KARL LEONHARD. *Briefe über die Kantische Philosophie*, vols. I–II. Leizpig: Georg Joachim Goshen, 1790–2.

Versuch einer neuen Theorie des menschlichen Vorstellungsvermögen. Jena: Widtman & Mauke, 1789.

Beyträge zur Berichtigung bisheriger Missverständnisse in der Philosophie. Jena: Widtman & Mauke, 1790-4.

Ueber das Fundament des philosophischen Wissens. Jena: Widtman & Mauke, 1791.

SCHAUMANN, J. G. *Ueber die Transcendentale Aesthetik: Ein kritischer Versuch*. Leizig: Weidmann, 1789.

[SCHMID, CARL CHRISTIAN ERHARD?]. "*Grundsätze der reinen Philosophie* von Christian Gottlob Selle." *ALZ* 3/212b (Sept. 1788): 606–16. [Review]

SCHMID, CARL CHRISTIAN ERHARD. *Critik der reinen Vernunft im Grundrisse*. Jena: Mauke, 1788.

Wörterbuch zum leichteren Gebrauch der Kantischen Schriften nebst einer Abhandlung, 4th ed. Jena: Cröker, 1798.

SCHÜTZ, C. G. "Verteidigung gegen Hn. Prof. Schellings sehr unlautere Erläuterungen über die A. L. Z." *ALZ* 5/57 (20 April 1800): 465–80.

[SCHULTZ, JOHANN]. "De Mundi Sensibilis atque Intelligibilis Forma et Principiis." *Königsbergische Gelehrte und Politische Zeitungen* (22 and 25 November 1771). Reprinted in Reinhard Brandt, "Materialien zur Entstehung der *Kritik der reinen Vernunft*," in Ingeborg Heidemann and Wolfgang Ritzel, ed., *Beiträge zur Kritik der reinen Vernunft 1781–1981*, 37–68; translated in Schultz. *Exposition*, 163–70. [Review]

"*Institutiones logicae et metaphysicae* by Jo. Aug. Henr. Ulrich." *ALZ* 4/195 (December 13, 1785): 297–9. [Review]

SCHULTZ, JOHANN. *Erläuterungen über des Herrn Professor Kant Critik der reinen Vernunft*. Königsberg: Dengel, 1784. Translated as *Exposition of Kant's 'Critique of Pure Reason,'* James C. Morrison, tr. Ottawa: University of Ottawa Press, 1995.

Prüfung der kantischen Critik der reinen Vernunft. 2 vols. Königsberg: Nicolovius, 1789–92.

SCHULZE, GOTTLOB ERNST. *Aenesidemus oder über die Fundamente der von dem Herrn Professor Reinhold in Jena gelieferten Elementarphilosophie: Nebst einer Vertheidigung des Skepticismus gegen die Anmassungen der Vernunftkritik*. 1792.

SELLE, CHRISTIAN GOTTLIEB. "Von der analogischen Schlußart." *Berlinische Monatsschrift* 4 (August 1784): 185–7.

"Nähere Bestimmung der analogischen Schlußart." *Berlinische Monatsschrift* 4 (October 1784): 334–7.

"Versuch eines Beweises, dass es keine reine von der Erfahrung unabhängige Vernunftbegriffe gebe." *Berlinische Monatsschrift* 4 (December 1784): 565–76. Reprinted in Hausius, *Materialien*, vol. 1, 98–106.

Grundsätze der reinen Philosophie. Berlin: Himburg, 1788.

TIEDEMANN, DIETRICH. "Ueber die Natur der Metaphysik: Zur Prüfung von Herrn Professor Kants Grundsätzen." *Hessische Beyträge zur Gelehrsamkeit und Kunst* 1 (1785): 113–30, 233–48, 464–74. Reprinted in Hausius, *Materialien*, vol. 2, 53–103.

TITTEL, GOTTLOB AUGUST. *Ueber Herrn Kants Moralreform*. Frankfurt: Pfahler, 1786.

Kantische Denkformen oder Kategorien. Frankfurt: Gebhardt, 1787.

Erläuterungen der theoretischen und praktischen Philosophie nach Herrn Feders Ordnung. Frankfurt: Gebhardt and Kurber, 1791.

ULRICH, JOHANN AUGUST HEINRICH. *Institutiones logicae et metaphysicae*. Jena: Cröker, 1785.

WEISHAUPT, ADAM. *Kantische Anschauungen und Erscheinungen*. Nürnberg: Gratenau, 1788.

Gründe und Gewissheit des menschlichen Erkennens: Zur Prüfung der Kantischen Critik der reinen Vernunft. Nürnberg: Gratenau, 1788.

Zweifel über die Kantische Begriffe von Zeit und Raum. Nürnberg: Gratenau, 1788.

Ueber Materialismus und Idealismus. Nürnberg: Gratenenau, 1788.

WIELAND, CHRISTOPH MARTIN. *Gesammelte Schriften*, vol 23. Berlin: Akademie Verlag, 1969.

Secondary Sources

Allgemeine deutsche Biographie. 56 vols. Leipzig: Duncker & Humblot, 1875–1912.

ALLISON, HENRY. *The Kant-Eberhard Controversy*. Baltimore and London: The Johns Hopkins University Press, 1973.

Kant's Transcendental Idealism: An Interpretation and Defense. New Haven and London: Yale University Press, 1983.

"On Naturalizing Kant's Transcendental Psychology." *Idealism and Freedom: Essays on Kant's Theoretical and Practical Philosophy*, 53–66. New York: Cambridge University Press, 1996.

AQUILA, RICHARD E. *Representational Mind*. Bloomington: Indiana University Press, 1983.

Matter in Mind. Bloomington: Indiana University Press, 1989.

BECK, LEWIS WHITE. *Early German Philosophy: Kant and His Predecessors*. Cambridge, Mass.: Belknap Press of Harvard University Press, 1969.

"Six Short Pieces on the Second Analogy of Experience." *Essays on Kant and Hume*, 130–164. New York: Yale University Press, 1978.

"Did the Sage of Königsberg Have No Dreams?" *Essays on Kant and Hume*, 38–60. New York: Yale University Press, 1978.

BEISER, FREDERICK C. *The Fate of Reason: German Philosophie from Kant to Fichte*. Cambridge, Mass.: Harvard University Press, 1987.

BRANDT, REINHARD. *The Table of Judgments: Critique of Pure Reason A 67–76; B92–101*, Eric Watkins, tr., NAKS Study in Philosophy, vol. 4. Altascadero, Calif.: Ridgview, 1995.

BREAZEALE, DANIEL,"Fichte's *Aenesidemus* Review and the Transformation of German Idealism." *Review of Metaphysics* 34 (March 1982): 541–68.

"Between Kant and Fichte: Karl Leonhard Reinhold's 'Elementary Philosophy.' " *Review of Metaphysics* 35 (June 1982): 785–821.

BROOK, ANDREW. "Realism in the Refutation of Idealism." In Hoke Robinson, ed. *Proceedings of the Eighth International Kant Congress*, 313–19. Milwaukee: Marquette University Press, 1995.

CARLSSON, ANNI. *Die deutsche Buchkritik*, Band I: Von den Anfängen bis 1850. Stuttgart: W. Kohlhammer Verlag, 1963.

DE VLEESCHAUWER, H. J. *La Déduction Transcendentale dans L'Oeuvre de Kant*. Paris: Librairie Ernest Leroux, 1936. Reprint, New York: Garland, 1976.

The Development of Kantian Thought. London: Thomas Nelson and Sons Ltd., 1962.

ERDMANN, BENNO. *Kants Kriticismus in der ersten und in der zweiten Auflage der Kritik der reinen Vernunft.* Leipzig: Verlag von Leopold Voss, 1878. Reprint, Hildesheim: Verlag Dr. H. A. Gerstenberg, 1973.

FALKENSTEIN, LORNE. "Was Kant a Nativist?" *Journal of the History of Ideas* 51 (1990): 573–97.

"Kant's Empiricism." *Review of Metaphysics* 50 (March 1997): 547–589.

Kant's Intuitionism: A Commentary on the Transcendental Aesthetic. Toronto: University of Toronto Press, 1995.

FÖSTER, ECKHART. "Kant's Refutation of Idealism." In A. J. Holland, ed. *Philosophy, Its History and Histeriography*, 287–303. Dodrecht: Riedel, 1985.

di GIOVANNI, GEORGE. "The Facts of Consciousness." In di Giovanni and H. S. Harrris, trs. *Between Kant and Hegel: Texts in the Development of Post-Kantian Idealism*, 1–50. Albany: State University of New York Press, 1985.

GUYER, PAUL. *Kant and the Claims of Knowledge.* New York: Cambridge University Press, 1987.

"The Transcendental Deduction of the Categories." In Paul Guyer, ed., *The Cambridge Companion to Kant*, 123–60. New York: Cambridge University Press, 1992.

HARPER, WILLIAM. "Kant on Space, Empirical Realism and the Foundations of Geometry." *Topoi* 3 (1984): 143–61.

HATFIELD, GARY. *The Natural and the Normative: Theories of Spatial Perception from Kant to Helmholtz.* Cambridge, Mass: MIT Press, 1990.

HINSKE, NORBERT AND MICHAEL ALBRECHT, EDS. *Was ist Aufklärung: Beiträge aus der Berlinischen Monatsschrift.* 4th ed. Darmstadt: Wissenschaftliche Buchgesellschaft, 1990.

KIRCHNER, JOACHIM. *Die Zeitschriften des Deutschen Sprachgebietes von den Anfängen bis 1830.* Stuttgart: Anton Hiersemann, 1969.

KITCHER, PATRICIA. *Kant's Transcendental Psychology.* New York and Oxford: Oxford University Press, 1990.

KOŠENINA, ALEXANDER. *Ernst Platners Anthropologie und Philosophie: der philosophische Arzt und seine Wirkung auf Johann Karl Wezel and Jean Paul.* Würzburg: Königshausen & Neumann, 1989.

KRONICK, DAVID A. *A History of Scientific and Technical Periodicals: The Origins and Development of the Scientific and Technical Press 1665–1790*, 2nd ed. Metuchen, N.J.: The Scarecrow Press, 1976.

KUEHN, MANFRED. "The Early Reception of Reid, Oswald and Beattie in Germany 1768–1800." *Journal of the History of Philosophy* 21 (1983): 479–96.

"Kant and the Refutation of Idealism in the Eighteenth Century." In Donald C. Mell, Theodore Braun, and Lucia M. Palmer, eds., *Man, God and Nature in the Enlightenment*, 25–35. East Lansing, Mich: Colleagues Press, 1988.

Scottish Common Sense in Germany: A Contribution to the History of Critical

Philosophy. Kingston and Montreal: McGill-Queen's University Press, 1987.

LONGUENESSE, BÉATRICE. "Kant et les jugements empiriques: Jugements de perception et jugements d'experience." *Kant Studien* 86 (1995): 278–307.

Kant and the Capacity to Judge. Princeton, N.J.: Princeton University Press, 1998.

MORGAN, MICHAEL. *Molyneux's Question: Vision, Touch, and the Philosophy of Perception*. New York: Cambridge University Press, 1977.

OST, GÜNTHER. *Friedrich Nicolais "Allgemeine Deutsche Bibliothek."* Berlin: 1928.

PRAUSS, GEROLD, *Erscheinung bei Kant: ein Problem der Kritik der reinen Vernunft*. Berlin: de Gruyter, 1972.

REICH, KLAUS. *The Completeness of Kant's Table of Judgments*, Jane Kneller and Michael Losonsky, tr. Berkeley: Stanford University Press, 1992.

ROBINSON, HOKE. "Two Perspectives on Kant's Appearances and Things in Themselves." *Journal of the History of Philosophy* 32 (1994): 411–41.

SASSEN, BRIGITTE. "Critical Idealism in the Eyes of Kant's Contemporaries." *Journal of the History of Philosophy*, 35 (1997): 421–55.

SCHNEIDER, UTE. *Friedrich Nicolais Allgemeine Deutsche Bibliothek als Integrationsmedium der Gelehrtenrepublik*. Wiesbaden: Harrassowitz Verlag, 1995.

STRAUSS, WALTER. *Friedrich Nicolai und die kritische Philosophie: Ein Beitrag zur Geschichte der Aufklärung*. Stuttgart: W. Kohlhammer Verlag, 1927.

STRAWSON, P. F. *The Bounds of Sense*. London: Methuen, 1966.

VAIHINGER, HANS. *Kommentar zu Kants Kritik der reinen Vernunft*. 2 vols. Stuttgart: Union Deutsche Verlagsgesellschaft, 1922.

WALKER, R. C. S. *Kant*. London: Routledge, 1978.

The Real in the Ideal: Berkeley's Relation to Kant. New York: Garland, 1989.

WISTOFF, ANDREAS. *Die deutsche Romantik in der öffentlichen Literatur*. Bonn: Bouvier, 1992.

WOLFF, MICHAEL. *Die Vollständigkeit der Kantischen Urteilstafel*. Frankfurt: Klostermann, 1995.

Reference and Citation Index to Translations

Feder, *Raum und Caussalität*

1–2, *KEC*, 106	128
2, *KEC*, 106	129
23, *KEC*, *110*	129
24, *KEC*, *110*	129–30
26, *KEC*, 111	130
27, *KEC*, 112	130
28, *KEC*, 112	131
30, *KEC*, 113	131
41, *KEC*, 116	131–2
48–9, *KEC*, 118	132
57–8, *KEC*, 121–2	133–4
59, *KEC*, 122	134–5
65, *KEC*, 140	160
76, *KEC*, 144	161–2
77, *KEC*, 144	162
77, *KEC*, 144	163

Critique A

Space Metaphysical Expositions

A22	139
A22ff	106
A23	83, 126
A23ff	109
A24	86, 86–7
A25	88

Space Conclusions from the Above Concepts

A26	90–1
A29	83

Time Metaphysical Expositions

A31	86
A32	88

Time Conclusions from the Above Concepts

A36–7, 37 note	171

Aesthetic §8

A42	106
A44	139
A46	139

Deduction

A100ff	207
A101	171
A114	106, 205
A125–7	172

Schematism

A137ff	204

Second Analogy

A193	211

Phaenomena and Noumena

A242	204
A256	126

Amphibolies

A277ff	203

Fourth Paralogism

A366ff	106
A370	140
A370ff	106
A370–80	169–70
A378	149

Antinomies

A429	126
A491	171

Doctrine of Method

A714	118

Critique B

Preface to

Bxliii	176
Bxxxv	177

Space Metaphysical Expositions

B38	129

Space Conclusion from Above Concepts

B42 128

Transcendental Logic and Transcendental Analytic

B89–90 228

Analytic of Concepts

B105 216, 218
B106 215, 218
B107 218
B109ff 217
B118 221
B119 225

Transition to Deduction

B126f 221
B127 226
B128 229

Deduction

B167 220

Refutation of Idealism

B275 and Bxxxix note 179–80
B276–70 181

Prolegomena

Ak. IV, 265 87–8
Ak. IV, 267 87
Ak. IV, 268 116, 118
Ak. IV, 268ff 82
Ak. IV, 272–3 118
Ak. IV, 280ff 82
Ak. IV, 285–6 90–1
Ak. IV, 287 123
Ak. IV, 287f 106
Ak. IV, 288 139
Ak. IV, 289 149
Ak. IV, 289–90 140–1
Ak. IV, 294 201
Ak. IV, 298 206, 213
Ak. IV, 374 167

Grundlegung zur Metaphysik der Sitten

Ak. IV, 453 103

Pistorius, review of B-edition

351, *KEC*, 180 185

Schmid, *Wörterbuch*

627, *KEC*, 236 256
637, *KEC*, 241 258
646–7, *KEC*, 245 261
647, *KEC*, 245 262
649, *KEC*, 246 263
650–1, *KEC*, 247 264
651, *KEC*, 247 265
653, note *, *KEC*, 248 265
667, *KEC*, 254 267

Selle, *Grundsätze der reinen Philosophie*

148–9 237 note 3
167 238 note 4

Index

affection: argument of, 23–4; problem of, 5, 12, 15, 20, 24–5, 173–4
Allgemeine deutsche Bibliothek, 1, 16, 42–7, 93, 176, 185
Allgemeine Literatur-Zeitung, 1–2, 11, 14, 17–18, 35, 42–8, 233
analysis, 82
anthropomorphism, 58
Antinomy(ies), 5n.25, 11, 15n.64, 69–70, 123
appearances: and representations, 19, 208; and things in themselves, 19, 26, 64, 99–102; as actual things that exist outside us, 139; as delivering data for objects, 61; causes of, 21; nature of, 19, 28; possibility of, 93–4; *see also* empiricism, as distinguished from purism
a priorism, 34
Aristotle/Aristotelian, 37, 93, 215–16, 218–19, 226; and prime matter, 25

Beck, J. S., 3, 275
Bering, J., 14, 275
Berkeley, G. /Berkeleyan, 7–9, 19, 23, 54, 149, 154–5, 167
Berlinische Monatsschrift, 43
Bertuch, F. J., 44, 275
Biester, J., 36, 275
bodies: and space, 123–5; as representations, 139–41, 147, 164, 166; as actual things, 53, 60, 141, 167
Bohn, K. E., 44, 275
Born, F. G., 19, 27, 270; on Molyneux Question, 18; response to Feder, 27–8, 133–5, 183–4; response to Pistorius, 29–30, 185–90

Canon of Pure Understanding, 73
Categories, 30–9, 62, 193–230; and heterogeneity from sensible intuitions, 204; applicability of, 30, 35, 37, 204–5, 212; Aristotle and Kant on, 215–6, 218–19; as abstractions, 220–1; as empty forms, 222–5; as forms for objects in general, 233–5; as logical functions of judgment, 203–4; as predetermined dispositions, 220; as preestablished, 214; as regulative, 224, *see also* applicability of; as schematized, 62; as systemically ordered, 216–8; causality, 224, 240; Deduction of, 35–6, 213–4; Locke and Kant on, 225–7, 229–30; Locke and Kant on origin of, 227–9; modality, 6, 63–4; nature of, 30, 37, 219–27; necessity of, 30–3; origin of, 30; quality, 63; quantity, 63; relation, 63; *see also* laws (concepts) of understanding
certainty, form and degree of, 253–4, 267–9
Cheselden, 96
cognitive capacities: cognition through, 247–3, 263–7; relation to each other, 245–6, 263; relation to objects, 246–7, 264–5
common sense, 57–8, 71, 140–1, 151
Copernican revolution (turn), 16, 25–6, 34, 177–9

Deduction: obscurity of, 35, 213
Descartes, R. 19, 125
Dialectic, 66–72
Doctrine of Method, 57, 72–3
dogmatism, 57, 140
dreaming argument, 23

Eberhard, J. A., 2, 275; and the *Philosophisches Magazin*, 2, 42, 47
empiricism, as distinguished from purism, 5, 34, 38–42, 233–69
extension, concept of, 91

fallacious inferences: in psychology, 55–6, 67–8; in cosmology, 56, 68–70; in natural theology, 56–7, 70–2
Feder, J., 1–3, 16–7, 27–8, 36, 39, 176, 217, 270; and idealism, 19, 139–54, *see also* Schaumann; and the Molyneux Question, 18, and the *Philosophische Bibliothek*, 42; and the Transcendental Aesthetic, 11–2, 17–8, 106–

26; defense of realism, 20–1; *see also* Born, *Göttingen* (Feder/Garve) review
Fichte, J. G., 2, 3
form (of intuition): as a priori, 83; as different from objects, 84; as responsible for order, 83–4; necessity of, 84
Fourth Paralogism, 6, 9, 20, 24, *see also* refutation of idealism, Jacobi
Fries, J. F., 17, 275

Garve, C., 2, 7, 271, *see also* Garve Review
Garve Review, 5–7, 9–11, 59–77; and Antinomies, 11; and attack on Kant's a priorism, 10, *see also* space (and time), as extraordinarily peculiar and incomprehensible ideas; and attack on Kant's architectonic, 10–1; and interpretation of Kant's project as psychological, not epistemic, 10; and Kant's terminology, 10, 59–60
geometry (mathematics): and apodeictic certainty, 75, 86–7, 96, 109, 113–4
Göttingen (Feder/Garve) review, 1, 5–9, 16, 19, 21, 43, 53–8; and Berkeley, 7–8, 54; and the idealism objection, 7
Göttingische Anzeigen von gelehrten Sachen, 43

Hamann, J. G., 3, 7, 275
Helmholtz, H. von, 17, 276
Herder, J. G., 3, 45, 47, 276
Hume, D., 2, 13, 36, 47, 56, 114–5, 200, 214, 226

idealism, 6, 18–30, 58, 139–90; and errors, 151–3; and imperfection of sensible knowledge, 150–1; and realism, 140; egoistic, 149; epistemological benefits of, 19; ontological, 19, 23; ordinary, 155; objection, 7, 9; refutation of, 19, 26–7, 30, 58, 68, 179–82, 185-9; simple, 23, 26; skeptical, 19; *see also* transcendental idealism
induction, 195
intentionality, 28–9
intuition: as subsumed under laws of understanding, 207; kinds of, 203; matter and form of, 24–5, 83–4, 90

Jacobi, F. H., 3, 12, 19, 22, 24, 27–8, 271; and transcendental idealism, 24–5, 169–75
Jakob, L. H., 36, 276
judgments: analytic, 194–5; objective, 206–7; of experience, 206, 211, 213–4; of perception, 36, 206, 211, 213–4; subjective, 206–7; synthetic 81–2, 195–7

Kant, I.: and concepts of understanding, *see* categories; and empiricism, *see* empiricism, as distinguished from purism; and Feder, *see* Feder; and Garve, *see* Garve; and intentionality, 28–30; and problems with his terminology, 59–60, 127, 166, 180, 187, 189; and response to Schultz, 36; and space and time, *see* Transcendental Analytic; and skeptical implications, *see* skepticism; and the idealism objection, *see* idealism, transcendental idealism; and the pantheism controversy, 3; as nativist, 17; as representationalist, 22; *Critique of Practical Reason*, 36; *Critique of Pure Reason*, 1–42 passim; debate with Herder, 3, 47; *Entdeckung*, 2–4, 16, 42; Inaugural Dissertation, 12,35, 43; on Tiedemann, 14; on Tittel, 36–7; *Prolegomena*, 1–42 passim

Lambert, J. H., 12, 35, 276
laws (concepts) of understanding: as a priori, 7, 54, 61; as subjective and objective, 102–5; as without objective content, 175; *see also* categories
laws of thought: as grounded in inner conviction, 194–5; as grounded in experience, 195
Leibniz/Leibnizian, 2, 34, 54, 65, 86, 94, 101, 146, 154; and metaphysical delusions, 65; monads, 65; and preestablished harmony, 117, 149
Locke, J./Lockean, 2, 20, 31, 36, 38–9, 221; *see also* categories
Lotze, R. H., 17, 277

Maaß, J. G. E., 2, 42, 277
magnitude: genesis of concept of, 98–9
Malebrance, 149, 154
materialism (materialist), 58, 153
mathematical judgments (propositions): as analytic or synthetic, 12–4, 82–3
mathematics: as distinguished from philosophy, 72–3, 75–6, 87–8, 116–9, 132, 193, 197–8
Meiners, C., 42, 277
Mendelssohn, M., 1, 6, 12, 35, 43, 277
metaphysical principles, 88
metaphysics: nature of, 193; completion of 81, 177–8

Molyneux question, 12, 18, *see also*, space and time, and the person born blind
moral feeling: and role in theology, 71–2

nature: as created by understanding, 54, 61; as sum total of appearances, 205, 207
necessary truths: ground of 114–6
neglected alternative argument, 5, 12, 15, *see also* space (and time), as objective and subjective
Neue Allgemeine deutsche Bibliothek, 44, 47
Nicolai, F., 1, 44–7, 277

objects: as appearances, 64; as conforming to our cognition, 178–9, 185–7; as distinct from ourselves, 24; as distinct from representations, 23–4; as made (formed) by understanding, 54, 61; as making impressions on the senses, 172–5; as producing representations, 173; as representations, 23, 66, 141, 171; as types of representations, 73–4; in general, 233–5; *see also* sensible objects (appearances), objects of outer sense, empiricism, as distinguished from purism
objective world: access to, 101–2
objects (transcendental): as ground of appearances, 157; as in space, 29, 188–9; knowledge of, 172–4; *see also* things in themselves
objects of outer sense: as actual, 141; as distinguished from those of imagination, 161; as representations, 141, 160; *see also* sensible appearances

pantheism controversy, 3
periodical publication in late eighteenth century Germany, 5, 42–8
perception: acts vs. objects of, 21, 149–50
Pistorius, H. A., 2, 5, 16, 19, 28, 34, 39, 47, 271; and response to Schmid, 41–2; and review of *Erläuterungen*, 14–6, 93–105; and skepticism, 41, 259–60, 267–9; and the Copernican turn, 25–6, 177–9; and the Molyneux question, 12; and the neglected alternative argument, 5, 12–13, 15–6; and the Refutation of Idealism, 26–7, 179–82, *see also* Born; and the Transcendental Aesthetic, 11–16; as defending empiricism, 255–69
Plato/Platonist, 117, 153
preestablished harmony, 36, 117
primary and secondary qualities, 21, 147–8
principle of contradiction, 62
principle of sufficient reason, 32–3, 174, 211; as synthetic or analytic, 196–7, 200–3; demonstration of, 200–2; objective validity of, 203

reality, as distinguished from illusion, 8–9, 28
realism: and idealism, 29; Berkeley's direct, 20; common sense, 2, 20–1; Locke's representationalist, 20
reason, 193–4; 242–5, 260–3; and understanding, 55, 66; use of, 72–3
Reid, T., 21, 28–9
Reinhold, K., L., 3, 47, 277; and the pantheism controversy, 2–3; Briefe *über die Kantische Philosophie*, 2–3, 43; *Elementarphilosophie*, 2–3
representations: and actual sensations, 143; and things in themselves, 27, 165; as distinguished from sensations, 205; as distinguished from objects, 60, as in us, 149; causes of 21, 26; nature of, 23–4; order and regularity of, 207

Schaumann, J. C. G., 22, 272; response to Feder, 5, 19, 22–4, 155–68, *see also* problem of affection
Schelling, F. W., 2, 48
schema, 241
schematism: doctrine of, 31
Schmid, C. G. E., 5, 31, 39, 47; and defense of purism, 39–40, 233–54, *see also* Pistorius and defense of empiricism; and skepticism, 40, 242; and sensation, 40
Schultz (Schulze Schultze), J., 1, 3, 12, 34, 43, 47, 272; and consciousness as thing in itself, 35; and Deduction, 35–6, 213; and *Erläuterungen*, 14, 34, 93–105; and review of Ulrich, 34–6, 210–4
Schütz, C. G., 44–8, 278
Schwab, J. C., 2, 42, 278
Schulze, G. E., 278, and the *Aenesidemus*, 3
Second Analogy, 38
Selle, C. G., 2, 33, 36, 39–40, 43, 273; and necessity of a priori concepts, 31–2, 193–98; and principle of sufficient reason, 32, 196–7; and relevance to Kant, 31; *see also* Schmid, Pistorius as defending of empiricism

sensation(s): and actuality, 141–2, 167; and conformity to understanding, 207–9; and empirical guidedness, 8–9, 25–6; and the reality/illusion distinction, 23; as criterion of truth, 9; as distinguished from illusions, 105 n. 21; as distinguished from imagination, 141; as distinguished from objects, 141; as distinguished from reason, 76–7; as mark (criterion) of actuality, 55, 57–8, 74, 76–7, 159, 163–4, 167; as matter of intuition, 24, 83; as modifications of ourselves, 53–4, 60; causes of, 23, 25, 53, 60; inner and outer, 58; order and regularity of, 207–8
sensibility, 193–4, 234–9, 255–6; *see also*, sensation
sensible objects (appearances): and independence from perceiving subjects, 143–6, 161–4; as distinguished from imagination, 142–3; as distinguished from other representations, 54; as representations in us, 148–50
skepticism, 57–8, 229–30, 242, 259–60, 267–9
space (and time): and actuality, 60; and bodies (appearances) in space, 123–6, 164; and mirror images, 89–90; and the person born blind, 95–6, 121–2, 130, 133–5, *see also* Molyneux question; as a priori, 17, 84–6, 106, 108–10; as a condition of intuitions of outer sense, 106–8, 128, *see also* as subjective conditions of sensible intuitions (appearances); as essentially one, 109, 119–20; as extraordinarily peculiar and incomprehensible ideas, 74–5, *see also* Garve review and attack on Kant's a priorism; as forms of sensation, 61, 71; as having arisen from sensible impressions, 129; as objective and subjective, 15–6, 94–103, 256, *see also* neglected alternative argument; as (pure) intuitions, 81–91, 97–8; as subjective, 15, 255–6; as subjective conditions of sensible intuitions (appearances), 53–5, 61, 74; empirical origin of, 11–2, 238; independence from objects, 18; infinite divisibility of, 18, 123–4; infinity of, 109, 120–1; necessity of, 86, 96–7, 109, 111–3, 130–1; psychological origin of, 17–8
subjectivity: problem of, 12, 14–5
synthetic principle: 62

table of categories: accuracy and completeness of, 30, 37, 62; basis of, 62
Tetens, J., 1, 6, 278
Teutsche Merkur, 2, 43
things in themselves: as causes of representations, 26, 211–2; existence of, 64, 100–1; knowledge of, 20, 101–2
Tiedemann, D., 2, 11–4, 33, 47, 273; and necessity of a priori concepts, 33; and possibility of objective reference, 33–4, 205–9; and principle of sufficient reason, 33, 200–3; and the Transcendental Aesthetic, 81–92; and the Transcendental Analytic, 199–209
time: as objective property of things in themselves, 212
Tittel, G. A., 2, 17, 35–9, 274; and applicability of pure forms of understanding, 38; and nature of pure forms of understanding, 37–8, 219–27
Transcendental Aesthetic, 11–8, 79–135
Transcendental Analytic 30–8, 193–230
transcendental consciousness: as thing in itself, 212
transcendental (Kantian) idealism, 18–30, 155–9; and speculative egoism, 175; and transcendentally real things, 20; as distinguished from empirical idealism, 153–4, 158, 184; as distinguished from other types of idealism, 23–4, 26, 167; in epistemological terms, 19; ontological implications of, 19
Trendelenburg, A., 12, 15

Ulrich, 34, 36, 278; and *Institutiones Logicae et metaphsicae*, 34, 210–14
understanding, 239–42, 257–60; as bringing order into sensible intuitions, 54, 61; misuse of, 54, 61; right use of, 66; work (task) of, 54, 62

Weishaupt, A., 2, 39, 278

CPSIA information can be obtained at www.ICGtesting.com
Printed in the USA
BVOW040012271211

279108BV00001B/11/A